Uncle John's
BATHROOM READER
Plunges into
California

The Bathroom Readers' Institute
Ashland, Oregon, and San Diego, California

OUR "REGULAR" READERS RAVE

"Before the BRI came along, I had a small library of just books. After BRI, I now have a great library filled with incredible books."
—**Green S.**

"I just happened to see one of these sitting on the back of a friend's toilet one time eight years ago. Instead of reading the shampoo bottle, I picked this up. I have been hooked ever since."
—**Angela D.**

"*Uncle John's Bathroom Readers* are the entire reason I started collecting rubber ducks. I have over seventy."
—**Sara C.**

"My hubby was on a couple of game shows, and I know we can thank his love of the *Bathroom Reader* books for the winnings."
—**Donna E.**

"I have them all, and cherish every one! My 20th anniversary edition sadly fell into the (clean) toilet. I managed to dry it out sufficiently enough to continue reading."
—**Butch H.**

"My friend in school was reading *Bathroom Readers*, so then I bought a couple, and now my mom says I'm just threatening her with my intelligence."
—**Chase O.**

"Your *Bathroom Reader* is like a high-powered flush—it sucks you in. I drink more liquids so I can make more pit stops. Thanks for all the fun!"
—**Kara D.**

UNCLE JOHN'S BATHROOM READER®
PLUNGES INTO CALIFORNIA

For information, write...
The Bathroom Readers' Institute
P.O. Box 1117, Ashland, OR 97520
www.bathroomreader.com
e-mail: mail@bathroomreader.com

ISBN 13: 978-1-60710-426-1 / ISBN 10: 1-60710-426-1

Library of Congress Cataloging-in-Publication Data

Uncle John's bathroom reader plunges into California.
    p. cm.
    ISBN 978-1-60710-426-1 (pbk.)
    1. California--Miscellanea. 2. California--Anecdotes. 3. Califor-
nia--Humor. 4. Curiosities and wonders--California. I. Bathroom
Readers' Institute (Ashland, Or.)
    F861.6.U5 2012
    979.4--dc23
                                                2011044531

Printed in the United States of America
First printing
1 2 3 4 5   16 15 14 13 12

v

THANK YOU!

The Bathroom Readers' Institute thanks the following people whose hard work, advice, and assistance made this book possible.

Gordon Javna

JoAnn Padgett

Melinda Allman

Sue Steiner

Jay Newman

Michael Brunsfeld

J. Carroll

Derek Fairbridge

Jack Mingo

Jeff Altemus

Carl Lavo

Stephanie Spadaccini

Jenness Crawford

Ryan Murphy

Terri Schlichenmeyer

Michael Conover

Laurie Mason Shroeder

Dan Mansfield

Brian Boone

True Sims

Lilian Nordland

Monica Maestas

Annie Lam

Ginger, Mana, and Jen

Bonnie Vandewater

Amy L. and Amy M.

Kim T. Griswell

Sydney Stanley

David Cully

Margaret Faherty

Robert Mondavi

Cynthia Francisco

R. R. Donnelley

M. Mouse

The Johns (Steinbeck and Sutter)

Roman Santos

The Beach Boys

Kelly and Bea

Sophie and JJ

CONTENTS

Because the BRI understands your reading needs, we've
divided the contents by length as well as subject.

Short—a quick read

Medium—2 to 3 pages

Long—for those extended visits, when something
a little more involved is required.

CALIFORNIA, HERE WE COME!

HANG LOOSE!
Once upon a time, many moons ago, when people still wrote letters and bought their books in stores, little Uncle John caught an episode of *Gidget* on his grandmother's black-and-white TV. He was transfixed by the lull of the ocean, the escapades of Moondoggie and his pals, and the bright California sunshine. As soon as the show was over, he climbed off the sofa, grabbed the "C–Ch" volume of the encyclopedia from the bookshelf, and announced to Grandma Uncle John that, with his trusty Wonder Dog as his witness, he would one day move his throne to the left coast.

He didn't. But years later, at a brainstorming meeting for the next book in the *Bathroom Reader* series, Uncle John handed us each a bottle of Napa Valley Chardonnay and a longboard keychain, and announced that the great state of California would be our next project.

So we dug deep into our tank of knowledge, looking for nuggets about all things California: history, pop culture, science, obscure facts, and some really strange stuff. Have you heard the story of Tahoe Tessie, Lake Tahoe's "Loch Ness monster"? Did you ever see the Laguna Niguel Amtrak mooning up close? Do you know that San Quentin Prison has a baseball team? We didn't, either. Here's what else awaits you on the pages of this book:

• California's greatest myths explained: Can you drive with your windshield wipers on and your headlights off? Did Ronald Reagan really hate trees? Does your dog know when the next earthquake is coming?

• Some of L.A.'s most notorious addresses—from the spot where Howard Hughes crashed his airplane to the site of the Charles Manson killings to Marilyn Monroe's last home.

• Mendocino County's secret language of "bootling."

- The aliens who live inside Mount Shasta, and the lizard people who live under L.A.

- The Golden State's glorious natural beauty—the redwoods, Death Valley, and some of America's most amazing waterfalls.

- The gold rush story that inspired Mark Twain to create one of his most famous characters.

- California inventions, including jeans, the Cobb salad, and the wave.

- The craziest pranks ever played on the Hollywood sign.

- The answer (finally!) to the burning question: "Is California really going to fall into the Pacific Ocean?"

ONE LAST THING

Before we go, we want to give a big California thumbs-up to Sue, Jay, Derek, Jack, J., and Dan, who deserve a fish taco and an extra handful of Jelly Bellies for all their hard work.

So now, let's take a trip over the mountains and through the redwoods, into the desert, up the freeway, and down the coast to catch the gnarliest wave of weird and interesting stories about the best state in the world. We love you, California!

And as always...

Go with the flow!

—Uncle John and the BRI Staff

CALIFORNIA DREAMING

*Putting such a culturally and geographically diverse state
into a few words is difficult, but we'll give it a try.*

"It shone on everyone, whether they had a contract or not. The most democratic thing I'd ever seen, that California sunshine."
—**Angela Carter**

"Everything is just better in California—the wine, the food, fruits and vegetables, the comforts of living. Even the instrumentalists are generous and curious. Everything is wonderful."
—**Beth Anderson**

"I arrived in California with no job, no car, and no money, but, like millions of other girls, a dream."
—**Victoria Principal**

"As one went to Europe to see the living past, so one must visit southern California to observe the future."
—**Alison Lurie**

"California has become the first American state where there is no majority race, and we're doing just fine."
—**Bill Clinton**

"Tip the world over on its side and everything loose will land in Los Angeles."
—**Frank Lloyd Wright**

"The mountains of California are so gigantic that they are not favorable to art or poetry."
—**Oscar Wilde**

"The days have been mostly of heavenly beauty, and the wild flowers…which fairly rage with radiance, are worthy of some purer planet than this."
—**Henry James**

"The wild mustard is like that spoken of in the New Testament. Its gold is as distinct a value to the eye as the nugget gold is in the pocket."
—**Helen Hunt Jackson**

"You haven't lived until you've died in California."
—**Mort Sahl**

"In a way, California has turned its back on the world, and looks into the void Pacific. It's sort of crazy-sensible."
—**D. H. Lawrence**

Humans have lived in what is now California for at least 48,000 years.

IT'S A TRUTH-QUAKE!

*The big one is coming...and your dog knows it! Better
hide in a doorway! And a lot of other common beliefs
about earthquakes that are mostly just plain wrong.*

RUMOR: Big earthquakes always hit in the morning when
it's hot and dry.
TRUE: No
REAL STORY: Earthquakes are the result of tectonic plates
shifting deep below the earth's surface. Neither the weather nor
the time of day has any effect on them. Big earthquakes have been
recorded at all times of the day and night, year round. The belief
that earthquakes typically hit when the weather is hot and dry
began with Aristotle, who theorized that earthquakes were caused
by air trapped underground. Before one hit, he thought, so much
air would be trapped that the air aboveground would be hot and
calm. (Aristotle was wrong.)

RUMOR: Scientists know when the big one's coming—they just
don't want to tell us.
TRUE? No
REAL STORY: So far, no one has ever been able to predict
exactly when an earthquake will happen. Groups like the United
States Geological Survey (USGS) can identify which areas are
most likely to have an earthquake at some point, based on an
examination of underlying fault lines. For example, the USGS
estimates that, in the next 30 years, there is a 67 percent chance
of a major earthquake in San Francisco. But exactly when is
anybody's guess.

RUMOR: The safest place during an earthquake is a doorway.
TRUE? No
REAL STORY: In many houses, the doorway is actually the
least safe place. The doorway is only the safest place if you live
in an unreinforced adobe house, where the doorway is the
strongest frame in the building. If you live in anything else (like

most people do these days), you're better off sheltering under a sturdy desk or table because the walls and doorframes of modern buildings are usually equally reinforced and will fall (or not) together.

RUMOR: Animals can sense an earthquake coming.
TRUE? Possibly
REAL STORY: Over the years, there have been numerous anecdotes about animals sensing earthquakes—including reports about animals at the National Zoo in Washington, D.C., sounding the alarm before the 2011 Virginia earthquake. But there's never been any consistent or reliable data to prove it.

RUMOR: Lots of little earthquakes mean that a big one is less likely.
TRUE? No
REAL STORY: The Richter scale, which measures the magnitude of earthquakes, is *logarithmic*. That means that for each digit increase on the scale, an earthquake lets off about 30 times more energy. In other words, to equal one 6.0 earthquake, you'd need 32 5.0s, 1,000 4.0s, or 32,000 3.0s. And it would take 729 billion 3.0 earthquakes to release as much energy as a single 9.0. There just aren't enough little earthquakes in the world to alleviate the need for a big one.

RUMOR: Someday California will fall into the ocean.
TRUE? No
REAL STORY: Most earthquakes in California are the result of the Pacific Plate and North American Plate rubbing against each other along the San Andreas Fault, which runs from the Mojave Desert to the San Francisco Peninsula...and the movement is horizontal. This means that Los Angeles and San Francisco are grinding toward each other at about 46 millimeters a year. So someday, your great-great-great-great-great-grandkids might be able to see the Golden Gate Bridge from the Hollywood Hills, but California will never fall into the ocean.

CONDORAMA

The California condor is the largest flying land bird in all of North America.
It's also one of the most endangered. Want to know more? Read on.

HOME ON THE RANGE. The California condor's range used to extend up and down the West Coast, into Mexico, and all the way across the continent to Florida. But today, that area has been cut significantly. In the wild, the birds now live almost exclusively in the mountainous areas of California, Arizona, and northern Baja, Mexico.

REBOUND. The California condor's numbers had declined so severely during the 20th century (due to poaching, habitat encroachment, and the condor's own naturally low birth rate) that by the 1980s, only 22 wild birds were known to exist...in the *entire* world. Those birds were all captured so they wouldn't die off, and then they were cared for and bred at the San Diego Zoo and the Los Angeles Zoo until 1992, when they and their offspring began to be released back into the wild. Today, there are about 180 free-flying California condors. Another 200 or so live in zoos and at other conservation sites.

AN AGING POPULATION. California condors are one of the longest-living birds in the world. On average, they can reach about 60 years of age. Some live into their 80s.

HI, MOM. These birds are extremely attentive parents. Their gestation period lasts about 56 days, and most females lay just one egg at a time. The adults then provide their young a lot of atten-tion and care—chicks begin flying when they're about six months old, but continue to live with Mom and Dad for a few months after that.

EAT ME. The condors are scavengers. That means their diet is made up mostly of *carrion* (dead, rotting animal carcasses). Their favorites? Deer, sheep, and cattle, though rabbits and rodents will do in a pinch.

A condor appears on the CA state quarter, along with John Muir and the Yosemite Valley.

CALI-FOLKS, PART I

*Computers…Hollywood…surfing…politics. The look, feel,
and personality of California culture has been
shaped by some very influential people.*

STEVE JOBS

Who's That? In 1976 Jobs sold his car for the $1,300 necessary to co-found Apple Computers. Working out of his parents' garage in Los Altos, Jobs and engineering whiz Steve Wozniak created the first successful, mass-produced personal computer; Jobs then went on to create companies and products that changed the world. A few of his inventions: the Macintosh (1984), the first commercial personal computer to feature a mouse, windows, icons, and an interface that allowed users to run programs without typing commands at the keyboard; NeXT Computers (1988), instrumental in the invention of Web browsers and the World Wide Web; Pixar Animation Studios (1986), home of *Toy Story*, the first fully computer-animated movie; and the iPod (2001), iTunes (2003), iPhone (2007), and iPad (2010).

Shaping California: Jobs led consumers into the computer age with products that changed their music, movies, phones, and relationships with computers. When Jobs started Apple, California's Silicon Valley—though already a center for electronics production—wasn't well known. Today, it's a high-tech leader. As of 2007, Silicon Valley had more millionaires and billionaires than any other part of the country, and in 2010 the area received almost a third of the billions invested in U.S. companies.

MARY PICKFORD

Who's That? Sixteen-year-old Gladys Smith changed her name to Mary Pickford just before she arrived in California in 1910 to act in Hollywood silent movies. Starring in nearly 200 films over a 25-year career, Pickford also became one of the industry's first female producers, co-founding United Artists.

Shaping California: During her lifetime, Pickford was Hollywood's most beloved and highest-paid actress. Nicknamed "America's sweetheart," she was the one who started the cult of Hollywood celebrity and the public fascination with the lives of movie stars.

The public was mesmerized by Pickford's "glamorous Hollywood lifestyle," which included a palatial estate in Beverly Hills where she lived with her husband, the swashbuckling actor Douglas Fairbanks. In what would also become a Hollywood tradition, Pickford kept many scandalous secrets. She and Fairbanks had both been married to other people when they began a clandestine affair. Pickford also hid her struggle with depression and alcoholism, along with the pain of a seemingly glamorous, but very unhappy, marriage that ultimately ended in infidelity and divorce.

JOHN STEINBECK

Who's That? Steinbeck wrote 27 books, most of them set in Northern California's Salinas Valley where he grew up. His best-known works include *Of Mice and Men* (1937) and the Pulitzer–Prize winning novel *The Grapes of Wrath* (1939). Steinbeck used his stories to represent life's struggles, and his sympathetic portrayals of the poor and oppressed made him one of the world's most famous authors. Steinbeck won the Nobel Prize for Literature in 1962

Shaping California: *The Grapes of Wrath* exposed the plight of California's "Okies" (*more about that on page 351*), dust bowl migrants who arrived during the Great Depression. Many traveled to California to pick crops and get a new start, but they ran into prejudice, low wages, and frequent layoffs. The homeless workers lived in migrant camps, where many died of starvation despite the fact that California continued to have decent harvests.

The Grapes of Wrath was a controversial best seller that told the story of the Joads, a fictional family from Oklahoma who endured hardship and tragedy as they worked the farms of California. Readers sympathized with the Joads and wanted to do something to ease the suffering of migrants. The book angered many of California's agricultural leaders, but also inspired congressional hearings that improved migrant housing and labor laws in the state.

For more personalities, turn to page 315.

ALMOST FAMOUS

California has so many world-famous attractions that many lesser-known ones get overshadowed...like these.

FLIGHTDECK AIR COMBAT CENTER
Location: Anaheim

If you ever wanted to be a fighter pilot but didn't have the patience for years of military training, this place is for you. Eight military simulators let visitors take off, shoot missiles, and land on an aircraft carrier. The center's staff even puts would-be pilots through "flight training" before allowing them to man a cockpit.

TREES OF MYSTERY
Location: Klamath

For some, a trip to see the redwoods along the Northern California coast wouldn't be complete without a sky tram over the treetops, a giant talking (and joke-making) Paul Bunyan, and gift-shop fudge. Trees of Mystery, just south of Crescent City, is California kitsch at its very finest—a roadside attraction nestled into the splendid redwood forest.

BIG BEAR LAKE
Location: San Bernadino National Forest

Sure, Lake Tahoe gets all the glory, but Southern Californians have been flocking to Big Bear Lake since cars were first able to climb the steep mountains. Big Bear is a year-round resort: There's fishing, water-skiing, autumn-leaf gazing, and downhill skiing, along with countless restaurants and hotels. How did the area get its name? When American explorer and (later) rancher Benjamin Davis Wilson arrived in California in the 1840s (on a mission to track down a group of Native American horse thieves), he stumbled on the lake and surrounding valley. At the time, the area was populated by the Serrano Indians and an enormous number of grizzly bears. The Indians cherished and worshipped the grizzlies, believing them to be tribal ancestors, but the Americans hunted the animals (eventually to extinction in the region) for their pelts. Wilson named the place Bear Valley in honor of the animals.

There are about 44 million bubbles in a bottle of sparkling wine.

A CAPITOL IDEA

Building California's state capitol was a project so elaborate and underfunded that could drive an architect crazy. In fact, it did. Such was the sad story of Reuben Clark.

THE IDEA MAN

San Francisco architect Reuben Clark was optimistic when he submitted plans for an ornate capitol building in 1856. It had been only six years since statehood, and California's politicians were tired of moving the capital city from town to town. They'd already relocated three times since the first territorial session in Monterey in 1849. After San Jose, Vallejo, and Benicia came up short, the government finally moved to Sacramento, a city that was growing quickly because of its proximity to the gold fields.

This time, the chosen city was good enough, but officials were tired of meeting in its cramped county courthouse. They wanted a permanent building. That's where Clark came in. His design was patterned after the U.S. Capitol Building, and the board set up to oversee construction of the new building liked its grandeur. Clark got the job.

After relocating from San Francisco, Clark hired workers and got going on the project right away. But just a week into the planning stages, he was told to stop. The state had run into financial trouble, and there was no money available for the project.

HURRY UP AND WAIT

That's how things stood for four long years, but finally the board met again in 1860, certain it had enough money to get the project going again. The time gap, though, had allowed the board's members a chance for second thoughts. They decided that instead of just going forward with Clark, they'd have an open competition to find an architect. Seven architects presented designs, but the one the board liked best looked remarkably familiar. Although it belonged to a San Francisco architect named Miner Frederick Butler, the design looked almost identical to the one Reuben Clark had come up with four years earlier.

The sorcerer to whom Mickey Mouse is apprenticed in Disney's *Fantasia* is called...

Butler was immediately accused of plagiarism, but he had a defense—Reuben Clark created his design while working as an employee of Butler's architectural firm, and that firm had a strict "no moonlighting" policy. Therefore, Butler argued, Clark's design legally belonged to him. Eventually, the board decided Butler was right and awarded him the $1,500 architecture fee for the capitol building. Clark got a consolation prize—he would be hired as the project's supervising architect and would share credit with his former employer.

Clark dove into the work with enthusiasm, moving forward despite frustrating delays, haphazard funding, and the difficulty of getting building materials from the East Coast because of the Civil War. Flooding from the American River also deluged the site, destroying Clark's plans and drawings and requiring that a whole new foundation be built that was six feet higher than the first.

WHISPERS AND RUMORS

The longer the project took, the more Clark came under heavy pressure from an impatient government. He began taking out his frustrations on his slow-moving work crews...a big mistake. The disgruntled workers started spreading rumors about him, saying he was really a Southern sympathizer. They pointed to his earlier work on Mississippi's capitol building, claimed he was hiring "secessionists," and quoted him as saying he didn't care if the North won the war.

Just as being called a Communist in the 1950s could destroy a career, being called a Confederate sympathizer in 1865 was a serious charge that was hard to refute. Shortly after President Abraham Lincoln's assassination, when anti-South sentiment was running high, the Sacramento Union League—a social club of upper-middle-class men dedicated to public projects, social drinking, and stanch pro-Union patriotism—accused Clark of being a traitor.

"HALLUCINATION" OR REALITY?

Tired of all the pressure, innuendo, and insubordination, Clark applied for a leave of absence for health reasons from the capitol building project. When he decided he still wasn't ready to return as planned on January 1, 1866, he was fired and replaced by his assistant. Clark didn't take the news well. On February 5, a doctor from the California Department of Mental Hygiene interviewed him and reported that he was "subject to violent outbursts of passion, incoherency of ideas, difficulty in communication, loss of memory, [insomnia]. He sometimes threatens the life of his family…His hallucination is that someone is supplanting him in his position as architect of the Capitol…Cause: Continued and too close attention to the building of the State Capitol. Class: Monomania [defined in 19th-century psychiatry as a pathological fixation on a single issue in an otherwise sound mind]; no particular treatment."

Clark never recovered from the breakdown, and neither he nor Butler lived to see the capitol finished. Clark was committed to the Stockton State Hospital and died on July 4, 1866; Butler died in 1871. The California State Capitol was finished in 1874, and today it houses the state legislature and the office of the governor.

* * *

WEIRD (BUT REAL) COURSES
AT CALIFORNIA COLLEGES

- Arguing with Judge Judy: Popular "Logic" on TV Shows (UC Berkeley)

- Underwater Basket Weaving (UC San Diego)

- Learning from YouTube (Pitzer College)

- The Unbearable Whiteness of Barbie (Occidental College)

- Queer Musicology (UCLA)

- The Joy of Garbage (Santa Clara University)

- The Science of Superheroes (UC Irvine)

- The Simpsons and Philosophy (UC Berkeley)

- Stupidity (Occidental College)

URBAN ORE

One man's trash really is another man's treasure.

THREE ACRES OF STUFF

Toilets. There are dozens of them—white ones, shiny ones, old ones, even porta-potties. And they're clean, and pretty cheap to boot. That's what caught Uncle John's attention when he strolled through Urban Ore in Berkeley. Chances are, whatever you're looking for, you'll find it there: clothes, furniture, books, tools, art, knickknacks, tents, surfboards, electronics, lumber, cabinets, doors (they sell *a lot* of doors), and much more. (Sorry—no guns, pornography, auto parts, or hazardous chemicals.)

Urban Ore is no mere thrift store. It's one of the world's largest "ecoparks." Located in a massive warehouse on a huge lot that spans three acres in west Berkeley, people go there to donate their old junk, buy building materials for a home project, or just look around and gawk at the enormity of it all. (And this being California, you might just spot a celebrity or two: Regular customers include singers Chris Izaak and Country Joe McDonald, and the Grateful Dead's Mickey Hart.)

A MAN WITH A PLAN

Urban Ore was started in 1980 by Daniel Knapp and his wife, Mary Lou Van Deventer. The idea came to Knapp a few years earlier when he was a sociology professor. He took some students to a landfill and was amazed by all the usable stuff people just threw away. Knapp's big idea: Salvage the trash and sell it. Urban Ore made about $150 its first year. In 2010 it made $2.7 million.

Knapp's goal with Urban Ore is loftier than mere profit, though; he's striving for what he calls "the end of the age of waste." Everything that would normally be thrown away is either repurposed, reused, or recycled. For his part, Knapp estimates that Urban Ore keeps about 8,000 tons of material out of landfills each year. He even has three full-time employees who go to landfills every day to salvage whatever items they can later sell. As Knapp likes to say, "Waste isn't waste until it's wasted."

DUNE TUNES

If we told you that there are sand dunes in California that can actually play music all by themselves, would you believe us?

WHEN IN DOUBT, BLAME EVIL SPIRITS
In the 13th century, while traveling through the Gobi Desert, explorer Marco Polo heard eerie sounds coming from the sand dunes around him. He described the noise as "all kinds of musical instruments, and also of drums and the clash of arms." After hearing the mysterious noises, Polo came to the "logical" conclusion that he must be in the presence of evil spirits.

These days, we know that all that music was nature, not spirits. Of all the sand dunes in the world, only a few have the ability to "sing" in the ways that so startled Marco Polo. Beach sand sometimes makes brief squeaking noises, but it's rare to find dunes that produce the magnificent instrumentals Polo described. There are actually only about 30 singing sand dunes on earth, and California has four noisy sets of them.

• The **Kelso Dunes** are the loudest of California's singing sands. Located in the Devil's Playground area of the Mojave National Preserve, the Kelso Dunes rise as high as 650 feet.

• The sounds of the **Dumont Dunes**, also located in the preserve, were filmed for the PBS *Nova* episode "Booming Sands." According to researchers, the Dumont Dunes "sing" the note of G.

• The **Eureka Dunes** in Death Valley National Park are the highest group of dunes in California. Rising 680 feet from the valley floor, the dunes are also thought to be the tallest in North America.

• Also found in the park, the **Panamint Dunes** have been known to produce noises, but are the least tuneful of all of California's singing sands.

SINGING SANDS

Why is it that some dunes sing while others are silent? Scientists are still trying to figure that out, but they know some things for sure. Singing dunes need a special recipe of sand, moisture, wind, and movement. In particular, the dunes must be created out of

---

California law prohibits women from driving a car while dressed in a housecoat.

grains of sand that have been windblown over long distances, making them unusually smooth and round. All the grains must be similar in size, and the dunes free of foreign particles. Humidity and moisture also affect the sound—too much moisture and the sand goes silent because the grains can't move. But the dune must have some rainfall so that its inner grains stay a little damp.

When a dune creates sound, its outer layer (a few feet thick) of sand grains are dry from the sun, but its inner core can be wet and hard as cement from previous rainstorms. Wind then pushes sand grains to the top of the dune and they accumulate there until the angle of the slope reaches a tipping point of about 35 degrees. That causes an avalanche of sand grains to fall, moving against one another, creating friction and producing the loud bass rumble of dune music.

At least, that's how it's done in nature. In the name of science, researchers usually produce their own avalanches and sandy symphonies by hiking to the highest spot on the dune and then sliding down on their derrieres.

SCIENCE FROM THE BOTTOM UP

California Institute of Technology professor Melany L. Hunt and many of her graduate students have been among those sliding down California's dunes to research the secrets of sand noise. By sitting on the dunes when they sing, researchers have learned that vibrations throughout the entire dune are part of the music. Often, even after the sand has stopped moving, the dunes continue to vibrate and boom for a few minutes. And by using radar, computers, and *geophones* (microphones that can be buried in sand), Caltech researchers have measured the frequencies and rates of vibration of the dune songs. They've discovered that older, higher dunes with steep slopes are most likely to produce music, which is louder in the fall than in the spring. Most importantly, though, they've found that dunes produce a tone similar to one produced by a stringed instrument, and they think they know how that happens.

Singing dunes have their outer layer of dry sand (about five feet thick) that conducts sound much better than the moist inner sand. The differences in conduction between the dry and hard sand causes the noise to bounce around in the dry layer, magnifying the vibrations and amplifying the sound. Hunt has compared the singing sand dunes to cellos: "In a cello, the musician bows the strings, and the sound is amplified through vibrations of the cello [body] and the enclosed air. In the dune, we excite the system by avalanching the sand on the upper surface, and the sound is amplified in the dry, loose upper layer of sand."

Scientific research has also shown that the windblown sands in California's singing dunes do have special, noisemaking properties. Put ordinary beach sand in a jar and shake it up, and you won't hear a peep. Put dry singing dune sand in a clean jar, shake it up, and you'll probably hear a sound. Next time you're in the Mojave Desert, give it a try.

* * *

GATHERING THE TRIBES

California's 1960s counterculture movement spawned several whimsical and innovative public gatherings:

• **The Renaissance Pleasure Faire:** The first Renaissance Pleasure Faire took place in 1962 in Agoura Hills near L.A., a joint project of schoolteacher Phyllis Patterson, her husband Ron, and the Living History Center. That spring festival quickly spawned a similar one each fall in Marin County. The fairs were very popular with hippies in the 1960s as one of the few places that actively welcomed long hair, beards, role-playing, and eccentric costumes.

• **Love-Ins and Be-Ins:** On October 6, 1966, the day LSD became illegal in California, thousands of people gathered in Golden Gate Park to protest. The Love Pageant Rally featured flowers, flutes, incense, and lots of LSD ingestion. The rally inspired the Human Be-In on January 17, 1967, which attracted 30,000 people to Golden Gate Park. This ultimately led to the counterculture and political "Summer of Love" protests, which brought the 1960s hippie revolution into the mainstream.

• **Fantasy Fair:** The Fantasy Fair and Magic Mountain Magic Festival, held in June 1967, was the first large-scale rock festival, featuring many groups playing over a long weekend.

The only California park accessible only by boat is...

THIS OLD $HACK, PART I

A bedroom or two, a bathroom or two, and a place to be a couch potato...that's all you really need, right? Not if you're a bazillionaire in California.

T**HE GREYSTONE MANSION**
Address: 905 Loma Vista Drive, Beverly Hills
Rich Residents: Ned Doheny and family
Why It's Famous: The Greystone Mansion began as a wedding present from oil baron Edward L. Doheny, who drilled L.A.'s first successful oil well in 1892, to his son Ned and new daughter-in-law Lucy. It was 12.58 acres of land where the Dohenys built a $3.1 million mansion in the late 1920s, the most expensive home ever built in California at the time. Ned was murdered just four months after they moved in, but his wife and children remained until 1955. After that, the mansion changed hands several times before it became part of the city's parks department and was listed on the National Register of Historic Places. But what makes Greystone really famous is that it's been a filming site for some of Hollywood's most famous movies and TV shows, including *X-Men*, *The Big Lebowski*, *There Will Be Blood*, *Batman and Robin*, *Gilmore Girls*, *The Witches of Eastwick*, and *Ghostbusters II*.
Can I Visit? Yes. The property is a now a public park and is open for tours.

THE HEARST CASTLE

Address: 750 Hearst Castle Road, San Simeon
Rich Residents: William Randolph Hearst, his wife Millicent, their five sons, and occasionally, his mistress Marion Davies
Why It's Famous: Possibly the most famous California mansion ever, the Hearst Castle took almost 30 years to build. Originally, newspaper magnate William Randolph Hearst intended to build a cabin on a stretch of land that his wealthy miner father left to him when he died, but ideas quickly spun out of control. In the end, the mansion grew to boast an airfield, a movie theater, a private zoo, 58 bedrooms, 60 bathrooms, and two swimming pools, one of which resembles a Roman bath and includes floor-to-ceiling mosaic tiles infused with gold.

...Ahjumawi Lava Springs State Park in Shasta County.

Can I Visit? Yes. The castle is open for business and offers several types of tours.

FALCON LAIR

Address: 1436 Bella Drive, Beverly Hills
Rich Residents: Rudolph Valentino, Gloria Swanson, Doris Duke, and Joe Castro
Why It's Famous: Italian actor Rudolph Valentino rose to fame in the 1920s playing dashing leading men in movies like *The Sheik* and *The Four Horsemen of the Apocalypse*. In 1925, he bought Falcon Lair, a mansion in Beverly Hills that he intended to share with his wife of two years, Natacha. But Natacha didn't actually want to be married (rumor was, she was a lesbian), and she divorced him before the home was completed. Ultimately, Valentino used the home as a retreat and furnished it with fabulous antiques purchased during his travels overseas. When he died of a perforated gastric ulcer in 1926, Falcon Lair was sold to pay his debts.

In the 1950s, actress Gloria Swanson rented the place for a while, and then Doris Duke (heir to a tobacco and energy fortune) moved in with her boyfriend, jazz pianist Joe Castro. Duke was an antiques collector, and she bought all the pieces to Napoleon's original war room, shipped them to California, and set them up in the house just as the emperor had displayed them in the 1800s. Duke died in 1993 under mysterious circumstances, and the butler everyone suspected of killing her (by drugging her with morphine) was named a beneficiary in her will. He lived there until his death in 1996…caring for the dogs Duke had left behind and to whom she had willed more than $100,000. After Duke's death the mansion was sold again…and again…and again, but was never really renovated or kept up. Finally, it fell into such disrepair that the main buildings were demolished in 2006.

Can I Visit? No. The house is gone, but the property and the outer gates are still there.

For more lavish California homes, turn to page 240.

Beach Boy Brian Wilson flunked a music class at Hawthorne High.

NOTABLE ASPHALT

*Living in California means spending a lot of time on the road.
How about some trivia about those freeways you're driving
on? (Please don't read this until the traffic has stopped.)*

THE START OF IT ALL

For better or worse, the Arroyo Seco Parkway connecting
Los Angeles and Pasadena got California's wheels rolling.
When it opened in 1940 (the first highway in the western United
States), it was just 3.2 miles long; later that year, it was expanded
to six miles long and could handle about 27,000 cars a day. As
people moved to the state, though, that setup quickly became out-
dated. Today, the Arroyo Seco is 8.162 miles long and can support
up to 122,000 cars each day...and that's still not enough. Traffic
often gets congested in its six lanes.

The Arroyo Seco (Spanish for "dry streambed") was named for
an intermittent stream that flowed from the San Gabriel Mountains to the Los Angles River. Originally, the road was a parkway,
meaning that it had a center island with trees and grass. Over the
years, the landscaping was removed to make way for more lanes,
and the road became known as the Pasadena Freeway. But in 2010,
the California Department of Transportation (Caltrans) changed
the name back to the original to honor its historic value.

THAT LONG AND WINDING ROAD

At 807 miles, U.S Highway 101 is the longest roadway in the
state...it's also one of the oldest. The original 101 stretched along
the Pacific coastline from the Mexican border to Olympia, Washington. In California, much of it followed El Camino Real (Spanish for "The Royal Road"), the trail from San Diego to San
Francisco that Spanish padres built in the 17th and 18th centuries
to connect their 21 missions. Today, the southern part of the highway has been shortened—it now begins near downtown L.A.—
but not much else has changed.

THE SHORT OF IT

According to Caltrans, the state's shortest highway is State Route

153. Located in El Dorado County in the Sierra Nevadas, the "highway" stretches just half a mile from the gold rush town of Coloma to a parking lot at Marshall Gold Discovery State Historic Park. The park contains a monument to James Marshall, who discovered gold along the American River in 1848. Many people believe that Marshall not only started the gold rush, but that he also launched California's notorious population growth—which has brought with it a whole lot of roads and cars.

CONGESTION FREEWAY

A 2011 study by the Texas Transportation Commission revealed what many California commuters already knew: The most congested stretches of highway in the U.S. are in Los Angeles. A three-mile piece of the northbound Harbor Freeway between I-10 and Stadium Way near Dodger Stadium "won" the title of most congested. The second most congested area in the country is the northbound six-mile stretch at the intersection of Harbor Freeway and I-10, just south of downtown Los Angeles. Third worst: a 13-mile stretch heading north on I-405 near L.A.'s Getty Center Drive.

IT'S CAR-NAGE OUT THERE!

Although California has plenty of freeways with dangerous interchanges and curse-worthy hairpin turns, the deadliest stretch of asphalt in the United States is a straight, 181-mile section of I-15 running through the open desert and connecting Los Angeles to Las Vegas. U.S. Department of Transportation reports show that over a period of 15 years, there were 834 accidents and 1,069 fatalities on this road. That's more than double the death toll of any other road in the country. Why? I-15 does go to Vegas, after all, and alcohol is a factor in about a quarter of the accidents. A third of the crashes involved speeding, and half the people who died weren't wearing seat belts. But officials claim the main problem is that people get careless on a straight road with miles of visibility—it tends "to put drivers to sleep."

For more freeway trivia, cruise over to page 159.

SOLD!

People will sell (and buy) just about anything on eBay. Need a haunted painting? Some fingernails from a serial killer? They're just a mouse click away.

CALIFORNIA COLLECTIBLE: A haunted painting
STORY: In 2000 an anonymous couple listed a painting for sale on eBay with a warning: "Do not bid on this painting if you are susceptible to stress-related disease, faint of heart, or are unfamiliar with supernatural events." The couple found the painting behind an abandoned California brewery, and it does look creepy—there's a boy with a vacant stare next to a spooky doll-like girl, with several hands grabbing at them from behind. Its title is chilling, too: Hands Resist Him. Naturally, the couple hung it in their four-year-old daughter's bedroom.

The girl soon complained that "the children in the picture were fighting and coming into the room during the night." Instead of taking the haunted work of art down, though, the parents set up a motion-sensor camera that did appear to capture the boy moving. Then the family learned about the painting's perilous past: For a time, it was on display in Los Angeles, but both the gallery owner and the *L.A. Times* critic who reviewed it died soon after. Finally the couple had had enough and onto eBay it went…with the warning and a disclaimer releasing the couple of all supernatural liability. E-mails poured in from people who felt sick or fainted after just looking at its listing. Still, the painting got 30 bids.

SELLING PRICE: $1,025

CALIFORNIA COLLECTIBLE: A town on the Northern California coast

STORY: In 2002 the Humboldt County hamlet of Bridgeville (population "about 30") made news as the first town ever to be offered for sale via eBay auction. A family had paid $150,000 for the former timber town in 1973 and could no longer afford its repairs. So they put together a deal that included more than 80 acres of land, a mile of riverbank, a post office that doubles as a library, an abandoned café, a cemetery, a stone bridge built in the 1920s, about a dozen houses, and its own ZIP code.

…A: He was the first non–Native American child born in California.

At first it seemed Bridgeville would sell quickly, but then *Time* magazine called it "a rural slum," overrun with uninhabitable shacks, broken septic tanks, and abandoned vehicles. The winning bidder got cold feet and disappeared. That's when Laguna Hills banker Bruce Krall stepped in and bought it for the bargain price of $700,000. Over the next four years, he got rid of 10 semi trucks full of debris, installed a septic system, and repaired buildings, hoping to turn Bridgeville into a coastal vacation spot. But eventually he couldn't afford to make any more renovations. So in 2006, he resold it (now with eight houses, three cows, and a population of about 20) on eBay...for more than $1 million. The new owner was a 25-year-old entertainment manager from L.A. who began construction on an elementary/middle school and a park... but then tragically, he killed himself later that year. The 140-year-old town was listed for sale on eBay *again* in 2007—this time at $1.3 million.

SELLING PRICE: No takers

CALIFORNIA COLLECTIBLES: Fingernails and a cut-up Christmas card from a convicted murderer

STORY: Southern California isn't all palm trees and sunshine. It was also the stomping grounds for 10 percent of the world's known serial killers during the 20th century. Among them were Lawrence Bittaker and Roy Norris, who met in prison in San Luis Obispo in the 1970s and, after their release, bought a windowless van they nicknamed Murder Mack. During the summer of 1979, they cruised beaches, photographing and picking up girls. They raped and murdered at least five. Norris eventually testified against Bittaker for a sentence of 45-years-to-life—Bittaker got the death penalty.

In the 1970s, collectors had begun seeking out "murderabilia," souvenirs from heinous crimes and killers. Bittaker sold his prison-issued socks, but Norris hoped to really cash in. While imprisoned, he clipped his fingernails and taped them to a piece of a cut-up Christmas card. He authenticated the card with a long handwritten note, his signature, and his fingerprint. It's unclear who or how many people the card belonged to over the years, but it turned up on eBay in 1999.

SELLING PRICE: The item got just one bid...for $9.99.

The departure point for the "3-hour tour" on *Gilligan's Island*: Alamitos Bay, Long Beach.

THE YEAST SAN FRANCISCO CAN DO

If you thought sourdough was invented in San Francisco...you'd be wrong! But the city did make it famous. Here's how.

A SOUR HISTORY

Sourdough is the oldest type of leavened (raised) bread in the world. The ancient Egyptians first baked it about 3,500 years ago by mixing flour, water, and a little salt, and then letting it sit at room temperature. Wild yeast (which was always in the air) settled, grew in the dough, and then fermented, creating the sour smell. That first batch was called the "starter" (or "sponge," or "mother dough") because it could be used for years as yeast for additional loaves of bread.

Sourdough probably came to California with Alaskan miners, many of whom kept a piece of starter with them at all times so they could always have fresh bread. As long as they added a little water and flour every other week or so, the starter would last for years. According to legend, many miners in the California gold fields kept a bit of starter in their cabins and even slept with it to keep the dough from freezing. Over the centuries, the recipe traveled the world and finally ended up in San Francisco in the 1840s.

MOTHER OF ALL SOURDOUGHS

Today there are about 60 commercial sourdough bread bakeries in San Francisco, and one of them is also the oldest continuously operating business in the city. Isidore Boudin, the son of a master baker from France, rolled into San Francisco around 1849 and opened the Boudin Bakery. He was just in time for the gold rush and the influx of single mining men who wanted someone to cook for them.

The miners taught Boudin about sourdough and how to make a starter. He combined that with what he knew of French baking and created his shop's mother dough, which the Boudin Bakery claims it still uses today to start every white sourdough loaf it

San Francisco is the birthplace of mall mainstays Banana Republic and Old Navy.

makes. (Boudin's official history includes a story of granddaughter Louise Boudin escaping the 1906 earthquake and fire and carrying the mother dough to safety in a bucket.) Many food historians debate this claim, saying it's possible that the present-day starter is the direct descendant of the original batch, but more likely, the original mother dough was lost long ago because it wasn't kept sterile during the early years. Either way, the Boudin Bakery laid the foundation for San Francisco's sourdough empire.

WHY IS SAN FRANCISCO SOURDOUGH SO GOOD?

Many people think that San Francisco sourdough is the best in the world, and the city definitely has some of the best weather conditions for creating the starter. Wild yeasts are abundant and can settle in any food and cause fermentation. But what San Francisco really has going for it is the crucial silent partner in sourdough: lactic acid bacteria. The bacteria are crucial to creating sourdough because they excrete glucose that the yeast feeds on, and they grow naturally in San Francisco. In fact, lactic acid bacteria are so abundant around the city that the dominant strain is even named *Lactobacillus sanfranciscensis*. These bacteria grow best in humid fog and temperatures between the low 60s and the low 80s... conditions that match San Francisco's weather perfectly.

SOME SOUR FACTS

• The bacteria in sourdough are "good" bacteria, also known as *probiotics*. They can help settle the symptoms of many digestive issues, including irritable bowel syndrome.

• On average, a slice of sourdough bread contains 96 calories.

• Sourdough starter is about 12 percent alcohol, the result of fermented sugars and yeast. Alaskan miners called the alcohol (some of which collects in a top layer of the dough) "hooch," after the Hoochinoo Native Americans, who liked to trade supplies for the booze.

• If a sourdough starter turns pink or orange, it's gone bad.

• The older the starter, the more tangy the bread will be.

• California gold rush miners were nicknamed "sourdoughs" because so many of them carried their starter in backpacks or in pouches worn under their shirts.

A SIGN OF THE TIMES

Technically, it's illegal to make "unauthorized alterations" to the famous Hollywood sign in Los Angeles. But over the years, a few pranksters have still managed to get noticed.

HOLLYWEED: On January 1, 1976, California's "relaxed marijuana law" decriminalizing adult use of the drug went into effect, and local stoner...er, Californian...Danny Finegood and some friends hung curtains painted with Es over the double Os to celebrate.

OLLYWOOD: Eleven years later, in 1987, Finegood and his buddies pulled another prank, covering up the H to protest of all the support Lieutenant-Colonel Oliver North received during the Iran-Contra scandal.

OIL WAR: Finegood draped the sign again in 1991 to protest the first Persian Gulf war. Of his efforts, his parents were said to have been "very proud."

HOLL+WOOD: In 1992, to promote their newest album *Wasted in America*, the band Love/Hate put up a large cross in front of the Y in Hollywood. Jizzy Pearl, the band's lead singer, then strapped himself to the cross in a mock crucifixion. The city was not amused, and Pearl was arrested for trespassing.

USCWOOD/GO UCLA: The rivalry between UCLA and USC is legendary, and before a football game in 1987, students at USC climbed into the Hollywood Hills to drape the sign so it read "USCWOOD." It took UCLA six years to retaliate, but in 1993, before another game, members of the school's Theta Chi fraternity got their revenge, draping the sign to read "GO UCLA."

HOLYWOOD: Hollywood has never been much of a "holy" town, but in 1987, when Pope John Paul II visited Los Angeles, someone (no one knows who) covered up one of the Ls to turn the city "holy" for the pope's visit.

WELCOME TO BAGDAD, CALIFORNIA

From A to Z, a tour of California cities and towns—some familiar, some not—and how they got their names.

ANAHEIM

Disneyland's hometown was founded by 50 German families in 1857 who came up with the name by combining Ana, after the nearby Santa Ana River, and the German word *heim*, meaning "home."

BAGDAD

Now a ghost town, Bagdad was originally a Mojave Desert train station along the Santa Fe Railroad line. The town got its name when the tracks were laid in 1883, but exactly who came up with it is unknown. Most people assume, though, that the name was chosen because the town's climate resembled Baghdad, Iraq.

BEVERLY HILLS

Before it became a haven for movie stars, Beverly Hills was ranch land where farmers raised sheep, cattle, and lima beans. A member of the real estate group that began subdividing the area in 1907 named it after a neighborhood called Beverly Farms in Beverly, Massachusetts—a favorite vacation spot of then-president William Howard Taft.

BURBANK

The city was *not* named after Luther Burbank, the famous plant breeder. He was still a teenager in 1867 when David Burbank, a New Hampshire–born dentist, drove his covered wagon across the plains to California and bought 10,000 acres north of L.A. In 1886 Burbank sold the land to a group of speculators who named the new town Burbank after its founder.

CALEXICO

The name Calexico is what's called a *portmanteau*, the joining of

---

California granted women the right to vote in 1911, nine years before the federal government.

two words into one: in this case, a combination of "CALifornia" and "mEXICO." OK, you may have guessed that. But did you know that Calexico's neighbor and sister city just across the border in Mexico is Mexicali?

COALINGA
Nestled in California's Central Valley, Coalinga was established in 1888 as a coaling station for the Southern Pacific Transportation Company—Coaling Station A. A railroad official decided it would sound a lot better by dropping the "Station" and adding the "A" to "Coaling."

EUREKA
The largest coastal city between San Francisco and Portland, Oregon, Eureka was named for the Greek word meaning "I have found it." What did the settlers find? Not the gold they were looking for, but lumber, fishing, and shipping—industries that kept the city afloat and thriving.

HERCULES
In 1869 the California Powder Works opened its dynamite factory in San Francisco (in what became Golden Gate Park the next year) and soon moved the facility to a more isolated area 20 miles to the northeast. Hercules was the name of the brand of dynamite the company produced, and they named the new town after it.

MALIBU
The area that became Malibu was originally home to the Chumash Nation, whose 7,000 square miles of prime real estate extended from San Luis Obispo in the north to Malibu in the south and inland to the San Joaquin Valley. The Chumash called the southern area *Humaliwo*, meaning "the surf sounds loudly." The "Hu" syllable was mostly silent, though, so the word sounded like "Malibu."

For more California place names, turn to page 147.

SALAD DAZE

*Salads were rare in the United States until the turn of the 20th
century, and they didn't become culinary works of art until the
1920s. Not surprisingly, California, with its year-round
sunshine and booming agricultural industry, gave the
world some of its most famous salad innovations.*

COBB SALAD. There are conflicting stories about who
actually created this salad in the 1930s: Bob Cobb, the
owner of L.A.'s Brown Derby, or the restaurant's chef.
Either way, the mixture of vegetables, diced chicken, eggs, bacon,
cheese, and French dressing was named after Cobb and quickly
became a staple all over the country.

TACO SALAD. According to author Jean Anderson in *The
American Century Cookbook* (1997), taco salad "arrived with the
Tex-Mex fast-food franchises, which began to pepper the country
in the '60s...The man who whetted our appetite for 'hot and spicy'
was Glen Bell, who opened the first Taco Bell in Downey, California. That was 1962. Did Taco Bell originate the taco salad? I've
been unable to prove it did. Or didn't. The first recipe I could find
for taco salad appeared in the May 1968 issue of *Sunset.*"

CAESAR SALAD. California gets only half the credit for this
one. Caesar Cardini lived in San Diego, but in the 1920s, he built
a restaurant just over the Mexican border in Tijuana to circum-
vent U.S. Prohibition laws. The result was a steady stream of
Southern California customers, and on July 4, 1924, Caesar's
restaurant had so many customers that he began running out of
food. The solution? According to his daughter, he put together a
quick, easy salad out of items in the kitchen: romaine lettuce,
croutons, lemon juice, Worcestershire sauce (which gave it a
slight anchovy taste), an egg, olive oil, and black pepper. He later
opened a restaurant in L.A. and sold the salad there too.

RANCH DRESSING. Hidden Valley Ranch was a real place—a
dude ranch outside Santa Barbara built by Gayle and Steve Hen-
son in 1954. At a time when meat and potatoes were king in

American kitchens and salads were considered "rabbit food," the Hensons created their own flavorful salad dressing so they could get their guests to eat inexpensive raw vegetables. The recipe called for buttermilk, mayonnaise, herbs, and spices, and the Hensons got so many compliments that they started selling the herb-and-spice mixture in envelopes that guests could take home and mix with their own buttermilk and mayo. In 1972 the Hensons sold the recipe and the Hidden Valley Ranch name to Oakland's Clorox Co. for $8 million. First, Clorox added buttermilk flavoring to the mix so buyers could use plain milk, but in 1983, the company began selling the dressing in bottles. In 1992 ranch became America's most popular salad dressing.

GREEN GODDESS DRESSING. Credit for Green Goddess (mayonnaise, sour cream, lemon juice, pepper, anchovies, chives, chervil, and tarragon) goes to Philip Roemer, a former chef at the Palm Court Restaurant in San Francisco's Palace Hotel. In the mid-1920s, actor George Arliss stayed at the hotel and often ate at the Palm Court while he starred in a William Archer play nearby. Chef Roemer concocted the dressing as a tribute to Arliss…and he named it after the play—*The Green Goddess*.

*　*　*

YOU KNOW YOU'RE A CALIFORNIAN IF...

- Your monthly mortgage payment is higher than your monthly salary.

- Your first-grader's teacher has an orange mohawk, multiple piercings, and insists that the children call her by her first name…Willow.

- You feel bad for anyone who doesn't have access to an In-N-Out.

- You can go surfing (in a wetsuit) and snow skiing (in shorts) on the same day.

- You would *never* call it "Cali."

- You're always forgetting…is pot legal?

Real name of L.A.'s Guns 'n' Roses guitarist Slash: Saul Hudson.

ROADSIDE ATTRACTIONS

Next time you're on a road trip and need a break,
consider one of these pit stops.

The Giant Clams: Pismo
Beach

Monopoly in the Park:
San Jose

The Bearded Muffler Man:
Hayward

The Giant Lemon:
Lemon Grove

The Circus Trees:
Gilroy

World's Largest Artichoke:
Castroville

**The Building Shaped Like a
Shoe:** Bakersfield

The Drive-Thru Tree:
Leggett

Bennie the Dinosaur: Benicia

Hobbiton: Phillipsville

The Moving Rocks: Death
Valley

Bosco, the Dog Mayor:
Sunol

Chicken Boy: Los Angeles

The Great Statues: Auburn

Santa Claus: Oxnard

The Giant Orange:
San Jose

The Petrified Forest:
Calistoga

**The Haunted Aircraft
Carrier:** Alameda

The One-Log House: Bear
Valley

The Ship House:
Encinitas

**Queen Califia's Magical
Circle Garden:** Escondido

Pink's Hotdogs:
Hollywood

**The Coffee Pot Water
Tower:** Kingsburg

The Big Doughnut: Inglewood

Salvation Mountain: Niland

GO, POETS!
BEAT SLUGS!

Are you a Dirtbag, an Anteater, or a Banana Slug? Do you know why?

THE BANANA SLUGS
School: UC Santa Cruz
Mascot: Sammy the Slug
Why they're called that: Students at UC Santa Cruz are lovers, not fighters, and originally they chose this slimy yellow mollusk (found mostly in the state's redwood forests) to represent them because they believed that it was more important to enjoy playing sports than to win games. The *Ariolimax dolichophallus*—the banana slug's scientific name—seemed to be the perfect counterpoint to the vicious predators most schools chose to represent their athletic teams.

The school's administration didn't like the mascot, however, and wanted something more "dignified" and "serious." So in 1980, when Santa Cruz graduated from a loose athletic program of intramural sports to real NCAA competition, the school changed its mascot...to the Sea Lions. But students remained loyal to the banana slug, and after a landslide vote in 1986, the administration changed it back. The Banana Slugs have received lots of love in the mainstream media ever since: Quentin Tarantino famously adorned John Travolta in a UCSC T-shirt in the movie *Pulp Fiction*, and *Reader's Digest* named it the NCAA's top mascot in 2004.

THE DONS
School: University of San Francisco
Mascot: The Don
Why they're called that: The athletic teams at the University of San Francisco were known as the Grey Fog until November 1931, when student body president George Ososke got an angry letter from the city's junior chamber of commerce. In it, the group complained that "Grey Fog" reinforced negative images of San Francisco and could discourage tourism. Ososke brought the issue to his superiors, and two months later, a committee of four under-

graduates, four alumni, and four administrators was established to select a new entity to represent them. The committee considered several promising names, including the Vigilantes, Golden Gaters, and Seagulls, but in the end, they decided to pick Dons. Why? The term is an honorific once reserved for Spanish and Portuguese royalty and nobility, and was chosen to reflect the area's Spanish roots. In the years since, it's morphed into the school's debonair Zorro-like mascot who can be seen supporting USF at sporting events.

THE ANTEATERS

School: UC Irvine

Mascot: Peter the Anteater

Why they're called that: The students at UC Irvine had a difficult decision to make on November 29, 1965, when they were asked to select a mascot for their school's athletic teams. On the ballot were four eclectic choices: an eagle, a unicorn, a seahawk, and an anteater. All the creatures had their merits, but students ultimately choose the anteater, in part because the feisty, long-nosed mammal was one of the stars of Johnny Hart's B.C. comic strip, which was extremely popular at the time.

It took administrators a while to embrace the choice, but eventually, they came around and today there is even a school-sponsored sign at Orange County's John Wayne International Airport proclaiming "Welcome to Anteater Country."

THE KEELHAULERS

School: The California Maritime Academy

Mascot: A pirate

Why they're called that: A "keelhaul" was an old form of corporal punishment on British and Dutch sailing ships, in which insubordinate sailors were tied to a rope and dragged under the keel of a ship while hundreds of barnacles scraped at their skin. The United Kingdom and the Netherlands officially abolished keelhauling in 1853. Before the 1970s, the school's teams were called the Seawolves, but a student vote showed that Cal Maritime athletes wanted something a little more menacing and unique, and the Keelhaulers were born.

"Californians are a race of people; they are not merely inhabitants of a state."—O. Henry

THE POETS
School: Whittier College
Mascot: Johnny Poet
Why they're called that: Few academic institutions have a more genteel nickname than Whittier College, where the athletic teams have been known as the Poets since 1907. The name is a tip of the cap to the celebrated Quaker poet and abolitionist John Greenleaf Whittier, for whom the college is named.

THE GAUCHOS
School: UC Santa Barbara
Mascot: Gaucho Joe
Why they're called that: In 1936 actor Douglas Fairbanks was so popular at UC Santa Barbara that the student body voted to change its name from the Roadrunners to the Gauchos in honor of his performance as a South American cowboy in the movie *The Gaucho*. The student body tried to change the name again many years later after Fairbanks's star had faded, but could never come up with a suitable replacement.

THE DIRTBAGS
School: Long Beach State University
Mascot: None
Why they're called that: Officially, the Long Beach State University teams are called the 49ers, but in 1989 the men's baseball team started calling itself the Dirtbags. That year, the team started practicing on an all-dirt field, and the switch left many Long Beach players covered in...well...dirt after practice was over. In the years since, the name has become a beloved part of the program's gritty identity. "Being a Dirtbag is more about the attitude that you play with," said former Long Beach pitcher Jeremy Ward. "You are required to give 110 percent all of the time." Of course, not everyone is a fan of the team's nickname: *Time* magazine included the Dirtbags on its 2009 list of the Top 10 Worst Team Names.

DIY ARCHITECTURE

A man's home is his castle...especially when he gathers
up a bunch of junk and builds it by hand.

N**ITT WITT RIDGE**
Location: 881 Hillcrest Drive, Cambria
Materials: To build this junk-heap castle, California artist
Arthur Beal (1896–1992)—also known as Captain Nitt Witt—
used rusted metal, broken TV sets, glass bottles, beer cans, abalone
shells, old toilets, and even golf balls (as ornaments for his bed-
posts). The stairway railings had working faucets at the bottom,
and a series of dirty sinks made up an outdoor waterfall. Legend
says that Beal—who sometimes worked as a garbage collector—
got a lot of his construction materials from the Dumpsters at nearby San Simeon, where newspaper publisher William Randolph
Hearst built his own sprawling castle.
History: Beal never really took his creation seriously. He was an
eccentric artist, and the idea for the house just came to him—one
day in 1928, he decided to stack some junk and make himself a
home. Beal lived at Nitt Witt Ridge until family members concerned about his mental state sent him to a nursing home in his
mid-90s. (He snuck out almost immediately, but caregivers found
him safe at his castle and brought him back.)
Bonus: There's a picture of Beal by Nitt Witt Ridge's front gate.
The black-and-white portrait shows a genial old man in a fur hat,
and it sits in a place of honor: taped to the lid of an old toilet bowl.

FORESTIERE UNDERGROUND GARDENS
Location: 5021 West Shaw Avenue, Fresno
Materials: Baldassare Forestiere (1879–1946) carved these gardens
out of the rock of the San Joaquin Valley and described them as
singalore come il mare (Italian for "as unique as the sea"). For 40
years, he etched out a sprawling 10-acre underground villa with
more than 10,000 square feet of grottoes, gardens, meeting rooms,
and bedrooms. (Some visitors say the structure reminds them of
the ancient catacombs in Forestiere's native Sicily.) Forestiere

---

Bandleader Lawrence Welk's personalized California license plate: A1ANA2.

could barely read or write, and he made up his designs as he went along, but those designs were elaborate. Hallways are curved to allow air to move around and create gentle breezes. Ceilings are cone-shaped so that hot air quickly rises from the floor. Even though it's completely underground, the design includes open vertical shafts to allow natural light to penetrate all three levels. Open areas are covered by glass to keep out the rain.

History: After an argument with his father about his career prospects, Forestiere left Sicily around 1900 and came to America to prove he could make his way as a winemaker or citrus grower. After taking jobs on the East Coast—he helped dig the Holland Tunnel, which connects New Jersey and Manhattan—he bought 70 acres of Fresno land, sight unseen. But instead of that land becoming a thriving winery, he learned that its soil was mostly clay and sand, totally wrong for the vineyard he had envisioned. Still the self-taught horticulturist kept digging. He managed to grow strawberries, lemons, six kinds of grapes, grapefruits, almonds, and kumquats...all in his underground garden. He even grafted two kinds of lemons, three kinds of oranges, and a grapefruit...onto the same tree. Forestiere died at age 67. His Underground Gardens are now a museum, and his orchard is still producing fruit.

RUBEL CASTLE

Location: 844 North Live Oak Avenue, Glendora

Materials: Michael Rubel (1940–2007) used river rocks, railroad ties, glass bottles, scrap steel, railroad track, cement, rubber gloves filled with sand, trophies, bedsprings, and a motorcycle to build his dream castle. Called "Rubelia" or "The Tin Palace," the castle features a pipe organ originally from Madison Square Garden and a working 1890s clock installed in a 70-foot rock tower. Rubel outfitted his castle with a portcullis, a miniature working railroad, a Santa Fe Railroad caboose, vintage cars, a printing press, a blacksmith shop...and cannons.

History: As a kid, Rubel loved to build forts at an orange grove in his L.A. county hometown of Glendora. In 1959, after a two-year tour of the world as a cabin boy, Rubel bought part of that orange grove with money he claimed came from an old Dutch sea captain. Then he started building. First, he drained a reservoir and

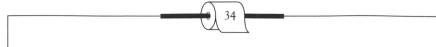

carted out the mud. Then he started piling up his junk...er, building materials...and invited in anyone to stay with him, as long as they lent a hand.

Over the next 25 years, there were thousands of visitors. Rubel called them "Pharm Hands" and schooled them in the main rule of Rubellian construction: "Safety Third." Rubel often sat on his porch or in a hammock, smoking a pipe and barking out architectural advice like, "Let's stick it here because it looks funny." Celebrities were common visitors to Rubel's castle: Jack Benny and Bob Hope stopped by, and Rubel's grandfather once played strip poker at the castle with a burlesque showgirl named Sally Rand. Construction ended in 1986, and Rubel willed his masterpiece to the Glendora Historical Society upon his death in 2007. "The castle really has no function, no purpose," said Rubel. "It's all a big, wild dream, just as the forts were when I was a kid."

*   *   *

THE SAN QUENTIN DRAMA CLUB?

On page 259, we'll tell you about San Quentin State Prison's baseball program, but that isn't the only extracurricular activity offered to inmates there:

• San Quentin's inmates produce the only prisoner-run newspaper in the state of California: the *San Quentin News*.

• The San Quentin Drama Workshop began in 1958. Its first production: *Waiting for Godot*, by Samuel Beckett.

• The San Quentin College Program has graduated more than 100 inmates since it began in 1996. The program is funded completely by donations (no federal or state money is allotted for prison college education) and offers an associate of arts degree in liberal arts/general education. It's also the only program in the state's entire prison system where inmates can earn a degree on-site.

Kentucky, Maryland, Missouri, and Pennsylvania all have a city called California.

THE GREAT JOKESTER

More than 30 years after his first inauguration, Ronald Reagan remains a polarizing figure: a hero to conservatives and a villain to liberals. But there's no doubt that he was a fantastic speaker who made some great jokes.

"It's true hard work never killed anybody, but I figure, why take the chance?"

"Politics is supposed to be the second-oldest profession. I have come to realize that it bears a very close resemblance to the first."

"You can tell a lot about a fella's character by whether he picks out all of one color or just grabs a handful."
—**When asked why he kept a jar of jelly beans on his desk during meetings**

"My fellow Americans, I am pleased to tell you I just signed legislation which outlaws Russia forever. The bombing begins in five minutes."

"Politics is not a bad profession. If you succeed, there are many rewards. If you disgrace yourself, you can always write a book."

"How can a president not be an actor?"

"Honey, I forgot to duck."
—**To his wife after surviving the assassination attempt**

"I have left orders to be awakened at any time in case of national emergency, even if I'm in a cabinet meeting."

"I have wondered at times what the Ten Commandments would have looked like if Moses had run them through the U.S. Congress."

"I want you to know that also I will not make age an issue of this campaign. I am not going to exploit, for political purposes, my opponent's youth and inexperience."

"I don't know. I've never played a governor."
—**When a reporter asked in 1966 what kind of governor he'd be**

"I am not worried about the deficit. It is big enough to take care of itself."

Ronald Reagan's last acting role before entering politics: *The Killers* (1964).

SINGIN' CALIFORNIA QUIZ

How well do you know California's songs? (Answers on page 368)

1. What's the title of the gold rush ballad about a miner's daughter who accidentally drowned while taking ducklings to the water?
Extra credit: How did the poor girl fall in?

2. Which California lockup gave a murderer the blues, and what legendary artist wrote and sang about them?
Extra credit: Name the movie that inspired this country classic.

3. Jan and Dean and the Beach Boys had hits about an old lady who was a fearsome drag-racer. What was the title?
Extra credit: What car did Granny drive?

4. Sheryl Crow won a Grammy for "All I Wanna Do." In that hit, where does the sun come up?
Extra credit: What does Billy do to his bottles of Bud?

5. In Tupac Shakur's "California Love," what three communities are listed as knowing how to party?
Extra credit: Who's the squeaky-voiced actor introducing the "Monster" in the song's video?

6. What's the title of the song in which the band Train seeks salvation from a five-year bender?
Extra credit: Where are the "ladies" from who lead Train up the coast?

7. This song about a fellow and his "sun-kissed" lady-love was written for the 1921 Broadway musical *Bombo*. Since then, the tune has been sung so often in association with California that most people think it's the state's official song. (It's not, though supporters keep trying.)
Extra credit: Who first performed this classic?

The synthetic element *berkelium* was named for Berkeley, where it was created.

8. What's the name of the official state song?
Extra credit: What does it claim is the color of California's sunsets?

9. San Francisco is one of the few cities with two official songs: For many years, the unofficial song was "San Francisco" from the 1936 movie *San Francisco* starring Jeanette MacDonald. In 1984, the city wanted to make that tune official, but a second song had to be added because the mayor preferred a worldwide smash hit by Tony Bennett. What's the title of the second official song?
Extra credit: Who was the stubborn mayor?

10. The Beatles introduced listeners to Blue Jay Way—where is it?
Extra credit: Who got lost in the fog trying to get there and inspired George Harrison to write the song?

11. Creedence Clearwater Revival constantly gets stuck in what little California town?
Extra credit: Why did John Fogerty pick this locale?

12. The music video for what pop song portrays California as a land of cotton candy beaches and extremely mean gummy bears?
Extra credit: Who's the naked lady singing in the video?

13. What legendary Depression-era protest singer wrote the lyrics for 1998's "California Stars"?
Extra credit: Who asked English singer/songwriter Billy Bragg to write the music?

* * *

DID YOU KNOW?

The kangaroo rat, which lives in Death Valley, never drinks water. It gets all its liquid from the seeds and other foods it eats, and by using special membranes in its nasal cavity to recycle the humidity given off when it breathes.

CALIFORN-ALIENS?

People believe a lot of strange things. One of the strangest happens to be a place about 75 miles south of the BRI's headquarters: picturesque Mt. Shasta in Northern California. It's known for its hiking, skiing... and the invisible people who live inside the mountain.

SACRED SPOT

Towering 14,179 feet above sea level, Mt. Shasta's snow-capped peak has been surrounded by mystery and legend since indigenous people first encountered it thousands of years ago. And ever since white settlers arrived in the area in the mid-1800s, the mountain—as well as the nearby town by the same name—has been the scene of some very weird sightings, including UFOs and mystical creatures roaming around the mountain's slopes. In fact, Shasta City was one of the first centers of the New Age movement in the United States. It's still home to hundreds of energy readers, spiritualists, psychics, and alien-seekers.

Shasta's New Age movement can be traced back to 1884, when teenager Frederick Oliver, from the nearby town of Yreka, first visited the mountain and fell into a trance. Under the control of "other forces," Oliver wrote A *Dweller on Two Planets*. And to thousands of people, the book—still in print today—is not science fiction, but the source material for their belief system.

THE LEMURIANS

Dweller tells the history of Mt. Shasta, which Oliver claimed was channeled directly to his mind by an immortal creature named Phylos, whose race, the Lemurians, once lived on a Pacific Ocean continent called Mu. Like Atlantis, Mu was a "lost continent" that modern scientists say never existed.

Lemurians, Oliver wrote, talk to each other telepathically in a language called Solara Maru, but Phylos spoke English to Oliver (curiously, with an English accent). Oliver described the Lemurians as physically stunning—more than seven feet tall with long, flowing hair and lean, graceful bodies. They wore white robes lined with sacred stones, and decorated sandals. Technologically advanced even by today's standards, the ancient Lemurians developed water generators, antigravity machines, high-speed trains, and devices comparable to cellular phones and televisions.

But for all their expertise, the Lemurians could not prevent the cataclysmic earthquake they knew was coming. One night about 12,000 years ago, Mu began shaking and sinking into the sea. But the 25,000 Lemurians were ready—they all boarded tall ships bound for the uninhabited land of what is now Northern California. Once there, their engineers hollowed out Mt. Shasta and constructed a subterranean city called Telos. According to Oliver/ Phylos, they chose that particular mountain because it's "the earthly incarnation of the Great Central Sun, the source of all physical and spiritual energy in the universe." And so, for twelve millennia, the Lemurians have lived peacefully inside the mountain.

BEAM ME UP

Floating in the sky directly above Mt. Shasta, Oliver went on, is yet another Lemurian city: "The Crystal City of the Light of the Seven Rays." It's visible only to the most tuned-in human psychics, who describe it as a huge, floating, purple pyramid, the point of which extends into space. From within the Crystal City, the Lemurians operate interplanetary, interdimensional spaceships called the "Silver Fleet" (which would seem to explain all of the UFO sightings near Mt. Shasta). The Lemurians represent our galaxy in the intergalactic "Confederation of Planets."

Good luck actually seeing a Lemurian yourself, or one of their spaceships, or their Giant Purple Pyramid City. Few people have. That's because the Lemurians exist on a "vibrational level" to which humans are not physically attuned (in other words, they're invisible). Thankfully, there are dozens of books out there about the mountain's inhabitants and its spiritual energy, all of them based on Oliver's...er, Phylos's *A Dweller on Two Planets*.

DAYS OF FUTURE PASSED

But time may be short for the city of Telos: The mountain the Lemurians moved into is actually a dormant volcano, which the United States Geological Survey warns may erupt again in the next 200 years. So if you happen to live in another area on earth that contains a massive pocket of spiritual energy, you may soon be getting some beautiful, seven-foot-tall, invisible neighbors.

CRUISIN' WITH CORTÉS

Before there was California the state, there was California the island,
which was supposedly full of beautiful warrior women, gold, and griffins.
That California existed only in fiction, but it inspired one Spanish
explorer to hunt down the area that became the Golden State.

STRANGE AS FICTION

In 1524 Spanish explorer Hernán Cortés petitioned his king for permission to explore the western coast of North America, writing this description of what he hoped to find: "The chiefs of the Ceguatan province [the area around present-day Cihuatlán on the southern Pacific Coast of Mexico] assure me that there is an island inhabited only by women, and that, at given times, men from the mainland visit them; if they conceive, they keep the female children to which they give birth, but the males they throw away. This island is ten days' journey from the province, and many of them have traveled there and told me also that it is very rich in pearls and gold."

Despite this intriguing description, King Charles I of Spain turned Cortés down. The prospect was intriguing, but it sounded familiar…perhaps the king had read that story somewhere before? Sure enough, what Cortés was describing was "California," not the state we know today, but a mythical land that had appeared in a popular work of fiction written about 14 years before.

A NOVEL IDEA

Around 1510 the Spanish writer Garci Rodríguez de Montalvo penned a series of adventure stories about a traveling knight. He imagined a *califa* (Spanish for a female *caliph*, or head of state) ruling an all-female island called a *califerne* (a Spanish word for kingdom). But what to call that kingdom? It didn't take long for de Montalvo to stretch out "califerne" to California. And so he began:

> "You should know that at the right hand of the Indies [North America], there is an island named California, very close to Terrestrial Paradise, populated only by black women, without a single man among them. They live in the manner of the Amazons,

robust in body, with strong and passionate hearts and great virtues...Their weapons are all of gold, as are the harnesses of the wild beasts they tame and ride, for on the island there is no other metal...The island everywhere is rich with gold and precious stones...

On this island, California, are many griffins of a type that are not seen in any other part of the world. In griffin birthing season, the women disguise and protect themselves in thick leather to catch the newly hatched griffins and raise them in their caves, feeding them male prisoners of war and any boy babies that they've given birth to. The training is done with such skill that the griffins do no harm to the women, but that any male who comes to the island is in danger of being killed and eaten."

With that introduction, de Montalvo coined the name California in his book *Las Sergas de Esplandián* (*The Exploits of Esplandian*). It was a novel of chivalry, adventure, and romance. When the protagonist—a brave Spanish knight—discovers California, he (spoiler alert!) overthrows the island's califa and converts her entire californe to Christianity, heterosexuality, and womanly modesty and subservience.

This sort of book was very popular during the 16th century, when crossing the ocean to explore new lands was at its peak. The New World, which had been in the public's imagination since Christopher Columbus first stumbled onto it 18 years earlier, and any new discoveries were sure to fascinate readers. But that posed a bit of a problem for de Montalvo. So much of the New World was being discovered—and it was happening so quickly—that people might have already heard stories about what the place was actually like, and they might not believe his tale. So he decided to set his story in a more distant New World near an unknown ocean. He claimed that his ocean was beyond the New World's known landmass, and since explorers had so far reached North America only via the Atlantic Ocean, his setting offered mystery and intrigue. It would be another three years before Vasco Balboa hiked through Panama to become the first European to even see the Pacific Ocean; 22 years before the Spanish traveled across Mexico to the Pacific coast and established a home base in Zacatula; and a quarter of a century before the Spanish arrived on the Pacific coast of North America. That's where Cortés comes in.

CORTÉS GETS HIS CHANCE

In 1535 Cortés finally wore down the royal resistance to letting him explore the western coast of North America, and he headed out. One of his goals was finding the "real California" that the Mexican chiefs had described to him 12 years earlier.

Sailing along what's now the coast of Southern California and Baja California, Cortés discovered what he thought was a big island, maybe even *the* island. It wasn't. Despite doing some exploring and talking with the natives, he didn't find the women and treasures he'd hoped for. In fact, the place wasn't tropical at all; it was mostly a barren desert. Still, he mapped it before moving on. Shortly afterward, he reached another landmass that he thought was an even larger island. But again, although he searched thoroughly, he never found the promised spoils.

WISH THEY ALL COULD BE CALIFORNIA GIRLS

Although Cortés was disappointed not to have found the mythical land of California, he at least could return with some new land to claim for Spain...and take a cut of any riches for himself. He named the area Santa Cruz ("Holy Cross"), which was something of a default name for Spanish explorers when they couldn't come up with something better...as evidenced by the hundred-plus places named Santa Cruz from Mexico to Chile. He then headed back to the Spanish colonial headquarters in New Spain (now Mexico City) to stake his claim to the region. Over the years, he returned twice more to Santa Cruz to do more exploring.

By 1540 Cortés knew that the hot, desolate area he'd found was nothing like the fictional California. But one of New Spain's leaders still remembered Cortés's claims from his earlier proposal to the king. Antonio de Mendoza, the royal representative in the colony, despised and distrusted Cortés, and wanted to be sure Spain wasn't missing out on the riches that the fictional California had to offer. So he sent explorer Hernando de Alarcón to check out Cortés's findings. De Alarcón came back with his own map that confirmed Cortés's claims, but he'd changed the region's name: Santa Cruz was now marked as Baja ("lower") and Alta ("upper") California. Some historians believe that de Alarcón specifically chose those new names to mock Cortés and his quest for a fictional island. What-ever Alarcón's intention, the name California stuck.

Swimming is not allowed in any San Diego County lakes.

FOREST GIANTS

Biologists have counted 175 coast redwoods (Sequoia sempervirens)
that are more than 350 feet tall. That's longer than a football field.
How do California's redwoods reach such great heights?

• The coastal region from central California to southern Oregon has the same conditions the dinosaurs thrived in: a humid, temperate climate. The region never freezes, never gets too hot, and receives up to 140 inches of rain per year.

• Farther inland, the annual summer drought keeps tree growth in check, but daily fog on the coast keeps the redwoods moist year-round.

• After the fog clears in the afternoon, it evaporates from the leaves and falls on the nutrient-rich soil below. That evaporation also creates a vacuum that sucks up groundwater through the trees' capillaries like a straw.

• All trees have capillaries, but gravity prevents them from pulling up water higher than about 100 feet. Redwoods can triple that height because their capillaries are much stronger.

• Redwoods also grow so tall because they're battling each other for sunlight. This race to the top helps the strongest ones grow two feet each year.

• It takes about three to five centuries for a redwood to exceed 300 feet. Keeping it alive this long: their fibrous bark, which in a mature tree can be a foot thick. It's full of tannins that are resistant to fungus and harmful insects.

• Redwood bark is also fire-resistant. In fact, periodic fires are beneficial because they clear out underbrush that would otherwise choke the trees by stealing water and nutrients from the soil.

• Even with the redwoods' enormous height, their root systems are relatively shallow, so a strong gust of wind could topple one of these giants. Redwoods combat this "weakness" by allowing their roots to intertwine with each other, making them all more stable.

SMOG STORY

Does L.A.'s smog make you tear up? Yeah, us too.

DISCOVERING SMOG

In 1905 a doctor at a London public health conference wanted a name for the blanket of smoke and fog that often polluted the city. He came up with "smog." In the 1940s, Southern Californians began using the term to describe the air pollution that often blanketed their city, irritated their eyes and throats, and caused breathing problems. Smog increasingly became a health concern, but nobody knew exactly what it was, what was causing it, or what to do about it.

Then, in 1948, Arie Haagen-Smit, a Dutch chemistry professor at the California Institute of Technology was helping Southern California farmers whose plants had developed bleached and discolored leaves from smog. His experiments revealed that when plants in sealed chambers were exposed to ozone gas, the leaves showed smog damage. When volunteers sat in chambers filled with the same gas, they suffered the watery eyes, burning throats, and breathing problems that were common in L.A. on smoggy days. Thus, Haagen-Smit concluded that ozone caused the smog to form.

SMOG DECONSTRUCTED

California's smog is specifically called *photochemical smog* because it's created by a photochemical reaction—a chemical reaction in which molecules and atoms absorb light. The smog begins to form when nitrogen oxides and other volatile organic compounds get into the air, either through auto exhaust or from machines and factories that burn fossil fuels. Then on Southern California's hot, sunny days, the sunlight "cooks" the chemicals. Their molecules break apart and then attach to oxygen molecules, creating the odorless, tasteless gas called *ozone*. That gas makes up about 90 percent of photochemical smog, and that's why smog is worse on hot, sunny days.

The confusing thing about ozone is that it can both protect human health and be very toxic. When ozone is up in the stratosphere (about 10–30 miles above the earth's surface), it's not part

---

Pioneer Cemetery in Coloma counts an actual samurai warrior among its "residents."

of the air we breathe, and it creates the ozone layer that protects humans from the sun's ultraviolet rays. But the ozone in smog is in the lower atmosphere where we do breathe, and it can make people sick.

Along with ozone, smog is made up of soot and chemicals that form *aerosols*, liquid or solid particles suspended in a gas. The aerosols are what make it hard to see through smoggy air and contribute to the phenomenon's "dirty haze." Volcanic eruptions and forest fires can also produce aerosols, but in big cities, most aerosols come from burning fossil fuels.

GAS MASK, ANYONE?

On July 26, 1943, Los Angeles was struck by what newspapers called an "enemy gas attack." It was during World War II, so everyone was on edge, and on that hot day, many city residents were blinded by hazy smoke and fumes that left them with weeping eyes and burning throats. Some could barely see—others were nauseous and vomiting. It turned out not to be an enemy attack at all. It was smog—the first real instance of severe smog in the city. Los Angeles, it turns out, is a perfect smog haven.

L.A.'s ocean breezes blow west to east. On hot days (when the sun burns brightly and cooks the ozone), those winds blow in the water's cool, moist air. Denser and heavier than the hot air above the L.A. basin, the breezes flow in underneath the warmer air. The warmer air on top creates what's called a "marine inversion layer." This layer acts like a cap on the atmosphere, keeping the air below it from rising. Without an inversion layer, pollutants like ozone can disperse into the atmosphere. With one, ozone is trapped close to the ground where people are breathing.

The city also sits on a low coastal plain surrounded by high mountains on three sides. When the wind blows east from the ocean, pollutants back up against the high mountains and remain trapped over the city. L.A.'s weather patterns and geography—combined with its large population, traffic, and industry—have given it the highest levels of ozone in the United States.

GIVING SMOG A SEND-OFF

Los Angeles is definitely California's smoggiest city, but Long

---

An estimated 200 languages are spoken in California.

Beach, Riverside, and Bakersfield are pretty bad, too. That means Californians have a lot of experience with the phenomenon and are leading the country in ways to get rid of it. The state's war on smog began in 1947, when Governor Earl Warren signed the Air Pollution Control Act, authorizing the creation of an Air Pollution Control District in every county. In 1959 Governor Pat Brown and the state legislature passed laws requiring new cars sold in California to meet state pollution control standards. If Detroit automakers wanted to sell cars to California's huge population, they were going to have to come up with ways to reduce emissions. So they did.

From then on, California continued to push the reluctant auto industry to meet ever-lower emission requirements. Thanks in large part to California's regulations, auto emissions all over the country improved—today, the pollution a new car emits is about 10 percent of the pollution levels allowed in 1990.

Smog has fought back, however, with the help of industry, politicians, and a growing population. In 1953 a state committee recommended that vehicles use fuels other than highly polluting diesel. But it wasn't until 2011 that diesel vehicles were finally subjected to emission requirements. As for population growth, by 2010 the greater Los Angeles population was about 11,874,000. With about 577 cars per 1,000 people, that puts more than 6 million cars on L.A. roads—creating pollution in the city's stagnant air.

But there's still good news: In L.A., smog emissions per person fall well below the national average. Plus, California's goal is to generate 33 percent of its electricity with renewable fuels like wind or solar by 2020. That's like taking millions of cars off the road. The war on smog has yet to be won, but California is still fighting.

* * *

"The formula for a happy marriage? It's the same one for living in California: When you find a fault, don't dwell on it."

—Jay Trachman

The world's first laser was successfully operated in Malibu in 1960.

16 CALIFORNIA EXTREMES

How much do you know about California's highest,
lowest, oldest, largest, and smallest stuff?

TALLEST LIVING THING: Hyperion, a 379-foot Sequoia (California redwood) tree located in the Redwood National Park near Eureka. Hyperion's location in the park is kept secret to prevent it from being damaged by tourists.

SMALLEST MOUNTAIN RANGE: The Sutter Butte Mountain Range near Yuba City. The buttes are a circular volcanic outcropping just 10 miles in diameter.

OLDEST LIVING TREE IN NORTH AMERICA: A 4,842-year-old bristlecone pine in Inyo National Forest outside Bishop. Named Methuselah (after the oldest person whose age is referenced in the Bible), this pine was a seedling during the Bronze Age, when the Pyramids were going up in Egypt.

LARGEST LIVING TREE: General Sherman, a giant sequoia in Sequoia National Park, east of Visalia. Named for Civil War general William Tecumseh Sherman, this tree weighs more than 2 million pounds, is 275 feet tall, and is the largest tree on earth when measured by its estimated volume of 52,513 cubic feet.

BIGGEST SOLITARY BOULDER: Giant Rock in Landers in the Mojave Desert. At about seven stories high, it weighs more than 23,000 tons.

LONGEST RUNWAY: At Edwards Air Force Base in the Mojave Desert. It's 7.5 miles long, and the first space shuttle landed there.

WORLD'S TALLEST ONE-PIECE TOTEM POLE: Built in 1962, the brightly painted 160-foot-tall pole in the McKinleyville Shopping Center was designed by Ernest Pierson, who carved it from a single 500-year-old redwood.

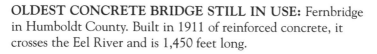

OLDEST CONCRETE BRIDGE STILL IN USE: Fernbridge in Humboldt County. Built in 1911 of reinforced concrete, it crosses the Eel River and is 1,450 feet long.

HIGHEST LANDING PAD ON A BUILDING: The U.S. Bank Tower in downtown L.A. is 1,018 feet high, making it the world's tallest building with a helipad on the roof. It's also America's tallest building west of Chicago.

NORTH AMERICA'S BEST VIEW OF THE WORLD: The 3,849-foot summit of Mt. Diablo in Contra Costa County. It reveals more of the earth's surface than any other peak in the world, except Mt. Kilimanjaro in Africa. Mt. Diablo looks west to the Farallon Islands in the Pacific, east to the Sierra Nevada mountain range, south to the Santa Cruz Mountains, and north to the Cascades.

NORTH AMERICA'S HIGHEST CONCENTRATION OF LAVA TUBE CAVES: Lava Beds National Monument near Tulelake. The beds formed thousands of years ago when the exterior lava flow cooled and solidified, while the inner hot lava flowed away—creating an empty center and a cave.

NORTH AMERICA'S LARGEST ALPINE LAKE: Lake Tahoe is 12 miles wide, 22 miles long, and 1,645 feet deep.

CALIFORNIA'S HIGHEST MEASURED WATERFALL: Yosemite Falls in Yosemite National Park is actually made of three separate parts: Upper Yosemite Fall, Middle Cascades, and Lower Yosemite Fall together create a 2,425-foot waterfall.

AMERICA'S HIGHEST UNINTERRUPTED WATERFALL: Ribbon Fall is a single waterfall that flows off El Capitan in Yosemite and makes a sheer drop of 1,612 feet.

AMERICA'S LARGEST NATURAL AMPHITHEATER: The Hollywood Bowl. In 1922 it was built into the hillside (like the amphitheaters of ancient Greece and Rome) to aid acoustics.

FIRST ROSE BOWL: The first Rose Bowl game was held on January 1, 1902, at Tournament Park in Pasadena. Michigan defeated Stanford 41–0, when the Stanford players quit with just eight minutes remaining.

Most of the state's agricultural revenue comes from tomatoes.

THE WAVE

Love it or hate it, we've all done the wave. Here's why.

NOW THAT'S JUST KRAZY

On October 15, 1981, during baseball's American League Championship game at the Oakland Coliseum, the A's were battling the New York Yankees to go to the World Series. The Yankees ended up winning the game 4–0 to capture the American League pennant, but Oakland came away with something a little more historic: the city is considered the modern birthplace of the sports phenomenon called "the wave."

You know what it is—that wacky stadium event where you're expected to jump to your feet, throw up your hands, and cheer a split second after the person sitting next to you, giving spectators on the other side of the stadium the impression that a human tsunami is washing through the stadium. California's "Krazy" George Henderson, a former teacher and professional cheerleader, was the one who introduced Oakland to the wave that day, but technically, he didn't actually come up with the idea.

According to many reports, people had been doing something like the wave since the 1960s, when students at basketball games at Pacific Lutheran University in Washington State stood up and sat down in unison. And hockey fans in Montreal and other Canadian cities kind of did it too. But it wasn't until that 1981 baseball game at the Coliseum that the phenomenon got national attention. Henderson became the wave's self-proclaimed inventor, and California its birthplace...until the University of Washington Huskies declared that they, not Henderson, had actually invented it.

WHO SAYS WASHINGTON CAN'T LIE?

The students at the University of Washington in Seattle claimed that they had invented the wave, also in October 1981, and they even put up a plaque at their stadium to commemorate the occasion. Then the school sent Henderson a letter demanding that he stop calling himself the wave's inventor on his Web site and in the national media.

The Huskies made a good case: The audience at the October

31 homecoming game against Stanford had indeed done an admirable wave, and there were those rumors that students at Pacific Lutheran had been doing it for decades. (Pacific Lutheran is in the town of Parkland, about 40 miles south of Seattle.) But there was one big problem with the Huskies' claim: Henderson had his wave on tape, and it had taken place 16 days before the Washington/Stanford homecoming game. In the end, the Huskies withdrew their protest, and Henderson continued to call himself the "inventor of the wave."

THE MEXICAN WAVE

Within a few years, the wave had rolled across North America, but the rest of the world didn't see it until 1986, during the FIFA World Cup in Mexico City. During lulls in the soccer play, spectators in the stadium began doing the wave. Their effort impressed television viewers worldwide, but also gave the impression that it was a Mexican invention. As a result, Henderson's wave became known as the Mexican wave in many parts of the world.

WAVE RESEARCH

In 2002 *Nature* magazine included an article about Hungarian professor Tamas Vicsek, who had analyzed videos of people doing the wave. He found that...

• It takes only a few dozen like-minded spectators to start a wave.

• The wave is usually about 15 rows wide and travels at a speed of 22 seats per second.

• The wave usually travels clockwise. (Reports that Australian waves travel counterclockwise have yet to be proven.)

* * *

DID YOU KNOW?

At the 1932 Olympics in Los Angeles, Japan's Takeichi Nishi and his horse Uranus won gold in the equestrian show jumping event, Japan's only equestrian gold medal ever. During World War II 13 years later, Nishi died in fighting for the Japanese at the Battle of Iwo Jima. Clint Eastwood's 2006 film *Letters from Iwo Jima* made Nishi its main character.

Robert Kennedy was killed in L.A.'s Ambassador Hotel...

WE ♥ BAKERSFIELD

*Bakersfield gets a bad rap. (Not fair!) Fortunately, Uncle John
is here to tell you some cool things about it.*

• **Holding onto its history.** Bakersfield has saved many historic
buildings and artifacts in the Kern County Museum. One is a
small portable jail that could be transported by railroad to wherever it was needed.

• **Get there from anywhere:** Once isolated by desert, distance,
and the Tehachapi Mountains, Bakersfield is now well connected.
According to the city's official Web site, it's within a four-hour
drive of 90 percent of California's population.

• **Missions impossible?** Bakersfield's isolation was a good thing for
the area's original inhabitants, though, because it helped keep the
Spanish missions away. Between 1769 and 1823, the Spanish laid
a chain of army presidios and missions along California's coastal
areas, enslaving the tribes, taking their land, and forcing them to
convert to Christianity. They hoped to do the same through Mexico, Arizona, and California's Central Valley, so in 1776, Father
Francisco Garces, the first known European in the area, crossed
the Kern River as a scout for the Spanish. But nothing came of it
because, in the meantime, the first inland California mission
turned out to be a disaster.

Founded on January 7, 1781, and destroyed six months later,
the mission—located near modern-day Yuma, Arizona—was too far
from supplies and army reinforcements. Plus, the Quechan Indians
who inhabited the region were none too pleased to have their land
stolen and their way of life destroyed. So they sacked that mission
and one other, killing at least 50 Spanish men (including Father
Garces), capturing the women and children, and thwarting plans
that the inland mission chain would keep moving north. As a
result, the Bakersfield tribe of Yokuts remained safe from European
settlers for another 40 years. Father Garces got the posthumous
consolation prize of being officially designated a Christian
martyr—he also got a 16-foot statue that stands atop a five-foot
pedestal on Bakersfield's North Chester Avenue.

• **The great wide ways.** Maybe you notice that some of the streets in Bakersfield seem unusually wide. When founder Colonel Tom Baker (*more about him on page 83*) laid out his city, he decided that the standard width of 66 feet was too narrow for carriages and wagons, so he made his streets 82 feet wide and his avenues 115 feet wide.

• **Missed amidst the mist.** A late fall and winter hallmark of Bakersfield's weather is an absurdly thick fog called "tule fog"—it comes from cold mountain air settling into the area's tule grass wetlands. The San Joaquin Valley acts like a bowl, holding the cold air, and when there's little wind over a long period of time, the tule fog can last for days or weeks, typically cutting visibility to 200 yards or less. Sometimes a *lot* less, like not being able to see your hands in front of your face and even resulting in massive pileups on major highways. Tule fog throughout the Central Valley is the leading cause of weather-related traffic fatalities in California.

• **It ain't the heat, it's...oh wait, it *is* the heat.** In an average year, Bakersfield's temperature rises above 90°F more than 100 times.

• **It thinks it's part of Texas.** Besides the heat, there are oil wells, agriculture, cheap land, rodeos, faux cowboys, rabid Dallas Cowboys fans...and the lowest sales tax of any big city in California (although still a hefty 7.25 percent, last we checked).

• **One good earthquake, and it might be underwater.** A dirt embankment called the Lake Isabella Dam is all that prevents Lake Isabella from engulfing Bakersfield and its outlying areas to a depth of about 30 feet. That might still be okay, except that the earthen dam sits atop an earthquake fault. In 2007 the Army Corps of Engineers elevated the dam to the twin status of highest risk and highest priority to fix. However, as of the end of 2011, the Army Corps was still "looking at ways to fix the dam."

To read about the musicians who created the famous Bakersfield Sound, turn to page 226.

Self-proclaimed Mule Capital of the World: Bishop.

THE STATE OF WINE

*California wines got no respect...until they
won big at a French wine tasting.*

VICTORY IN PARIS

In June 1976, journalist George Taber wrote a short piece for *Time* magazine called "Judgment of Paris." It reported on a small wine tasting at the Intercontinental Hotel in Paris, just down the street from the Louvre. Taber reported that the French judges at the tasting were leaders in the world of wine, with years of experience judging France's finest vintages. Their job was to sample several of France's greatest Burgundies to find the best white wine, and several of France's finest Bordeaux to find the best red wine. There was one twist: In honor of the American bicentennial that year, several California wines were also being included in the tasting...just for fun. No one actually expected them to win.

The tasting was blind so that none of the judges knew which wines they were tasting and could, therefore, give objective opinions. The judges were disdainful of the California wines, though. The French were sure they'd be able to spot California products due to their inferior taste and lack of "nose" (aroma). Then the results were announced, and the judges were stunned. Taber wrote: "The unthinkable happened: California defeated all Gaul."

The judges chose Napa's 1973 Chateau Montelena Chardonnay as the best white wine. For the reds, their choice was Napa's 1973 Stag's Leap Wine Cellars S.L.V. Cabernet Sauvignon. Even more remarkable, three of the top four white wines and two of the top five red wines were from California.

FOR WHOM THE BELL TOLLS

California's triumph was all the more remarkable because the state's modern wine industry was so young. It hadn't really begun until 1933, when bells tolled in Napa Valley to celebrate the end of Prohibition. The 18th Amendment to the U.S. Constitution prohibiting the manufacture, sale, and distribution of alcohol had lasted more than 13 years, and although a few wineries had

The Red Hot Chili Peppers most successful album: *Californication* (1999).

remained open to produce wines for religious ceremonies, most had been forced to shut down. U.S. wine production dropped by 94 percent during Prohibition, and many of California's vineyards were replaced with prune orchards.

Recovering from Prohibition was a slow process. Nearly all the good wineries were gone. Most vineyards that appeared in the early 1930s produced low-quality wines, and there wasn't much incentive to make them better. Unlike Europeans, Americans often associated wine with winos—not luxury or fine living. And when Americans did buy great wine, they splurged on French imports.

So for the 30 years after Prohibition ended, most California wineries produced cheap jug wines or poorly made, fortified wines (with added brandy). Only a few pioneers believed that California could produce great wines.

WINE ICONS

• **André Tchelistcheff.** One of the best and most influential post-Prohibition winemakers was a refugee from the Russian Revolution. In 1938 Tchelistcheff was hired by Beaulieu Vineyards, one of the few great wineries that had survived Prohibition. Having learned winemaking in France, Tchelistcheff pioneered techniques that were new to many Californians: He aged wine in small oak barrels and used cold fermentation to improve the flavor of white wine. In the vineyards, he knew where to plant the different varieties of grapes so that they would do best (the area's rich volcanic soil gave the grapes a distinctive taste) and developed systems to protect grapes from frost.

• **Lee Stewart.** After establishing Souverain Cellars atop Napa's Howell Mountain in 1943, Stewart became one of the first California winemakers to produce estate-style varietals, wines made primarily from a single grape variety. He was a traditionalist and a perfectionist whose attention to detail helped Souverain win competitions throughout the state.

• **Robert Mondavi.** Probably the greatest champion of California wines, Mondavi's self-titled winery was the first great one to open in California after Prohibition, and Mondavi spared no expense bringing in the best equipment, talent, and techniques. (*More about him on page 315.*)

THE MEN WHO CONQUERED PARIS

Tchelistcheff, Stewart, and Mondavi were the teachers of the two winemakers who won the 1976 Paris tasting. Mike Grgich of Chateau Montelena created the Chardonnay that bested France's greatest Burgundy, and Warren Winiarski of Stag's Leap Cellars produced the winning Cabernet Sauvignon. Although Grgich and Winiarski came from very different backgrounds, both had arrived in California nearly broke, but armed with big dreams of making world-class wine.

Born in Croatia, Miljenko "Mike" Grgich grew up making wine on his father's farm and later studied the business. He hated the communists who'd taken over his home country and longed to take up his craft in California, which he'd heard was a paradise. After some luck and years of work, Grgich made it to Napa in 1958. He worked for Lee Stewart, went on to become an assistant to Tchelistcheff, and finally became chief winemaker for Robert Mondavi.

In 1972 Jim Barrett was restoring Napa's neglected 90-year old Chateau Montelena winery and hired Grgich as chief winemaker. Chateau Montelena was so run-down that Grgich had to design a whole new space and install equipment before he could create the 1973 Chardonnay that he sent to the French tasting.

Warren Winiarski left his academic life in 1964, quitting his job as a professor of political theory at the University of Chicago, packing up his family, and moving to Napa to find work in the wine business. Like Grgich, Winiarski's first job was as an apprentice for Stewart, and he next worked for Mondavi as an assistant winemaker. All the while, he dreamed of having a chance to make his own great Cabernet.

In 1969 Winiarski visited a vineyard and liked its homemade Cabernet so well that he bought the adjoining land, believing that the area would produce great Cabernet grapes. He was right. In 1970 he founded Stag's Leap Cellars with Tchelistcheff as his consultant. His harvest in 1973 produced the wine that went to Paris.

THE JUDGMENT OF PARIS

The first winning vineyard owner to learn of the results of the 1976 Paris tasting was Jim Barrett of Chateau Montelena, who was visiting France at the time. Taber asked for a comment, and

...their headlights at night in order to avoid detection by potential Japanese bombers.

Barrett was modest, saying, "Not bad for kids from the sticks."

When *Time* magazine hit the stands on June 7, 1976, the cover story was about cheating at West Point, but everyone was talking about "Judgment of Paris." Newspapers across the country picked up the story. The *New York Times* pointed out that California wines had bested the French in earlier tastings in the United States too, but the French had complained their wines suffered from travel and that the American judges were either biased or incompetent. The *Times* asked, "What can they say now?"

Wine sellers across the country were overwhelmed with requests for Montelena Chardonnay and Stag's Leap Cellars Cabernet, as well as all the other California wines that had impressed the French judges. Before the tasting, California wineries had trouble convincing stores to take their wines. Now, customers were angry that the award-winning wines were so difficult to find. Between 1980 and 1990, the number of wineries in California soared to 900…from about 25 in 1975. By 2001 the yearly value of California retail wine was estimated at $14 billion, and the wine country north of San Francisco was attracting 10 million tourists a year.

SAVORING VICTORY

Winiarski and Grgich's lives were forever changed by their winning vintages. Winiarski had gone deeply in debt to finance Stag's Leap, but after Paris, orders poured in for his wines. Stag's Leap Cellars became famous for its great Cabernets, and in 2007, when Winiarski retired, he sold the winery for $185 million.

Grgich's win allowed him to finally buy a piece of California "paradise." With a business partner, he founded the Grgich Hills Estate in the Napa Valley town of Rutherford, and began making the type of Chardonnay that won the Paris tasting. Grgich Hill's very first Chardonnay won the *Chicago Tribune*'s "1980 Great Chardonnay Showdown." It bested 221 Chardonnays from around the world—including French Burgundies—and earned Grgich the nickname "the King of Chardonnay." And in 1996 the Smithsonian's National Museum of American History put on display bottles of the 1973 Stag's Leap Wine Cellars' Cabernet Sauvignon and the 1973 Chateau Montelena Chardonnay. California wines had really arrived.

A DAY AT THE RACES

If you've got a pair of good sneakers—and maybe a gorilla costume—head to Northern California, which offers some of the country's most amazing, bizarre, and time-honored footraces.

DIPSEA
COURSE: The race's 7.4 miles begin in the Marin County town of Mill Valley, head north through the ancient redwood forests at the Muir Woods, climb the forested trails of Mount Tamalpais, and finally end at the Pacific Ocean in Stinson Beach.

WHAT IS IT? In 1904 a group of San Francisco athletes took a ferry to Marin County and then a train to the depot in Mill Valley. They made a bet to see who could make it to the Dipsea Inn, which had just opened in Stinson Beach, first, and then they started running. The racers had so much fun that the Olympic Club in San Francisco (the fancy health club all the original participants belonged to) decided to make it an annual event. The next year, it became official, making Dipsea the oldest trail race in the nation. It's also one of the country's few handicapped races, with participants getting a head start based on their age and gender.

Today, Dipsea is held every second Sunday in June, and it has not changed much over the years, though the train depot in Mill Valley is now a bookstore. It's also one of the most challenging races in the state. Dipsea runners climb 2,700 feet. At the beginning, they attack "the stairs"—three flights of 676 steps that rise as high as a 50-story building. There are steep trails with names like Cardiac Hill and Insult Hill. And the twisting, narrow trails can be dangerous, so even though thousands apply to run Dipsea each year, for safety's sake, only 1,500 are allowed to participate.

ONLY AT DIPSEA

• The handicapping has made for some interesting winners, especially the 100th Dipsea race in 2005, which was won by eight-year-old Reilly Johnson.

• The most famous Dipsea runner is Jack "the Dipsea Demon" Kirk, who ran 67 consecutive races and won two of them. Kirk last ran the Dipsea in 2002—he was 95 years old. He died five years later at the age of 100.

• Blind runner Harry Cordellos tackled Dipsea several times in the 1970s and '80s.

• The Dipsea record is 44:49, set by Ron Elijah in 1974

THE WESTERN STATES 100

COURSE: This race covers 100 miles in the Sierra Nevadas, from Squaw Valley to Auburn.

WHAT IS IT? The Western States Endurance Run, better known as the Western States 100, is America's original 100-mile trail run. Its story is linked to the Tevis Cup, a 24-hour, 100-mile endurance horse race that began in 1955 and follows the same course. In the Tevis Cup's early days, the idea that a human could run that trail on foot in 24 hours seemed impossible. But in 1974, veteran rider Gordy Ainsleigh knew he wouldn't be able to participate on horseback because his new horse had a tendency to go lame. So he trained to make the run on foot. Ainsleigh finished in 23 hours and 42 minutes, proving that a human could finish the rugged course (in 108°F heat) in less than a day. After that, other people began running with the horses, and in 1977, the Western States 100 became official. Since 1978, the human race has been held on the last weekend in June, a month earlier than the horse one.

The Western States 100 starts in Squaw Valley at 5:00 a.m. on Saturday. Those who reach the finish line at Placer High School in Auburn by 5:00 a.m. on Sunday win a silver belt buckle. Those who finish by 11:00 a.m. get a bronze buckle. To accomplish that, runners have to cross the Sierras, at times climbing more than 15,000 feet. They follow trails used by gold rush miners and spend nearly half the race running in the dark with a flashlight. Most of the race passes through magnificent but lonely territory, accessible only on foot, by horse, or by helicopter. Sometimes, even in June, there's snow in the mountains. So many athletes from all over the world want to participate in this ultramarathon that lotteries are held every year to see who the lucky masochists…er, runners… will be.

ONLY AT THE WESTERN STATES 100

• Gordy Ainsleigh said he almost didn't finish that first race in

1974. He saw a horse dying along the route, and thought that if a horse couldn't make it, his own chances weren't good. Ainsleigh did finish, of course, running the last miles while talking to "a hot item on a pretty chestnut Arab, a lady I had had my eye on."

• Among the hazards listed in the race's welcome pamphlet: heatstroke, rattlesnakes, bears, mountain lions, and poison oak.

• From 1974 to 1977, the footrace was run in conjunction with the horse race, and the runners were monitored by veterinarians.

ZAZZLE BAY TO BREAKERS

COURSE: The race's 7.46 miles begin at the Embarcadero (on the San Francisco's "bay" side) and end at the Great Highway at the western edge of Golden Gate Park (the "breakers," because that's where the Pacific's waves "break" onto the shore).

WHAT IS IT? Six years after the 1906 earthquake, San Francisco was still stuck in the depressing and seemingly never-ending process of rebuilding. To lift people's spirits, the *San Francisco Bulletin* sponsored a footrace. On a New Year's Day in 1912, 186 runners started at the Embarcadero Ferry Building and raced across the city to the beach. (The winner, college student Robert Vlught, credited his victory to his mom's good meals.) Since then, the race has been run every year.

Over the years, that race evolved into the annual Zazzle Bay to Breakers, held every third Sunday in May. It's a respectable race that attracts world-class runners every year, but it's also become known as one of San Francisco's biggest parties. Many of the runners don outrageous costumes—everything from Kermit the Frog to bananas to fuzzy pink gorillas. Nudists clad only in sneakers always make an appearance, and block parties pop up all along the route.

ONLY AT BAY TO BREAKERS

• Tortillas are thrown around like Frisbees as runners wait for their start.

• A prize is awarded to the World Centipede Running Champion. "Centipedes" are groups of at least 13 runners who move as one unit. They can be connected by anything from a costume to a bungee cord, but according to the rules, "feelers" must appear on the first runner's head, and a stinger has to be attached to the "tail" of the last runner.

The Cobb salad's namesake Robert H. Cobb was a first cousin of baseball legend Ty Cobb.

MAP OF THE (INFAMOUS) STARS' HOMES

Think nothing interesting ever happens in your neighborhood? Maybe you should just thank your lucky stars that you're not living with the stars.

ADDRESS: 426 North Bristol, Brentwood
NOTORIOUS HAPPENING: Actress Joan Crawford moved into this house in the 1940s, lived there for 26 years, and raised four children in it. Her daughter Christina wrote the 1978 book *Mommie Dearest*, detailing the abuse she suffered at Crawford's hand during this time. It was the first big "tell-all" Hollywood memoir.

ADDRESS: 810 Linden Drive, Beverly Hills
NOTORIOUS HAPPENING: Mobster Bugsy Siegel met his maker here on June 20, 1947. Rumor has it, his ghost still haunts the seven-bedroom abode.

ADDRESS: 808 Whittier Drive; and 803 and 805 North Linden Drive, Beverly Hills
NOTORIOUS HAPPENING: Billionaire Howard Hughes lost control of his airplane and crashed into these three houses on July 7, 1946. Hughes survived but was injured, and among the wounds was a cut on his lip—and to cover up the scar that was left behind, he grew a thin moustache.

ADDRESS: 730 North Bedford Drive, Beverly Hills
NOTORIOUS HAPPENING: Actress Lana Turner's teenage daughter Cheryl Crane stabbed and killed Turner's boyfriend Johnny Stompanato in this house in the early morning hours of April 5, 1958.

ADDRESS: 12305 Fifth Helena Drive, Brentwood
NOTORIOUS HAPPENING: Marilyn Monroe was found dead

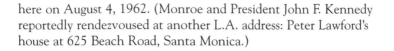

here on August 4, 1962. (Monroe and President John F. Kennedy reportedly rendezvoused at another L.A. address: Peter Lawford's house at 625 Beach Road, Santa Monica.)

ADDRESS: 10050 Cielo Drive, Beverly Hills
NOTORIOUS HAPPENING: In one of L.A.'s most horrific and famous murder cases, actress Sharon Tate, her unborn baby, and four other people were killed at this address in 1969 by followers of Charles Manson. Various buyers purchased the house over the years, but it was demolished in 1994.

ADDRESS: 9402 Beverly Crest Drive, Beverly Hills
NOTORIOUS HAPPENING: Actor Rock Hudson's last home, known as "The Castle," it's where he died of AIDS in 1985.

ADDRESS: 722 North Elm Drive, Beverly Hills
NOTORIOUS HAPPENING: Spoiled rich kids Lyle and Erik Menendez murdered their parents Jose and Kitty at the family home in August 1989.

ADDRESS: 1270 Tower Grove Drive, Beverly Hills
NOTORIOUS HAPPENING: "Hollywood Madam" Heidi Fleiss ran her...um...business out of this house on in the 1990s.

ADDRESS: 875 South Bundy Drive, Brentwood
NOTORIOUS HAPPENING: O. J. Simpson's ex-wife Nicole Brown Simpson and her friend Ronald Goldman were murdered outside this condo on June 12, 1994. In the wake of all the publicity surrounding the case, the townhouse was extensively renovated and got a new address: 879 South Bundy.

*　　*　　*

"The average Hollywood film star's ambition is to be admired by an American, courted by an Italian, married to an Englishman, and have a French boyfriend."

—**Katharine Hepburn**

Golf carts are street-legal in Palm Desert—even on highways.

LOCKEDOWN
IN CHINATOWN

After a fire destroyed much of Walnut Grove's Chinatown, some of the residents decided that they needed a new home. So they founded Locke, the only town in America built by Chinese people for Chinese people.

GO EAST, YOUNG MAN

Before the mid-1800s, the Chinese had little reason to emigrate to America and only a few merchants, students, and sailors did. In 1848 the total U.S. Chinese population was just 325 people. But that changed very quickly in the 1850s. Plagued by years of floods, famine, and suffering from battling warlords and political turmoil, China also fought two wars with Great Britain during that time. The causes? Trade and opium imports—the British were bringing the drug illegally into China and huge numbers of Chinese citizens were becoming addicts. The Chinese didn't fare well during those wars, and suddenly, the United States—with its booming California gold rush and offers of railroad, mining, and farm jobs—started to look really good. Thus began an exodus of young Chinese men, anxious to make their fortunes abroad in order to keep their families back home from starving. By 1852 more than 20,000 Chinese immigrants lived in the United States, mostly in California—by 1880 that number was 300,000.

The Chinese made up a sizable workforce that was willing to work long hours cheaply, a boon for large industries of the day. But many white laborers panicked, fearing they were losing valuable job opportunities to the immigrants. That panic lead to widespread racism.

EXCLUSION

Anti-Chinese fear and racism ran so deep that, beginning in 1882 with the Chinese Exclusion Act, the U.S. Congress passed a series of laws prohibiting any new Chinese immigration for 10 years. When the law was extended a decade later, the effect was not only to exclude new laborers, but also the wives and children of those

---

The San Francisco 49ers team colors are an homage to...

who were already here. Further laws prevented Chinese immigrants from gaining citizenship, marrying non-Asians, and owning land.

As if these laws weren't bad enough, there were plenty of regular Americans also willing to make life even more difficult for the Chinese. Some went on killing sprees, and Chinese homes all over California were destroyed by arson. So when the Asian section of Walnut Grove burned down in 1915—even though it looked like the result of an accident—some of the town's residents feared they were being targeted.

MULTIPLY BY DIVIDING

In the early 20th century, Walnut Grove was a large town on the Sacramento River in the Central Valley. It was an unusual place for a couple of reasons: First, it was the only municipality that straddled the river. Connected first by a riverboat and then a bridge, the two halves made for another unusual situation. The west side was reserved for people of European descent, the east for people of Asian descent. The Asian half was divided even further into Japanese and Chinese sections. The Chinese section was likewise divided into two: the Chung San and the Toi Shan. The groups came from two different regions of China, had somewhat different cultures, and spoke different dialects of Cantonese.

The Chung San group was smaller and less politically powerful than the Toi Shan. After the 1915 fire, the Toi Shan and Japanese rebuilt in Walnut Grove, but the Chung San people wanted something new. Led by a successful Chinese businessman named Lee Bing and a handful of others (mostly labor brokers who connected the local labor pool with temporary jobs), they decided to relocate and start a town of their own. Since Chinese people weren't allowed to own land, Bing and his group rented 14 acres from a sympathetic local named George Locke. (Legend has it that Locke and Bing "sealed" their agreement with only a handshake.) The Chinese residents named the town after the landowner, built businesses and houses, and made Locke the only American town designed and built by Chinese architects, builders, and workmen for their own people.

NOT EXACTLY MAYBERRY

It would be nice to imagine Locke as being a stable, healthy family town. But most of the Chinese workers who lived there had been stranded without families, thanks to the immigration laws. That created a population that was mostly young, unattached, and male...in other words, a little rowdy. Locke's residents generally numbered around 600, but on weekends, that could swell to more than 1,200 people looking for food, diversion, companionship, and excitement. Locke also had no police force, and the county sheriff stopped by only occasionally. So during Prohibition, speakeasies, opium dens, brothels, and gambling halls became a large part of the local economy.

Still, the residents of Locke thrived during the 1920s. Bing Lee ran a headquarters for the Chinese Nationalist Party that was supported financially by revolutionaries in China. Rooming houses, grocery stores, barbershops, a theater, bakeries, and clothing stores all sprung up in town. As some women and children were finally allowed to immigrate, Locke also became a haven for Chinese families.

LOCKE DOWN

The town's heyday lasted only about a decade. The Depression and the repeal of Prohibition both hit Locke hard, and it went into decline. Most second-generation Chinese left as they grew up, seeking out better employment opportunities in large cities.

Locke is still there...though barely. Many of its wooden buildings—built cheaply a century ago—are in a state of disrepair. But its historic Main Street and River Road buildings attract contemporary tourist traffic, as do the surviving Chinese and Japanese parts of Walnut Grove. Locke was designated a National Historic Landmark District in 1990 and has been listed on the National Register of Historic Places since 1971. Of the 70 or so people who live there today, about 10 are of Chinese descent...and the land below their houses still belongs to somebody else.

*　　*　　*

I FEEL THE EARTH MOVE

The National Earthquake Information Center records 12,000 to 14,000 earthquakes every year—more than 30 a day—all over the world, but most are too small for humans to feel.

California's lowest recorded temperature: -45°F in Boca (1937).

UNCLE JOHN'S PAGE OF LISTS

Some random information from the BRI trivia files.

3 CALIFORNIA CITIES ON LISTS OF AMERICA'S 10 MOST POPULOUS
1. L.A. (#2)
2. San Diego (#8)
3. San Jose (#10)

5 MOST EXPENSIVE CALIFORNIA ZIP CODES
1. 91008: Duarte/Bradbury (L.A County)
2. 94027: Atherton (San Mateo County)
3. 90274: Rolling Hills (L.A. County)
4. 90210: Beverly Hills (L.A. County)
5. 94920: Belvedere/Tiburon (Marin County)

3 ARNOLD S. CATCH PHRASES
1. "I'll be back."
2. "Hasta la vista, baby."
3. "It's not a tumor."

7 CLAREMONT COLLEGES
1. Pomona
2. Scripps
3. Claremont McKenna
4. Harvey Mudd
5. Pitzer
6. Claremont Graduate
7. Keck

3 ROLLER COASTERS ON THE SANTA CRUZ BOARDWALK
1. Giant Dipper
2. Hurricane
3. Sea Serpent

5 SEASONS OF *THE REAL WORLD* THAT WERE SET IN CALIFORNIA
1. Los Angeles (1993)
2. San Francisco (1994)
3. San Diego (2004)
4. Hollywood (2008)
5. San Diego (2011)

4 MOST POPULAR SPRINKLES CUPCAKE FLAVORS
1. Red velvet
2. Sweet cream butter
3. Belgian chocolate
4. Madagascar bourbon vanilla

Disneyland's floral Mickey Mouse portrait at the entrance is replanted nine times a year.

THE CAL–STANFORD PRANK WAR

When it comes to college football, few teams feud quite as passionately as the ones at UC Berkeley (Cal) and Stanford. One writer even went so far as to call the rivalry "miniature warfare." And hey, what good is a war if you don't dish out some pranks?

SEIZING THE AXE

Cal and Stanford typically do their most furious battles on the football field, but the biggest prank in the schools' histories actually began at a baseball game. In 1896 Stanford student Will Irwin got his school's fans chanting, "Give 'em the axe!" at a game. The cheer caught on, and three years later, before a baseball game against Cal, Stanford's cheerleaders brought onto the field a real 10-pound lumberjack's axe. They used it to chop up blue and gold ribbons (Cal's colors) after every great Stanford play, and then marched the axe past the stands where the Cal fans were seated. The stunt didn't do any good, however; Cal won the game, 9–7.

But Cal's fans were still mad, so when the game was over, a group of them waited at the exit and then jumped the Stanford students carrying the axe. In the tumult, Cal made away with the axe. Sprinter Billy Drum ran with it through the winding streets of San Francisco, with both Cal and Stanford men pursuing. After additional skirmishes in which the axe changed hands several times, the Cal students reached a butcher shop, ran inside, and cut the axe blade away from the handle. Then Clint Miller stuffed the axe under his overcoat, put the handle down his pants leg, and headed for the Ferry Building to board a ship back to Berkeley. At the landing, Stanford students were waiting with police, who frisked those boarding the ferry. For a few minutes, it looked like Cal was sunk, but Miller managed to sneak aboard and cross the bay. Back at campus, Stanford's axe was stored first in a safe and then under the pillow of the baseball team's trainer. It was later moved to a bank vault, where it remained for 30 years…brought out only for an annual spring pep rally, to which it was transported in an armored car.

California was the first state to adopt an official insect: the dogface butterfly (1972).

THE IMMORTAL 21

Stanford wanted its axe back, of course, but the opportunity to get it didn't present itself until 1930. In what's known to many fans as the "most perfectly executed axe theft of all time," 21 Stanford students arrived outside the bank where the axe was stored. On that day, it was scheduled to be transported (in its armored car) from a baseball rally. It never made it back.

Disguised in Cal colors, the Stanford raiders set off tear gas and flash powder just as the axe emerged from the armored car. In all the confusion, they overpowered Cal's baseball team captain (officially known as the "Grand Custodian of the Axe") and grabbed the axe from him. (Stanford legend says he was so distraught that he started to cry, though it might have been the tear gas.) The students spirited the axe back to Stanford's campus outside Palo Alto, where they were hailed as heroes and nicknamed the "Immortal 21." Angry and stunned Cal students called them the "Immoral 21" instead.

Stanford students kept the axe in a bank vault for three years while the arguing over who was its rightful owner continued. Finally, in 1933, the two schools came to an agreement: The axe would become a trophy, awarded every year to the winner of the Big Game, the football game the two schools played each fall. All those feelings of goodwill didn't stop students from stealing the axe, however. Over the years, Stanford has stolen it three times, and Cal, four times. And it didn't stop the students from pulling other pranks, either.

MORE LEGENDARY CAL–STANFORD PRANKS

- In 1982 the Big Game featured a kickoff returned by Cal for a score to win in the closing seconds. Stanford students avenged the loss four days later by replacing thousands of copies of the *Daily Californian*, the Cal student newspaper, with a fake issue. The mock front page reported that the NCAA had overruled officials and declared that Stanford had actually won the game by a score of 20–19. Another story described how the Cal football coach broke down in tears after being informed of the decision.

- In 1990 Cal lost the Big Game in the final seconds. Berkeley student Theodore B. Kelly seized the moment—he hacked into the referee's microphone system and announced over the stadium's sound system, "Penalty. Unsportsmanlike arrogance. Stanford Sucks."

- In 1998 five Cal students stole the 10-foot-tall costume for Stanford's mascot: a redwood tree. They then recorded a video featuring one of their own dressed in the tree costume with a blindfold on. They also took a picture and sent it to Stanford, demanding a ransom for the costume's release. After about two weeks—during which Cal's chancellor threatened to bench Berkeley's mascot at the upcoming Big Game if the tree costume wasn't returned—the Cal students "released the tree unharmed."

For the UCLA–USC rivalry and its pranks, check out page 142.

* * *

DON'T MESS WITH HEARST

In 1941 Orson Welles starred in and directed the movie *Citizen Kane*, which has often been called the greatest movie ever made. It paints a very unflattering (though technically "fictional") picture of California media mogul William Randolph Hearst, and Welles, always one who enjoyed pushing buttons, hoped the movie would make a statement about Heart's capitalist greed. But Welles underestimated the depth of Hearst's power, which the mogul used to discredit Welles and the film. Hearst threatened the studio (RKO), saying he'd expose its scandals in his newspapers if the film were released. He threatened movie theaters until they were too afraid to show it. And his newspapers conducted a public smear campaign of Welles himself, accusing the actor/director of being a communist who was disloyal to the United States.

It worked. Hearst's accusations got Welles into trouble with the FBI, and *Citizen Kane* tanked at the box office. When the movie was announced at the 1942 Oscars (it received nine nominations), people booed. It wasn't until the 1960s that audiences discovered *Citizen Kane* on a mass scale and turned it into a hit.

At nearly three million acres, San Bernardino is the largest county in the U.S.

GHOST COAST

California is known for sun, surf, sand...and some
of the most haunted real estate in the United States.

WHO: At least six ghosts, including a dog and a criminal named "Yankee Jim" Robinson
WHERE: The Whaley House, Old Town San Diego
STORY: If Thomas Whaley could do it all over again, he probably wouldn't have built his house on the site of San Diego's former public gallows. In 1855, though, that was the land he bought—probably for a bargain. He built a large, elegant brick structure that served as a home for his wife Anna and their children. The house also had enough room for him to use or rent out parts of it as a store, courthouse, school, and theater. All in all, it was a perfect house...except for the ghosts.

Today the Whaley House is called the "most haunted house in California," and the people who work there report smelling burning tobacco and lavender perfume, and seeing chandeliers swinging on their own, windows flying open, and what appear to be actual people dressed in 19th-century clothing who walk by and then disappear around corners. Sometimes an empty rocking chair even rocks on its own, and a piano plays by itself. The home became a museum in 1960, and over the years, visitors have reported feeling a noose tightening around their necks while they're inside. The identified ghosts include...

• **"Yankee" Jim Robinson** was executed on the site in 1852 for stealing a boat. His heavy boots can be heard tramping up and down empty stairways and hallways. According to some reports, Thomas Whaley witnessed Robinson's execution.

• **Violet Whaley**, one of Thomas Whaley's daughters, was so depressed after her marriage ended in divorce that, in 1885, she shot herself in the heart.

• **A child**, who supposedly died after accidentally ingesting poison, sometimes haunts the kitchen.

• **Dolly Varden**, the Whaleys' fox terrier, was once seen "running" down a hallway with her ears flapping.

Q. What did Anton LaVey found in 1966 in San Francisco? A. The Church of Satan.

WHO: Crushed sailors, a child, and others

WHERE: The RMS *Queen Mary* Hotel, Long Beach

STORY: Making its maiden voyage in 1936, Britain's *Queen Mary* was the biggest, fastest, and most powerful ocean liner of its time, but during World War II, the ship was painted gray, reassigned to ferry soliders to the front, and nicknamed the "Gray Ghost." By the end of the war, it had carried about 800,000 troops across 600,000 miles of water. After the war, a refurbished *Queen Mary* made more than 1,000 additional cruises before retiring to Long Beach Harbor to become a hotel and museum in 1967.

It's also a gathering place for ghosts. According to the Discovery Channel, the *Queen Mary* is the "most haunted ship in America," and hundreds of ghost sightings have appeared over the years. Guests and employees have heard disembodied footsteps, knocking, voices, laughter, and singing. They've seen doors open and close on their own, wet footsteps appear near empty swimming pools, and World War II soldiers hanging out in the hallways. Some of the spectral stowaways may have died on the ship—there were at least 49 deaths reported on the *Queen Mary* during its sailing days. Famous apparitions include...

• **John Pedder**, an 18-year-old engineer who was crushed to death by watertight door number 13 in the engine room.

• A child named **Jackie**, said to have drowned in the second-class swimming pool.

• And **sailors** from the HMS *Curacoa*, who died when the *Queen Mary* collided with their ship. Visitors have claimed to hear the men screaming from the lower decks.

More ghost stories on page 213.

*   *   *

SHOW US THE MONEY!

California has America's largest state economy. As of 2010, California's gross domestic product (GDP) was $1.9 trillion.

THE DELINQUENCY OF MINERS

Theft, drugs, shanghaiing, and even murder were all in a night's work on old San Francisco's Barbary Coast.

MAIDEN LANE'S NAUGHTY PAST

Today, San Francisco's Maiden Lane, an alley off Union Square, is a chic place for shoppers, but most people don't know that it's named for ladies of the night. In fact, Maiden Lane was once home to the most notorious dens of prostitution in the city's infamous red-light district, the Barbary Coast.

From 1850 to 1917, the Barbary Coast spanned about 40 blocks from the Embarcadero to the Presidio. Attractions like the Transamerica Pyramid, Ghirardelli Square, and Fisherman's Wharf, as well as parts of Chinatown, North Beach, and the Financial District, are all built on the former "wickedest" place in North America. Named after the pirate-plagued Barbary Coast of Africa, the neighborhood was filled with taverns, opium dens, casinos, dance halls, and brothels.

GOLDEN BEGINNINGS

In 1848 San Francisco's population was about 800; by 1853 it was more than 50,000. Most were young men between 20 and 40, and they often came to town fresh from a successful bout of prospecting and with gold to burn. But where to spend it?

During the first years of the gold rush, few women lived in San Francisco. As news of the strike in California traveled around the world, however, thousands of prostitutes arrived from Mexico, Europe, Asia, and other parts of the United States to "help" the miners spend their money. So many "ladies of the night" descended on the city during the mid-1800s that by 1850, only about a third of San Francisco's females were "honest" women.

At first, women could get rich simply by sitting next to a man and supplying him with drinks. Actual prostitution was much too

---

1.3 million acres of California are designated as state parks.

expensive. The men even complained that in San Francisco, the going rate for a Parisian prostitute was about 100 times what she charged back home. But as more and more working girls arrived, the men had more choices.

YO, BARBARY COAST CRIBS!

The Barbary Coast's notorious brothels varied from glamorous "parlor houses" to grim one-room shacks called "cribs." One famous parlor house belonged to Madam Bertha Kahn and catered to an extremely wealthy clientele. Madam Kahn tolerated no liquor, no swearing, and no vulgarity of any kind. When a man came to visit, she called out, "Company, girls!" and the women trooped downstairs to sit demurely on the couch while the customer made his choice.

For most prostitutes, though, life in the Barbary Coast was brutal…and short. In Chinese cribs, young girls who had been bought or kidnapped in China were forced into sexual slavery until they were no longer useful—at which point they were killed. Other prostitutes were controlled by madams or pimps who used violence to keep them in line. It wasn't unusual for a prostitute to be murdered by a client who decided not to pay. And of course venereal diseases were rampant.

BARBARY'S BAD BOYS

The Barbary Coast didn't actually get its nickname until the 1860s. Before that, the neighborhood was called Sydney Town in honor of a fierce gang of convicts from Australia called the Sydney Ducks. With so many people constantly arriving in San Francisco, officials had a tough time keeping a lid on crime, and gangs like the Ducks flourished. From 1849 to 1855, there were usually about two murders a night in Sydney Town, but few people were prosecuted. Some of the crimes perpetrated by the Ducks included arson—amid the confusion and spreading fire, the gang would rob empty stores and houses.

Finally in 1851, a group of locals formed a vigilante committee that went after the Ducks. They held secret trials and lynching, and drove the gang from San Francisco. Of course, other criminals simply stepped in to take their place. In 1876 a writer described the Barbary Coast as "the haunt of the low and the vile of every kind. The petty thief, the house burglar, the tramp, the whore-monger, lewd women, cutthroats, murderers, all are found here."

As crime thrived, it was the rare greenhorn sailor, miner, or farmer who entered the neighborhood's streets and got out with his money. There was always a girl to ply him with drinks and get him to spend all his cash. Or a bartender ready to put knockout drops in his drink so that his pockets could be picked. If all else failed, a bouncer could throw a patron out for being a poor spender...but not before clocking him over the head and cleaning out his wallet. There were also worse fates than losing money—ruthless thugs made big bucks by supplying captains of sailing vessels with men. They shanghaied, or kidnapped, unlucky drunks who later woke up at sea bound for ports unknown. The kidnappings happened so often that the Barbary Coast coined the term "shanghaied."

"LEWD WOMEN AND BEASTLY MEN"

Reformers did try to clean up the Barbary Coast. After the 1906 earthquake destroyed much of the neighborhood, concerned San Franciscans tried to keep the saloons, dance halls, and brothels from rebuilding. The most famous reformer was Reverend Terence Caraher, who fought against the evils of prostitution for years. (He seemed to find evil everywhere, though, even launching unexplained crusades against trolley cars and complaining that they encouraged "lewd women and beastly men.") By 1911 Caraher had shut down some of the Barbary Coast's largest brothels, including one that was run by local politicians.

But it wasn't until 1914, when the state government in Sacramento passed the Red Light Abatement Act, which allowed authorities to seize property being used for prostitution, that things really started to change. The law was challenged and upheld in 1917 by the California Supreme Court. That year, San Francisco police were able to shut down the city's brothels for good, and the long party in the Barbary Coast was finally over.

*   *   *

DID YOU KNOW?
Yosemite National Park has more than 700 miles of hiking trails.

WE ♥ MODESTO

Modesto is California's 18th largest city and seventh in terms of agricultural production. But those claims to fame are nothing when compared to these.

• **Cruisin' for a bruisin'.** Filmmaker George Lucas grew up on a walnut ranch in Modesto, and a bronze sculpture in Lucas Plaza downtown commemorates his place as the city's favorite son. The sculpture is a life-size teen boy/girl car scene inspired by Lucas's 1973 movie about cruising up and down the city's streets. *American Graffiti* triggered a huge wave of 1950s nostalgia and made stars of the cast: Harrison Ford, Richard Dreyfus, Ron Howard, Cindy Williams, Paul Le Mat, and Mackenzie Phillips. What it didn't do was make a star of Modesto—nearly all of the city scenes were filmed in Petaluma.

• **Full of nuts.** Once called the A's and the Colts, Modesto's minor-league baseball team got its latest name in 2005 in honor of the nuts that grow outside the town. (We especially like that the Modesto Nuts have two mascots: Wally the Walnut and Al the Almond.)

• **Arch friends, Arch enemies:** Straddling I Street at Ninth is the famous Modesto Arch. In 1911 the Modesto Business Men's Association wanted to erect something that would welcome visitors with a message that Modesto wasn't just some backwater but a great place to live and do business. Somebody suggested an arch—maybe something like the Arc de Triomphe in Paris, but not so expensive—that spelled out the town's name and included an immodest boast about the city. So the group petitioned the city council for permission to erect an "Ornamental and Electric Arch…to be constructed of brick, reinforced concrete, and steel."

The city agreed, mainly because the Business Men's Association was willing to shell out the $1,200 (about $30,000 today) to build it. But what about the motto? Somebody suggested a slogan contest that would be judged by local luminaries. Entries streamed in. When the judges met, they decided that a contemporary, infor-

---

76 of the 500 volcanic vents in California have erupted during the last 10,000 years.

mal, fun motto was just what Modesto needed. So they awarded the grand prize of $10 to James Hanscom for his slangy tribute to his hometown's stoic unflappability: "Nobody's got Modesto's goat!" But people didn't like that. It was too...contemporary, informal, and fun. So the city council and the Business Men's Association stepped in and declared that the arch would be better served by the runner-up: clerk Sam Harbaugh, who got the glory but only a $3 prize as payment.

- **Family's everything...unless you're selling salami.** Modesto's E. J. Gallo Winery is the largest family-owned winery in the world. It employs 3,300 people in its wine factory and headquarters, making E. J. Gallo the largest employer in town. The founders, Ernest and Julio Gallo, had a reputation of ruthless competitiveness—not just with other wineries, but also with their own workers and family members. For example, they successfully sued another brother for selling Gallo brand salami, arguing that his product would confuse consumers and dilute the Gallo wine trademark. The brothers also fiercely fought unions, inspiring a "Boycott Gallo" campaign by the United Farm Workers in the early 1970s that eventually brought the company to the bargaining table.

Today, Gallo makes 900 million bottles of wine every year and dominates retail shelf space countrywide by stealthily packaging its wine under more than 60 brands, including Barefoot Cellars, Carlo Rossi, Boone's Farm, Turning Leaf, Andre Cellars, Bridlewood Estate, Clarendon Hills, and Frei Brothers. As the largest exporter of California wines, Gallo sells more than half of its bottles overseas, but keeps enough to provide about 33 percent of all the bottles of wine sold in the United States. Is Gallo big enough yet? Not if you ask Ernest Gallo, who was once quoted as saying, "We don't want most of the business. We want it all."

- **#12! Let's raise a toast!** Given E. J. Gallo's dominance, it might not be surprising that, in 2010, Modesto was rated #12 in *Men's Health's* listing of "America's Drunkest Cities."

Pip-pip: There are seven municipalities in the UK named California.

MURDER, HE
WROTE, PART I

*Once upon a time, two writers discovered the dark side of
sunny California and gave it to the rest of the world.*

WEST COAST MURDER

When Dashiell Hammett and Raymond Chandler
began writing in the 1920s and '30s, detective stories
were "soft-boiled" (i.e., sentimental) and usually revealed a com-
plicated, puzzling murder with important clues. The puzzle was
solved by a genius amateur—like Agatha Christie's Hercule
Poirot, who appeared in more than 30 of her novels and caught
murderers with this famous "grey cells." But Hammett's and Chandler's gumshoes were hard-boiled (i.e., gritty), seasoned pros who
dealt with corruption, crooks, and thugs. They were loners because
government and police often sold out to the highest bidder, and
they solved crimes with fists and guns.

Hammett is especially famous for creating the hard-boiled
detective story and turning it into great literature. Chandler continued Hammett's tough realism and added poetry and heart.
While making literary history, Chandler and Hammett were also
famous for moving the mystery world away from the English country mansions that most of the stories inhabited and placing them
on the mean streets of San Francisco and Los Angeles. For the
first time, California was portrayed as a place full of injustice and
corruption.

SAMUEL DASHIELL HAMMETT

In 1915, 21-year-old Dashiell Hammett began working as a detective for the Pinkerton Agency, a national private law-enforcement
agency. Army service during World War I and a bout of tuberculosis interrupted that career—Hammett was sent to a hospital in
Washington State and told he'd probably never fully recover from
the illness. So he gave up being a Pinkerton, moved to San Francisco, and turned to writing. But because of his experience at the
agency, detective stories were a natural fit.

In 1922 Hammett became a regular contributor to a mystery pulp magazine called the *Black Mask*, and the detectives that he created were unlike any other lawmen in fiction at the time. The point of the story wasn't so much to solve murders, as to follow the exploits of a tough P.I. as he took on the bad guys. Hammett's work was realistic; his talent made his stories popular with critics and the public. Hammett went on to write five novels, and might have written more if bad health, heavy drinking, and run-ins with the anti-Communist McCarthy hearings of the 1950s hadn't slowed his progress. Despite all those problems, though, Hammett became one of the most influential authors in the United States, and his "hard-boiled" mystery style is still going strong.

THE MALTESE FALCON

Background: Dashiell Hammett's most famous book was 1930's *The Maltese Falcon*, which introduced readers to a foggy, murderous San Francisco. It's considered by many to be America's greatest detective novel and appears on Modern Library's list of the top 100 novels of the 20th century.

The Premise (Spoiler Alert!): The story revolves around investigator Sam Spade, "a pleasant, blonde Satan"—the kind of guy who's having a secret affair with his partner's wife, even though he doesn't much like her. Into Spade's (and his partner, Archer's) agency comes beautiful Brigid O'Shaughnessy. She asks them to follow a man who's run off with her sister, and after the detectives take the case, both Archer and the man he was following are killed. Brigid then admits she hasn't actually been looking for her sister after all, but for a priceless jeweled sculpture called the Maltese Falcon...and she's in trouble. Spade keeps her as a client and takes on gangsters and con men who are also searching for the valuable bird. Along the way Spade falls for Brigid, but he still turns her in to the police for murder because she killed his partner so that she could get the Falcon.

SAM SPADE GOES TO THE MOVIES

If the character of Sam Spade seems familiar, that's probably because Humphrey Bogart played him in the movie. *The Maltese Falcon* was released in 1941, and remains one of the most famous films ever made. Bogart's portrayal of slick Sam Spade, who can outfox the police and the crooks, is one of the actor's best-known performances. The movie became so popular that the U.S. atomic bomb "Fat Man" was named for *The Maltese Falcon*'s rotund villain, played by Sidney Greenstreet. *The Maltese Falcon* was nominated for a Best Picture Oscar, and is #23 on the American Film Institute's top 100 list of best movies.

SAM SPADE'S SAN FRANCISCO

• Spade's San Francisco is filled with fog, mystery, and murder…as well as good food. John's Grill, where Spade ordered chops, baked potatoes, and sliced tomatoes about 80 years ago, is still in business at 63 Ellis Street.

• Spade's apartment, where Spade and Brigid had their romance, can still be found at 891 Post Street, which just happens to be the same apartment building once occupied by Dashiell Hammett.

• And just a few blocks away, Burritt Alley is marked with a plaque dedicated to three of the story's fictional characters. It reads: "On approximately this spot, Miles Archer, partner of Sam Spade, was done in by Brigid O'Shaughnessy."

For an L.A mystery and the story of Raymond Chandler, head over to page 152.

* * *

MEET YOU AT THE FOUNTAIN

At the intersection of Market, Geary, and Kearny Streets in San Francisco is a cast-iron fountain that 19th-century entertainer Lotta Crabtree gave to the city in 1875. A lover of animals, she had the sculpture created to include a drinking fountain for people and a water trough for thirsty horses. Crabtree's fountain became a meeting point for survivors after the 1906 San Francisco earthquake, and eventually, it became a tradition for locals and tourists to meet there every year on the morning of April 18—the anniversary of the earthquake.

An average day at Disneyland yields about 30 tons of garbage.

FREEDOM RIDE

On August 9, 1961, a group of 11 college students from Los Angeles boarded a train at Union Station. Their destinations: Louisiana and Mississippi. Their goal: to protest racism and segregation.

THE TIMES THEY ARE A'-CHANGIN'

The Freedom Riders were people—black and white, generally male and under 30—who traveled on buses into the American South to protest racial inequality and violence. In the 1960s, even though nearly 100 years had passed since the end of the Civil War, the South was still a stronghold of prejudice and segregation, supported by Jim Crow laws, a series of state and local laws that discriminated against African Americans and maintained "separate but equal" facilities for whites and blacks. There were segregated water fountains, bathrooms, restaurants, public schools, and public transportation. In the 1950s and '60s, Americans began challenging those laws, maintaing that separate facilities were inherently unequal. There had been a little change already—in 1954, with its famous *Brown v. Board of Education* decision, the U.S. Supreme Court declared segregated public schools to be illegal. But in the Deep South, racial prejudice, segregation, and violence still reigned.

In 1960 the Supreme Court issued another decision, stating that segregating trains, buses, and other forms of public transportation or their facilities (stations, bathrooms, and so on) was also illegal, but the southern states simply ignored the ruling. On trains and buses throughout the South, African Americans were required to sit in the back or give up their seats to white patrons on demand. The goal of the Freedom Riders was to bring attention to this injustice and encourage the federal government to start enforcing the Supreme Court's 1960 decision.

GET ON THE BUS

On May 4, 1961, the first group of Freedom Riders—seven African Americans and six whites—left Washington, D.C., on two Greyhound buses. Their plan was to ride through the entire Deep South (Virginia, North Carolina, South Carolina, Alabama,

---

First California-born state governor: Romualdo Pacheco (elected 1875).

Georgia, Mississippi, Tennessee, and Louisiana). But they were so severely harassed and attacked—beaten, bloodied, and jailed, their buses firebombed and destroyed—that they made it only as far as Birmingham, Alabama. In a response on behalf of the U.S. government, Attorney General Robert Kennedy called for a "cooling-off period," essentially asking the Freedom Riders to abandon their cause. They refused. Instead, more and more Freedom Riders volunteered throughout the summer—eventually, more than 400 in all, including 100 from California—and 11 of them were organizing in Los Angeles.

Life for African Americans on the West Coast during the 1950s and '60s was slightly better than for their counterparts in the South—for one, there were no Jim Crow laws in California—but it wasn't great by any means. During World War II, many African Americans had moved west in search of jobs in industry and defense, but when the white soldiers came home, black workers were pushed out. That created a racial divide and deep poverty in traditionally black areas of California's cities. In Los Angeles especially, African American residents were more likely to be poor and uneducated than their white peers. As a result, the city had become one of the epicenters of the civil rights movement. Pastors and activists held rallies all over L.A., and Reverend Martin Luther King Jr. visited several times. So it wasn't surprising that the Freedom Rider movement found a sympathetic ear in Los Angeles.

COLLEGE STUDENTS ON A MISSION

"The call went out to students around the country," said Robert Farrell, a member of the Los Angeles City Council from 1974 to 1991. "Let's save the Freedom Riders." In 1961, Farrell was 24, a UCLA graduate who was interested in civil rights. He and 10 others from various L.A. colleges joined the cause. Supported by the Congress of Racial Equality (CORE), a group dedicated to ending racial discrimination, the students met at Union Station in downtown L.A. on August 9, 1961, and boarded a train bound for Houston, Texas. Their plan was to disembark there, desegregate the lunch counter at the train station, and then board buses that would take them into Mississippi and Alabama, the heart of Jim Crow country. Said Farrell, "We were going to carry out a mission...and we understood what the risks were. We knew there

[were] going to be arrests and jailing. But it was worth taking a risk."

At the train station in Houston, the L.A. students met up with another group from Texas Southern University. They all sat together at a segregated coffee shop lunch counter inside the station. Like the rest of the South, Houston was under the thumb of Jim Crow—black and white students sitting together in a coffee shop drew a lot of attention. The cooks and waitresses refused to serve them, and pretty soon, a group of angry segregationists assembled outside. Within an hour, the group had morphed into a mob that shouted and spit racial epithets at the students. Police quickly arrived...and arrested the students, hauling them off to the Harris County Jail.

In jail, the students were booked and placed in holding cells, where several of them were attacked by fellow inmates...all under the watchful eye of the guards. According to Freedom Rider Steve McNichols, "We were in there for two days, living by our wits and trying to make as many friends as we could."

"A SIGNAL OF VICTORY"

The 11 Freedom Riders from L.A. never made it beyond Houston. CORE bailed them out of jail, and the battered, exhausted, hungry group returned to California. But that was no sign of defeat. As the American people watched the nonviolent Freedom Riders being beaten on TV, outrage began to spread, and by September, the federal government agreed to enforce the 1960 Supreme Court decision. Farrell said, "We took that as a signal of victory."

Other victories would follow: In many cases, the Freedom Riders didn't just focus on transportation. Like the L.A. group, they sat together at segregated restaurants and coffee shops in the cities they visited. They were especially successful when they targeted big businesses, many of which had headquarters in the North. Unwilling to face boycotts or trouble at home, the businesses often voluntarily desegregated their southern establishments. And then finally, in 1964, President Lyndon Johnson signed the Civil Rights Act, which outlawed all forms of racial discrimination. The struggle for civil rights continued for at least another decade, but finally, at least, the protesters had the law on their side.

BY THE BAY

We left our heart in San Francisco. (These people did too.)

"God took the beauty of the Bay of Naples, the Valley of the Nile, the Swiss Alps, the Hudson River Valley, rolled them into one, and made San Francisco Bay."
—**Fiorello La Guardia**

"The Bay Area is so beautiful, I hesitate to preach about heaven while I'm here."
—**Billy Graham**

"When I lived in Oakland, we would think nothing of driving to Half Moon Bay and Santa Cruz one day and then driving to the foothills of the Sierras the next day."
—**Tom Hanks**

"As many of you know, I came from San Francisco. We don't have a lot of farms there. Well, we do have one—it's a mushroom farm, so you know what that means."
—**Nancy Pelosi**

"Isn't it nice that people who prefer Los Angeles to San Francisco live there?"
—**Herb Caen**

"L.A.? That's just a parking lot where you buy a hamburger for a trip to San Francisco."
—**John Lennon**

"San Francisco is poetry. Even the hills rhyme."
—**Pat Montandon**

"If you're alive, you can't be bored in San Francisco. If you're not alive, San Francisco will bring you to life."
—**William Saroyan**

"Just one look at any of those streets, and you couldn't be anywhere else—it's so beautiful. Who couldn't become ravenous in such a place?"
—**Julia Child**

"You are fortunate to live here. If I were your president, I would levy a tax on you for living in San Francisco!"
—**Mikhail Gorbachev**

"Leaving San Francisco is like saying good-bye to an old sweetheart. You want to linger as long as possible."
—**Walter Cronkite**

Beat novelist Jack Kerouac once worked as a railroad brakeman in San Francisco.

TWO SIDES OF BAKER

The town of Bakersfield gets its name from early settler and founder Colonel Thomas Baker, who might be considered a hero or a crook…depending on what story you tell.

THE FABULOUS BAKERSFIELD BOY

The most often told history of Bakersfield goes like this: In 1832 Ohio-born Colonel Tom Baker—a 22-year-old surveyor and fledgling land lawyer—decided to head west. In Iowa, he stopped off for a little while to work as a district attorney and president of the state senate before continuing on to California in the 1850s. By 1863, he'd gotten himself elected to the state legislature and had successfully taken on an audacious project of draining the swamps along the Kern River. An expert consultant had written a report calling that task impossible, but Baker rolled up his sleeves and did it anyway, creating a small town called Kern Island that was surrounded by farmland.

Indifferent to riches, though, he gave away almost all of the reclaimed land, sometimes for a dollar an acre or even less, and kept only 80 of the 31,000 acres for himself. His goal: To bring in settlers. Baker was equally generous to travelers and immigrants, letting them stop, camp, and graze his fields of vegetables and fruits while their livestock feasted on his alfalfa. According to legend, he told them only to "Help yourself, but don't waste anything." The story has it that the travelers told each other to "stop and stay at Baker's field." So gradually, the settlement adopted Bakersfield as its official name.

THE MAYBE NOT-SO-FABULOUS BAKERSFIELD BOY

As with most laudatory histories, however, a few facts were left out of that story. In particular, the expert consultant who called the swamp drainage project impossible was Thomas Baker himself. Having been appointed to the U.S. Land Office in Visalia, his report drove away investors and doomed the partnership that owned rights to the swamp reclamation project. Soon the office was desperate to sell the rights for pennies on the dollar and could find only one willing buyer: Thomas Baker. He paid $10,000 for the chance to claim 200,000 acres of swamp. (He ultimately took 31,000.)

If that makes Baker sound dirty, he was. He often used his experience and contacts from the California legislature to get laws written in his favor. And he wasn't above a bit of bribery either: In 1865, when he reported that the swampland had been claimed and should be deeded to him, California's governor sent a civil engineer named A. R. Jackson to check out Baker's claims. Remembering his own sketchy swamp drainage report from years earlier, Baker realized just how risky outside experts could be, so he took no chances. When Jackson returned to Sacramento, he reported that Baker had fulfilled all requirements and was due the deed. What Jackson didn't report was that, thanks to Baker's "generosity," he was now the proud owner of a nice parcel of that land himself.

* * *

HOLLYWOOD GOSSIP

From the 1940s to the 1990s, actor Robert Mitchum played tough guys in more than 100 movies, and those roles weren't too far from his real personality. Mitchum grew up poor and came of age during the Great Depression. He spent some time riding around the country on freight trains and even did a stint as a prisoner on a Georgia chain gang. His attitude was coarse, and compared to his real life, he found acting dull and Hollywood phony. In 1948, just as his career was taking off, Mitchum was arrested for attending a party where drugs were found. He fully expected to be fired from his studio contract, and told police that his occupation was "ex-actor." When Hollywood welcomed him back, Mitchum seemed almost sorry. He spoke nostalgically about jail, calling it "Palm Springs without the riffraff."

In the late 1940s, that kind of attitude ran up against actress Loretta Young, a powerful and savvy star who was famous for her glamorous beauty and ladylike ways. Young, Mitchum, and actor William Holden costarred in the 1948 Western *Rachel and the Stranger*. Young kept a "swear box" on set, and anyone who used profanity had to drop in money, which was given to charity at the end of filming. Her "rates" started at 50¢ for "hell" and went up from there. Supposedly, Mitchum would stuff the box with change in anticipation of using lots of foul language.

JOHN MUIR'S YOSEMITE, PART I

Naturalist John Muir first visited Yosemite in 1868, and he wrote all about it in the 1912 book The Yosemite.

NATURAL WONDER

Located in central California, in the western Sierra Nevada Mountains, Yosemite is one of the world's most popular national parks—more than 3 million people visit every year. It's also home to some famous natural attractions: Half Dome, Yosemite Falls, Bridalveil Fall, El Capitan, and the Mariposa Grove among them. But in 1868, when famed naturalist John Muir first visited, Yosemite was untouched wilderness. In 1912, Muir wrote *The Yosemite*, a travel memoir about his experiences in the valley. Here are some excerpts from that book.

A "TEMPLE LIGHTED FROM ABOVE"

"The most famous and accessible [valley in the Sierra Nevada], and also the one that presents [the] most striking and sublime features on the grandest scale, is the Yosemite, situated in the basin of the Merced River at an elevation of 4,000 feet above the level of the sea. It is about seven miles long, half a mile to a mile wide, and nearly a mile deep in the solid granite flank of the range. The walls are made up of rocks, mountains in size, partly separated from each other by side cañons [canyons], and they are so sheer in front, and so compactly and harmoniously arranged on a level floor, that the Valley, comprehensively seen, looks like an immense hall or temple lighted from above.

"But no temple made with hands can compare with Yosemite. Every rock in its walls seems to glow with life. Some lean back in majestic repose; others, absolutely sheer or nearly so for thousands of feet, advance beyond their companions in thoughtful attitudes, giving welcome to storms and calms alike, seemingly aware, yet heedless, of everything going on about them. Awful in stern, immovable majesty, how softly these rocks are adorned, and how fine and reassuring the company they keep: their feet among beautiful groves and meadows, their brows in the sky, a thousand flowers leaning confidingly against their feet, bathed in floods of water, floods of light, while the snow and waterfalls, the winds and avalanches and clouds shine and sing and wreathe about them as the years go by, and myriads of small winged creatures—birds, bees, butterflies—give glad animation and help to make all the air into music. Down through the middle of the Valley flows the crystal Merced, River of Mercy, peacefully quiet, reflecting lilies and trees and the onlooking rocks; things frail and fleeting and types of endurance meeting here and blending in countless forms, as if into this one mountain mansion Nature had gathered her choicest treasures, to draw her lovers into close and confiding communion with her."

BRIDALVEIL FALL

"Entering the Valley, gazing overwhelmed with the multitude of grand objects about us, perhaps the first to fix our attention will be the Bridal Veil, a beautiful waterfall on our right. Its brow, where it first leaps free from the cliff, is about 900 feet above us; and as it sways and sings in the wind, clad in gauzy, sun-sifted spray, half falling, half floating, it seems infinitely gentle and fine; but the hymns it sings tell the solemn fateful power hidden beneath its soft clothing.

"The Bridal Veil shoots free from the upper edge of the cliff by the velocity the stream has acquired in descending a long slope above the head of the fall. Looking from the top of the rock-avalanche talus on the west side, about one hundred feet above the foot of the fall, the under surface of the water arch is seen to be finely grooved and striated; and the sky is seen through the arch between rock and water, making a novel and beautiful effect...

"The rainbows of the Veil, or rather the spray- and foam-bows, are superb, because the waters are dashed among angular blocks of granite at the foot, producing abundance of spray of the best quality for iris effects, and also for a luxuriant growth of grass and maiden-hair on the side of the talus, which lower down is planted with oak, laurel, and willows."

For more of John Muir's musings on Yosemite, turn to page 176.

California was the first state to have a trillion-dollar economy.

CAN YOU SPEAK BOONTLING?

Teen slang, passwords, quarterback calls, spelling in front of the kids—they all spring from the same impulse. Sometime after inventing language to express information, humans began adapting it to limit the people who would know what they were saying. But very few went as far a small town in Mendocino County, which deliberately made up more than a thousand new words.

SOMETHING NEW UNDER OL' SOL

Boontling is a 1,000-word language spoken in and around Boonville, a tiny town of about 700 people located 115 miles north of San Francisco. In the mid-1800s, settlers began moving into the Anderson Valley, an isolated spot of Mendocino County, to pursue a life of farming, fishing, and logging. Without a lot of outside influences, the new settlers found whatever intellectual stimulation and amusement they could. The town changed names several times—first it was the Corner's, then Kendall's City, and finally Boonville, after W. W. Boone, a local merchant—and sometime in the 1870s, the locals began replacing standard English words with words they'd invented. Eventually they amassed at least 1,300 of them.

The reasons they created Boontling (from "Boonville lingo") remain mysterious, but the most likely explanation is that Bootling was mostly just a word game to stump friends and pass the time. "You don't just go and pick a random word out," explained one of Boonville's codgy kimmers (old men), who spoke in the 1960s. "It has to have a meaning or a background or something. Someone might go and think all week about something to make a word out of. He might come to the bar on Saturday night and just drop the word into conversation. Nobody would ask what that word meant, they'd have to go figure it out."

If the word was funny, clever, or memorable, it might be adopted into the language of a small circle of friends as an inside joke before eventually being revealed and spreading around town. Over time, the words would also spread up and down the Ander-

---

Oldest lake in North America: Clear Lake, estimated to be 2.5 million years old.

son Valley to even smaller towns like Yorkville, Navarro, and Philo. Even today, some Boonville residents still use the language.

A BIT OF BAHL LINGO

Sometimes Boontling words made straightforward sense…like *briny*, which means "seaside" or "ocean." Other times, figuring out a word required knowledge of things outside the village. For example, understanding the term *bulrush*, meaning a "foundling child," required the knowledge that the King James Bible told the story of baby Moses being abandoned by his desperate mother in a floating basket woven from bulrushes (or, papyrus). More often, though, you needed to know Boonville's personalities and goings-on to understand the words. Many local names and notorious anecdotes became sources. For example…

• **Apple head:** Girlfriend. The word "doll" has long been slang for an attractive woman, and a common homemade toy in the 19th century was a doll with a dried apple for the head.

• **Bahl:** Very good. This comes from Red Ball shoes, which were considered around Boonville to be the best brand.

• **Bill Nunn:** Maple syrup. Comes from the name of a man who poured syrup on everything he ate.

• **Borp:** Hog. Shortened from "boar pig."

• **Brightlighter:** An outsider, particularly someone from the bright lights of the big city.

• **Can-kicky:** Angry.

• **Chigrel:** A meal…from "child's gruel."

• **Cloddies:** Boots…from "clodhoppers."

• **Frati:** Wine. Frati was the surname of a local winemaker.

• **Gorm:** Food. This comes from the French words *gourmet* and *gourmandise* (to eat greedily).

• **Gray-matter:** A college professor or other brainy person.

• **Greeley:** Newspaper. Horace Greeley was a famous editor of the *New York Tribune* from 1841 to 1872.

- **Heelch:** An unfairly large portion. Some Boontling words were adapted from English by changing certain vowels to an *ee* sound. For example, the word for day is "dee," dime is "deem," and an unpleasant person is an "eesole." Other terms combined words. So *heelch* was a truncated form of the expression "(taking the) whole cheese."

- **Horn of zeese:** Cup of coffee, named after a local cook known as Zeese—from his initials Z.C.—who made unusually strong coffee.

- **Jeffer:** Big fire. This term honored the big fires owner Jeff Vestal used to build in the main fireplace of the Boonville Hotel.

- **Keloppity:** Travel by horse. No explanation necessary.

- **Neemer:** No more, formed by adding the *ee* and combining words.

- **Piked:** Well traveled. This may come from the word "turnpike," or from the 19th-century Rocky Mountains explorer Zebulon Pike, for whom Colorado's Pikes Peak was named.

- **Shied:** To quit, or be scared away. The word is usually used while deer hunting.

- **Shoveltooth:** A medical doctor. There was a Boonville doctor who had protruding front teeth, so....

- **Skullsey:** A desolate area, the sort of dry and deserted place someone in a movie might run across a cow skull.

- **Skype:** Preacher...short for "sky pilot."

- **Strung:** Killed. This comes from stringing fish and hangings.

- **The dusties:** Death. From the phrase "ashes to ashes, dust to dust."

- **Tidrik:** A social gathering. It's a combination of "tea drink."

- **Toob:** A quarter...short for "two bits."

- **Walter:** A telephone. Businessman Walter Levi was the first person in Boonville to have a phone installed.

Fires have caused San Francisco to be rebuilt seven times.

FAST-FOOD FOUNDERS

*You probably know that McDonald's got its start in San Bernardino,
but what about the rest of these fast-food joints?*

IN-N-OUT BURGER

Now: There are more than 250 In-N-Out Burgers in California, Nevada, Utah, Arizona, and Texas. In 2008 the business made about $420 million in revenue.

Then: In 1948, the same year that McDonald's started using an assembly line to prepare its food, a different kind of revolution began in the L.A. County town of Baldwin Park. In-N-Out Burger founders Harry and Esther Snyder opened one of the first drive-thru restaurants without carhops and featuring a two-way speaker box so people could order right from their car. In-N-Out soon caused "burger jams," with cars forming a line out into the street.

Despite their success, the Snyders bucked the fast-food trend and refused to expand rapidly or franchise their success. Instead, they insisted on overseeing the business to make sure that only fresh meat and produce went into their meals. When other fast-food companies began using frozen patties, Harry Snyder turned to a group of butchers who sold him high-quality meat. Instead of keeping prepared food warm, everything was made fresh, including the French fries. To maintain quality service, the Snyders trained their employees well and paid higher wages than other fast-food companies. Their emphasis on quality has turned In-N-Out into a beloved West Coast institution and made fans of famous chefs like Gordon Ramsay and Julia Child.

A&W ROOT BEER

Now: A&W is the world's best-selling root beer, and there are hundreds of A&W fast-food restaurants in the U.S. and Canada.

Then: On a hot June day in 1919, during a World War I veterans' parade, Roy Allen opened a root beer stand in Lodi. Allen had tasted root beer in Flagstaff, Arizona, and liked it so much that he bought the formula from its inventor. Now he wanted to see how well the drink would sell in California. As it turned out, pretty well. Allen charged just a nickel a serving, and so many people loved his root beer that he opened another stand in Sacramento. Business continued to grow, and in 1922, he brought in a partner, Frank Wright. The men combined their initials and A&W Root Beer was born.

Much of their success came from the drinks and hamburgers they sold, but they were also shrewd businessmen who took advantage of the Prohibition laws. Allen and Wright sold their root "beer" in large frosty mugs and decorated their restaurants to look like saloons. Many drinkers seemed to enjoy the ambience even without the alcohol. A&W was also one of the first hamburger joints to offer drive-up carhop service. In 1924 Allen bought out Wright and started selling franchises so that people could open their own A&Ws, a move that turned the small collection of California eateries into one of the first nationally successful restaurant chains.

BOB'S BIG BOY

Now: There are more than 455 Bob's Big Boy restaurants in the U.S. and Canada.

Then: In 1936 Bob Wian sold his DeSoto convertible for $350 and used the money to open a 10-seat burger stand in Glendale that he called Bob's Pantry. One day, one of his regular customers asked for a hamburger that was "completely different," so Wian sliced a sesame-seed bun into three slices rather than two and added two hamburger patties, extra cheese, lettuce, and his own relish and dressing to create the Bob's double-decker. That burger was a hit with customers. In 1938 Bob's Pantry became Bob's Big Boy in honor of that double-decker, and there was enough money to convert the tiny stand to a drive-in. In the 1940, '50s, and '60s, Wian franchised the Bob's Big Boy chain, and his restaurants became so popular that security guards had to be hired to handle traffic. In 1968 he sold the business to Marriott for $7 million.

JACK IN THE BOX

Now: Jack in the Box is one of the nation's largest hamburger chains, with more than 2,200 restaurants in 19 states.

Then: In 1941 Robert Oscar Peterson founded Topsy's drive-in restaurant in San Diego. Over the next decade, he opened several more Topsy's, which he renamed Oscars', creating a chain of drive-ins in Southern California. Then in 1951, Peterson remodeled the original Topsy's into a Jack in the Box. The major change was an intercom placed inside "Jack" the clown, allowing drivers to talk directly to the service crew. Many customers weren't used to drive-thrus back then, though, so signs directed them to "pull up to Jack and place your order." Peterson eventually converted all his restaurants to drive-thrus, and the fact that patrons just picked up their food and drove off helped Peterson keep his overhead costs low. It also helped revolutionize fast food as other chains took up the idea.

TACO BELL

Now: Taco Bell serves more than 36.8 million customers a week in nearly 5,600 restaurants in the U.S., Europe, Asia, the Middle East, and South America—but not in Mexico.

Then: The first fast-food taco was invented at a San Bernardino hamburger stand. Glen Bell Jr., who owned Bell's Hamburgers and Hot Dogs, was a fan of McDonald's efficient system and an even bigger fan of Mexican food. He believed that fast-food tacos could give burgers "a run for their money." But the standard soft tortilla taco shells took too long to prepare. So in 1951 Bell came up with a nifty idea: Instead of the soft tortilla, he used a crispy fried taco shell that could be stuffed quickly. He knew he was on to something when his first customer finished a taco and came back for another…even though that first one had dripped sauce all over his shirt and tie.

The 19¢ tacos were so popular that, by 1954, Bell had decided to sell only Mexican food. He started restaurants called Taco Tia and El Taco with partners, but sold out of both enterprises to finally go it alone. In 1962, with $4,000, Bell opened the first Taco Bell in Downey. By the time he sold the company to PepsiCo in 1978, there were 868 Taco Bells across the country. But Bell's biggest claim to fame may be that he gets credit for introducing most Americans to their first taco.

*   *   *

With more than 270 state parks, the California State Park System is the largest state park system in the U.S.

COMEDY CENTRAL

How many Californians does it take to screw in a lightbulb? Keep reading.

AND THEN THERE WAS CALIFORNIA

On the sixth day of the Creation, God announced to his archangel underlings, "Today, we're creating a place called California. Pull out all the stops. Give it beautiful mountains, lakes, forests, the redwoods, the ocean, incredible wildlife, and vast sandy beaches. Give it gold and a perfect climate. And whatever you do, make sure the people are beautiful and brilliant."

"But sir," interjected one archangel. "Aren't you being overly generous to these Californians?"

"Don't worry," said God. "I'll balance it out. Wait until you see who I'm going to put in charge in Sacramento."

VALLEY GIRL CAR MAINTENANCE

OMG. One day, a Valley girl was driving home when her car was like, totally pelted with hailstones. The next day, she took the car to the repair shop and the mechanic decided to have a little fun. He told her that to fix the car, she needed to take it home and blow really hard into the tailpipe to pop out all the dents.

"Like, for real?" asked the Valley girl.

"Like, totally for real," said the mechanic.

So she drove the car home, parked in the garage, and then went around back and started blowing into the tailpipe. She tried once. No luck. Twice. Nothing.

Just then, her Valley girl roommate came home and asked what she was doing. When the first Valley girl repeated what the mechanic had said, the second one rolled her eyes, propped a hand on her hip, and said, "Like, duh! You have to roll up the windows first."

THE LIGHTBULB MOMENT

Q. How many Californians does it take to change a lightbulb?
A. None. Californians can't afford to have lights.

WE ♥ CATALINA

About a million people a year hop onto a boat or a helicopter and head over to one of California's best-known playgrounds of the rich and famous: Catalina Island.

• The island's official name is Santa Catalina because Spanish explorer Sebastian Vizcaino arrived there on November 24, 1602, the eve of Saint Catherine's Day.

• Catalina is part of L.A. County, even though it's about 20 miles offshore.

• It's also part of the Channel Islands chain, an archipelago off the Southern California coast that stretches 160 miles from San Clemente Island in the south to San Miguel Island in the north.

• Catalina has just two towns: Avalon (population about 3,700) and Two Harbors (population about 200).

• Besides its casino and tourists, Catalina is famous for the herd of wild bison that roams the island's bushland. The bison aren't native to Catalina, though. They arrived in 1924 with a film crew making a movie called *The Vanishing American*, starring...no one we've ever heard of. When filming wrapped, the production company decided it was too expensive to ship the bison back to the mainland and so just left the animals there. Over the years, the bison herd grew...and grew—at one point, the animals numbered several hundred—and began to threaten the native species. Wildlife conservationists have been trying to limit the herd for years and have it to a mostly manageable 150 today. The kicker: The scene the bison were brought over to film never even made it into the movie.

• Want to bring your car over on a ferry to Catalina? Forget it. Most people get around the island in golf carts or on foot, and very few cars are allowed. The ones that are must be electric, and even those are strictly regulated. The waiting list to register a vehicle on Catalina: about 25 years.

Catalina Island was once owned by chewing-gum baron William Wrigley.

CALIFORNIA Q & A

We had a lot of questions about the Golden State. Let's get started.

HOW DID MODESTO GET ITS NAME?

A: In 1870 an engineer was mapping out land plots along new Central Pacific tracks for a not-yet-existent station and town. He called over a young man named George Cosgrove, who was on-site as an assistant, and told him ask around for suggestions for a town name. Cosgrove asked the crew, but came up empty and was about to give up when he saw an engine approaching slowly on the track. Out stepped the Central Pacific's founders and directors: Charles Crocker, Mark Hopkins, and William Ralston. To the shock of his bosses, Cosgrove stepped up and asked if *they* had any ideas. Hopkins joked, "Name it, Ralston." Ralston simply said, "I thank you for the honor, but must ask that some appropriate name be chosen." Then a man named Tony, who supervised the Mexican workers, remarked quietly, *"Esta senor es muy modesto!"* ("That man's very modest!") Crocker heard him, and suggested that Modesto would be a great name for the town.

DID CALIFORNIA REALLY HAVE A TOWN WHOSE MAYOR WAS A DOG?

A: Honorary mayor, but yes. Sunol—a small unincorporated town in Alameda County, about 45 miles southeast of San Francisco—made history in 1981 when a black Lab/Rottweiler mix named Bosco beat out two human candidates to become the town's "mayor." The election was meant to be a joke (the result of a conversation in a local bar), but Bosco became a treasured public servant: He was always eager to take walks with his constituents, showed up to social events in a specially designed tux, and became famous as America's first elected canine. Like all good politicians, he even got some bad press: In 1990 the *Beijing People's Daily*, a newspaper in China, claimed that Bosco's election proved the failure of American democracy because the voting public couldn't distinguish people from dogs. Sunol shot back that the Chinese editors clearly didn't understand democracy, Americans, or their sense of humor. Bosco's human "mother," Pat Stillman, insisted that most Chinese would prefer Bosco to communist dictators anyway, and students at Stanford and UC Berkeley invited Bosco to appear at a pro-democracy rally in front of the Chinese consulate in San Francisco.

Bosco served as an honorary mayor and symbol of democracy until his death in 1994. In 2008 Sunol's residents placed a bronze statue of him under the town clock. Another memorial appears at the town's only bar, Bosco's Bones and Brew. There, bartenders lift the rear leg of a long-dead, stuffed black dog that pees beer for the customers.

WHERE DID THE CONCEPT OF "MURPHY'S LAW" GET STARTED?

A. At Edwards Air Force Base in the Mojave Desert. The base's Flight Test Center opened during World War II as a place to research, develop, and test aerospace systems for the U.S. military. In 1949 Captain John Paul Stapp was the lead on a project to test how the g-force (the force of gravity acting on the body at sea level) affected pilots during plane crashes, and how much g-force they could tolerate. To simulate the force of crashes, Stapp acted as his own guinea pig and rode in a rocket-powered sled called the Gee Whiz that accelerated to speeds of about 200 mph and then slammed to a stop. An engineer named Captain Edward A. Murphy Jr. arrived at the base with sensors that he called "strain gauges." Murphy's sensors could measure the g-force on various parts of Stapp's body when he rode the Gee Whiz. However, the sensors were wired wrong during one test run, thus producing data that was incorrect.

Over the years, there have been differing accounts about Murphy's reaction, but most people agree that he grumbled about the installation technicians, saying, "If there's any way they can do it wrong, they will." As Murphy's complaint made its way around the base, it became, "If anything can go wrong, it will," the basic principle of Murphy's Law. The first time the public heard the phrase was at a press conference a few weeks later, when Stapp praised the project's engineers for their good safety record. A belief in what they were all now calling "Murphy's Law," Stapp claimed, made them work to eliminate any possible problems.

A standard oak barrel holds enough wine to fill about 300 bottles.

SOCAL SANTA ANA-GRAMS

Southern California's notorious Santa Ana winds have blown in and scrambled these city names into anagrams. Can you decode them? (Answers on page 368.)

L **OS ANGELES COUNTY**
1. BEHEAD CONDOR: _____
2. MANIC SONATA: _____
3. PANDA SEA: _____
4. NOODLE WIG: _____
5. AHA! STUD NOOKS: _____

INLAND EMPIRE
1. RIDER VISE: _____
2. BANNERS IN ROAD: _____
3. DERMAL PEST: _____
4. FAT ANON: _____
5. CUTE MALE: _____

SAN DIEGO COUNTY
1. IDEA SONG: _____
2. A LAVISH CUT: _____
3. DISCOED ON: _____
4. CANOES DIE: _____
5. ALAS ME! _____

THE CENTRAL COAST
1. VAN SLOG: _____
2. PIANO SUBSOILS: _____
3. A SLIMY VEIL: _____
4. OPERA SLOBS: _____
5. AS A BAN BAR RAT: _____

For Northern California's cities, head over to page 179.

Q. What's the most southwesterly city in the U.S.? A. Imperial Beach.

MANZANAR MEMORY

*During World War II, the United States decided to lock up about
120,000 Japanese Americans in internment camps. This is the
story of the American teenager who chose to go with them.*

R EMEMBER PEARL HARBOR?
On the morning of December 7, 1941, Japanese bombers
attacked the U.S. at Pearl Harbor, Hawaii, one of America's largest military bases in the Pacific. More than 2,000 American soldiers died in the surprise attack, and the country's Pacific
Fleet was severely crippled. That left the United States vulnerable, and many people—civilians and government officials—feared
that another attack was coming. Their fear led to paranoia, which
in turn led to one of the most appalling decisions in American
history. On February 19, 1942, President Franklin Delano Roosevelt signed Executive Order 9066, authorizing the imprisonment
(or, internment) of all Japanese Americans living on the West
Coast. Official notices were posted in Japanese neighborhoods
from San Diego to Seattle, explaining that residents had about a
week to gather basic supplies and then report to "War Relocation
Camps" for the duration of the war against Japan.

SACRIFICING THE FEW TO SAVE...NO ONE

The FBI had already concluded that Japanese Americans were
no security threat, however, and many Japanese residents were
second- and third-generation U.S. citizens, loyal to their actual
home country instead of the country of their forefathers. Even
babies and children of Japanese descent who had been adopted by
Caucasian parents and clearly posed no threat were relocated.

The truth didn't matter much, though, as newspapers up and
down the West Coast whipped up racial hysteria. Americans
already had a long-held dislike of Asian immigrants, whom they
accused of stealing jobs and being disloyal. The attack on Pearl
Harbor just intensified that hatred. An *L.A. Times* editorial stated,
"A Japanese American...with the rarest exceptions grows up to be
a Japanese, and not an American...Thus, while it might cause
injustice to a few to treat them all as potential enemies...such

treatment should be accorded to each and all of them while we are at war with their race." Following suit, the United States set up internment camps in seven western states. Two of the biggest— Tule Lake and Manzanar—were in California.

A FRIEND IN NEED

In 1942 Ralph Lazo was 16 years old. He wasn't Japanese, but he lived in the Bunker Hill section of Los Angeles, a mixed neighborhood where residents were of Jewish, Korean, Basque, and Japanese descent. Although young, he was used to taking care of himself. His mother, a Mexican immigrant, died when he was five. Lazo's father worked two jobs to support his son and daughter, and the family struggled for money.

Lazo was a skinny kid, eager to please, who raised pocket money delivering magazines, collecting bottles for deposit, and sweeping floors. He was friendly and naturally gregarious, and some of his closest friends at Belmont High School—the ones whose parents let him eat, sleep, and hang out in their homes when his father worked late—were Japanese.

When Executive Order 9066 went into effect, Lazo helped his friends and their families pack up what they could carry and put everything else up for sale. Lazo watched with disgust as white buyers paid next to nothing for fully equipped farms, factories, warehouses, homes, and stores, as well as furniture and other personal belongings. "It was immoral," he told an interviewer years later. "These people [Japanese Americans] hadn't done anything wrong. They were Americans, just like I am."

As the day of departure got closer, one of his friends asked Lazo how he was going to survive without them. "Maybe I'll go with you," he replied. His friends assumed he was joking.

"DAD, I'M GOING TO CAMP"

Over the next couple of days, though, Lazo formed a plan. One night at dinner, he casually announced, "Dad, I'm going to camp with my friends." His father, tired from working all day, assumed his son was talking about a weekend trip and said, "Okay."

In May 1942 Lazo arrived at the scheduled departure location. He was prepared to lie to anyone in authority who asked what he was doing there, but nobody asked. Carrying just a few personal possessions like everyone else, he boarded a crowded train headed for the Manzanar camp located 230 miles northeast of Los Angeles at the foot of the Sierra Nevada Mountains.

WELCOME TO THE APPLE ORCHARD

The word *manzanar* means "apple orchard" in Spanish, and at one time, the name fit the area perfectly. However, by the 1940s, the once-lush farm area had dried up after the City of Los Angeles bought up the valley's water rights during the early 20th century and diverted most of the area's water supply to its growing urban population. That process turned the Owens Valley where Manzanar is located into a dry alkali flat that was prone to dust storms. Farms, ranches, and most of the town itself had been abandoned by 1929. As far as the U.S. government was concerned, it was a perfect place to imprison a bunch of possible enemy combatants.

As Lazo disembarked the train into the dismal surroundings, he discovered that he wasn't the only non-Asian there. Some non-Asian wives and husbands had joined their Japanese spouses and children who had been ordered to the camp. Plus, some of the Japanese people who were forced into the camps were barely so— the order included people who were as little as 1/16th Japanese (i.e., one of their great-great-grandparents was Japanese). The big difference was that he was only person who was there completely by choice. After standing in a line of new arrivals that snaked through rows of shacks and barracks hastily slapped together, Lazo received his housing assignment—he'd be living with the older unmarried men.

JIVE BOMBERS TAKE FLIGHT

Life in the camp wasn't easy or fun. Families, who had been promised individual cabins before being relocated, discovered instead that they'd actually be living in 20' x 100' tar-paper barracks, divided with curtains into 20' x 25' "apartments." They all shared bathrooms and showers, the barracks were uninsulated (and therefore, sweltering in the summer and freezing in the winter), and dust blew everywhere year-round. By July 1942, about 10,000 people were crowded into the camp.

Still, despite their circumstances, the inmates at Manzanar did their best to make the camp experience feel like home. They planted trees, organized baseball teams, and even planned parties with entertainment by the camp's jazz band, the Jive Bombers (a bit of dark humor that recalled the dive bombers that attacked Pearl Harbor and inspired the governmental overreaction that put them there). They set up schools and baseball tournaments, opened a hospital, went to church, raised fruits and vegetables, and published a newspaper called the *Manzanar Free Press*. They even had a post office, shops, and factories for making artificial rubber and camouflage nets. Workers were paid between $8 and $19 a month (about $110–$250 in today's money). Lazo became a mail carrier making $12 a month, eventually upgrading to a recreational director and a $4 raise. In that job, he organized dances and intramural sports teams and got to leave the camp briefly to attend a YMCA conference in Colorado.

UNCLE SAM WANTS YOU!

Eventually Lazo told his father where he was. He sent a note saying that he was being taken care of, eating well, and going to school. He was a little surprised, however, when his dad didn't object: "He knew...that I was safe," Lazo said. "You couldn't ask for more protection than barbed wire, armed guards, and searchlights."

Although imprisoned as potential traitors and saboteurs, the camp's young men were still subject to the draft. In 1944 Lazo graduated from Manzanar High School and was drafted into the army, which sent him to fight Japanese in the South Pacific. He survived the war, returned home with a Bronze Star, entered college on the G.I. Bill, and became a high school teacher, but he never forgot his Japanese friends or his time in Manzanar: Lazo was among the first people to donate money to fund a class-action suit against the government on behalf of the incarcerated Japanese. In 1988, more than 40 years after the war ended, the U.S. government settled that suit, paying out about $20,000 per survivor.

Ralph Lazo died in 1992, and one of his Japanese friends from Manzanar, William Hohri, spoke about him at a memorial service: "When 140 million Americans turned their back on us and excluded us into remote, desolate prison camps, the separation was almost absolute—almost. Ralph Lazo's presence among us said, 'No, not everyone [thought that was all right].'"

WATERFALLIFORNIA

Our state has some amazing waterfalls. Here are a few standouts.

MOSSBRAE FALLS. Located near Mt. Shasta in the town of Dunsmuir, Mossbrae looks like a scene from a fairy tale. Groundwater seeps out of a mossy cliff and gently cascades down into the Sacramento River. The falls are 150 feet wide, and nearly 50 feet high. (At last report, the trail to the falls was closed, but they're building a new one away from the railroad.)

McWAY FALLS. As if Big Sur needed any help to be California's most idyllic coastal getaway, it boasts a beautiful 80-foot waterfall that plunges from the top of a tree-lined cliff onto the beach.

CRYSTAL ICE CAVE. Lava Beds National Monument (just south of the Oregon border) has an impressive frozen waterfall, but it's a bit of a chore to see it. Why? It lives deep inside an ancient lava tube where the environment is so fragile that the location is kept secret. You can only access it via a guided tour in the winter. The icy formations, some centuries old, make it worth it.

LOWER YOSEMITE FALLS. Yosemite Falls boasts one of nature's most ethereal light shows. Go there in late spring (when the water flow is the strongest) on the night of a full moon. If the sky is clear, you'll be able to witness a rare "moonbow"—all the colors of the spectrum floating in the mist of the waterfall.

HEART ROCK FALLS. Located in the western San Bernardino Mountains near Crestline, this pretty waterfall sits right next to an amazing geological feature: the perfect shape of a heart that's been carved out of the rock—not by humans—but by water.

DARWIN FALLS. The last thing you'd expect to see in arid Death Valley National Park is a lush, wooded waterfall reflecting in a gentle pool, and that's what makes Darwin Falls so special. The three-mile hike begins in the desert and ends up in paradise.

THE JUMPING FROG
OF JACKASS HILL

Here's how a California frog gave America's greatest author his jump-start.

FROM CAPTAIN TO PROSPECTOR

Mark Twain—one of the greatest American writers of all time—penned books like *The Adventures of Tom Sawyer*. But before Twain became famous, he was just Sam Clemens, a young man who had trouble keeping a steady job. By the time he decided to go west, Twain had already given up on a number of occupations: he'd been a disgruntled typesetter, printer, and sometimes writer for his brother's newspaper. He finally found a job he liked as a Mississippi riverboat captain, but when the Civil War broke out in 1861, military blockades on the river ended that career. So the 26-year-old Twain volunteered with a ragtag unit of the Confederate cavalry, mounted a mule, and went off to war. After less than a month, though, he realized that he hated both soldiering and mule riding, so he quit. Jobless and anxious to avoid fighting, Twain learned that his older brother Orion (a staunch Lincoln supporter) had been appointed as secretary of the Nevada Territory. Twain accompanied Orion to Nevada, where he intended to find great wealth as a miner.

In the early 1860s, millions of dollars in silver and gold were being discovered near Virginia City, Nevada, but Twain had no luck. When he loaded his pockets with shiny flakes, they turned out to be mica rather than than gold. When he tried silver prospecting, he quickly learned that drilling, blasting, and shoveling added up to backbreaking work with little reward. Twain quit mining even faster than soldiering.

In September 1862, he went back to newspaper work at the *Territorial Enterprise*, a Virginia City newspaper. Readers loved Twain because when there was no exciting news, he just invented some—including one story about the "discovery" of a petrified man who was preserved while leaning against a rock. Twain sold some humor pieces to California newspapers and magazines, and began using his pen name. "Mark Twain" came from his days on the river and was a term that meant the depth of the water was two fathoms (12 feet) deep, enough for a riverboat to pass through safely.

CALIFORNIA, HERE I COME!

Twain might have lasted longer in Virginia City, but one night after drinking too much, he accused some of the town's society ladies of being liars (and in favor of interracial relationships, a major taboo at the time), and his comments accidentally made it into the paper. The editor of the *Virginia City Daily Union*, a rival paper, then accused Twain of slandering the women. Twain was so angry that he challenged the man to a duel, but before they could meet with pistols at dawn, Twain decided to leave town. He headed to California, where he got a job at the *San Francisco Daily Morning Call.*

When Twain arrived in San Francisco in 1864, gold from California and silver from Nevada were pouring into its banks, quickly making the city the West's most sophisticated metropolis, with a population of more than 100,000. The young reporter enjoyed San Francisco, where he met writers like Bret Harte and attended the opera. And he praised the food at the oceanfront Cliff House (now part of the Golden Gate National Recreation Area and famous even in those days), saying that patrons there could "eat one of the best dinners with the hungry relish of an ostrich."

As much as Twain enjoyed San Francisco, though, he hated his job. Reporting for the *Call* was the dull recording of the daily minutiae of the city. Twain spent hours in San Francisco's courthouse, watching boring proceedings. He also showed up at civic meetings, weddings, and funerals. "It was fearful drudgery—soulless drudgery—and almost destitute of interest," he said of the job. "It was an awful slavery for a lazy man."

THE FUTURE: A FROG

Pretty soon, Twain got himself into trouble again...this time, for writing letters to newspapers protesting local police corruption. Finding himself on the wrong side of San Francisco's chief of police, Twain quit the *Call* and disappeared into Tuolumne County's gold country, where his friends Steve and Jim Gillis had a cabin on Jackass Hill—sonamed for the male donkeys that the miners used for transportation.

By 1865 California's gold rush (which began in 1848) had wound down considerably, but there were still "pocket miners" like the Gillis brothers. These men usually hunted for small "pockets" of high-grade gold ore that would bring in a few thousand dollars, lived off the profits until they were broke, and then went pocket mining again. Twain stayed at Jackass Hill for 12 weeks trying to find gold. As usual, he had no luck.

By then, Twain was almost 30, nearly broke, and drinking too much. He longed to make a fortune and impress his mother and sister back home in Missouri, but he hadn't been successful since his steamboat piloting days. Then, in the nearby town of Angels Camp, a bartender told Twain and his friends a tall tale making the rounds at the miners' camps. The story went like this: Jim Smiley's champion jumping frog—named Dan'l Webster—couldn't make it off the ground after a competing frog's owner secretly poured quail shot down Dan'l Webster's throat. The bartender's story was dry, but when Twain returned to Jackass Hill, he gave up mining to spend all his time writing about the frog. He told his friends that if he could get the story just right and make it funny enough, "that frog will jump around the world."

Until then, Twain had been dissatisfied with his humorous articles, which he considered a "low" form of writing that wasn't quite respectable and certainly wasn't literary. His work hadn't brought him the pride or income he wanted, but after hearing the frog-jumping story, Twain decided that writing, even if it was lowbrow, would be his future. And he decided that the frog was going to launch his career.

THE GOOD HUMOR MAN

On November 18, 1865, Twain's short story "Jim Smiley and His Jumping Frog" was published in New York's *Saturday Press*. Newspapers reported that it "set all New York in a roar." The story was reprinted in newspapers and magazines around the country, and Dan'l Webster took Mark Twain from obscurity to national fame in one giant leap. The following year, Twain's first book was published—it was a compilation of his short stories and articles and was entitled *The Celebrated Jumping Frog of Calaveras County and Other Sketches*.

Once Twain made up his mind that he was a writer, his career took off. He scored a job with one of California's most prestigious newspapers, the *Sacramento Union*, which sent him to the Sandwich Islands (now Hawaii) for a few months "to write four letters a month at twenty dollars apiece." By the time Twain returned to San Francisco, his island pieces had made him even more famous, and the editor of another San Francisco paper, the *Alta California*, urged him to capitalize on his notoriety by lecturing on the Sandwich Islands. The idea terrified Twain: "I thought of suicide, pretended illness, flight...I was very miserable and scared."

Despite the stage fright, Twain rented out San Francisco's Academy of Music and planned a performance for October 12, 1866. He wrote the following ad for the show: "A splendid orchestra is in town but has not been engaged. Also, a den of ferocious wild beasts will be on exhibition in the next block. A grand torchlight procession may be expected; in fact, the public are privileged to expect whatever they please. The doors open at 7. The trouble will begin at 8."

Not surprisingly, the place was packed, and the reviews of Twain's lecture were glowing. No one had ever seen anything like it before—the performance was peppered with jokes, satire, and silly stories, and Twain made the audience's laughter his main priority. He was, essentially, America's first stand-up comic. A lecture tour was hastily organized in California's gold towns, and for once, Twain struck it rich, making about $1,200 (more than $17,000 in today's money).

TRAVELING TWAIN

By the end of 1866, Twain had been hired as a traveling correspondent for the *Alta California*. The paper sent him east by boat to New York and paid him to write letters about the journey, which included a trek to the Midwest and his home in Missouri. Twain was then supposed to return to San Francisco, but he persuaded the *Alta California* to finance a trip to Palestine.

The letters Twain wrote on that trip became the basis of his first best-selling book, *Innocents Abroad*. His career firmly established, Twain never returned to California, but he left behind a famous description of the state that is quoted today: "America is built on a tilt and everything loose slides to California."

WE ♥ BURBANK

This story comes to you from beautiful downtown Burbank.

• **"Media capital of the world."** Once the butt of Johnny Carson's jokes—in the 1970s, he liked to say *The Tonight Show* was filmed in "beautiful downtown Burbank"—the city just northeast of Los Angeles is now home to several major media companies, including ABC, the Walt Disney Company, and Warner Bros.

• **World's largest dwarfs?** Disney's headquarters (officially known as the Team Disney Michael D. Eisner Building) features seven 19-foot-tall dwarfs as columns, holding up the building's pediment. It's more appropriate than you think. The success of the 1937 animated film *Snow White and the Seven Dwarfs* saved the studio and provided the money to build the Burbank property.

• **It's a small space after all.** Walt Disney originally wanted to build his theme park in Burbank on land next to the studio. The city government wasn't happy about hosting the "Happiest Place on Earth," however—one council member said, "We don't want a carny atmosphere in Burbank." So Disney bought up a bunch of cheap farmland in a little backwater named Anaheim instead.

• **Flying sausage, hard to swallow.** In 1910 farmer Joseph Fawkes patented the country's first monorail, which he called the "Aerial Swallow." He designed it to look like a giant sausage and built it in Burbank. The monorail hung from an elevated track and looked a little like an airplane without wings, complete with propeller in the front. The flying sausage might have revolutionized transportation if it had fulfilled Fawkes's promise of a 10-minute trip from Burbank to downtown Los Angeles. Instead, it broke down almost immediately.

• **What's in a name?** Burbank's airport has had a continuing identity crisis, running through seven names in 80 years. In 1928 the private airstrip opened as the Angeles Mesa Drive Airport. In 1930 it became the United Airport, and then, four years later, the

---

Creosote bush, a plant that grows in the Mojave Desert, can live to be 43,000 years old.

Union Air Terminal. Bought by Lockheed in 1940, it was the Lockheed Air Terminal until 1967, when the airplane manufacturer decided it needed a more glamorous name and started calling it the Hollywood-Burbank Airport. That lasted until 1978, when Lockheed sold the airport to the local airport authority which changed its name to the Burbank-Glendale-Pasadena Airport. That unwieldy name stuck until 2003, when the airport authority voted to honor a local actor and comedian, renaming it the Bob Hope Airport.

• **A myth is just a myth:** Movie buffs once thought that the Burbank airport was the filming site for *Casablanca*'s thrilling airport scenes. It wasn't. The shot of an airplane taxiing was filmed at Van Nuys Airport, and the rest was on an artificially fogged sound stage. Oh well, we'll always have Paris: The streets used for *Casablanca*'s flashback love scenes can still be seen on the Warner Bros. back lot tour.

• **Now you see it, now you don't.** During World War II, the Lockheed factory in Burbank employed 80,000 people making bombers for the war. But because it was so close to the coast, the U.S. government worried that the factory was vulnerable to an enemy attack. The solution? Camouflage the entire plant. One problem: Lockeed was surrounded by tract housing, rather than a forest or jungle, which might offer easy camouflage. And so, this being Southern California, the movie business came to the rescue. The factory and parking lot were covered with a massive movie set made largely of latex and chicken wire and disguised to look like a typical Burbank neighborhood: houses, streets, lawns, and cars. The factory's chimneys and ventilation outlets became trees, bushes, and fire hydrants. From the air, the whole setup was surprisingly convincing.

* * *

Stanford University is sometimes called "The Farm" by locals, because it was once a horse farm belonging to former California governor and Stanford founder Leland Stanford.

Milton Latham served as California's sixth governor for five days in 1860...

WHO'S THAT BAND?

The stories behind two of California's most-beloved musical groups.

THE GRATEFUL DEAD. Originally called Mother McCree's Uptown Jug Champions and then the Warlocks, the Grateful Dead have one of the most debated band names in American musical history. Legends abound about where the term came from, but, according to Jerry Garcia himself, the story goes like this: "We were standing around in utter desperation at Phil [Lesh]'s house in Palo Alto. There was a huge dictionary, big monolithic thing, and I just opened it up. There in huge black letters was 'The Grateful Dead.' It...just canceled my mind out." What was that book? Probably a collection of folk tales. The story of the "grateful dead" has been around for centuries and tells of a traveler who, after paying the debts of a deceased pauper (whose body a group of townspeople refused to bury because, in life, the man owed them so much money), was brought good luck by the ghost of the deceased.

JAN AND DEAN. When it comes to California surf music, most people immediately think of the Beach Boys, but Jan and Dean did it first. William Jan Berry and Dean Ormsby Torrence met as teenagers in West L.A., where they formed a band with a group of guys from their high school and started covering popular songs of the time. The pair were clean-cut, blond, and very popular with the local girls, so when one of them told Berry that it would be "really cool" if he recorded a song, he decided to go for it. That song—1958's "Jennie Lee"—included Berry and another friend (because Torrence was away in the army), but it laid the foundation for Jan and Dean. By the next year, Torrence had returned, and he and Berry recorded "Baby Talk," which reached #10 on the 1959 charts. The pair released a couple of less popular songs over the next few years, but in the early 1960s, Berry and Torrence met another California surfer named Brian Wilson, who had his own band (The Beach Boys) and had written a song called "Surf City," but couldn't seem to get the melody just right. Jan and Dean helped him out, they recorded it (with Wilson on backup vocals), and the guys had their first #1 hit.

...He resigned to become one of the state's U.S. senators.

WHAT A RUSH!

The California gold rush began on January 24, 1848, when sawmill operator James Marshall found gold flakes at Sutter's Mill in Colma. From there, the gold rush became a game of numbers.

1: Percentage of the American population that migrated to California between 1848 and 1854. That's about 285,000 people, the largest free migration in U.S. history. (The population of San Francisco alone soared from 459 in 1847 to 100,000 in 1849.)

$3: Price *per* egg in a typical mining camp in 1848. (By the way, that's about $74 today.)

5–7: Number of months it usually took would-be prospectors to travel from New York to California by ship. The vessels had to go around Cape Horn at the tip of South America because there was no direct water route to the West Coast. Some pioneers also went overland. That trip took about four months if conditions were right (if they weren't, it could take as much as a year), but more people died along the route—scurvy, cholera, and starvation made it very risky.

7: Total Chinese population of California in 1848. The number rose to 11,794 by 1852 as immigrants flooded to the gold fields.

$16: Cost of a can of sardines in a typical California mining camp in 1849 ($398 today). In 1849, an ounce of gold also brought in about $16.

$20: Average daily earnings for California placer miners in 1848 ($500 today). By comparison, men working on the Erie Canal earned anywhere from 37¢ to 80¢ a day.

30: Percentage of prospectors who died from disease, accidents, or violence between 1848 and 1852.

$45: Cost of a pair of overalls in a typical California mining camp in 1848. Other necessities, like a pair of boots, could go for as much as $100.

160: Weight, in pounds, of the largest gold "nugget" discovered during the California gold rush. The massive nugget was found in Calaveras County in 1854.

200: Number of deserted ships in San Francisco Bay on June 4, 1849. The crews had all abandoned them to seek their fortunes in the gold fields.

515: Percentage that wages for unskilled workers (clerks, dishwashers, street sweepers, and so on) increased in California between 1847 and 1849. As many workers abandoned their jobs and turned to mining, only a handful of Californians stayed behind, and they were able to make a lot of money by picking up those old jobs.

1851: Year that Wah Lee opened the first Chinese laundry in San Francisco. Before that, there were so few laundries in the city that prospectors often sent their dirty clothes on ships to Hong Kong, where they would be cleaned, pressed, and returned...about three months later.

$40,000: Reward offered by Commodore Thomas Jones of the U.S. Navy Pacific Squadron in 1848 for sailors who deserted to go to the gold fields. (The reward didn't stop anyone, though; the men just kept leaving.)

150,000: The Native American population of California in 1846. The number dropped to 30,000 by 1860, as entire villages succumbed to smallpox, influenza, and measles introduced by immigrants. Others also starved or became fatally ill as gravel, silt, and toxic chemicals from mining camps seeped into the water supply and destroyed traditional hunting grounds. Native Americans were the only group to lose population during the gold rush.

$10 million: Money made from gold extracted from California in 1849 alone. The number rose to $41 million in 1850...and $81 million in 1852.

IT'S JUST GOOD BUSINESS, DUDE

In the 1960s, a young entrepreneur and his surfing buddies pushed a photocopier onto the sidewalk…and formed a billion-dollar company.

A ROCKY START

A In 1969, when 22-year-old Paul Orfalea opened a tiny copy shop next to a hamburger stand at UC Santa Barbara, he had no idea it would become the phenomenon that is Kinko's. Orfalea was an unlikely candidate for big business success: he was dyslexic, had ADHD, and couldn't even work a copy machine very well. But the store he opened—which was often so busy that customers spilled out onto the sidewalk—became one of the most successful self-service office supply companies ever.

Orfalea was born in Los Angeles in 1947 and grew up in a time when, he said, "they didn't even have a word for dyslexia." It was many years before he discovered a name for his learning disabilities he had, but he always knew two things: he had a lot of trouble reading, and it was tough to pay attention in class. Orfalea failed second grade and, even after repeating it, couldn't learn the alphabet. By the third grade, he'd been put into a school for developmentally disabled students. His parents spent years trying to help him, sending him to eye doctors and speech therapists. Finally, a remedial reading teacher discovered his problem and taught him phonics and other techniques.

He eventually caught up with his classmates, but Orfalea was still a terrible student. He was often restless, bored, and rebellious. He failed the ninth grade, was expelled several times, and finally graduated high school with a D average. Only the fear of being drafted and sent to Vietnam—and his parents' willingness to pay tuition—sent him to college. At the University of Southern California, Orfalea majored in "business and loopholes," and he always signed up with the easiest professors he could find. Still school was hard. During his first philosophy class, Orfalea recalled thinking, "'I don't understand any of that.' I put my pen down and said, 'I'm never going to make it in this world.'"

Last film Roman Polanski made in the U.S.: *Chinatown* (1974).

THE BRIGHT IDEA

Orfalea often worried about his future. He'd already been fired from a gas station because he couldn't write legible receipts. He still couldn't read easily or spell at all. He couldn't even fix things. He was basically unemployable. On the other hand, one of his professors praised his business ideas, and he knew how to sell things. Orfaela was determined to own his own business—if he could just figure out what it should be.

One afternoon, after watching students using the copy machine at the university library, Orfalea had an epiphany. Copy machines were durable and necessary, and many students didn't have easy access to them. So he took out a $5,000 bank loan and opened a copy shop in the tiny beachside town of Isla Vista, on the main road to the UC Santa Barbara campus. Why there? It had the market he was looking for: college kids in need of a copy shop. And there was easy beach access...he and his buddies loved to surf. Orfalea leased a photocopier and sold copies for 2.5¢ a page, undercutting the university library by 7.5¢. His shop quickly became so successful that he often had to take the copier outside because there were just too many customers to fit inside the tiny store.

Along with copiers, the shop did a brisk business in pens, pencils, highlighters, and notebooks. Orfalea even took the merchandise to the students—in the early days, he'd pack school supplies in a backpack and sell them in the dorms in the evenings. (It was, he said, also a good way to meet girls.) And when it came time to choose a name for his shop, he went with his college nickname: Kinko's, after his curly (kinky) red hair.

THE ONE-MINUTE MANAGER

For the next two years, Orfalea ran Kinko's with the help of his hippie and surfer pals. He developed a business style influenced by his dyslexia and ADHD. That meant Orfalea relied heavily on his workers. They had focus when he didn't, understood the machinery better than he did, and could run the shop when he got restless and needed a break. So he needed to make sure "they were happy and that they would continue working for me." Orfalea called the staff at Kinko's, "coworkers," rather than "employees" (a term he considered demeaning). He asked for their input about day-to-day operations and improvements and paid them a percentage of the business so they'd be dedicated to helping grow the profits.

The business approach worked. Profits from the first Kinko's paid off Orfalea's bank loan in four months. It also paid for a 27-foot sailboat that the boss could live on. He knew that he was onto something good.

HOW TO SUCCEED IN BUSINESS: TAKE A VACATION

Orfalea also wanted to expand Kinko's to other college towns, but he didn't have enough cash to finance the idea. So he decided to gain perspective by backpacking around Europe as "a getaway cure." When he returned to Santa Barbara a few months later, he had a solution: he reached out to his friends and coworkers, and together they formed partnerships to open new Kinko's, with Orfalea keeping a controlling interest in each one.

Orfaela and the new Kinko's partners took off in old cars and VW vans. They traveled from college campus to college campus, scouting good places for copy shops. One early partner was Bradley Krause, a long-haired surfer and Vietnam veteran majoring in graphic arts. Krause drove north up the West Coast—he was the first person to open a Kinko's internationally (in British Columbia, Canada) and eventually became president of the company's Northwest Division. Another partner was Jim Warren, a surfer who'd met Orfalea at a keg party. Warren headed out to Georgia and became president of Kinko's Southeast Division. Orfalea continued to encourage his partners to grow their businesses, and as they did, Kinko's kept expanding.

WANDERER-IN-CHIEF

As the stores spread throughout the country in the 1970s, Kinko's became a national corporation. Orfaelea, with his controlling interest in every store, was the head of that corporation, but instead of calling himself the "chief executive," he became "chief wanderer." Every three weeks, the restless Orfalea left his confining office and took a tour of his stores. He paid attention to "what they were doing right" and then used that information to keep the whole corporation on the right track. In one case, a Chicago store had customers banging on the doors to get in after closing time, so it started offering 24-hours-a-day, seven-days-a-week operations.

Orfalea thought that was a great idea and expanded it to other Kinko's.

Orfaela also used his travels to check out the competition and to spot new trends. During the 1980s, he noticed that there was a market for home office and home business services like full and self-service copying, computer rentals, and desktop publishing services. Kinko's was among the first to offer them.

WHAT GOES AROUND, COMES AROUND

By the 1990s, there were 420 Kinko's and more were still opening. By 1996, there were stores in every state and in Canada, Japan, South Korea, and the Netherlands. As his company grew into a billion-dollar enterprise, Orfalea never changed the "dyslexic" style of business he'd developed in Isla Vista: He kept an emphasis on delegating responsibilities to coworkers and encouraging their creativity. He also "made them happy," so that they treated his customers well. Kinko's offered excellent benefits, including profit sharing, health insurance, opportunities for promotions, scholarships for employees' children, education and training stipends, and even well-stocked refrigerators in the days before payday…for employees who ran out of money before they got their next check. From 1999 to 2001, Kinko's earned itself a spot on *Fortune Magazine*'s list of "America's Best Companies to Work For."

In 2004 FedEx bought Kinko's for $2.4 billion, and Orfalea turned his energies to charity. He coauthored three books about business, and in a strange twist of fate also returned to school—teaching his business methods at UC Santa Barbara.

*   *   *

BUMPASS WHAT?

Bumpass Hell in Mt. Lassen Volcanic National Park is named for a settler named Kendall Vanhook Bumpass, who, in 1864, stumbled upon the site, which was filled with fumeroles and boiling pools of water. He described the steamy area as "hell" to a reporter, and for him it really was: While showing his discovery to the press, Bumpass stepped onto a thin crust of ground covering a boiling pool. He burned his leg so badly that it had to be amputated.

The L.A. Dodgers introduced plastic batting helmets to the major leagues.

HOT TIMES

*If you've ever wanted to say, "Take this consumer-driven life and
shove it," and you don't mind extreme temperatures, a lot of dust,
and being miles away from civilization, you might consider
going to Burning Man. Just don't bring any money.*

THE SPARK

Okay, technically, the annual Burning Man festival—
which attracts hippies, techies, New Agers, campers, and
just about anyone who loves the idea of peace, communal living,
and a lack of consumerism—takes place in Nevada. But it began
in San Francisco in June 1986, when Larry Harvey and Jerry James
decided to build something to honor the summer solstice. From
scrap wood, they constructed an eight-foot-tall "man" with a triangular face and brought it to Baker Beach, a wide expanse with a
view of the Golden Gate Bridge. The area was mostly deserted,
and it was the perfect setting to douse the man in gasoline and
burn him. About 20 bystanders who caught sight of the flaming
structure ran over to watch.

For the next summer solstice, Harvey and James did it again.
This time, though, they advertised with a simple flyer and held a
potluck beforehand. The wooden man more than doubled in size
that year, and the number of gawkers quadrupled. By 1988 the
event was officially named Burning Man, and up to 200 people
came to watch the now 30-foot-tall man burn. During those first
few years, Harvey says they set the man afire as an offering or gift.
Later, its destruction became symbolic of personal evolution, and a
way to "stick it to the man."

LIGHT MY FIRE

The gathering in 1989 also included sculptures and about 300
attendees. It featured the largest man thus far—40 feet tall. At that
size, though, the man couldn't really be burned on Baker Beach
covertly anymore. The event caused such a scene that it attracted
news crews—and police arrived to keep everything under control.

The next year, Harvey and James held the gathering again, but
decided not to actually burn the man because officials had warned

---

Q: What L.A. band was originally known as Tony Flow and the...

them that big fires were prohibited. That's when a burn-crazy throng moved in and tried to light the man anyway. Someone even assaulted Larry Harvey while the crowd shouted, "Burn it now!" That was all a bit too much. The event was postponed until the organizers could find a venue where they could burn their man and run amok without interference.

BAD DAYS AT BLACK ROCK

Enter the Cacophony Society, a group of San Francisco pranksters who suggested a dusty lakebed, or *playa*, in Nevada's Black Rock Desert. It's the largest flat surface in North America and was the perfect party spot. Battling heat during the day, cold at night, wind, and a lack of water, 80 "burners" created an entire town, the first Black Rock City, over Labor Day 1990. Black Rock City was transitory—it would last only as long as the festival. To protest what Harvey called the "commodification of our culture," vendors weren't allowed, and within the camp, no money exchanged hands. Harvey said, "Imagine you are put upon a desert plain, a space which is so vast and blank...Imagine it is swept by fearsome winds and scorching temperatures, and only by your effort can you make of it a home. Imagine...nothing that's for sale. These challenging conditions represent the chief appeal of our utopian experiment."

AFTERGLOW

Burning Man on the playa is still going strong today—in 2011 more than 50,000 burners showed up. The festival typically lasts from the Monday before Labor Day, through the holiday, though people arrive for a week or so beforehand. It's still an experience like none other. The harsh climate is survivable only because the city becomes a tight-knit community where people help each other out. Everyone volunteers to keep free food, drinks, music, and attractions going 24/7. They build elaborate stages, design costumes from recycled materials, host workshops, and book world-class musicians...all on their own. Organizers now also charge an entrance fee to cover services: Burning Man has rangers, a public works department, an airport, and newspapers— for two weeks. When it's over, the burners pack up everything and leave without a trace.

In 2011 the idealistic vision of Burning Man seemed to be in jeopardy when, for the first time ever, the festival sold out before it even started. Scalpers sold tickets for thousands of dollars, and tour packages went for $95,000, virtually spitting on Harvey's non-commerce culture. But once it began, the festival went off as it always did, with attendees biking around the town, eating together, camping together, having fun together…and on the second-to-last night, they all burned the man together too.

* * *

THE GAMBLE HOUSE

Architect brothers Henry and Charles Greene designed the Gamble House, a bungalow in Pasadena, in 1908 as a retirement residence for David Gamble of the Proctor and Gamble Company and his wife Mary. Today, the structure is a National Historic Landmark and a masterful example of American Arts and Crafts architecture.

Mostly built between about 1907 and the 1920s, Arts and Crafts houses are elaborate, decorative structures, meant to be works of art, rather than simply a place to live. The Gamble House, in particular, is spectacular. Its teak-framed front door is made of three panels of inlaid Tiffany glass. The exterior uses dark shingled siding to blend into the natural surroundings, and the gardens include winding pathways and stones meant to look like brooks running across the lawn. The interior is often described as "a symphony of wood." Hand-rubbed mahogany, teak, oak, and cedar create the walls, trim, and cabinetry. Everything was crafted by hand, and there's so much attention to detail that even the shapes of the picture frames on the walls are part of the design.

The Gamble house eventually passed down to family heirs Cecil and Louise Gamble, who intended to sell it…until they overheard the buyers planning to "lighten the house" by painting everything white. Shocked, the Gambles decided to preserve the house instead by donating it to the City of Pasadena in 1966. Since then it's attracted fans from all over and has shown up on TV and in movies—the Gamble House was used as the exterior of Doc Brown's mansion and garage in 1985's *Back to the Future*.

Oldest art museum west of the Mississippi: the Crocker, in Sacramento (est. 1885).

TOPS IN CROPS

If you ate vegetables, fruits, dairy products, or nuts today, they probably came from California. Some facts about the state's agricultural industries.

• California is America's largest producer of agricultural products and ranks second in livestock. (Texas is first.)

• More than half of California farms are smaller than 50 acres, and 90 percent are family-owned.

• California is the country's leading producer of strawberries, dairy, green onions, artichokes, figs, dates, almonds, walnuts, raisins, kiwifruit, pomegranates, pistachios, garlic, olives, and marijuana.

• In the last decade or so, marijuana has become California's top cash crop. In some counties, it accounts for a majority of the local economy, making more than grapes, almonds, and citrus. No one knows for sure how much marijuana is grown in the state (because it's still illegal except for medicinal purposes), but estimates claim that it's worth nearly $14 billion a year.

• In the early 1870s, the newly minted U.S. Department of Agriculture gave Eliza and Luther Tibbets two tiny navel orange trees as an experiment. Eliza had once been a neighbor of botanist William Saunders, who worked at the Department of Agriculture, and she and Luther had heard of a plant that bore sweet fruit. Saunders was having no luck planting oranges in Washington, D.C., so Eliza wrote to him and asked for a few saplings…to see if oranges could grow in California soil. According to legend, the trees thrived with dishwater and a little help from nearby nurserymen. The Tibbets harvested their first orange crop in the mid-1870s and later sold buds from their trees.

• California farmers grow three kinds of rice: short-grain varieties (7 percent of the crop), medium-grain (90 percent of the crop), and specialty rices such as arborio, jasmine, and basmati (about 3 percent). Each variety has a different texture and a different use in cooking.

California surpassed Wisconsin as the top dairy-producing state in 1993.

• The first olive trees came to California from the Mediterranean by way of monks who settled in Mexico in the 1700s. The hot product back then was olive oil, but when the market dropped due to oversaturation in the late 1800s, a widowed German immigrant named Freda Ehmann experimented with the olives themselves. On her farm in the Northern California town of Oroville, Ehmann discovered that if she cured her olives just so, they were delicious. By the late 1890s, she was selling her product as far north as Vancouver and all over the East Coast, and California olives became a much-sought delicacy.

• In the 1920s, California artichokes caused an "artichoke war" in New York, when Mafia kingpin Ciro Terranova, also known as "the Artichoke King," cornered the import market and began overcharging his New York customers. Things got so bad that New York City mayor Fiorello La Guardia declared the possession or sale of artichokes to be illegal, but dropped the ban after a week because La Guardia himself loved the vegetable and couldn't bear to be without it.

*　*　*

FUN-LOVING FAIRFAX

• In the 1960s the tiny Marin County town of Fairfax was a hotbed of counterculture and free love. One year, residents even watched members of the bands Jefferson Airplane and the Grateful Dead play "stoned softball" at the Fairfax Little League baseball diamond.

• California's first communal hot tub also appeared in Fairfax. In 1966, local Al Garvey, who'd enjoyed communal baths during a trip to Japan, built a redwood tub in his backyard for himself and his wife Barbara. "The whole thing started out as just a place for Barbara and me to relax. We called it a Japanese bath," Garvey said. "But it was so much fun, we started inviting friends over." Jazz musician John Handy was one guest. Soon the Garvey parties became famous and friends wanted Al to build them their own hot tubs. He did, eventually turning "communal hot tubbing" into one of the most popular pastimes of California's New Age culture.

DYING TO GET IN

*There are some places in California that you might
like to visit, but you wouldn't want to live there
because...well...no one actually "lives" there.*

HOLLYWOOD FOREVER CEMETERY, LOS ANGELES

Famous "residents": Movie lovers often visit the graves
of Rudolph Valentino, Tyrone Power, Douglas Fairbanks, Jayne
Mansfield, Faye Wray (without King Kong), and Marion Davies
(mostly famous for being William Randolph Hearst's mistress).
There's also a memorial to African American actress Hattie
McDaniel, who won an Oscar for playing Mammy in *Gone With
the Wind.* Unfortunately, McDaniel's tomb is empty; she wanted to
be buried here, but she was excluded because of her race. Young
hipsters pay their respects to punk rocker Johnny Ramone, whose
grave includes a life-size statue of him wailing on the guitar.
Another famous stop is the grave of Mel Blanc, the voice of Bugs
Bunny—his headstone reads "That's All Folks."

Claim to fame: Established in 1899, the cemetery was *the* place to
be buried from the 1920s through the late '40s. These days, Hollywood Forever has more than just famous corpses, though. It boasts
all kinds of activities: On summer evenings, thousands of visitors
come with blankets and picnic baskets to watch movies screened
on the white mausoleum walls. On weekends, there are concerts,
and annual Day of the Dead celebrations feature sacred ceremon-
ial tributes, musical entertainment, and lots of gourmet Mexican
food. Hollywood Forever is also probably the only cemetery in the
country that's recommended by local magazines as a great place to
bring a date.

THE CITY OF SOULS, COLMA

Famous "residents": Colma hosts 17 cemeteries and crematori-
ums. Baseball great Joe DiMaggio, former governor Pat Brown,
and one of San Francisco's most famous murder victims, Mayor
George Moscone (assassinated in 1978 along with activist Harvey
Milk) are buried at Holy Cross Catholic Cemetery. Wyatt Earp

rests in the Hills of Eternity. William Randolph Hearst's grave is at Cypress Lawn Memorial Park. Also at Cypress Lawn: Harry "the Horse" Flamburis, a former Hells Angel gang leader whose pals supposedly buried his chopper with him.

Claim to fame: Located just south of San Francisco in San Mateo County, Colma is known as the "City of Souls" because it has about 2,000 live residents, but nearly 2 million resting "souls." Colma's Japanese, Chinese, Italian, Serbian, Catholic, Jewish, Greek Orthodox, and nondenominational cemeteries all have one thing in common besides death: their story begins in San Francisco.

In the late 1880s, San Francisco's cemeteries were nearly full, but real estate was becoming more and more expensive. So city residents turned to nearby Colma, an easy carriage ride to the south. In 1887 the first cemetery opened in the town, and in 1914 (because many old cemeteries were deteriorating), many of San Francisco's dead were moved to mass graves in Colma, which became the city's necropolis.

MOUNTAIN VIEW MEMORIAL PARK, OAKLAND

Famous "residents": Located near the top of the hillside, the section of the cemetery known as Millionaires Row has spectacular views and mausoleums. The largest of these monuments is the tower dedicated to businessman Charles Crocker, who owned Crocker Bank (later acquired by Wells Fargo) and a share of the Central Pacific Railroad. It's said his widow kept an eye on his resting place from her Nob Hill mansion.

Other famous occupants include Domingo Ghirardelli of Ghirardelli chocolate; Henry Kaiser of Kaiser Permanente; James Folger of Folgers Coffee; architect Julia Morgan, who designed the Hearst Castle; and Art Lym, who trained with the Wright brothers and became the first Chinese American aviator.

Claim to fame: The 226-acre Mountain View Memorial Park was designed by Frederick Law Olmsted, the most famous American landscaper of the 19th century and one of the designers of New York's Central Park. Olmsted liked to combine buildings and landscapes to bring out a location's natural beauty, and he had plenty to work with in Oakland's hills, with their sweeping views of San

In 1908 Long Beach became the first city in the state with an organized lifeguard service.

Francisco Bay. As a result, many people come to Mountain View to walk, meditate, enjoy nature, and even get married.

MISSION DE ALCALÁ, SAN DIEGO

Famous "residents": Hundreds of Native Americans who labored at this San Diego mission are buried in the courtyard, though none of their names were recorded. Today, they are remembered only with a small stone marker. The recorded graves belong to five of the padres who ran the mission. The earliest marked grave in California is that of Padre Luis Jayme, who was killed by the Kumeyaay in 1775. The tribe had launched a failed uprising that tried to oust the missionaries and Spanish soldiers.

Claim to fame: No one knows the site of the oldest cemetery in California because there aren't any records of the resting places of the Native Americans who occupied the area for thousands of years before Europeans arrived. But the Mission Basilica de Alcalá, founded in 1769 by Catholic priest Junipero Serra, is the oldest recorded cemetery in the state.

THE OLD CITY CEMETERY, SACRAMENTO

Famous "residents": Among the prominent Californians buried here is John Sutter, best known for being one of the owners of Sutter's Mill, where the first California gold was found.

Claim to fame: Founded in 1849 on land donated by Sutter, this cemetery is famous for its gold rush residents—many of whom wound up here after accidents or brawls involving too much liquor. But no list of cemeteries is complete without a ghost story, and one of the most interesting tales comes from Old City. The cemetery is supposedly home to one of Sacramento's best-known ghosts, May Woolsey, who was born in 1866 and was almost 13 years old in 1879 when she died of encephalitis. After Woolsey's death, her grieving mother packed a trunk with her possessions—clothes, books, toys, and trinkets—and placed it in a compartment above a stairway in the family's home. When the trunk was found in 1979, it was said to also include a message to May's mother from beyond the grave. The person who wrote the note claimed to be happy and not dead...only waiting.

IF AT FIRST YOU DON'T SUCCEED...

When the American navy's Tom Jones sailed into Monterey Bay in 1842, he demanded that Mexico surrender California to the United States. One problem: There wasn't any war...yet.

PEACEFUL POST

During the 18th century, when Spain ruled California, it made Monterey the colony's capital. Monterey Bay was an important port with a good climate and fertile land, and the town, though sleepy, was home to the region's governors. Because Monterey's location was so good, though, the Spanish worried that it wouldn't be theirs for long. In particular, they were concerned that the Russians—just across the ocean to the northwest—wanted the port. So in 1770, Spain set up a military fort to defend Monterey "from the atrocities of the Russians." Except those "atrocious" Russians never showed up. Instead, Monterey remained quiet for decades...so quiet that the Spanish spent very little on its deteriorating fortifications.

THE ARGENTINIANS ARE COMING!

Then, in 1818, an Argentinian privateer named Hipólito Bouchard arrived. Argentina was battling for independence from Spain, and Bouchard had his government's permission to plunder Spanish ships in the area and harass the Spanish any way he could.

Bouchard arrived with two armed ships: the *Argentina* and the *Santa Rosa*. After a quick look around, Bouchard saw no wealthy Spanish merchant ships to raid, so he decided to attack the town, hoping the Spanish governors were storing some riches there. He wanted to take Monterey by surprise, but a watchman saw him coming and sent word to California's governor, Pablo Vicente de Sola. By the time Bouchard arrived in the bay, the governor had evacuated all the women and children and added a new battery of cannons. When the *Santa Rosa* attacked Monterey, the privateers were the ones who got a surprise. The new cannons crippled the *Santa Rosa* and forced its surrender.

But when the governor started demanding that the crew come ashore, the Argentinians realized that de Sola lacked the boats and firepower to come get them. So they just left in lifeboats and headed back to Bouchard, who was still on the *Argentina*.

Bouchard docked near Monterey and, with a few cannons and 400 men, he marched overland and attacked from behind the city's crumbling fortress. Governor de Sola and his few soldiers fled while Bouchard plundered Monterey. The Argentinians stayed for six days before moving on to attack other ports along the coast.

EYES ON THE PRIZE

It wasn't until the 1840s that another naval officer tried to take control of the city. By then, Monterey was in the hands of Mexico (which gained independence from Spain in 1821), and it was a crucial port. Mexico didn't have the resources to defend California, though. And it was no secret that France, England, and the U.S. all wanted to oust Mexico and take the region for themselves.

In 1841 the U.S. government appointed the feisty Thomas Catesby Jones as commander of the U.S. Pacific Fleet. The next year, Jones got a message from an American official in Mexico who believed war was about to break out between the two countries. Jones had also heard rumors that Mexico owed England a great deal of money and had offered up most of California to settle the debt. So Jones decided to take the port before England did, speeding off toward Monterey with his marines. Meanwhile, the rumored declaration of war between the U.S. and Mexico never happened.

ON HIS BUCKET LIST

On October 19, 1842, Jones's squadron sailed into Monterey Bay and captured a Mexican merchant ship as a "prize of war." The captain of the ship told him that there was no war, but Jones didn't believe him. The commodore continued on, notifying the city's officials that Monterey had to be surrendered. Since the town had only 29 soldiers and 11 cannons, it wasn't much of a fight—Jones won immediately. The next morning, Mexican officials and a prominent American merchant, Thomas Larkin, came aboard Jones's ship to work out terms of surrender. Larkin also told Jones there was no war and he read quotes from some recent newspapers for proof. But when Larkin couldn't find an actual copy of a newspaper to show him, Jones suspected the man of conspiracy and moved forward with his plan. The surrender papers were signed, the Mexican soldiers were locked up, and the American flag was raised in California for the first time. Commodore Thomas Catesby Jones was in his glory…for about 24 hours.

The next day, Jones found some newspapers and finally realized there was no conspiracy and no war. He had to lower the Stars and Stripes, raise the Mexican flag, and make amends to the people of Monterey. Jones did this mainly by throwing lots of parties for everyone.

CALIFORNIA DREAMIN'

While Monterey danced, however, many Mexican officials were furious. California's incoming governor, Manuel Micheltorena, demanded $15,000 in restitution. He also wanted 1,500 new uniforms for his soldiers and (maybe to keep the dancing going after Jones's band left town) a full set of military musical instruments. None of the reparations were ever paid, and even though the United States apologized and Jones lost his command, bad feelings between the two countries increased.

One person who noticed how easy it was for Jones to capture Monterey was politician James K. Polk. In 1845 Polk was elected president, and at his inauguration, he announced that the acquisition of California was at the top of his presidential to-do list. Polk also knew that Jones had been right when he suspected England would try to take California. So in 1846, after war finally did break out between the U.S. and Mexico, Polk's government sent Commodore John D. Sloat and the U.S. Pacific Fleet to Monterey.

Sloat sailed into Monterey Bay with the intention of claiming it before the English could. Once again, there was a battle—the Battle of Monterey—that was really no battle at all. Sloat's 250 armed officers landed with no shots fired and raised the American flag. (This event is widely known as the first time the Stars and Stripes flew in California, but technically, it was the second time.) Two weeks later, the British arrived, but when their commander found the Americans entrenched in Monterey, he sailed off again rather than start a conflict.

The last duel in California took place in 1859 between a…

HOT ENOUGH FOR YOU?

Death Valley is a place of extremes, so
here are five extreme facts about it.

• Death Valley got its name 1849 from a group of gold prospectors who decided to take a shortcut on their way to the gold fields of Northern California and got lost. After spending months wandering thirsty and hungry in the desert, they finally made their way over the Panamint Range (along the northern edge of the Mojave Desert) to safety. Amazingly, only one person in their party died. Still, as they left the desert behind, one of the pioneers declared, "Good-bye, Death Valley!" The name stuck.

• The average annual rainfall in the valley is 2.5 inches. In 1929 and 1953, no rain was recorded at all. Oddly, the average evaporation rate is 150 inches. (No one seems to know where all that moisture comes from.)

• Death Valley holds the record for the lowest spot (282 feet below sea level) and the hottest place (with a record high temperature of 134°F) in North America. Death Valley's record low—set in 1913, the same year as the record high—was 15°F.

• The most lucrative discovery ever made in Death Valley came in 1881, when businessman William T. Coleman discovered sodium borate, or borax, in the rocks near Furnace Creek. With many uses, including in detergents, fire retardants, and cosmetics, and as an antifungal agent, borax proved to be hugely profitable for Coleman, thanks to the Harmony Borax Works he founded and the famous "twenty-mule teams" he used to haul the stuff out of the desert between 1883 and 1889.

• Death Valley's hot, dry climate is home to more than 1,000 plant species, more than 50 species of mammals, and nearly 350 kinds of birds, in addition to fish, amphibians, and reptiles. Nearly all of the mammals are nocturnal, to escape the heat.

MOTOR INN

California practically invented the motel industry...not surprising since, during the early 1900s, the state was America's most popular travel destination.

CALIFORNIA, HERE I COME!

In the 1920s, World War I was over, and Americans were living large. The economy was booming, and people had money to spend. What did they buy? Cars. Ford's Model T made automobiles affordable for the masses, and the road trip became America's newest pastime. Tourists packed their cars and hit the open road. Many of them—enticed by year-round sunshine and ocean air—headed for California. But when the tourists arrived, they discovered that there wasn't really anywhere to stay. California was a relatively young state—initially built by a gold rush—so the inns and hotels that were common on the East Coast were rare in the West. Most travelers had no choice but to stay in auto-camps, where they basically had to live out of their cars.

For many, the lack of accommodations was an inconvenience, but for Los Angeles architect Arthur Heineman, it was an opportunity. In 1925 Heineman opened California's first roadside motor hotel near San Luis Obispo. Called the Milestone Mo-Tel, it was specifically designed for travelers on road trips. It cost just $1.25 a night for two rooms with a kitchen and a garage. There was even a restaurant on-site, complete with linen napkins and fine china.

GET YOUR KICKS

Within about a year of the Milestone's opening, Route 66 was established. This historic highway—one of the first highways in U.S. history—covered more than 2,000 miles and stretched from Chicago to L.A. It opened up the West to road travel, and with gas at just 17¢ a gallon, driving vacations to California became inexpensive, easy, and relatively quick. The adventuresome and optimistic middle class was eager to see the country...for a while.

The onset of the Great Depression in the 1930s and World War II in the early 1940s stalled American automobile travel. But

The ashes of author Henry Miller were scattered off the coast of Big Sur.

when the war ended and the economy boomed again in the 1950s, the road trip was as popular as ever. Baby boomers and their parents headed for California, and they needed new places to stay once they got there. So motels opened up and down the Golden State. Some of the most famous and unique include...

THE WIGWAM MOTEL. Frank Redford—a Kentuckian with an interest in Native American history—opened seven Wigwams around the United States in the 1940s and early '50s—the San Bernardino location began accepting customers in 1949. Located on Route 66, the 11 tepee-shaped units featured everything you'd find in a square room, including air-conditioning. The San Bernardino location is one of just three Wigwam Motels left in the United States (the other two are in Kentucky and Arizona).

THE MADONNA INN. This motel has nothing to do with either the singer or the saint. Opened on December 24, 1958, in San Luis Obispo by Phyllis and Alex Madonna, the inn originally had just a dozen rooms. Over time, it expanded and now includes more than 100 rooms, each with a different decor: The Caveman Room is decorated with solid rock. The Kona Room includes faux lava. The Tack Room, with its brilliant red walls, is horse-themed. And so on. There's also leaded glass throughout the inn, a staircase with a marble balustrade in the dining room, and a 28-foot-tall gold-and-copper tree in the main dining room.

TRAVELODGE. This chain got its start in San Diego in 1935. Owned by Scott King and originally called King's Auto Court, it was a motel empire by 1940. Today there are 71 motels across California.

BEST WESTERN. In 1946, M. K. Guertin—a co-organizer of the first motel association back in the 1920s—founded Best Western Motels in Long Beach.

MOTEL 6. The very first Motel 6 opened in Santa Barbara in 1962. Builders William Becker and Paul Greene wanted to attract budget-conscious travelers, so they charged $6.60 per night for a single room with no frills: pay phones only, coin-operated black-and-white TVs, no on-site restaurant, and minimal maid service.

First movie filmed at the Hollywood Bowl: *Jazz Mad* (1928).

CALIFORNIA'S FIRST HIPPIE

He had long hair, wore sandals and a white robe, ate a raw vegetarian diet, and lived under the first L of the Hollywood sign. Not all that unusual in California, right? Except this was the 1940s, and it was considered very, very strange.

HEAVEN AND L

Consider the case of eden ahbez (no capital letters— ahbez believed that caps should be reserved for "God," "Life," "Love," "Peace," and other divine words). He lived an eccentric's life and probably would've continued doing so undisturbed except that he wrote a hit song and brought the world to his door...or what would've been his door, if he'd actually had a front door.

Born George Alexander Aberle in Brooklyn, New York, in 1908, he traveled across the country, eventually settling in Southern California. He had always been musical, had played piano, and even led a dance band in the 1930s. So when he arrived in Los Angeles, he offered to play piano at Eutropheon, a small health-food store and restaurant on Laurel Canyon Boulevard in exchange for food. Its owners, John and Vera Richter, were from Germany and were followers of a movement called *lebensreform* ("life reform") that encouraged healthy food, nudity, sexual liberation, alternative medicine, Eastern religion, and living close to nature. Aberle came to agree with the lifestyle and joined a small group of followers who lived in the desert and called themselves "Nature Boys." They lived wild, didn't shave or cut their hair, and ate a diet made up mostly of raw vegetables.

It was about that time that Aberle also changed his name to eden ahbez and began sleeping under the first L of the famous Hollywood sign. He met a woman named Anna Jacobsen, who appreciated him and his philosophies, and they married and continued to live outdoors even after they had a son.

Look out below! In San Francisco's financial district, it used to be a...

A SONG IS BORN

During this time, ahbez was still playing at the food store/restaurant and also began writing songs. One of them was called "Nature Boy" and had a haunting melody and lyrics about a "strange enchanted boy" who learned this important lesson after he had "traveled very far": the most profound thing in the world "is just to love and be loved in return." (No one is sure if ahbez was writing about himself or someone else.) The message was simple, and a disc jockey named "Cowboy" Jack Patton, who happened to hear ahbez perform it, thought the tune would be perfect for Nat King Cole's voice. During one of Cole's concerts in Los Angeles, Patton urged ahbez to go backstage and give the music to the singer's manager, Mort Ruby.

The only copy of the song ahbez had was rumpled and soiled from use and outdoor living, but he went backstage that night anyway and insisted that Ruby give it to Cole. Ruby did, and Cole liked the song well enough to try it out in a few live shows to see how the audience reacted. Quite positively, it turned out. So Cole added it to his repertoire and on August 22, 1947, he recorded "Nature Boy."

There was only one problem: Neither Cole nor Ruby had any idea how to get in touch with ahbez to get his permission to release it. In fact, nobody in the music business seemed to know who the guy was, and he wasn't listed in the phone book. Eventually, they tracked ahbez down under the Hollywood sign, and he granted permission. But Cole had started second-guessing the song. It wasn't like anything else on the radio at the time, and he was thinking that recording such an unusual tune might not be wise.

A STAR IS TORN

So Nat King Cole put away the recording for a while, not quite knowing what to do with it. Despite those doubts, his live audiences still seemed to enjoy it, and he started to get asked when he was going to record it. Finally, Capitol Records, Cole's record company, came up with a solution—in 1948, they put "Nature Boy" on the B-side of what they thought would be Cole's next big hit, "Lost April." In most cases, that's the well-deserved ending for a mediocre song, but not this time. A radio deejay in New York played the B-side instead of the A-side, and the phones lit up. People wanted to hear it again. When word got out to other radio stations, "Nature Boy" quickly became Capitol Records' #1 single. Other music stars rushed out to record their own versions of it.

Luckily, ahbez didn't need much money to be happy, because "not much" is reportedly about what he made from the song. Some of it was his own fault: he'd signed overlapping agreements with several music publishers, and each claimed their share. Worse, the melody that he said came to him in the "mist of the California mountains" turned out to be very similar to a Yiddish song called "Schwieg Mein Hertz," and ahbez had to pay a substantial settlement to its publisher. None of this made much difference in ahbez's lifestyle, though. He and his family continued camping outside and lecturing on street corners about the benefits of vegetarianism and Eastern philosophy.

BACK TO NATURE

After "Nature Boy," ahbez did a little more work in the music business, but he also became part of a media whirlwind as magazines and newspapers covered his strange lifestyle. He gave many mystical-sounding quotes like this one reported by a writer from *Life*: "I am the wind, the sea, the evening star. I am everyone, anyone, no one." He also wrote a few more songs, including "Land of Love" and "Lonely Island," that Nat King Cole and some others recorded, but only "Lonely Island" made it into the Top 40. Later, he recorded a couple of albums himself in which he recited his poetry over a lush "cocktail-lounge-meets-nature-sounds" music track. That didn't do very well, either.

In the end, ahbez became less of a curiosity and more of an elder as younger hippies adopted the lifestyle he had pioneered. The modern world eventually overtook him, however. In 1995, at the age of 86, ahbez died after being struck by a car. But "Nature Boy" lived on. It's been recorded by dozens of artists over the years and appeared in movies like *The Talented Mr. Ripley* and *Moulin Rouge!*

WELCOME, SPACE BROTHERS! PART I

The aliens are coming! The aliens are coming! Okay, maybe not.
But members of these California cults might disagree.

WHAT: The College of Universal Wisdom
WHERE: The Morongo Basin, in the desert near Joshua Tree

WHAT THEY'RE ABOUT: The first big wave in flying-saucer cults can be laid at the feet of a man named George Adamski. In 1952, responding to psychic messages from space people, Adamski led six seekers into the Southern California desert. He briefly became separated from the group and, as luck would have it, met up with a spaceship driven by a handsome blond alien named Orthon. Soon Adamski was being visited regularly by people from other planets...and it wasn't just him. When his story hit the newspapers, lots of people reported similar psychic messages and mysterious visitations...so many that 10,000 contactees began attending an annual gathering in the California desert called the "Giant Rock Spacecraft Convention."

That convention was organized by George Van Tassel, a former Hughes Aircraft mechanic who claimed he'd been in contact with aliens for a year before Adamski. Not just that, but Van Tassel said he was instructed by the aliens to collect donations for a college (the College of Universal Wisdom) where he would build an "Integratron," a machine that would rejuvenate human cells, take years off a person's age, and might even make humans immortal. (Alas, he warned that it wouldn't actually make you look any younger, though, and if you got too high a dose of the magic rays, you might spontaneously combust.) Despite being "based on the design of Moses' Tabernacle, the writings of Nikola Tesla, and telepathic directions from extraterrestrials," the only good the Integratron did for Van Tassel was financial—he died in 1978 at age 67 after collecting tens of thousands of dollars from believers, who paid up before the Integratron was even finished. The college never happened, but the Integratron—a big wooden dome, minus the spinning metal part that would've made people young again— is still around in the desert near Joshua Tree. Visitors can rent it for a night or a weekend, or just take a healing "sound bath," a series of glass bowls played within its echoey dome.

P.S. For a quarter of a century, Adamski's description of the handsome human-looking alien became the prototype of what most other contactees reported during the 1950s and '60s. That changed in 1977 with the movie *Close Encounters of the Third Kind*—suddenly, contactees began describing the aliens they met as short creatures with large, slanting eyes.

WHAT: UNARIUS Academy of Science (technically making the name the "Universal Articulate Interdimensional Understanding of Science" Academy of Science)

WHERE: El Cajon

WHAT THEY'RE ABOUT: Since its founding by engineer Ernest Norman and his wife Ruth in 1954, UNARIUS has claimed to have a direct line to the wisest beings of the universe…who sent Ernest their thoughts at a speed much faster than light and ultimately dictated "through him" more than 100 books of cosmic and universal wisdom. The beings also answered questions about human origins: Asians, for example, supposedly descended from interstellar gypsies who colonized Mars and moved to Earth a million or so years ago. When attacked by Earth natives, however, the space transients retreated to their underground cities on Mars, apparently not having developed the self-defense mechanisms to trump the earthlings. In their panic, they left behind a small group that managed to survive, thrive, and became the Asians of today.

After Ernest died in 1971, Ruth took over the organization. Through her and a "sub-channeler" named Louis Spiegel, the strange messages continued. Spiegel predicted a 1976 landing of spaceships from 33 planets. When they didn't show up, he said that they would actually arrive in 2001. That didn't happen either, but it didn't matter. Spiegel died in 1999, and his followers believed he had traveled to Venus to wait for his next reincarnation.

For more California space cults, turn to page 335.

Shasta Dam has enough concrete to build a three-foot-wide sidewalk around the equator.

WHO KILLED JANE STANFORD?

A wealthy woman cofounds a prestigious university as an homage to her son, but soon finds herself embroiled in a bitter fight with the university's president over the school's direction...and then she ends up dead. But who did it?

MIRACLES AND TRAGEDIES

Located in Palo Alto, Stanford University is considered one of the country's top schools—in 2011, *U.S. News and World Report* ranked it fifth. But Stanford's academic reputation isn't nearly as interesting as the school's great murder mystery.

New York–born Jane Lothrop married a young lawyer named Leland Stanford in 1850, and the couple meandered across the country until they settled in California. Leland eventually made a fortune, not in law, but by selling supplies to gold miners at exorbitant prices. By the 1860s, Leland was also California's eighth governor and president of the Central Pacific Railroad. Soon, the Stanfords were one of the wealthiest couples in the nation, and gossips said the only thing their charmed life lacked was a child.

Then, in 1868, when Jane was 39 years old, she gave birth to a son, Leland Jr. At that time, it was uncommon for new mothers to be approaching 40, so the Stanfords called Leland their "miracle baby." He was a cheerful kid who spent happy days on his father's horse farm in Palo Alto. The boy also loved antiquities and wanted to be an archaeologist. His parents thought that was a great idea, so they took him to the Mediterranean to visit several archaeological sites. But during the trip, Leland Jr. got typhoid fever. He died in Italy in 1884.

"I WANT YOU TO BUILD A SCHOOL..."

The Stanfords were heartbroken, but decided to honor their son by establishing a university in his name. How exactly they got it all going, however, remains up for debate. According to the 1903 U.S. Congressional report on education: "While Stanford was watching his boy by his bedside and wearied out asleep, he dreamed that his son said to him, 'Father, do not say you have nothing to live for, you have everything to live for. Live for humanity.' While he thus dreamed, the child died." Leland Stanford later said the dream inspired him to say to Jane, "The children of California shall be our children."

But famous psychic Maud Drake always disputed that story. She told newspapers that the idea for the school came from the spirit of Leland Jr. himself, who appeared to his parents during a séance. According to Drake, Leland Jr. instructed his parents to build the school. The Stanfords denied Drake's story (and according to many accounts, they'd already started the school before they saw her), but it was true that they'd attended séances. Like many people in late 1800s (including Victor Hugo, Sir Arthur Conan Doyle, and Queen Victoria), Jane Stanford turned to spiritualists who claimed they could communicate with the dead. She even held séances in her grand mansion on Nob Hill.

Harvard University president Charles Eliot, who advised the Stanfords on how to set up a university, offered a third theory: He believed that the main reason Leland decided to fund a school was because Jane was interested in education. Her husband hoped a school would keep Jane busy and keep her from obsessing about her son's death or the séances that might allow her to talk to him.

SCHOOL DAZE

Whatever the reason for its founding, Leland Stanford Junior University opened in 1891 with an enrollment of 559 students. The school was co-ed, one of the first in the nation to admit women. Less than two years later, however, Leland Stanford died and the government sued his estate to recoup money borrowed by the Central Pacific Railroad. Stanford's assets were frozen and the school suddenly had no access to any of the family money that had been keeping it going. The university was on the verge of being shut down.

No one expected much from Jane. Everyone figured she'd be too overwhelmed by her husband's death to do any good. Instead, she single-handedly kept Stanford open. She slashed her own allowance so that she could give the school nearly all her earnings

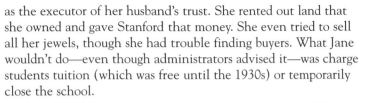

as the executor of her husband's trust. She rented out land that she owned and gave Stanford that money. She even tried to sell all her jewels, though she had trouble finding buyers. What Jane wouldn't do—even though administrators advised it—was charge students tuition (which was free until the 1930s) or temporarily close the school.

It worked. Thanks to Jane, the university made it to 1895, when the government dropped its case against the Stanford estate. Jane took over her late husband's fortune and suddenly had about $30 million to devote to Stanford.

THE PLAN'S AFOOT

Once the money problems were behind her, though, Jane found herself at odds with Stanford's president, David Starr Jordan. They disagreed over the school's educational policies—he wanted more science; she wanted liberal arts. They also fought about money, how Stanford hired and fired its professors, and many other things. Jane took every battle personally because she ran the school the way she thought her son and husband would have wanted her to. She was also very rich and powerful…and she wasn't the compromising type. By 1904 there were rumors she planned to fire Jordan.

Then in January 1905, Jane Stanford was nearly murdered. Every night before bed, she drank a bottle of mineral water that was placed on her nightstand by someone on her household staff. But on this particular night, Jane took a sip and immediately spit out the liquid—and then tried to make herself vomit anything she might have ingested. She thought the water tasted strange and, after having it tested, discovered that it contained enough strychnine to kill a person in minutes. Police and private detectives investigated the poisoning but couldn't find the culprit.

MURDER MOST FOUL

Jane decided she wasn't safe in San Francisco, so the next month, she and her secretary Bertha Berner left for Hawaii and moved into the Moana Hotel in Honolulu. But their escape didn't last long—on February 28, Jane drank a bicarbonate of soda that Berner had prepared, and then went to bed. Within a couple of hours, she woke up convulsing and screaming, "I think I have been poisoned again…This is a terrible death to die!" Several doctors tried to help her, but Jane didn't make it. She died that night.

Seven doctors conducted an autopsy in Honolulu, and all agreed on the cause of death: strychnine poisoning. But President Jordan wasn't buying it. He left for Honolulu at the news of Jane's death and hired his own doctor to write a report that debunked the poisoning. Then Jordan announced to the press that Jane had died of heart failure and any doctor who said otherwise was incompetent. Following his statement, the San Francisco police department dropped its investigation into the original strychnine incident. He also discredited Jane herself, implying that her claims that she was poisoned were the emotional ravings of an irrational woman (her history with séances didn't help matters). In the end, everyone accepted Jordan's theory. Few people knew he and Jane had been at odds, and Stanford was a prestigious university. Its president carried a lot of weight.

A "MYSTERIOUS DEATH"

History accepted the verdict of heart failure until 2003 when Robert Cutler, a physician and professor emeritus at the Stanford School of Medicine, published *The Mysterious Death of Jane Stanford*. Cutler made a good case for the fact that David Starr Jordan had a motive to kill Jane Stanford—according to Cutler, she was close to gaining enough support from the board of trustees to fire Jordan. As a result of Cutler's investigation, most historians now believe she was poisoned and that Jordan covered up the crime.

But *who* actually bought and administered the strychnine remains a mystery. Over the years, some have accused a maid and a butler, but the two main suspects have always been Bertha Berner and David Starr Jordan. Berner was there at both poisonings, but she had no motive. As Jane's personal secretary, Berner was treated like a friend. She traveled the world, was paid a good salary, and seemed quite fond of her employer.

Jordan, however, had a lot to gain. With Jane Stanford out of the way, he kept his job and he had access to millions of dollars left for the school in trust. But there was no proof Jordan had access to Jane's mineral water or the bicarbonate of soda. If he bribed one of her employees, a friend, or the pharmacist to poison her, no one ever said a word. And so the case remains cold.

DESTROYING CALIFORNIA

Hollywood movies are always trying to blow up, burn down, or otherwise wreak havoc on this great state, but just how plausible are these disaster scenarios?

VOLCANO (1997)

Plot: An earthquake hits Los Angeles and causes little damage aboveground. But when a group of utility workers burns to death in a storm drain in MacArthur Park, the head of the Office of Emergency Management, Mike Roark (Tommy Lee Jones), knows something's rotten in the City of Angels. Over the course of the next few days, another earthquake shakes the city, this time causing massive damage; thick smoke rises from the La Brea Tar Pits; more city employees burn in the sewers; and a volcano caused by all the seismic disturbances erupts, spewing lava onto Wilshire Boulevard. Only geologist Amy Barnes (Anne Heche) and Roark can save the city. But can they do it in time?

Could it happen? According to geologist Ronald R. Charpentier, "Los Angeles and Southern California may have a lot of potential for earthquakes, but are probably safe from volcanoes for a while."

CONTAGION (2011)

Plot: A fast-moving, previously unknown virus kills Beth Emhoff (Gwyneth Paltrow) of Minnesota, and the Centers for Disease Control (CDC) jumps on the case in an effort to stop the disease from spreading. They fail, and the virus moves across the country and the world. In San Francisco, conspiracy blogger Alan Krumwiede (Jude Law) is convinced (or at least, tries to convince the public) that the government is exploiting the average American and trying to profit from a rush to create a vaccine. Despite the fact that San Franciscans mob local drugstores to get Krumwiede's homeopathic remedies, people in the city keep dying, local services are suspended, and trash and diseased debris pile up in the streets. Can the CDC come up with a vaccine and treatment in time to save the world?

Could it happen? W. Ian Lipkin, the director of Columbia University's Center for Infection and Immunity and the film's scientific advisor, says, "It is a plausible scenario—and it's also something in the way of a wake-up call."

THE BIRDS (1963)

Plot: Melanie Daniels (Tippi Hedren) buys a pair of lovebirds at a pet store, travels by car and boat to the seaside village of Bodega Bay, and leaves them as a gift for lawyer Mitch Brenner (Rod Taylor). While she's there, a seagull nips her head. As the next few hours turn into days, and days turn into weeks, the birds of Bodega Bay seem to lose their birdbrains and start attacking residents: Seagulls dive-bomb a children's birthday party, sparrows go after Brenner, and various townspeople have their bodies mauled and their eyes pecked out. Will Californians ever figure out what caused the rash of avian violence or how to stop it?

Could it happen? Maybe. In 2005 Alicia Craig of Indiana's Bird Conservation Alliance said, "There's been an increase in the number of times that people report incidents like, 'I had this weird thing happen where a bird attacked me.'"

MONSTERS VS. ALIENS (2009)

Plot: In this family-friendly animated disaster-ish movie, Reese Witherspoon plays Susan Murphy, a bride-to-be whose wedding day is ruined by a meteorite strike. The meteorite emits a bizarre fictional chemical called *quantonium*, which causes Murphy to grow...and grow...and grow into a giantess. When the military finds out about her, they capture her and take her to a super-secret, clandestine facility for study. There, she meets a bunch of other "monsters" like herself, including a gelantinous blob (Seth Rogen) and a half-cockroach/half-human scientist (Hugh Laurie). Meanwhile, from a compound in space, the alien Gallaxhar (Rainn Wilson) detects the quantonium radiation and sends a giant robot to Earth to check it out. Hilarity and wackiness ensue, but at one point the giant robot chases the giant Susan Murphy to the Golden Gate Bridge and into San Francisco, where the question becomes, "Who will win this battle royale?"

Could it happen? Well, it's monsters...and aliens. And did we mention that the movie is a cartoon?

HODGEPODGE

Quick! Some facts about California.

• California's population: 38 million...and growing by about 420,000 people every year. That means one out of every eight Americans lives in the Golden State.

• Currently listed as an endangered species, the riparian brush rabbit of California, a species of cottontail, lives in only one place in the world: Caswell Memorial State Park in San Joaquin County.

• The Country Store in Baker claims to have sold the most winning lottery tickets in California history.

• On February 9, 1960, actress Joanne Woodward was awarded the very first star on the Hollywood Walk of Fame—a stretch of 15 blocks along Hollywood Boulevard and three blocks along Vine Street. Since then, more than 2,400 more stars have been molded into the sidewalk.

• California boasts more theme and amusement parks (47) than any other state.

• San Diego has the world's largest military complex: More than 100,000 active-duty soldiers live in the city, including 35 percent of all U.S. Marines and 32 percent of all members of the U.S. Navy.

• Three of America's top five oil fields are located in Kern County, which produces 10 percent of all U.S. oil.

• Only wild (undammed) river in the state: the Smith in the Klamath Mountains.

• The practice of bringing home a "doggie bag" from a restaurant began in the 1940s, when World War II rationing made wasting food a no-no and diners were encouraged to save money and supplies by feeding their dogs (or cats) their dine-out leftovers. San Francisco was one of the first (some say *the* first) places to offer patrons an easy way to take their scraps home. The city's Restaurant Association created cartons called Pet Pakits in 1943 and began distributing them to local eateries.

The band Van Halen formed in Pasadena in 1972 under the name Mammoth.

THE UCLA–USC PRANK WAR

On page 66, we introduced the Cal–Stanford rivalry, one of the most brutal in college sports. But for Southern Californians, nothing…and we repeat, nothing…is more of a battle than the annual UCLA–USC football game. And the pranks these schools have pulled over the years aren't too shabby either.

• In 1947, just before the annual USC (Trojans) vs. UCLA (Bruins) football game, a group of Bruins kidnapped USC's mascot, a mutt named George Tirebiter. With kickoff only hours away, the perpetrators returned the canine safe and sound, but with an entirely new look—they'd shaved a large "UCLA" into his fur. The Trojans didn't panic, though. Instead, they called to action several USC sorority sisters who quickly knitted a red-and-gold sweater for Tirebiter to wear…thus saving the Trojan faithful from humiliation.

Uncle John Extra: Tirebiter met a sad end under the wheels of a car a few years later and was followed by a succession of other Tirebiters until 1961, when a white stallion in the Rose Parade caught the attention of a USC official. The official asked the rider to participate in the next home game, and thus was born Traveller, the current USC mascot.

• At the 1958 matchup, USC interlopers managed to steal all of the game-day editions of the *Daily Bruin*, UCLA's student newspaper. The thieves replaced them with newspapers that looked real, but included a front-page interview with the UCLA coach in which he was quoted as saying, "I can't see any hope for our team."

• The life-size bronze statue of Tommy Trojan, an ancient soldier wearing a helmet and holding a sword, is a revered icon that typically stands in the middle of the USC campus. But before the big UCLA–USC football showdown in 1953, a group of enterprising UCLA students sneaked Tommy off campus under the cover of night. They sawed off the arm that carried the sword, and then welded it back on so that it looked like Tommy was stabbing himself in the back. (And then they returned it to USC.)

Legoland California's largest model (a dinosaur) contains more than 2 million blocks…

• In 1939 the UCLA Alumni Association gave the school a beautiful brass bell for cheerleaders to ring every time the Bruins scored. A relic from an old Southern Pacific freight locomotive, the "Victory Bell" became controversial two years later when six members of USC's Sigma Phi Epsilon fraternity dressed as Bruin fans slipped into the UCLA rooting section at the annual football matchup. With the crowd distracted by the game, no one noticed the brazen six loading the bell onto a truck and driving off with it. USC managed to hide the bell for a year—initially in a frat basement, but then at several homes in the Hollywood Hills and Santa Ana. At one point, the students stashed it in a haystack to outwit investigators. Finally, in 1942, the bell was returned and the two schools reached a truce: Henceforth, the bell would be a trophy, awarded to whomever won the annual football game between the two schools. As of 2011, the score was 46–28 in favor of the Trojans.

• During finals week, 1989, a group of USC students bought 20,000 crickets and divided them into two groups: 10,000 were painted a bright cardinal red, and the other 10,000 a brilliant gold (USC colors). Then the merry pranksters set out for the UCLA campus, where they released the crickets in the school's main library. Just before making a hasty retreat, the Trojans also posted signs on the library walls that proclaimed, "Hope you enjoy studying, Bruins. USC beat UCLA!"

• In 1958 UCLA students designed what they believed would be the greatest prank ever. The plan: Hire a helicopter, swoop down on Tommy Trojan, and dump 500 pounds of manure on the statue. But it was football season, and since Tommy was the frequent target of UCLA vandals, student guards were camped out nearby to provide 24-hour surveillance. On the eve of the big game, the rented whirlybird appeared suddenly over Tommy. The Bruins aboard slid the door open and then let loose with the manure, taking aim at Tommy's head below. But the pranksters hadn't accounted for the effect of the helicopter blades. Their rotation sucked the manure upward...back into the helicopter, splattering it all over the perps' faces, while the Trojan guards cheered from the ground below.

WHEN ANIMALS ATTACK!

Cougars and rattlesnakes and bears, oh my! California's backcountry is full of dangerous animals. How can unsuspecting hikers protect themselves? Read on.

MOUNTAIN LIONS
Puma, cougar, panther—all are names for the same animal, best known in California as the mountain lion. These cats can be huge—up to six feet long and 225 pounds. Mountain lions roam all over the state (and into Mexico and Central and South America), but attacks are rare: the California Department of Fish and Game reports only 16 mountain lion attacks in the state since 1890, and only six of those were fatal. Still, park officials (and regular people) consider mountain lions dangerous enough to warn hikers about them. A few tips:

• Never hike alone; mountain lions are less likely to attack groups. And don't hike at dusk or dawn, when the cats are more likely to be out hunting.

• Make noise while you're hiking.

• If you see a mountain lion, don't run, don't turn your back on it, and never approach it. Leave plenty of space for it to escape.

• If the animal attacks, stand tall, yell, fight back...and keep fighting. According to some, mountain lions don't have a lot of endurance. The hope is that they'll give up on you and go looking for something weaker, like deer.

RATTLESNAKES
California is home to nine different species of rattlesnakes: the northern Pacific, western diamondback, sidewinder, speckled, red diamond, southern Pacific, great basin, Mojave, and Santa Catalina Island rattlesnake, which actually has no rattle. (The Santa Catalina climbs trees and eats birds on Catalina Island, so it evolved over time to lose the noisy rattle that let prey know it was coming.) Rattlers make their homes in a variety of habitats: grasslands, rocky hills, deserts, swamps, scrub brush, and meadows, and they're a common sight for hikers, especially in Southern

California. For the most part, these snakes are pacifists—they rarely attack unless provoked. Some tips:

• Never stick your hands anywhere that you can't see, and be careful of picking up "sticks" when you're in the water. Rattlesnakes are able to swim.

• Always wear hiking boots when you go into the wilderness, never sandals, flip-flops, or bare feet.

• If you see a rattlesnake in the wild, don't attack it. Most bites occur when people try to harass or kill the animals. Snakes really are more afraid of humans than we are of them, so leave them alone.

• Give the snake a wide berth so it doesn't feel threatened.

• If you are bitten, get medical help right away. Most rattlesnake bites aren't fatal, but they should always be treated.

BEARS

Like mountain lion attacks, bear attacks are rare in California—since 1980, the Department of Fish and Game has recorded only 13 incidents. But for lots of Californians who like to hike and camp in the state's wilderness, that's 12 too many. So what should you do to protect yourself in the wild?

• Make a lot of noise while you're hiking to let bears know you're around. Most likely, they'll keep their distance.

• While camping, always store your food, toiletries, and trash in bear-proof containers or in your car's trunk. Never feed bears or leave food out at your camp.

• If you encounter a bear and it attacks, don't run. Some bears can run as fast as racehorses. Instead, fight back—turn to face the animal, make a lot of noise, and try to appear as large as possible.

• Never approach a bear or pick up a cub...the mother will probably be nearby.

*　　*　　*

California has its own state tartan registered with the Scottish Tartan Authority.

Of the 5,000 Californian plant species, about 30% are unique to the state.

WHY DO THEY HATE US?

They're just jealous.

"There is science, logic, reason; there is thought verified by experience. And then there is California."
—**Edward Abbey**

"Whatever starts in California unfortunately has an inclination to spread."
—**Jimmy Carter**

"California is like an artificial limb the rest of the country doesn't really need."
—**Saul Bellow**

"This is California. Blondes are like, the state flower or something."
—**Steve, *Beverly Hills 90210***

"El Salvador has the scenery of Northern California and the climate of Southern California plus—and this was a relief—no Californians."
—**P. J. O'Rourke**

"I especially like California when it's not moving. The idea of the ground opening up and sucking me in is not my idea of a good time."
—**Matina Bevis**

"It's a scientific fact that if you stay in California you lose one point of your IQ every year."
—**Truman Capote**

"California is a great place to live if you're an orange."
—**Fred Allen**

"Los Angeles makes the rest of California seem authentic."
—**Jonathan Culler**

"Southern California, where the American dream came too true."
—**Lawrence Ferlinghetti**

"There's nothing wrong with Southern California that a rise in the ocean level wouldn't cure."
—**Ross MacDonald**

"I wouldn't want to live in California. All that sun makes you sterile."
—**Alan Alda**

"California is the land of perpetual pubescence, where cultural lag is mistaken for renaissance."
—**Ashley Montagu**

"I love California. I practically grew up in Phoenix." —Dan Quayle

WELCOME TO ZZYZX, CALIFORNIA

Our A to Z tour of California place names continues.
(Anaheim through Malibu appears on page 24.)

MANHATTAN BEACH

A man named John Merrill owned a lot of the land that eventually became Manhattan Beach, and named the town around 1900 after his hometown—not the New York borough, but Manhattan Beach, a residential section of Brooklyn.

MENLO PARK

In the 1850s, two Irish immigrants named their 1,700-acre Northern California spread for Menlo, their native village in County Galway. They put up a big sign in front of their adjacent houses that read "Menlo Park." When the railroad came through in 1863, the government made it official.

NEEDLES

Located in the Mojave Desert on the western banks of the Colorado River, the city of Needles is named for "the Needles," a group of pointed rocks just across the river in Arizona.

PASADENA

Pasadena was first settled by a group of Midwesterners who called it "the Indiana Colony"…until the postal service told them they'd have to change the name if they wanted their own post office. So one of the town fathers suggested four names that someone had translated into Chippewa: "Crown of the Valley," "Key of the Valley," "Peak of the Valley," and "Hill of the Valley." The town fathers decided that they liked the word that all of the names ended in: "pa-sa-de-na," which means "of the valley."

PLACERVILLE

The lure of riches attracted a lot shady characters to California's

---

Snoopy's brother Spike hails from Needles.

gold country, and many of them reached an unpleasant end by hanging in a mining center in northeastern California that came to be called Hangtown. But a bunch of do-gooders from the local churches and the temperance league didn't like the name. They pushed for a change, and in 1854, it was good-bye Hangtown, hello Placerville. The town's new, more respectable name referred to a *placer* (pronounced PLASS-er), a deposit of sand or gravel in the bed of a river or lake that contains valuable minerals.

SCARFACE

This name honors a Native American warrior known as Scarface Charley, who served on the Native American side during the Modoc War of 1872–73, a conflict between the Modoc tribe and the U.S. Army around the Oregon–California border.

TARZANA

According to legend, Edgar Rice Burroughs, the author of *Tarzan of the Apes*, bought 550 acres in the San Fernando Valley in 1919 and named his new spread Tarzana Ranch, in honor of the book that had made his new life as a land baron possible. A few years later, Burroughs sold 100 acres of the ranch to be turned into a subdivision called Tarzana Tract. Finally, in 1927, the locals petitioned for a post office and held a contest to name their new town: Tarzana won by a landslide.

TRUCKEE

The town of Truckee's claim to fame is that it's where the famous and unfortunate Donner party spent their last winter. But a happier story is how Truckee got its name: Pioneers crossing the Sierra Nevadas in the 1840s encountered a tribe of friendly Paiutes. To welcome the travelers, the Paiute chief rode toward them calling, "Trokay," which was both his name and the Paiute word for "everything is all right." The visitors started calling him "Tru-ki-zo," and the town of Truckee—after a little fiddling with the spelling—was named in his honor.

VOLCANO

There is no volcano in or near Volcano, California, but early prospectors assumed the bowl-shaped valley the town was set in was the crater of a once-active volcano. It's not. It's just a valley.

WHITTIER

First settled by Quakers, Whittier was small and isolated in the early days. But as the city grew in the late 1800s, the locals decided to name it after Quaker poet John Greenleaf Whittier, who felt honored enough to write a poem called "My Name I Give to Thee" for the town's dedication.

YOU BET

Founded as a mining town in 1858 in the Sierra Nevada Mountains, You Bet had its own post office until 1903. "You bet!" was the favorite expression of a local saloon keeper—hence the name.

YREKA

The name Yreka (pronounced why-REE-kuh) comes from the Shasta Indian *wáik'a*, which is what the local indigenous people called nearby Mount Shasta, meaning either "north mountain" or "white mountain." But Mark Twain spun his own tale of how the town got its name: His story goes that a stranger walking by saw a canvas sign for a bakery. The sign had been folded over and showed all the letters backwards except the B, so it looked like this: YREKA.

ZZYZX

At one time, Zzyzx (rhymes with "pie mix") was a health spa built around mineral springs in the Mojave Desert. The spa was the brainchild of Curtis Howe Springer, a radio evangelist and self-proclaimed medicine man (and alleged quack) who squatted on the land there in the 1940s. Thirty years later, the government reclaimed the acreage and arrested Springer for misuse of public lands. The spa buildings were eventually converted for the use of California State University's Desert Studies Center. The name Zzyzx, which Springer had advertised as "the last word in health," still gets the last word—it's the last place name listed in the United States Board of Geographic Names. And where did the word actually come from? Springer made it up.

WE ♥ CHICO

Herb Caen, the late San Francisco columnist, once famously said that Chico was a place "where you find Velveeta in the gourmet cheese section." But Chico isn't really that unsophisticated—it even has a college (with the reputation of being a party school, but still...).

• Chico, located in Northern California's Butte County, was named after a language spoken by Native Americans who lived in the region. Today, the language is extinct.

• Bidwell Park may not be well known outside of Chico, but it should be. It's the third largest municipal park in California, and 13th largest in the United States, making it bigger than more famous outdoor areas like Golden Gate Park and New York's Central Park.

• Streets named after trees are pretty common, but Chico has a sly variation on the theme: The "tree" streets that run through California State University, Chico, are Chestnut, Hazel, Ivy, Cherry, and Orange, making a nifty acronym of the city's name.

• The world's largest buyer of organic hops is Chico's Sierra Nevada Brewing Company. It's the sixth largest brewery in the country, roiling and fermenting since its founding in 1980.

• Chico tempted fate by opening a Titan missile site on April Fool's Day, 1961. The U.S. Air Force bought farmland about six miles outside the city limits and began work on a $40 million Titan missile base—digging out 600,000 cubic yards of soil and rocks, and installing 32,000 cubic yards of concrete, 300 tons of pipes, and 90 miles of wiring. Although the site officially opened in April 1961, it wasn't until a year later that the missiles were all in place. Then, on May 24, an explosion rocked Chico and destroyed one of the missile silos. Two weeks later, a flash fire destroyed another silo and killed a worker. Rebuilding the silos and fixing the errors took a year and at least $1 million more, but finally the Chico Titan Base became operational on March 9, 1963. It lasted only two years. In May 1964, the secretary of

---

Given name of legendary 49ers quarterback Y. A. Tittle: Yelberton Abraham.

defense announced that Titan missiles were going to be phased out. By the next year, the very expensive base was deactivated and abandoned.

• Chico's Warner Street was named for the Warner Bros. movie studio. The actual Warner brothers (Jack, Harry, Albert, and Sam) never lived in the city, but during the 1930s, their studio filmed parts of two huge movies there—*The Adventures of Robin Hood* and *Gone With the Wind*. That inspired Chico to rename the north end of Ivy Street in the hopes that more big-budget movies would be filmed there. (They weren't.)

• Chico got a lot of press in November 1921 when mysterious stones of various sizes (some as small as peas, others as large as baseballs) began falling in front of a warehouse at Fifth and Orange Streets, often from a cloudless sky. The stones continued through March of the next year and often increased in frequency when newspaper reporters or city officials came by to inspect the site. The bombardment stopped abruptly in the spring of 1922. Why? It was all a hoax. A local resident later confessed to using a catapult to launch the rocks over the building.

• Not as easily explained was a report on August 20, 1878, by a local newspaper, later reprinted in the *New York Times*, that "more than a dozen men" saw hundreds of various types of fish measuring one to three inches fall from the afternoon sky across several acres. Residents never did find out what had actually happened in that case.

*   *   *

DID YOU KNOW?

On May 7, 1943, in a Richmond shipyard, actress and singer Lena Horne christened the SS *George Washington Carver*. It was only the second U.S. Navy ship in history to be named for an African American. (The first was the SS *Harmon*, which honored Mess Attendant First Class Leonard Roy Harmon, a posthumous winner of the Navy Cross for heroism in the 1942 Battle of Guadalcanal.)

Richard Nixon's favorite movie: *Patton*.

MURDER, HE WROTE, PART II

On page 76, we told you about author Dashiell Hammett's
spooky foray into the mysterious underworld of the detective
novel. Now, we'll get to know his successor.

R AYMOND THORNTON CHANDLER
Born in Chicago but raised in England, Raymond Chandler's
classic British education left him with a lifelong love of literature. After graduation, he tried to make a living in London as a journalist and a poet, but soon realized that he wasn't very good at either occupation. So he moved to the United States and eventually settled in Los Angeles. Unlike Dashiell Hammett, Chandler had no experience as a detective. He did have experience with violence and death, though: Chandler fought for Great Britain during World War I and was the only member of his unit to survive. As for greedy con men, cops, and politicians, Chandler learned all about them as an executive for Dabney Oil during the L.A. oil boom.

After a drinking problem cost Chandler that executive job in 1932, he began writing detective stories for the *Black Mask*, the same pulp magazine Hammett wrote for. By 1939 Chandler was writing successful novels, and he went on to write three screenplays for Hollywood.

Chandler brought some literary romanticism to his stories. His investigator Philip Marlowe was "a more honorable man than you or I," a modern knight trying to protect the helpless and bring them justice. Chandler was also famous for brightening up the detective tale with unique descriptions like this one: "It was a blonde. A blonde to make a bishop kick a hole in a stained-glass window."

THE BIG SLEEP
The Premise (Spoiler Alert!): In Chandler's first and most famous novel, *The Big Sleep* (1939), Los Angeles is a bleak, corrupt town. An invalid named General Sternwood, who's being blackmailed with scandalous photos of his younger daughter Carmen,

hires investigator Philip Marlowe to look into the case. Sternwood asks Marlowe to stop the blackmailer. During their conversation, the general also mentions that his older daughter's husband, Rusty Reagan, has gone missing. Having taken a liking to the ailing general, Marlowe not only goes after the blackmailer, but also tries to find Reagan. After dealing with murders, gamblers, and double crosses, Marlowe winds up protecting the old military man from the knowledge that Rusty Reagan is sleeping the "big sleep" because Carmen killed him.

MARLOWE AT THE MOVIES
Humphrey Bogart played Phillip Marlowe in the 1946 film version of *The Big Sleep*. This film noir is most famous for the steamy relationship between Marlowe and Vivian, Sternwood's older daughter, who was played by Lauren Bacall, Bogart's real-life wife. *The Big Sleep* was so full of murderous twists that Bogart himself had a question about the plot: Did Sternwood's chauffeur kill himself or was he murdered? No one on the set knew the answer, so they called Chandler. He didn't have the answer either.

The Big Sleep returned to theaters in 1978 in a remake starring Robert Mitchum as a tough, honorable Marlowe.

MARLOWE'S LOS ANGELES
• Marlowe had an office on the top floor of the six-story Cahuenga Building in Hollywood.

• Angelenos still enjoy the Musso & Frank Grill on Hollywood Boulevard, where Marlowe (and Chandler) enjoyed a good meal

• Not far from Musso's, on the 6600 block of Hollywood Boulevard, was Stanley Rose's bookstore...transformed by Chandler into a porn store operated by the villain who was blackmailing General Sternwood.

* * *

"Hollywood is the kind of town where they stick a knife in your back and then have you arrested for carrying a concealed weapon."

—**Philip Marlowe**

HORSING AROUND

When it comes to horse racing, California has some of the world's coolest tracks.

• Seabiscuit ran his last race at Santa Anita Park in Arcadia in 1940.

• In 1942 Santa Anita Park became a holding area for 20,000 Japanese Americans scheduled to be interned throughout the western United States.

• From 1942 to 1944, there was no horse racing at Del Mar either, but the site was used as a Marine training area and a manufacturing site for B-17 bombers.

• The Del Mar Racetrack, located across the street from the beach just north of San Diego, is famously known as the place "where the surf meets the turf." In 1937 Bing Crosby wrote and recorded a song by that name as a way to commemorate the track's opening. It's still played before the first race of every season.

• Before 1933, gambling was illegal in California, so most celebrities and high rollers crossed the Mexican border at San Diego and headed for Agua Caliente, a resort that also operated a horse racetrack between 1929 and 1992. That track introduced many innovations to the sport of horse racing, including safety helmets for jockeys and starting gates.

• The longest continuously operating racetrack in California: Bay Meadows in San Mateo ran races from November 1934 until August 2008, when it closed.

• Among the original 600 shareholders of the Hollywood Park Racetrack were some Tinseltown stars: Walt Disney, Bing Crosby, Al Jolson, Darryl Zanuck, and Jack Warner (one of the founders of Warner Bros.), among others.

• Frank Vessels Sr., who opened Orange County's Los Alamitos Race Course in 1947, had only $19 in his pocket when he arrived in California in 1920. He made a fortune in construction, though, and today, Los Alamitos runs an annual race with a $2 million purse, among the highest payouts of any track in the United States.

SURF'S UP!

A tanned surfer ripping a cresting wave has become one of Southern California's most iconic images, but the craze really began in Hawaii. Here's a history of surfing. Shaka, brah.

HE'E NALU

There's some evidence that the first surfers may have been from Peru, but all of the sport's known history comes from the Polynesians, who settled the many island chains in the Pacific Ocean and have been surfing for at least 3,000 years. The Hawaiian Islands were among the last that the settlers reached, sometime around AD 400. These pioneers depended on the ocean for their livelihood and were skilled at navigating the white water that surrounded their island homes. Their surfing skills were a byproduct of their canoeing skills—the ability to pilot a canoe through heavy surf onto an unprotected beach was key to their survival. Early Hawaiians called the sport *he'e nalu*, or "wave sliding," and rode two different types of boards: *Olo* boards were 16 to 18 feet long (or even longer) and could weigh 150 pounds or more. More common was the shorter type of board called *alaia*. At 8 to 10 feet long, it was lighter and more maneuverable than the olo, and is the forerunner of the modern surfboard.

WALKING ON WATER

Surfing played a huge role in Hawaiian culture. The most revered wave riders were members of the *ali'i*, or "noble class." They were often political leaders who competed against each other while entire communities cheered from the beach. The priests, or *kahunas*, would pray each morning for good waves. But it wasn't just the leaders who surfed—nearly everyone in old Hawaii rode the waves, regardless of age, gender, or class.

When British explorer Captain James Cook's Third Pacific Expedition arrived there in 1778, his men were amazed—the natives were zipping through the sea while standing upright on wooden planks. One sailer wrote, "The boldness and address with which I saw them perform these difficult and dangerous maneuvers was altogether astonishing and is scarcely to be believed."

California's oldest amusement park: the Santa Cruz Beach Boardwalk.

WIPEOUT

Although the Europeans who first landed in Hawaii were awed by the native surf culture, the missionaries who came later were not amused. They disliked the idea of scantily clad natives frolicking on the beach, so they tried to suppress the sport. In the century after Captain Cook's arrival, the native population of Hawaii dropped from an estimated 300,000 to just 40,000—and surfing nearly vanished. Fortunately, the determined Hawaiians who survived 19th-century colonialism refused to stop riding the waves.

Later visitors were just as impressed as Cook's men had been. On a trip to Hawaii in the 1860s, Mark Twain gave "surf-bathing" a try. "I got the board placed right," he wrote, "and at the right moment, too; but missed the connection myself. The board struck the shore in three-quarters of a second, without any cargo, and I struck the bottom about the same time, with a couple of barrels of water in me."

By the turn of the 20th century, tourism had become integral to the Hawaiian economy for both natives and non-natives. White businessmen romanticized the island culture, and native Hawaiians found that one of the few ways to earn a living was by providing tourists with an "authentic" island experience. One such tourist was novelist and newspaper correspondent Jack London, who took a surfing lesson at Waikiki Beach in 1907 with a 23-year-old "beach boy" of mixed Hawaiian and Irish descent named George Freeth. In a magazine article titled "A Royal Sport," London described Freeth as "a young god bronzed with sunburn" who "leaped upon the back of the sea" and stood "calm and superb, poised on the giddy summit…flying as fast as the surge on which he stands."

CALIFORNIA DREAMIN'

Twain's and London's colorful accounts caught the attention of mainlanders looking for new adventures. In a bid to bring that island culture to the States, wealthy California businessman Henry Huntington (for whom the Huntington Library in Pasadena and the Orange County town of Huntington Beach are named) hired Freeth to come to California and give regularly scheduled surfing demonstrations. Huntington's goal: To promote the seaside town of Redondo Beach. He'd recently built a rail line connecting it to Los Angeles, and he wanted to convince the citizens of L.A. that a weekend at the beach was a good way to spend their leisure money. Once the idea caught on, Huntington made a fortune selling oceanfront property. Southern Californians came out in droves to see Freeth ride the waves—and many didn't want to go back home at the end of the weekend.

Another surfing ambassador, Olympic swimming star Duke Kahanamoku, came to California in 1912 and gave similar demonstrations. He went on to become the most famous surfer of the early 1900s.

Solidifying surfing's place as a viable sport, Californians organized the Pacific Coast Surfriding Championships in 1928 at Corona Del Mar and held the event annually until 1941, when it was interrupted by World War II. After the war, California culture exploded. Americans from all over the country headed west in droves to take advantage of the good jobs and booming economy. With an ever-increasing number of people on the beach, just one last piece remained to move surfing from a niche hobby to a national phenomenon: the development of cheap, lightweight, mass-produced surfboards.

BUSTIN' SURFBOARDS
Until the late 1940s, boards were made of solid wood and weighed 80 to 100 pounds. It took a lot of physical strength and determination to wrestle one of those old planks through the waves. That all changed when board makers figured out how to seal lightweight balsa wood inside a thin layer of fiberglass resin. These new boards were about 10 feet long, weighed only 20 to 35 pounds, and were far more buoyant than their heavier predecessors. In time, expensive balsa wood was replaced by molded plastic foam, making true mass production possible for the first time. With that, surfing suddenly became a lot cheaper...and a lot easier.

Just as it had in Hawaii centuries before, surfing became more than just a sport; it was also the center of an entire culture—in this case, pop culture. It began in 1957 when Hollywood screenwriter Frederick Kohner created a character based on his teenage daughter's exploits in the burgeoning surf scene at Malibu Beach.

He named the character Gidget, short for "Girl Midget." The Gidget franchise went on to include six novels, three films, and a television series. Surf movies became drive-in staples: Elvis Presley rode the waves in 1961 in *Blue Hawaii*; and in 1966 filmmaker Bruce Brown made what has become the classic surf documentary, *The Endless Summer*, which followed two surfers as they spent the summer chasing waves around the globe.

By the mid-1960s, teenagers from the quiet shores of the East Coast to the landlocked Midwest were watching Gidget movies and listening to the Beach Boys. Those kids dreamed of moving to California to take up the surfing lifestyle. And as they did—in droves—California boomed.

WAVE GOOD-BYE

But for the old guard of surfers who'd pioneered California's version of the sport, all this new attention wasn't necessarily a good thing. More than the Hollywood sanitization of their lifestyle, they grumbled that their once-pristine beaches had become crowded overnight. Many of them left California and relocated to Hawaii…or to wherever on earth they could find big waves.

RANDOM FACTS

• George Freeth was the first to bring surfing to the masses, but as far back as 1885, a group of princes from Hawaii took a trip to Santa Cruz and rode the waves on surfboards made of redwood.

• California has one of the biggest big-wave surf spots in the world: Mavericks, a break off Pillar Point in San Mateo County, often sees waves 25 feet high…and 80-footers on a really good day.

• Dale "Daily" Webster of Bodega Bay, California, surfed every day from September 3, 1975, to September 3, 2010—12,784 days in a row. (He worked nights so he'd never miss an opportunity to catch a wave.)

* * *

"Surfing soothes me, it's always been a kind of Zen experience for me. The ocean is so magnificent, peaceful, and awesome. The rest of the world disappears for me when I'm on a wave."

—**Paul Walker**

Only Beach Boy who ever really surfed: drummer Dennis Wilson.

MORE NOTABLE ASPHALT

*Like any good traffic jam, our list of freeway trivia just goes
on and on...and on. (Part I appears on page 17.)*

THAT SINKING FEELING

Constructed in 1937, Devil's Slide is not for the faint of heart. According to many California engineers, the stretch of Highway 1 between Pacifica and Half Moon Bay should never have been built on the steep, rocky outcropping above the Pacific. Every few years, Devil's Slide is closed due to landslides—in 2006 the road was closed for four months. Environmentalists, developers, and Caltrans engineers have argued for decades about the solution. Finally, in 2007, Caltrans began boring two tunnels through the mountain behind the sinking roadway. These tunnels, scheduled to open in 2012, will be 30 feet wide and 4,200 feet long, and they'll permanently divert traffic from Devil's Slide.

CHICKEN RUN

The Hollywood Freeway—along U.S. 101/170, between U.S. 110 and I-5—in Los Angeles has a flighty reputation, but that's got nothing to with show biz weirdness. In 1969 a poultry truck turned over on the freeway, and hundreds of chickens on their way to the slaughterhouse made their escape. The driver tried to round them up, but at least 200 got away and set up homes in the brush along the road, affectionately known to commuters as "the Freeway Chickens." The birds found a savior in Minnie Blumfield, and elderly woman who brought them food and water. By 1976 Minnie was 90 and could no longer care for them. So she agreed to let Caltrans round up the birds and take them to a farm (a real farm...not a slaughterhouse disguised as a farm). To this day, Caltrans maintains that the roundup was a success, but commuters along the Hollywood Freeway still report sightings of feral chickens.

THE FRIENDLIEST FREEWAY

Every morning (and some afternoons) on various overpasses along the Fresno section of Route 41, Cheryl "Monique" Turks gives morning commuters a break from road rage with enthusiastic

---

The original United Nations charter was drafted and signed in 1945 in San Francisco.

smiles and friendly waves. Drivers usually respond in kind, honking their horns or waving back.

THE SPOOKY STRETCH

Highway 152 between Los Banos and Gilroy is the most direct route from many parts of the Central Valley to the Bay Area. About 15 miles of the road climbs over Mt. Diablo along a route called Pacheco Pass, a scenic and dangerous road with a reputation for accidents. But some people don't blame the winding highway for the misfortune—they wonder if drivers are plagued by supernatural distractions because the pass is famous for being haunted.

Historically, the route was the trail of choice for the Ausaymus Indians, wagon trains, and bandits, and Pacheco Pass has a bloody history. When famous psychic Sylvia Browne traveled on the pass she called it "hell," claiming that she could "feel" the suffering wrought by battles between the Spaniards, Mexicans, Americans, and Native Americans. Other psychics (and ordinary drivers) have reported seeing ghosts on the mountain, including a screaming woman in Victorian dress searching for her child, and another screaming woman who appears as a passenger in a phantom car.

* * *

SIG ALERTS

A "sig alert" is a warning broadcast by radio and TV stations, Web sites, and electronic signs to alert drivers to a traffic jam or other unusual or hazardous traffic conditions. But where did the term come from? Many Californians seem think that it's short for signal alerts, but it's actually named after the man who came up with the idea, the late Loyd C. Sigmon, an executive at KMPC radio in Los Angeles. In the 1950s, in an attempt to boost ratings, Sigmon installed a receiver linked to the LAPD so that whenever there was an accident, a signal would alert the KMPC radio engineer. The engineer could then pick up the information and relay its affect on traffic to listeners. They called those broadcasts "Sigmon traffic alerts," and other stations started doing them, too.

OPENING LINES

Here are some great opening lines from some quintessentially California books. How many have you read?

"My father has asked me to be the fourth corner at the Joy Luck Club. I am to replace my mother, whose seat at the mah jong table has been empty since she died two months ago. My father thinks she was killed by her own thoughts."

—Amy Tan, *The Joy Luck Club*

"The Santa Anas blew in hot from the desert, shriveling the last of the spring grass into whiskers of pale straw."

—Janet Fitch, *White Oleander*

"My childhood ended the day I woke up with my underwear missing."

—Amy Asbury, *The Sunset Strip Diaries*

"Everyone is born with some special talent, and Eliza Sommers discovered early on that she had two: a good sense of smell and a good memory."

—Isabel Allende, *Daughter of Fortune: A Novel*

Afterward, he tried to reduce it to abstract terms, an accident in a world of accidents, the collision of opposing forces—the bumper of his car and the frail scrambling hunched-over form of a dark little man with a wild look in his eyes—but he wasn't very successful."

—T. C. Boyle, *The Tortilla Curtain*

"Samuel Spade's jaw was long and bony, his chin a jutting v under the more flexible v of his mouth. His yellow-grey eyes were horizontal."

—Dashiell Hammett, *The Maltese Falcon*

"The Salinas Valley is in Northern California. It is a long narrow swale between two ranges of mountains, and the Salinas River winds and twists up the center until it falls at last into Monterey Bay."

—John Steinbeck, *East of Eden*

Only Californian to win the Nobel Prize for Literature: John Steinbeck (1962).

THE SUPER BALL INVASION

The year: 1989. The place: Fullerton. The problem: The streets were flooded with thousands of bouncing elastic balls.

THE AMAZING ZECTRON

In the 1960s, chemists at the Wham-O toy company outside Los Angeles perfected a type of synthetic rubber called Zectron. Its primary benefit: The rubber in Zectron was so compressed that it held 50,000 pounds of pressure, making it extremely bouncy. That made Zectron the perfect substance to create a toy ball called a Super Ball. Pretty soon, kids all over America were bouncing them off of ceilings and rooftops, chasing them around the house, even breaking chandeliers and vases. The balls had an amazing 90 percent recovery, so if a kid dropped one from shoulder level, it would spring back almost as high. And when a Super Ball was thrown, it could jump a three-story building. Wham-O's headquarters in San Gabriel couldn't make them fast enough and had to hire four additional factories to help. One was on East Santa Fe Avenue in Fullerton.

But as fads do, Super Balls faded out a few years later. Schools banned them for causing disruptions. At least one father demanded a refund ($1 at the time) after he bounced one and got smacked in the face on its rebound. In the end, the Fullerton factory still had thousands of Super Balls it couldn't sell stored in a warehouse. For years, the building and its stock were abandoned.

INVASION OF THE BALL SNATCHERS

Then, in 1989, a strange thing started happening. Parents coming home from work, students at Fullerton College, kids at Acacia Elementary and Troy High School, pedestrians on the streets— all were bouncing Super Balls. Red, blue, multicolor, small, medium, large, even the less-bouncy Firetron version had invaded the town. Mischievous teens filled the beds of their trucks and dumped them in the courtyards of rival schools. Some drivers let the toys fly onto busy streets, filling up fields and gutters. As people tossed them at friends and strangers, balls overran the city. But where had they come from?

Pretty soon, a rumor began that the old Super Ball factory had exploded. (Some Fullerton residents still believe it today.) But no one had seen or heard anything like that. Finally some curious locals went to investigate. They found the old factory under construction...and quickly discovered where all the balls had come from. Workers had uncovered the stash of toys when they started building, and someone classified them as "hazardous waste." But instead of actually disposing of the balls, the lazy crew just opened up the containers and dumped them. One lot was more than two feet deep in Super Balls.

THE REAL DEAL

These weren't just any old Super Balls, either. The balls found in 1989 were the original, larger balls made at the old Wham-O factory (not the cheaper, less-bouncy ones made later in China). The balls were printed with the original Atom logo (which Wham-O had used to convey how explosive the balls were, and copyrighted in 1965). There were also some special Super Ball Golf Balls in the mix. These were the highest-bouncing of all because their dimples create additional compression. Today, some sell for more than $100. Eventually, all the balls in Fullerton were either collected or lost. Some sold to collectors. But kids who grew up there still remember the days of the Super Ball bonanza.

*   *   *

SUPER BALL BOWL

Super Balls aren't all bounce and no substance. In fact, the toy loaned its name—sort of—to a modern American sports institution. In the 1960s, when Lamar Hunt, founder of the American Football League (later part of the NFL), observed his kids playing with bouncy Super Balls, he thought up the name Super Bowl as a joke. (College football championships had been called "bowl games" since the 1920s.) When it came time for the first pro football championship in January 1967, no one had a better name for the game, so the Super Bowl it was.

CALI-FORE-NIA

California is home to more than 1,000 golf courses, and many of them have at least one interesting story. Here are a few.

FORE!
Course: Bel Air Country Club
City: Los Angeles
Claim to Fame: In 1921 silent film actor Fatty Arbuckle was charged with raping and killing a young woman he'd met at a party in San Francisco. Even though Arbuckle was acquitted, the scandal followed him for the rest of his life, and the Bel Air Country Club went so far as to ban celebrities from membership. Officials worried that the fast-living Hollywood types might cause trouble or bring shame on the club. The ban was reversed during the Great Depression, and in 1936 new member Howard Hughes showed the club what kind of trouble he could make: Late for a golf-date with Katharine Hepburn, Hughes landed his Sikorsky Amphibian airplane on the eighth fairway and then joined her for the back nine.

A BIT OF SCOTLAND IN YOUR CALIFORNIA?
Course: The Links at Spanish Bay
City: Pebble Beach
Claim to Fame: Course codesigner and six-time PGA Tour Player of the Year Tom Watson said, "Spanish Bay is so much like Scotland, you can almost hear the bagpipes." And actually, you really can hear the bagpipes. Every night before sunset, golfers at the Links—a Scottish word that means "sandy wasteland, usually by the sea"—hear the skirl of a bagpiper as he parades in full tartan over the first tee and out along the water.

HOLE-IN-102
Course: Bidwell Park Golf Course
City: Chico
Claim to Fame: On April 5, 2007, a 102-year-old woman named Elsie McLean became the oldest person to hit a regulation hole in

one (with witnesses!). "For an old lady," she said, "I still hit the ball pretty good." McLean knows the course well—she's been playing there since 1934.

CAN I TRADEMARK THIS TREE?
Course: Pebble Beach Golf Links
City: Pebble Beach
Claim to Fame: The Lone Cypress, a 250-year-old tree, was made famous by American photographer Ansel Adams, who took a well-known picture of it. It's also the symbol of Pebble Beach Golf Links, and in 1990 the club's lawyers tried to stop people from photographing the tree for commercial purposes. In the end, the trademark went through because the tree is on land owned by the Pebble Beach Company. Today, visitors have to pay to drive up to see it and must sign a statement agreeing not to commercialize its images. Lawyers for Pebble Beach said, "It's not the physical ownership of the tree [that we claim], but the ownership of the intellectual concept of the tree." (Lawyers for the tree could not be reached.)

GREENS THAT STAY GREEN
Course: Del Monte Golf Course
City: Pebble Beach
Claim to Fame: Opened in 1897, this is the oldest continuously operating golf course west of the Mississippi. Del Monte became popular in the 1920s, before courses were well-irrigated—golfers realized the Bay Area climate kept the greens green all year long.

WATER HAZARD
Course: Ocean Trails (now Trump National) Golf Club
City: Rancho Palos Verdes
Claim to Fame: On June 2, 1999, Ocean Trails' 18th hole fell into the ocean as part of a mudslide. The club fixed it by installing an underground retaining wall that Donald Trump (who later bought the course) said makes it the most expensive golf hole in the world. (The cause of the slide is still up for debate, but one local claimed it was the work of the Palos Verdes aliens, "telepathic brain-globs" who are rumored to have an underwater landing base off the coast of San Pedro.)

WEIRD NEWS

Californians do the strangest things.

THEY VANT TO SUCK YOUR BLOOD

As if vampire movies, books, TV shows, perfumes, and energy drinks (packaged in blood bags) weren't strange enough, now your own blood can be used to make you younger (though not immortal). Dr. Andre Berger, a plastic surgeon in Beverly Hills, performs a procedure called Dracula Therapy. It works like this: The doctor draws some of your blood, puts it into a machine that separates plasma from the blood cells, and then injects the plasma into your wrinkles. According to Berger, the plasma stimulates collagen growth in the skin that then smooths out the wrinkles. But does it work? Berger says it does, and not only that—it lasts longer than other antiwrinkle procedures. Plus, some women who've had it done say, "it's organic."

THAT'S ONE WAY TO AVOID TRAFFIC

In April 2011, drivers on I-405 North in West Los Angeles got a little something extra to go with their morning traffic: a nearly naked man (he was wearing black socks) jogging between cars on the freeway. The man eventually exited at Santa Monica Boulevard and argued with a woman who refused to give him $10 to buy clothes. (She also said he stole her cell phone when she tried to call the police.) Eventually, police did arrive and arrested the naked jogger for indecent exposure.

DEAR MR. PRESIDENT...

In November 2008, San Francisco residents were faced with a loaded decision: whether or not to vote for a ballot measure that would rename one of the city's sewage plants after President George W. Bush. It's no secret that San Francisco was firmly in the anti-Bush camp during his eight-year presidency, and although supporters needed only 7,200 signatures to put the measure on the ballot, they easily gathered 8,500. Why a sewage treatment plant? According to one supporter, it would be "a fitting monument to the president's work." (The measure didn't pass.)

The *Star of India*, docked in San Diego, is the oldest active tall ship in the world.

CALIFORNIA DID IT FIRST!

*Entertainment, politics, aviation, fashion, technology…
all have California firsts.*

FIRST PAIRS OF "PENTS." Levi Strauss was an immigrant from Germany whose brothers owned a dry-goods store in New York. He carried their merchandise around in packs on his back, peddling it on the streets. In 1853 Strauss moved to California and set up a dry-goods store in San Francisco. He built a local reputation for honesty, so when Nevada-based tailor Jacob Davis visited the city and wanted to start a business, he asked Strauss to be his partner. Davis had sewn heavy cotton work pants, or "waist overalls," that he made especially strong by hammering rivets in the pockets. In 1872 he pitched the product to Strauss: "The secret of them Pents, is the Rivits that I put in those Pockets…I cannot make them up fast enough." The pitch worked. Davis moved to San Francisco, and by 1873 the men were partners, manufacturing what came to be known as Levi's. Soon Californians were wearing America's first jeans.

FIRST LONG-DISTANCE PHONE LINE. In 1877 the world's first long-distance phone line connected the two towns of French Corral and French Lake, California. Built by the Ridge Line phone company, the line was strung for 58 miles along trees and poles and was built for the Milton Mining Company, which was looking for an easy way for people at its hydraulic mines to communicate with the dams upstream. (After hydraulic mining was outlawed in 1884, the miners at Milton used the phone line to warn illegal miners of unexpected visits by federal inspectors.)

FIRST FRISBEE. Technically, kids had been playing catch with metal pie tins for years when two former World War II fighter pilots, Warren Franscioni and Walter Morrison, arrived on the scene. But in 1948, the pair made the first aerodynamic, round-edged, plastic platter in Franscioni's San Luis Obispo basement. They called it the "Flyin' Saucer" and sold it for $1 each. Unfortunately, their company went under, and Franscioni went back to the air force. But Morrison kept selling a variation of the disk as the "Pluto Platter," and when Wham-O Toys took an interest in 1957, Morrison signed on with them—cutting Franscioni out of the millions the toy eventually earned. The saucers' sales soared when Wham-O mass-produced and renamed them Frisbees—after he found out that Yale students who liked to play with the platters had started calling them "Frisbie's" after a local bakery that used to supply its own pie tins for the cause.

FIRST MARTINI. New York may be home to the first three-martini lunch, but the martini itself is a California contribution. Legends abound about the origin of the drink, but the most popular goes like this: Sometime in the 1860s, Jerry Thomas, an inventive San Francisco bartender, created a new drink for a prospector on his way to the gold fields in Martinez. The miner had offered a gold nugget in exchange for "something special," and Thomas whipped up a mixture of gin, vermouth, bitters, and maraschino. Later, he called it a "martini" in honor of where the miner was headed. The cocktail was so successful that Thomas published the recipe in 1887.

Residents of Martinez, however, claim the prospector was headed *to* San Francisco and killing his thirst in a Martinez tavern in the 1870s when he asked for that "something special." Either way, California edged out the cocktail's New York version, which didn't appear until 1911.

FIRST TV BROADCAST. When he was 14 years old, Philo Farnsworth showed his Idaho science teacher a plan to use electronics to create something the teacher (and nearly everyone else) had never heard of—television. Seven years later, in 1927, Farnsworth had moved west and created the first electronic TV camera in a San Francisco laboratory. (He called it the "Image Dissector" because it transmitted an image by dissecting it into a series of pulsating currents.) He'd also invented the first TV receiver from a laboratory flask. On September 7, 1927, Farnsworth painted a thick black line on a glass slide and asked his wife and an investor, George Everson, to watch the world's first TV broadcast. The glass slide was placed between the Image Dissector and an *arc lamp* (a type of lamp encased in a glass tube that creates a bright arc of electricity). In the other room, the line showed up on the receiver, and as Farnsworth turned the slide, its image on the flask turned, too. Farnsworth's comment after the transmission was a calm, "There you are—electronic television." His wife had a more enthusiastic reaction: "The damned thing works!"

FIRST HEALTH CLUB. As a kid, San Francisco–born Jack LaLanne was a self-described "sickly junk-food junkie." He was also a certified meanie who attacked his brother with an axe and tried to set his house on fire. Fortunately at 15, LaLanne got into nutrition and exercise. He felt better—and nonviolent—and went on a mission to make America healthy. In 1936 LaLanne opened the nation's first health club, the Jack LaLanne Physical Culture Studio in Oakland. He got a blacksmith to help him create the world's first exercise machines, including leg extension machines and cable-pulley weights. Doctors thought LaLanne's exercise regimen was dangerous and warned that working out with weights could give people "heart attacks, and they'd lose their sex drive." But LaLanne persevered. In 1951 he created and starred in the world's first televised exercise and fitness TV program—funded with his own money because everyone was sure it wouldn't last more than a few weeks. They were wrong: *The Jack LaLanne Show* went national in 1959 and ran until 1985.

FIRST FLIGHT? In the 1880s, San Diego's John Montgomery studied the physics of flight and the wings of birds so that he could build a successful glider. He learned that planes were more successful if their wings, like those of birds, were shaped like cones. In 1883 he tested a glider with wings that were curved toward the front like a gull's wings. He flew over a hill in Otay Mesa, just outside San Diego, and glided for about 600 feet. It was the Western Hemisphere's first, heavier-than-air, manned, controlled flight...and it occurred 20 years before the Wright brothers' engine-driven flight in North Carolina. By 1905 Montgomery had built tandem gliders that were launched from hot-air balloons, flew at up to a 4,000-foot elevation, and could coast to a landing.

THE MOTHBALL FLEET

San Franciscans don't take water pollution lying down…not even when the biggest offender is the U.S. government.

GIVE A HOOT, DON'T POLLUTE

During World War II, the United States created one of the largest naval fleets in the world, but after the peace treaty was signed, the U.S. government decided to mothball the ships. All the cruisers, destroyers, transports, supply ships, and tankers were put into reserve, and one of the largest collections was parked in Suisun Bay, a tidal estuary just north of San Francisco. Some of the ships were called back into service for Korea and Vietnam, but most just sat derelict after 1946.

The navy's ships are marvels of engineering, but they were never designed to sit, unused, in a small bay for more than 60 years. To the locals, the fleet was, as one environmentalist called it, a "floating toxic waste dump." In 2007 more than 70 ships were still there, and on many of them, the lead paint was slowly flaking off into the water. It wasn't just lead, either. More than 20 tons of toxic materials—lead, copper, zinc, and barium among them—had already made their way into the water. And 65 tons of paint remained on the ships, an environmental time bomb left by the U.S. government for the citizens of San Francisco.

YOU CAN'T FIGHT CITY HALL...

The Maritime Administration, the division of the federal government that oversees the reserve fleet, had left the ships in Suisun Bay long past the time when it would have been easy to remove them. The fleet was old and decrepit, and simply towing them to a scrap heap wasn't possible. For one, environmentalists worried that any attempt to move the ships would cause even more paint to flake off into the water. Plus, there were no facilities for recycling a ship's scrap metal on the West Coast. So the ships would have to be towed through the Panama Canal to a facility on the gulf coast of Texas...trailing lead paint all the way.

The coast guard also insisted that the ships be cleaned of barnacles before they were towed into the open ocean. The decades

of barnacles on their hulls could introduce non-native species to
the distant the waters during journey. But the ships were so rusted
that scraping the barnacles off the hull would also scrape off sheets
of metal, causing even more pollution. And the whole process
would be very expensive and wasn't something for which San
Franciscans thought they should have to foot the bill.

The area's Water Quality Control Board, alarmed at the continuing contamination, first just asked the Maritime Administration to clean up its mess. That request was ignored. As the local
board continued to pressure the Maritime Administration, they
were told that "nothing could be done." So in 2007, they sued.

...EXCEPT WHEN YOU CAN

Several environmental groups joined the water board in its law-
suit, which claimed that the federal government was violating its
own Clean Water Act by leaving the ships to pollute the bay.
After more than two years of battling, in January 2010, a federal
judge agreed. San Francisco: 1. U.S. government: 0.

The Maritime Administration then had to begin a program to
remove 52 of the festering ships from Suisun Bay by 2017. It also
had to clean the remaining ships every three months to prevent
further waste from running off into the bay. So far, the agency has
been keeping to schedule, and if all goes according to plan, Suisun
Bay's ghost ships will soon finally be at peace.

* * *

CALIFORNIA BUMPER STICKERS

- Save California. When you leave, take someone with you.
- American by birth. Californian by the grace of God.
- Power up with hemp. Don't be fuelish.
- Welcome to California. Now go home!
- Don't hassle me. I'm local.
- The 405 sucks!
- Taco connoisseur
- California is gorges!

CHAMPAGNE WISHES AND GONDOLA DREAMS

"I have always had a dream of building an ideal city...it was only mere accident that it was built in California." —Abbot Kinney

VENICE MARSHES ON
Venice, California—with its sandy beaches and funky boardwalk scene—is one of the biggest tourist attractions in Los Angeles. But once upon a time, Venice was just a barren marshland that nobody thought was habitable...except Abbot Kinney, a millionaire with a crazy dream. Kinney was born in 1850 in New Jersey. He grew up middle class but quickly got rich when he became a junior partner at the Kinney Brothers Tobacco Company. Having made a fortune in cigarettes, the 27-year-old decided to take a trip around the world.

In December 1879, on his way home, Kinney got stuck in San Francisco. He couldn't catch a train to the East Coast because of heavy snow in the Sierras. His travels seemed stalled...until he heard about a health resort in the Sierra Madres, in what's now eastern L.A. County, and impulsively decided to check it out. Kinney suffered from terrible asthma and insomnia, and was always looking for a cure. When he arrived at the Sierra Madre Villa Hotel, business was booming and all the rooms were full. The best they could offer was a pool table to sleep on. He took it, and the next morning, Kinney reported having had "the best night's sleep of my life." Better yet, he woke up with no asthma.

So he decided to stay. Kinney bought land nearby and started a citrus ranch that he called Kinneloa (Hawaiian for "Kinney's Hill"). He also invested in real estate. In 1891 Kinney and his partner, Francis Ryan, bought a 1.5 mile stretch of oceanfront land, which included the empty, barren marshes that would become Venice.

KINNEY'S FOLLY
Kinney and Ryan created a subdivision in what is now the Santa Monica neighborhood of Ocean Park. To entice buyers and

---

Ed Cox from San Francisco invented S.O.S. pads in 1917...

tourists, they added entertainments to the area: a 500-foot pier, golf courses, and a racetrack. Kinney had even more projects in mind when Ryan died in 1898, but the men who bought Ryan's half of the business didn't like those ideas. By 1904 everyone wanted to dissolve the partnership. They decided to divide the land with a coin toss. Kinney won and shocked everybody by taking the swamp.

But he had a plan. On July 7, 1904, Kinney announced that on the swamp, he was going to build a grand resort city like Venice, Italy. It would have canals and gondolas and Italian Renaissance buildings. He called it the "Venice of America," but the locals (who watched construction crews trying to dig up the marsh's hard clay) called the venture "Kinney's Folly."

At first, it seemed like the locals were on to something. Venice of America was scheduled to open in May 1905, but then came two bad storms. Waves more than 20 feet high destroyed the nearly completed pier and littered the beach with broken planks.

CRAZY LIKE A FOX

Instead of giving up, though, Kinney hired 1,000 men to work in shifts around the clock. They rebuilt and lengthened the pier, and then constructed a stone breakwater to deflect the force of the waves away from Venice. On July 4—just two months behind schedule—about 40,000 visitors (nearly half the population of L.A. at the time) arrived for the town's grand opening.

Angelenos immediately fell in love with the place. Venice really did feel a little like a bit of Italy on the Pacific. There were vast, sandy beaches, and Kinney had imported Italian gondolas— and even Italian gondoliers—to ferry people along 16 miles of saltwater canals. The canals all flowed out from the large Grand Lagoon with an amphitheater on its shores so audiences could watch swimming races and diving shows. Visitors could stroll along Windward Avenue under colonnaded walkways while they admired buildings that had domes, spires, and towers like the one in the Piazza (Saint Mark's Square) in Venice, Italy. And if they didn't want to walk, they could always ride on Venice's own miniature train. The evening brought fireworks, but people seemed most impressed with the thousands of electric lights (rare in 1905) that illuminated the canals.

Crazy Kinney turned out to be an astute businessman. He sold lots along the canals for $1,000 to $1,250. Even the lots on dirt roads at the edge of his development were being snapped up for $500 each. During the opening month, Kinney sold $405,000 worth of real estate—more than $9 million today.

"THE CAPITOL OF JOYLAND"

Pretty soon, competitors sprang up at other Southern California beaches, and an amusement pier war began. But Kinney kept dreaming up new attractions: camel rides, freak shows, a dance hall, a roller coaster, a Ferris wheel, an aquarium, and even professional baseball. Kinney's imagination kept Venice going.

His former partners were more of a problem. They had a competing pier and political control of Ocean Park, which had jurisdiction over Venice. The ex-partners often delayed Kinney's permits, shortened his business hours, and refused requests for public services. It seemed like they were doing everything they could to put Venice out of business. But Kinney fought back—he funded his own group of politicians, and in 1911 they made Venice an independent city.

From 1905 until the early 1920s, Venice basked in its golden era. Hundreds of thousands of visitors showed up annually. They rode in gondolas, on camels, and on trains. They swam in the heated saltwater plunge, visited the pier, and had fun at the beach. Venice was—as postcards proclaimed—"the Capitol of Joyland!"

VENICE'S DECLINE

Kinney died in 1920, and although his family kept Venice going, it wasn't the same. Prohibition ended liquor sales and affordable cars gave people a choice of new vacation destinations. But the real downward spiral came when the residents of Venice voted in 1925 to allow their small town to become part of Los Angeles. They'd hoped to benefit from city services, but L.A. paved paradise instead. In 1929 the city filled in the canals north of Venice Boulevard with concrete. It taxed the residents who lived on the canals to pay for the paving—even though many of them had protested it. The south side of Venice Boulevard had canals too, but that area wasn't as developed and didn't have enough residents to pay for the paving. So those canals were just left to deteriorate.

In 1946 the L.A. Parks and Recreation Department refused to renew the Kinney family's lease for the pier, and it was torn down. Venice lost tourists and revenue, and over time, it got a new nickname: the "Slum by the Sea." The town came back to life in the 1980s, but Venice of America—the place where busy Angelenos could take a quick Italian vacation—was no more. It had been replaced by Muscle Beach, a boardwalk filled with characters, and many free-spirited residents.

EVERYTHING OLD IS NEW AGAIN

Some of the canals left in Venice today were built by Kinney, but most were part of a construction plan in the early 20th century that created a completely different subdivision. By the 1940s, those neglected canals were crumbling too, and the area had some of the cheapest rents in town. In the 1960s, though, many of the houses on the canals were attracting counterculture artists—most famously, Jim Morrison and the Doors. In 1982 preservationists managed to get the canals listed in the National Register of Historic Places. Ten years later, they were finally drained and repaired. In 2010 homes along the rebuilt canals were among the most expensive in Los Angeles....listing for more than $2 million each.

* * *

HOLLYWOOD GOSSIP

Jack Warner, film executive and president of Warner Bros. Studios from 1927 until 1972, wasn't easy to work for and often suspended actors (meaning they didn't work and weren't paid, but were still under contract and so couldn't work elsewhere either) when they didn't do what he said. During World War II, Warner suspended so many actors that the studio was running low on talent and his brother Harry finally had to write him a memo: "You must bear in mind that everyone is preaching liberty and freedom, and the actors are getting to believe it. When the war is over and all the actors and help have come back, you can at that time suspend anyone you want.'"

The name Alcatraz comes from the Spanish *La Isla de los Alcatraces*, "the Island of the Pelicans."

JOHN MUIR'S YOSEMITE, PART II

Naturalist John Muir first visited Yosemite in 1868, and he wrote all about it in the 1912 book The Yosemite. *(Part I appears on page 85.)*

YOSEMITE FALL

"During the time of the spring floods the best near view of the fall is obtained from Fern Ledge on the east side above the blinding spray at a height of about 400 feet above the base of the fall. A climb of about 1,400 feet from the Valley has to be made, and there is no trail, but to any one fond of climbing this will make the ascent all the more delightful. A narrow part of the ledge extends to the side of the fall and back of it, enabling us to approach it as closely as we wish. When the afternoon sunshine is streaming through the throng of comets, ever wasting, ever renewed, fineness, firmness, and variety of their forms are beautifully revealed. At the top of the fall, they seem to burst forth in irregular spurts from some grand, throbbing mountain heart. Now and then, one mighty throb sends forth a mass of solid water into the free air far beyond the others which rushes alone to the bottom of the fall with long streaming tail, like combed silk, while the others, descending in clusters, gradually mingle and lose their identity. But they all rush past us with amazing velocity and display of power though apparently drowsy and deliberate in their movements when observed from a distance of a mile or two. The heads of these comet-like masses are composed of nearly solid water, and are dense white in color like pressed snow, from the friction they suffer in rushing through the air, the portion worn off forming the tail between the white lustrous threads and films of which faint, grayish pencilings appear, while the outer, finer sprays of water-dust, whirling in sunny eddies, are pearly gray throughout. At the bottom of the fall there is but little distinction of form visible. It is mostly a hissing, clashing, seething, upwhirling mass of scud and spray, through which the light sifts in gray and purple tones while at times when the sun strikes at the required angle, the whole wild and apparently lawless, stormy, striving mass is

---

Q: What do jazzman Art Pepper, country singer Merle Haggard, and...

changed to brilliant rainbow hues, manifesting finest harmony. The middle portion of the fall is the most openly beautiful; lower, the various forms into which the waters are wrought are more closely and voluminously veiled, while higher, towards the head, the current is comparatively simple and undivided. But even at the bottom, in the boiling clouds of spray, there is no confusion, while the rainbow light makes all divine, adding glorious beauty and peace to glorious power. This noble fall has far the richest, as well as the most powerful, voice of all the falls of the Valley, its tones varying from the sharp hiss and rustle of the wind in the glossy leaves of the live-oak and the soft, sifting, hushing tones of the pines, to the loudest rush and roar of storm winds and thunder among the crags of the summit peaks."

WINTER IN YOSEMITE

"Every clear, frosty morning loud sounds are heard booming and reverberating from side to side of the Valley at intervals of a few minutes, beginning soon after sunrise and continuing an hour or two like a thunder-storm. In my first winter in the Valley, I could not make out the source of this noise. I thought of falling boulders, rock-blasting, etc. Not till I saw what looked like hoarfrost dropping from the side of the Fall was the problem explained. The strange thunder is made by the fall of sections of ice formed of spray that is frozen on the face of the cliff along the sides of the Upper Yosemite Fan—a sort of crystal plaster, a foot or two thick, racked off by the sunbeams, awakening all the Valley like cock-crowing, announcing the finest weather, shouting aloud Nature's infinite industry and love of hard work in creating beauty."

A RIDE ON AN AVALANCHE

"Few Yosemite visitors ever see snow avalanches, and fewer still know the exhilaration of riding on them. In all my mountaineering, I have enjoyed only one avalanche ride, and the start was so sudden and the end came so soon I had but little time to think of the danger that attends this sort of travel, though at such times one thinks fast. One fine Yosemite morning after a heavy snowfall...I set out early to climb by a side cañon [canyon] to the top of a commanding ridge a little over three thousand feet above the Valley. On account of the looseness of the snow that blocked the cañon I knew the climb would require a long time, some three or four hours as I estimated; but it proved far more difficult than I had anticipated. Most of the way I sank waist deep, almost out of sight in some places. After spending the whole day to within half an hour or so of sundown, I was still several hundred feet below the summit. Then my hopes were reduced to getting up in time to see the sunset. But I was not to get summit views of any sort that day, for deep trampling near the cañon head, where the snow was strained, started an avalanche, and I was swished down to the foot of the cañon as if by enchantment. The wallowing ascent had taken nearly all day, the descent only about a minute. When the avalanche started I threw myself on my back and spread my arms to try to keep from sinking. Fortunately, though the grade of the cañon is very steep, it is not interrupted by precipices large enough to cause outbounding or free plunging. On no part of the rush was I buried. I was only moderately imbedded on the surface or at times a little below it, and covered with a veil of back-streaming dust particles; and as the whole mass beneath and about me joined in the flight there was no friction, though I was tossed here and there and lurched from side to side. When the avalanche swedged and came to rest, I found myself on top of the crumpled pile without bruise or scar. This was a fine experience."

For Part III of Muir's Yosemite musings, turn to page 273.

*   *   *

EARTHQUAKE Q & A

Q. Is it true that we're having more earthquakes now than ever before?

A. No. With all the coverage major earthquakes get in the news these days, it can seem like their frequency is increasing, but actually the opposite is happening. Since reliable records of earthquakes started being kept in 1900, there have been an average of 18 earthquakes with a magnitude of 7.0 to 7.9 and one earthquake with magnitude of 8.0 or greater every single year. But for most of the last 30 years, there have been fewer than 18 such earthquakes each year.

Many of the giant redwoods in Sequoia National Park are more than 2,000 years old.

NORCAL SANTA ANA-GRAMS

The Santa Ana winds blew all the way up the state and have scrambled Northern California's city names. Can you sort them out? (Answers on page 369.)

THE BAY AREA
1. NASAL FEAR: _____
2. SO JEANS: _____
3. DANK-OLA: _____
4. OPAL A LOT: _____
5. SIRS OF CAN-CAN: _____

THE CENTRAL VALLEY
1. FABLED SKIER: _____
2. NO SERF: _____
3. COT KNOTS: _____
4. ED MOOTS: _____
5. I SALIVA: _____

GOLD COUNTRY
1. CAMERA SNOT: _____
2. BY ACUITY: _____
3. CUT REEK: _____
4. VAGARY SELLS: _____
5. KEG LOVER: _____

WAY UP NORTH
1. NERD DIG: _____
2. BLED RUFF: _____
3. ECCENTRIC STY: _____
4. VISUAL LENS: _____
5. FOG TAG, BRR! _____

The SoCal scramble appears on page 97.

The official color of the Golden Gate Bridge: international orange.

HOW L.A. SAVED THE OLYMPICS

*More Summer Olympics have been held in the United States than in any
other nation, but so far, Los Angeles is the only U.S. city to host
the Summer Games twice. And the Olympics came twice to
Los Angeles only because it had nowhere else to go.*

THE 1932 SUMMER OLYMPICS

Tough Problems: Los Angeles tried to host the Olympics in
1924, but lost out to Paris. In 1928 the city tried again, but
Amsterdam was chosen. In the early 20th century, most Olympics
were held in Europe because many of the participating countries
were European, and they considered to be California too far away
and the travel costs to get there much too expensive. Then came
the Wall Street crash in 1929, bank failures, and massive unemployment. By 1932 Americans were stuck in the Great Depression,
and the financial crisis had spread to the entire world. Times were
so bad that Los Angeles was the only city that offered to host the
1932 Summer Games.

L.A. was also suffering from high unemployment and other
financial problems, but city officials were determined to show off
its sophistication and beauty. Downtown was decorated with
Olympic flags and banners, and 10th Street—stretching from
Santa Monica to East L.A.—was renamed Olympic Boulevard.
Pink and cream bungalows were constructed and landscaped in
Baldwin Hills, just southeast of Culver City, creating the first
Olympic Village. The village included training fields, a recreation
hall that showed movies, and kitchens that served international
fare. Only the male athletes stayed in that first Olympic Village,
though; the women were housed separately in the elegant Chapman Park Hotel on Wilshire Boulevard.

Despite all this extravagance, the Great Depression did force
the Los Angeles Olympic Organizing Committee (LAOOC) to
make some frugal decisions. Local athletes stayed in their own
homes instead of in the village, and Americans from other cities
left the village as soon as their events were finished. The LAOOC

Oakland Airport was the starting point for Amelia Earhart's final flight.

also changed the length of time the Games lasted: previous Olympics lasted well over two months, but the 1932 Games were cut back to 16 days, from July 30 through August 14. The LAOOC also tried to avoid expensive stadium construction and held many events at existing structures: the Coliseum, the Rose Bowl, in parks, and even cycling on the Pacific Coast Highway.

Still, there were problems. Some critics claimed that this was not a time to spend money on sports. Others predicted that the Games would be an embarrassing failure. Economic woes also made it difficult for countries to send athletes, and the lowest number of Olympians showed up to compete since 1904. President Herbert Hoover also declined an invitation (he was too busy campaigning for re-election, which he lost)—the first time a head of state didn't appear at the Olympics. And at first, very few tickets were sold.

Tough Competition: But to the relief of the LAOOC, once newspapers reported the arrival of the athletes, Americans caught Olympic fever. In all, 37 nations—including first-timers China and Colombia—sent about 1,300 athletes to the Olympics. People traveled to Los Angeles, and the Coliseum filled to capacity with more than 100,000 watching the opening ceremonies.

The athletes wowed the crowds with fierce competition, shattering world and Olympic records:

• American runner Eddie "Midnight Express" Tolan set new Olympic records in the 100-meter and 200-meter events.

• American swimmer Helene Madison set an Olympic record for the 100-meter freestyle and a world record for the 400-meter freestyle, and she led the U.S. women's swim team to a world record in the 400-meter freestyle relay.

• Italian runner Luigi Beccali managed to beat the Olympic record in the men's 1,500 meter and add a touch of scandal, too— he gave the fascist salute at the award ceremony.

• Fourteen-year-old swimmer Kusuo Kitamura from Japan won the 1,500-meter freestyle, becoming the youngest male to earn a gold medal in an individual event.

• The United States' Mildred "Babe" Didrikson took gold in the javelin and the 80-meter hurdles, and silver in the high jump, and went on to become the most celebrated female athlete of her day.

Van Nuys High School alumni: Marilyn Monroe, Jane Russell, and Robert Redford.

- Clarence Linden "Buster" Crabbe likely got the biggest boost from the Olympics—after he set a world record in the 400-meter freestyle swim, Hollywood came calling, putting him in starring roles like Flash Gordon and Buck Rogers.

Result: Despite Depression woes, the L.A. Olympics were considered a huge success. Several of their innovations became traditions, including the shorter length of the Games, a village for athletes, and a dramatic victory ceremony (1932 was the first time winners stood on podiums while their nation's flag was raised).

Americans went home happy since the United States won 41 gold medals, but the LAOOC was a big winner, too. Newspapers reported that the Games had made a profit $1 million.

THE 1984 SUMMER OLYMPICS

Tough Problems: Los Angeles was, once again, the only city to bid for the 1984 Summer Games, and once again, it got the Olympics because of money issues. This time, though, the problem was the cost of the Games themselves. The bid for the 1984 Games was actually placed in 1978 to give the winning city enough time to build whatever structures might be needed. Only one city from each country could make a bid, and most of the world was scared away by the financial disaster of the 1976 Montreal Games.

Montreal mayor Jean Drapeau had once famously declared, "The Olympics can no more have a deficit than a man can have a baby." But cartoons of a pregnant Mayor Drapeau popped up in Montreal newspapers after the 1976 Olympics left the city with $1 billion of debt that wasn't paid off until 2006. So when Los Angeles residents learned they were getting the Games in 1984, some were angry, nicknaming the LAOOC "Lost And Out Of Control." However, LAOOC president Peter Ueberroth had some clever ideas: He financed the Games through private donors rather than taxes. He raised big bucks selling television rights, and even more money selling endorsements and sponsorships. Ueberroth also cut costs by filling many jobs with volunteers and keeping building to a minimum—UCLA, USC, and UC Santa Barbara all were used as Olympic villages to house athletes.

Things were looking good, but 12 weeks before the opening

Ronald and Nancy Reagan once lived at 666 St. Cloud Road in Bel Air, but Nancy...

ceremonies, a new problem arose: the Soviet Union announced a boycott. In 1980 the United States had boycotted the Moscow Games over a Soviet invasion of Afghanistan, and in 1984, Moscow retaliated. Fourteen socialist and communist nations, including Cuba, were no-shows. Only communist Romania agreed to come. Since the USSR had some of the world's greatest athletes, the boycott was a blow. Financial woes hadn't killed the Olympics, but many feared politics might.

Tough Competition: Despite the boycott, a record 140 countries sent athletes to the Games that year, including China, which returned for the first time since 1932. The spectacular opening ceremonies—which included everything from test pilot Bill Suitor flying with a jet pack to 84 pianists simultaneously playing "Rhapsody in Blue"—ended with athletes spontaneously breaking from their processional formation to dance. Their excitement helped ease any tensions of the boycott and created a mood of good will that lasted the entire Games.

The 1984 Games were also filled with firsts:

• The very first event made international news when China's Xu Haifeng won his nation's first gold medal ever in the men's free pistol event. The celebrating Chinese called the gold medal "a break through zero," and went on to win 14 more.

• Los Angeles held the first Olympic windsurfing, synchronized swimming, and rhythmic gymnastic events, as well as the first women's marathon, won by America's Joan Benoit.

• Portugal's marathon man, Carlos Lopes, won his country's first gold medal and set an Olympic record that remained unbroken for 24 years.

• Morocco's Nawal El Moutawakel won her country's first gold medal, becoming the first female Olympic champion from a Muslim nation.

• New Zealand archer Neroli Fairhill was the first paraplegic Olympic contestant; she competed in a wheelchair.

• History-making Olympians also included American runner Carl Lewis, who won four gold medals—in the long jump, the 100-meter, 200-meter, and the 4 x 100-meter relay. And a young Michael Jordan, who was still playing as an amateur, led the

...had the house number changed to 668 to remove any connections to the Antichrist.

United States basketball team to gold, averaging a team-high of 17.1 points per game.

• But America's darling in the 1984 games was 16-year old gymnast Mary Lou Retton, who earned perfect 10s in her vault and floor exercises and became the first American to win gold in the women's all-around event.

Result: Without any Soviet competition, the United States won an incredible 83 gold medals, but the L.A. Olympics were most remembered for their financial success. Although critics called them too commercial, they brought in a whopping $222.7 million for the city. LAOOC president Peter Ueberroth became *Time* magazine's Man of the Year, and other cities began bidding enthusiastically for the Olympics again.

* * *

WILLIAM RANDOLPH'S HEART

California media mogul William Randolph Hearst had a lot of faults—he (and fellow newspaper magnate Joseph Pulitzer) practically invented "yellow journalism," selling papers with salacious headlines that were loose with the facts. But Hearst also pursued many idealistic causes in his newspapers. One of the least known is his attempt to save the victims of the Holocaust during World War II. When news of the Nazis' mass murder of European Jews reached the United States in 1941, Hearst made sure his newspapers gave it prominent coverage—nearly all other American newspapers relegated the issue to the back pages.

In 1943 advocacy groups began urging the U.S. government to create an agency to rescue the Jews before it was too late, and Hearst was a big supporter. He even served as an honorary chairman of the Emergency Conference to Save the Jewish People of Europe. He also gave Jewish rescue advocates permission to print all their material with no charge and no page limit in his newspapers, and ran editorials that proclaimed, "Remember, Americans, this is not a Jewish problem. It is a human problem." Ultimately, Hearst was instrumental in convincing Congress and President Franklin Delano Roosevelt to establish the War Refugee Board, which helped save an estimated 200,000 people from the Nazis.

First capital of California after U.S. occupation: San Jose.

SURREAL CITY

*Lurking on the sides of many buildings in downtown
Palo Alto are some very suspicious characters.*

SEEING IS DECEIVING

An alien in a baby carriage. A burglar falling off the side of a bank. A boy with his fishing line caught on a window. If you take a walk around the city of Palo Alto, you'll see these and many other murals...all part of the Palo Alto Pedestrian Series by artist Greg Brown. In 1976 Brown got some grant money to work as an artist in residence in the city, and he had one thing in mind: he wanted to paint *trompe l'oeil* murals (French for "deceives the eye") on the walls of local buildings (and a few private ones)

Trompe l'oeil paintings are three-dimensional and meant to look real...unless you study them very closely. At first, Brown's work startled passersby—one city councilman even tried to get them painted over. But as the years passed, they became favorites of the locals, and State Senator Joe Simitian even named Brown Artist of the Year in 2007. As the buildings have been sold, renovated, and torn down, some of the murals have been lost. But Palo Alto residents have fought to preserve many of them. Brown, who still lives there, has re-created some and restored others himself. If you're ever in Palo Alto, see if you can find...

• A UFO that has crashed into the side of a building.

• A suspicious-looking man in a trench coat...with a bird sitting on his head.

• A pelican with a few dollars in its bill.

• A nun launching a model airplane.

• A painted woman watering a real bush.

• A levitating man with a bucket on his head...playing with a yo-yo.

• A mustached man sawing his way through elevator cables.

• A polar bear on crutches consulting an elderly nurse.

Barbie's official birthday: March 9, 1959.

NUDES, NO PRUDES

Need a place to get naked in California? Try one of these beaches.

BLACK'S BEACH. Sure, some people come for the scenery—Black's is a two-mile stretch of remote beach located just north of San Diego in the seaside town of La Jolla. It's accessible only by hiking down a 300-foot sandstone cliff (while ignoring posted signs declaring the cliffs unsafe) or by trekking in about two miles from the closest road access...a walk that's not even possible at high tide. But most people come to bare it all. Named for a family that once owned a horse farm on the bluffs overlooking the ocean, Black's has been nudist-friendly since the 1970s. Today, it's the largest nude beach in the United States, and a group called the Black's Beach Bares sponsors nude volleyball, nude sunbathing, nude Frisbee, nude...you get the idea.

BAKER BEACH. Part of San Francisco's Presidio, a park on the city's very northern tip, Baker has one of the best views in the state: a rocky shore that looks out at the Golden Gate Bridge and the hills of Marin County. The area feels isolated and private, even though it's part of the city, and the beach is considered one of the cleanest in San Francisco. The half-mile stretch of sand is also "clothing-optional," though many visitors claim that the nudes tend to keep to themselves and congregate at the north end of the beach near the bridge. Bonus: Parking is free.

SECRET HARBOR CREEK BEACH. If you think the idea of a nude beach in North Lake Tahoe is a little bit crazy, you're not alone—after all, there *have* been reports of bears passing by while "free-bathers" catch some rays in their birthday suits. And then, of course, there's the weather; nude swimming at Lake Tahoe in the winter would be out of the question. But according to North Swanson, head of a group called the Tahoe Area Naturists, "If it's above 40 degrees and there's no wind, it's okay." Lots of other people agree with him: Every summer, the society hosts a naked potluck and a festival called "Only Wear a Hat Day." And despite the "secret" in its name, Harbor Creek is the only nude beach in Lake Tahoe, so it's pretty well known.

Figs were introduced to California by Armenian immigrants.

OLD NEWS

If you think Hollywood is rife with scandal, breakdowns, and practical jokes these days...you're right! But it's nothing new—it's just Old Hollywood in reruns.

DING-DONG, THE PRODUCER'S DEAD

Hollywood's most legendary tyrant was Louis B. Mayer of MGM, whom 15-year-old Elizabeth Taylor once famously told to "go to hell!" From the 1920s through the early '50s, movie actors were at the mercy of the studios that employed them. Contracts controlled stars' careers and private lives. But no studio head was ever as tyrannical as Mayer. As far as he was concerned, nothing was worth risking the studio's bottom line—he even considered things like pregnancies to be "interruptions" of actress's work schedules. (At their weddings, Mayer gave grooms a "no babies" warning.) He was also known to ruin the careers of people he didn't like: Actor John Gilbert once punched Mayer for insulting Greta Garbo, and Mayer held a grudge. When Gilbert made the transition from silent films to talkies, Mayer reportedly tampered with the audio equipment to make Gilbert's voice squeaky and feminine, thus ending his career as a leading man. Mayer's meddling was so extreme that producer Samuel Goldwyn once joked, "The reason so many people showed up at Mayer's funeral was because they wanted to make sure he was dead."

THE JOKE'S ON WHO?

Actor Errol Flynn became famous in the 1930s for playing swashbuckling characters in movies like *The Adventures of Robin Hood*, but he was also well known for being a practical joker. In the 1940 film *Santa Fe Trail*, he costarred with a young Ronald Reagan. During one take, the actors jumped on their horses and galloped away...except Reagan, who went flying in the air because Flynn had loosened his saddle girths.

Friends liked to get their revenge on Flynn, too. Film director Raoul Walsh, actor John Barrymore, and Flynn were drinking buddies, and after Barrymore died in 1942, Walsh stole the corpse from the funeral parlor. He put a bottle of booze in Barrymore's

---

TV's **Dragnet** was based on real cases from the L.A. Police Department.

hand and propped up the body on a chair in Flynn's house. When Flynn returned home (after a night of drinking to console himself over his friend's death) and saw the scene, he "let out a delirious scream...My heart pounded. I couldn't sleep the rest of the night."

A YOUNG SCANDAL

Loretta Young began her career in 1917 at just four years old, and she continued to be a huge box-office draw into her 40s. But her appeal hinged on her personal and professional reputation, which was one of feminine purity. However, in 1935, she was cast opposite a still-married Clark Gable in the movie *Call of the Wild*. The pair fell in love (at least Young did) and had an affair. After the movie wrapped, Young took a long "vacation" in Europe and then "adopted" a daughter. Hollywood, however, was abuzz about the child, whom many said looked just like Clark Gable—right down to his famous large ears. (Young often tried to cover her daughter's ears with hats.)

Young knew that her career would be over if she admitted that she'd had an illegitimate child with a married man. Desperate to stay employed and respectable, Young denounced all the "ugly rumors." Many years later, though, she finally acknowledged having a child with Gable in an authorized biography—which was published just after she died in 2000.

LESSONS FROM JOAN

In 1953 Esther Williams, the MGM star who was famous for her lavish swimming musicals, was in her dressing room when actress Joan Crawford came by for a visit. Crawford had once been a big star for MGM but hadn't worked there for 10 years. She told Williams she'd be making a comeback with her new film *Torch Song*.

Sometime later, Williams heard yelling from one of the soundstages, which had been built to look like a theater. Williams went to investigate and found the darkened stage empty...except for Joan Crawford, who was yelling at the empty theater seats: "Why have you left me? Why don't you come to my movies? Don't turn your back on me!" Crawford wailed. Watching Crawford (who had won an Oscar seven years earlier) plead with imaginary fans made an impression on Williams. When her own career began to falter in the 1960s, she left MGM, created her own line of swimsuits, and became a successful businesswoman.

DOWN THE HATCH!

In 1959 heartthrob Tony Curtis costarred with bombshell Marilyn Monroe in the comedy *Some Like It Hot*, and they had to kiss onscreen. But the two had shared a brief romantic fling when they were young and just starting out in Hollywood, and there may have been some bad feelings left over on Monroe's part. According to Curtis, the kiss "was awful. She nearly choked me to death by deliberately sticking her tongue down my throat into my windpipe."

THAT'S AMORE

In 1950 Senator Walter Johnson of Colorado launched a tirade against *Casablanca* star Ingrid Bergman, calling her "Hollywood's apostle of degradation" and "a powerful influence for evil." Why? In 1949 Bergman left her husband, neurosurgeon Petter Lindström, and their 10-year-old daughter Pia so that she could live with Italian film director Roberto Rossellini. Worse, Bergman had a son with Rossellini out of wedlock (and two more children after they married). When an angry Lindström made the scandal public, Bergman became such a pariah that she wasn't seen in a Hollywood film again until 1956. Her comeback: the movie *Anastasia*, where she played an impostor passing herself off as the long-lost daughter of the Russian czar Nicholas II. The role won Bergman her second Best Actress Oscar. (The first was for the 1944 film *Gaslight*.)

*   *   *

NOT BONSAI, BUT ONLY THIS HIGH

You'll feel like Paul Bunyan when you stroll through Van Damme State Park's pygmy forest near Albion on the Mendocino coast. The fully matured pines and Mendocino cypress growing there measure less than six feet tall, thanks to soil 1,000 times more acidic than normal and a hard subsoil that doesn't allow much root growth. Some of the stunted trees are more than 100 years old.

EXPLOSIVE INFORMATION

Don't have enough to worry about? Try volcanoes and
their connection to California's red-hot underground.

THREE TO WATCH

Normally the chambers of boiling, molten magma lying miles under the earth have little to do with our daily lives. The earth's crust ranges from three to four miles thick, so the magma can't penetrate it...except where there are volcanoes.

Volcanoes are actually weak spots—breaks or holes in the earth's crust that open down to the molten magma. Pressure from shifting tectonic plates can push that magma up and out through the opening of a volcano. And at temperatures of 1,000°F or more, it can do a lot of damage.

"Very high threat" volcanoes are monitored by the United States Geological Survey (USGS) because they have the potential to devastate large areas or cause high fatalities. Out of 169 volcanoes in the United States, 18 have been rated as very high threats...and three of those—Mount Shasta, Lassen Peak, and the Long Valley Caldera—are in California.

MOUNT SHASTA

Where: Siskiyou County, at the southern end of the Cascades

Last erupted: About 200 years ago

Type of volcano: Capped by icy glaciers, Shasta is a solitary mountain that rises to 14,162 feet and dominates the landscape for miles. Mount Shasta's beauty has been acclaimed by artists and poets, but like many of the world's most beautiful and inspiring mountains, Shasta is actually a stratovolcano, a tall conical volcano that includes many layers of debris. Shasta's eruptions have been leaving behind *strata* layers of lava flow, ash, and rock fragments for about 450,000 years.

Volcanoes like Mount Shasta are especially dangerous because they have a very thick, "pasty" magma surrounded by volcanic gases. When these volcanoes erupt, it's because gas pressure creates an explosion inside the cone, filling the air with thick chunks of scalding lava that race down the side of the volcano—picking up rocks, water, trees, and other debris—at speeds of up to 450 mph. The result is a deep mud flow rushing down the mountain that can bury the surrounding area for miles.

Might erupt again? Yes. Mount Shasta's last eruption was well before the I-5 freeway and thousands of homes were built in the mountain's shadow. The freeway and the towns of Weed and Mount Shasta are all built on forests burned and buried by previous eruptions. Predicting eruptions is difficult, but the USGS constantly monitors Shasta for earthquakes, one of the most important clues of a coming eruption.

LASSEN PEAK

Where: Near Redding, at the southern tip of the Cascade range

Last erupted: On May 30, 1914, after a mostly quiet 27,000 years, Lassen woke up. Great clouds of steam exploded from the peak along with some lava and ash. The steam explosions were caused by groundwater heated by rising magma. For nearly a year, there were more than 180 steam explosions that ranged from a few seconds to half an hour. The explosions formed a new 1,000-foot crater that filled with lava.

Then, on May 19, 1915, a large eruption shot chunks of hot lava onto Lassen's snowy summit. The melting snows picked up volcanic rock, mud, and debris, creating a mudflow that surged down the volcano and destroyed forests and buildings miles away. Fortunately, no one was killed. Two days later, Lassen saw its most powerful eruption, which sent lava, rocks, and even boulders 30,000 feet into the air and devastated a three-mile area. After that, Lassen had a few small steam explosions through 1921 and gradually quieted down again.

Type of volcano: Lassen Peak, located in Lassen Volcanic National Park, is a lava dome plug volcano. These volcanoes begin as vents on much larger stratovolcanoes. Their lava flow is so thick and pasty that it plugs up the vent and a new volcano begins to expand and grow under the vent's surface. At 2,000 feet high, Lassen Peak is one of the largest lava domes in the world.

Might erupt again? The USGS is sure that another eruption will

Author Jack London once ran for mayor of Oakland on the Socialist ticket.

occur at or near Lassen Peak. To monitor when that might happen, the agency checks for seismic activity and watches for increases in areas of the park where small openings in the ground (called *fumaroles*) release steam and volcanic gases. So far, Lassen has proven to be active, but there are no signs of an imminent eruption.

THE LONG VALLEY CALDERA

Where: Mono County, eastern California

Last erupted: 76,000 years ago

Type of volcano: Long Valley is a "supervolcano." Instead of rising like mountains, supervolcanoes are broad depressions in the earth called calderas. These are the planet's largest volcanoes and sometimes cover hundreds of square miles. During the Pleistocene era, about 760,000 years ago, the Long Valley Caldera formed after a volcanic eruption that created a crater about 20 miles across.

Might erupt again? In May 1980, a series of about 30,000 earthquakes—including four that registered at least 6.0 on the Richter scale—rattled the caldera and the scientists watching it. The USGS began monitoring Long Valley for more signs of activity… and found a lot. Within the 200 square miles of the caldera floor, a dome of about 100 square miles was rising. Since 1980, that dome has risen more than two feet—a sign that magma is filling the chambers that were emptied out by that eruption in the Pleistocene era. There's also been an increase in carbon dioxide, a gas that's present in magma chambers. In fact, so much carbon dioxide has been created that it's killing trees on Mammoth Mountain, the highest spot on the caldera. Long Valley also has many hot springs, fumaroles, and enough geothermal energy to run three power plants.

When could all this molten magma cause Long Valley to blow? USGS data indicates the caldera can continue at this level of activity for decades—even centuries. But they can't say for sure exactly when the caldera will erupt next.

BERKELEY AND THE BOMB

During the dark days of World War II, Nazi Germany and the
United States raced to create the world's first atomic bomb. Fortunately
for the Allies, a group of scientists at UC Berkeley got started first,
and there were four key locations in and around the university
that played a role in changing the course of world history.

PLACE: Two-story, wooden building on South Drive, adjacent to LeConte Hall
    BACKGROUND: At age 29, Ernest O. Lawrence was the
youngest full professor ever hired at UC Berkeley. In 1929, in a
two-story wooden building near the center of campus, he built the
cyclotron, a machine that could accelerate subatomic particles like
protons at extremely high velocities in a confined tube. The goal?
To break the original elements apart and re-fuse the particles to
create new elements.

IMPACT: The cyclotron in Berkeley's Radiation Laboratory was
so revolutionary that it earned Lawrence the 1939 Nobel Prize for
Physics and made UC Berkeley the world's leading center for
atomic research. Other scientists around the globe began dupli-
cating Lawrence's patented invention...particularly physicists in
German-occupied territories of Europe.

By that time, most scientists (Lawrence included) could see
the bomb-making potential of the new elements created in the
cyclotron, and the United States, Great Britain, and their allies
worried what would happen if the Germans figured out how to do
it first. Famously, Albert Einstein (who was Jewish and lived in
Germany until 1933, but fled to the U.S. when Adolf Hitler came
to power) warned of the consequences: In a letter to President
Franklin D. Roosevelt, he wrote, "It is conceivable—though much
less certain—that extremely powerful bombs of a new type, carried
by boat and exploded in a port, might very well destroy the whole
port together with some of the surrounding territory." As a result,
a terrified Roosevelt ordered several universities to work together

---

The California gray whale has the longest migration route of any mammal (12,000 miles).

to investigate the possibility of building such a bomb. Lawrence joined the effort, and by September 1941, he'd devoted himself and his machine to a crash program to beat the Nazis.

PLACE: One Eagle Hill

BACKGROUND: A UC Berkeley professor and the "Father of the Atomic Bomb," J. Robert Oppenheimer lived with his wife Kitty in a multistory home at this address in the North Berkeley hills. The house inspired awe—picture windows overlooked San Francisco Bay and the Golden Gate Bridge—and it was there that the Oppenheimers entertained guests, often the most prominent scientists in the world. During these parties, no topic was off-limits, even the A-bomb, and Oppenheimer often expressed concern about Nazi Germany. Visiting physicist Edward Teller recalled, "I remember specifically Oppenheimer's prediction that only an atomic bomb could dislodge Hitler from Europe."

IMPACT: By 1942 Oppenheimer had been hired to head the effort to create a workable atomic bomb. That same year, the secret scientific operation was code-named the Manhattan Project, and Oppenheimer began inviting top physicists from all over the U.S. to join him at Berkeley for a conference about the bomb. He called his group "my luminaries" and converted his own garage into a temporary living quarters for one of them—former student Robert Serber, who took leave from his teaching job at the University of Illinois and became the chief assistant and group facilitator.

PLACE: The attic above Room 219 in LeConte Hall

BACKGROUND: Oppenheimer's group met daily in the fourth-floor attic above his office in LeConte Hall, an imposing four-story administrative office building that housed the physics department. Discussions began with a study of the largest man-made explosion at that time, the accidental detonation of an ammunition ship in Halifax, Nova Scotia, in 1917. An estimated 5,000 tons of TNT destroyed 2.5 square miles of the city's downtown, killing 4,000 people. The group calculated that an atomic bomb would release 200 times as much energy and that a radioactive uranium core (created in a cyclotron) would be what ignited it. The next obstacles were to determine what the bomb would look like, how much uranium was needed, and whether the bomb could be carried in a plane.

IMPACT: One of the group's scientists, Edward Teller, worried that the intense heat of an atomic bomb blast might ignite the atmosphere and destroy the world. Shocked, Oppenheimer halted the project until the group could study that possibility. They ran a series of mathematical calculations that convinced Oppenheimer the chance was virtually nil. By the end of the summer, the scientists also concluded that a bomb could be relatively small and could include an 8-inch-thick core of radioactive uranium surrounded by a heavy metal shell. At ignition, the shell would liquefy and then vaporize. An enormous explosion would result. The question remained: Where to find enough specialized uranium for such a bomb?

PLACE: The UC Radiation Laboratory (now the Lawrence Berkeley National Laboratory)

BACKGROUND: Cyclotron creator Ernest O. Lawrence provided the answer. Under a massive domed roof in Strawberry Canyon was a building that looked a little like a UFO. Inside, the physicist had created a "super" cyclotron, almost three times larger than any previous version. Using enormous electromagnets to whip subatomic particles into a high-energy beam, the machine smashed elementary uranium to bits and created enriched uranium isotopes plus a new element, plutonium, both of which could ignite a bomb. But the cyclotron could harvest only small quantities of both elements.

IMPACT: Lawrence convinced the government that many more super cyclotrons were necessary to make enough enriched uranium and plutonium to create a bomb. Construction got underway immediately to build them at uranium-processing plants in Oak Ridge, Tennessee, and Pasco, Washington. Simultaneously, Oppenheimer found a remote desert plateau in New Mexico called Jornada del Muerto ("Journey of the Dead") to build and test the bomb. It was there the government built the city of Los Alamos to bring it to fruition.

The world's first atomic bomb detonation took place at 5:30 a.m. on July 16, 1945, at a test site called Trinity on the white sands near Los Alamos. Looking on were Oppenheimer and Lawrence, who said, "Life suddenly became more serious."

WE ♥ SACRAMENTO

Sure, it's the center of California's political gridlock, but it's also a historic city with lots to love. No, really…it is.

• **Oldie and goodie.** Officially, Sacramento is the oldest incorporated city in California. That means its city charter was the first accepted by the state. When? 1850.

• **The name game.** Sacramento has earned an impressive number of nicknames…some flattering, many not. Here are a few: the Big Tomato, River City, Sack Toe, Sac Town, City of Trees, Sack O' Tomatoes, and Excramento (ouch).

• **Let it snow, let it snow…** Sacramento has a pretty mild winter climate (highs average in the 40s), but snow flurries do occasionally appear in the city's skies, and since its founding, there have also been a handful of measurable snowfalls. The last was in February 1976, when about two inches fell on the city. The most significant snowfall? January 4–5, 1888, when Sacramento officially recorded a whopping three inches.

• **Everything's comin' up roses.** According to the All American Rose Selections Committee (a nonprofit group "dedicated to the introduction and promotion of exceptional roses"), Sacramento boasts one of the top ten rose gardens in the United States: the World Peace Rose Garden in downtown Capitol Park. More than 650 roses grow there.

• **Animal house.** The Sacramento Zoo opened in 1927 and today is home to more than 600 animals and about 30 endangered species. One of the zoo's most popular residents: a desert tortoise named Herkimer who turned 83 in 2011.

• **The almond king.** Blue Diamond Almonds, established in Sacramento in 1914, calls itself the "largest almond processing plant in the world." They certainly are huge—Blue Diamond can produce as many as 12 *million* pounds of almonds in one day.

California is home to approximately 300,000 Native Americans—more than any other states.

BRAGGING RIGHTS, PART I

From the world's largest thermometer, to the Bigfoot Capital, these California towns have made some strange achievements.

CLAIM TO FAME: World's largest thermometer
WHERE: Baker
STORY: Located in San Bernardino County and often called the "Gateway to Death Valley," the town of Baker regularly sees summer days that reach 120°F. This may not seem like a reason to visit, but the small (population under 1,000) town has used this fact to attract thousands of tourists and secure itself a place in the record books. Baker boasts 134-foot-tall digital thermometer that shows its current temperature on three sides. (The thermometer's height commemorates the United States' hottest temperature of 134°F, recorded in nearby Furnace Creek in 1913.)

The thermometer was the idea of local Will Herron, who owned the nearby Bun Boy restaurant (now a Bob's Big Boy). He wanted to get motorists speeding by on nearby I-15 between L.A. and Las Vegas to stop in Baker. Remembering the many times he'd heard the question "How hot is it around here anyway?" he decided to create a giant thermometer.

In 1991 Herron hired the Electric Sign Company in Las Vegas to build the thermometer—it took 33 tons of steel, 4,943 lamps, and cost about $700,000. Neighbors thought he was a little crazy (maybe from the heat) and weren't thrilled with the brightly lit "eyesore." Some even expressed joy when the thermometer cracked in the furious Mojave winds and part of it came crashing down. But Herron rebuilt and filled the thermometer's metal core with concrete to keep it stable. It's been standing upright ever since and is such a hot tourist attraction that *Time* magazine includes the structure on its list of top U.S. roadside attractions.

CLAIM TO FAME: The center of the world
WHERE: Felicity
STORY: Located in Imperial County's Sonoran Desert, the town

The world's tallest thermometer in Baker is only 17 feet shorter than the Statue of Liberty.

of Felicity sports a 21-foot-high granite pyramid with a circular bronze plaque built into its base. The dot in the center of the plaque marks what Felicity claims is the world's "center." Visitors pay a small fee to stand on the spot and make a wish, and they get a certificate from the town as proof that they've been there.

Sure, technically we're all standing on a sphere, so any spot could be the center, a fact that Felicity's mayor and founder, Jacques-Andres Istel, admits. But he also points out that Felicity has the law on its side. Legal recognition of Felicity's world centeredness was granted by both the supervisors of Imperial County and the French Institut Geographique National. Felicity is also described as the center of the earth in the children's book *Coe the Good Dragon at the Center of the World*—though Istel wrote the book himself.

Born in France, Istel moved to Imperial County in the late 1950s and founded Felicity on about 3,000 acres of desert. He named the tiny town (today's population: about 30) for his wife Felicia. In addition to the centering pyramid, the couple added other landmarks to the region, including a salvaged staircase from the Eiffel Tower and a sundial with a *gnomon* (that's the name of the part that casts the shadow) resembling the arm of God in Michelangelo's painting on the Sistine Chapels ceiling.

For more bragging, turn to page 261.

*　　*　　*

DID YOU KNOW?

The *Sacramento Union* became famous in the 1860s for publishing a series of letters that author Mark Twain wrote during a trip to Hawaii, but there's very little evidence that he ever actually worked for the newspaper (some sources say that he may have briefly held a job in the editorial office). Still, whenever the *Union* was in financial trouble, its editors would find an old desk, call it "the desk where Mark Twain sat," and put it up for sale. According to one local paper, "Almost always, those desks sold quickly."

Oldest bar in California: Groveland's Iron Door Saloon (est. 1896).

HOORAY FOR HOLLYWOOD?

Greta Garbo once said, "If only those who dream about Hollywood knew how difficult it all is." Well, these people can tell you.

"In Hollywood, brides keep the bouquets and throw away the groom."
—**Groucho Marx**

"You get tough in this business, until you get big enough to hire people to get tough for you. Then you can sit back and be a lady."
—**Natalie Wood**

"If all the people in Hollywood who have had plastic surgery...went on vacation, there wouldn't be a person left in town."
—**Michael Jackson**

"It's said in Hollywood that you should always forgive your enemies—because you never know when you'll have to work with them."
—**Lana Turner**

"Hollywood is where they shoot too many pictures and not enough actors."
—**Walter Winchell**

"In Hollywood, an equitable divorce settlement means each party getting fifty percent of publicity."
—**Lauren Bacall**

"I don't think I can handle being here all the time. It's pretty nutty."
—**Johnny Depp**

"Hollywood amuses me. Holier-than-thou for the public and unholier-than-the-devil in reality."
—**Grace Kelly**

"You can take all the sincerity in Hollywood, place it in the navel of a fruit fly, and still have room enough for three caraway seeds and a producer's heart."
—**Fred Allen**

"In Hollywood, now when people die, they don't say, 'Did he leave a will?' but 'Did he leave a diary?'"
—**Liza Minnelli**

The letters of the Hollywood sign are 45 feet tall.

BURN, BABY, BURN

The largest wildfire in California's history was the 2003 Cedar Fire that burned 273,246 acres of San Diego County and killed 15 people. But the state sees numerous fires every year. Here are three other damaging fires that sent Californians' running for their water buckets.

SANTIAGO CANYON FIRE

Where: Orange and San Diego Counties

What: Wildfires have been ravaging California for centuries, but the Santiago Canyon Fire of 1889 was one of the first blazes to affect a large part of the state's population. Fanned by Santa Ana winds, more than 300,000 acres went up in flames during the last week of September, including numerous ranches and a California Southern railway bridge.

The Santiago Canyon Fire began in a sheepherders' camp and raged for three days. Telephones were new and rare, so firefighters relied on the telegraph to spread the news of the encroaching flames. A message sent to the *Riverside Daily Enterprise* warned: "Mountain fires!" Farmers lost the most in the blaze, as acre after acre of barley, hay, and other crops ignited in the fields. But amazingly, no human deaths were recorded. (About 3,000 sheep were killed, though.)

Aftermath: Early newspapers called the Santiago Canyon Fire "the Great Fire," and it occurred during a year when Californians were already dealing with a five-month drought, frequent small earthquakes, and a flood. To this day, historians consider the Santiago Canyon Fire to be one of the largest blazes ever to hit the state.

THE RATTLESNAKE FIRE

Where: Mendocino National Forest

What: It started out as a grass fire, one of the dozens that spark up each year in Northern California's brush-filled canyons. Around 10:00 p.m. on July 9, 1953, dozens of firefighters were battling the small blaze about 90 miles north of Sacramento when the wind suddenly shifted. The fire swelled and roared into the canyon…straight for a crew of 24 firefighters who had stopped for a dinner break. An alarm went off, but it was too late. The men scattered—15 headed deeper into the canyon, and the rest scrambled up a trail. From the canyon lip, the other firefighters watched as the lights from their coworkers' headlamps disappeared one by one.

Aftermath: The Rattlesnake Fire killed the 15 firefighters who ran into the canyon and left a lasting impression on the Forest Service, which oversees fire control in California's parks. The agency assembled a task force that came up with a list of firefighting rules called the Ten Standard Fire Orders, which remains in place today. The initiative seems to be a success; firefighter fatalities dropped dramatically after 1957, and double-digit deaths were not seen until 1966, when 12 men were killed in the Loop Fire in California's Angeles National Forest.

And how did the Rattlesnake Fire start? It was arson. Stan Pattan, the son of a Forest Service engineer, later confessed to setting the blaze in order to get a job on the fire crew. He was working as a cook in the firefighter camp when he was arrested, and later served three years in San Quentin.

PAINTED CAVE FIRE

Where: Los Padres National Forest

What: In 1990 one of the fastest-moving fires on record consumed 4,900 acres, 427 homes, 11 public buildings, and more than $400,000 worth of vehicles just north of Santa Barbara. It also took the life of 37-year-old Andrea Gurka, a wildlife artist who had sprained both ankles shortly before the fire started and wasn't able to escape her home in time.

The Painted Cave Fire—named for the roadway where it began—burned on June 27, a day when temperatures soared to 106°F. There hadn't been a fire in the area in 35 years, and the brush was thick and dry. High winds whipped the blaze into a frenzy, and the flames traveled nearly four miles in less than two hours, burning across U.S. 101 toward the Pacific Ocean.

Investigators quickly determined that the fire was the result of arson, and suspicion settled on Lenny Ross, a reclusive artist who made a living constructing solar-powered butterflies and selling them at craft fairs. Ross had been feuding with his neighbor,

Michael Linthicum, for years. In an effort to get the man to move, Ross started the fire in a patch of brush just off Linthicum's property. But police couldn't link Ross to the blaze and the case stymied.

Aftermath: Then, in 1996, Peggy Finley, Ross's ex-girlfriend, confessed a secret to her minister: Ross told her that he'd started a big fire. He only wanted to burn out one neighbor, she said, but the fire got out of control. Finley allowed the minister to tell the church's lawyer, who then called police. Detectives began assembling a case against Ross, but the district attorney balked, saying there wasn't enough evidence to warrant murder charges.

The case might have ended there, but Ross sued the county over a police search of his property. The county countersued over the cost of fighting the fire, allowing investigators to put their evidence before a civil jury. The ex-girlfriend testified against him, and Ross was found liable for the fire damage. Even though he escaped criminal charges, he was ordered to pay $2.75 million.

* * *

HOW DO YOU LOSE A WATERFALL?

It's hard to imagine losing a 400-foot waterfall, possibly the largest in Shasta County, but that's what happened in the Whiskeytown National Recreation Area. In the 1960s, park rangers had discovered the falls 15 miles into a vast stretch of wilderness while on a scouting mission to decide whether or not to buy the property. They didn't tell the owner about the waterfall in order to keep the price low. But just before the purchase was finalized, there was a staff shakeup at the park and the men who'd actually seen the waterfall were let go, causing the waterfall to be forgotten for more than three decades. Then, in 2005, park ranger Russ Weatherbee, having heard rumors about a large waterfall somewhere on Crystal Creek in the recreation area, decided to go searching for it, using a map he had found in an old cabinet. The map was wrong, but it was enough of a clue to lead him to a batch of aerial photos. Finally, on one of those pictures, he saw a glint of a white strip about two-thirds of a mile from where the map had indicated the falls was. He bushwhacked to the site, and bingo—that's how a found, then lost, waterfall was found again.

Abe Lincoln's nephew William Todd designed the first California state flag.

GIVE ME LIBERTY, AND GIVE ME HEALTH

Before capitalism and HMOs became dirty words, Richmond's Henry Kaiser made them work for both businessmen and employees, proving you could be rich and compassionate.

L ANDING IN CALIFORNIA
By the mid-20th century, Henry John Kaiser was among the most famous industrialists in the world. Born in 1882, he dropped out of school at 13 to help support his struggling family and eventually went on to found more than 100 companies in many different industries: engineering, construction, aviation, and electronics. Kaiser built roads, part of the San Francisco Bay Bridge, aqueducts, dams, and the locks on the Panama Canal. But he earned his greatest acclaim building hundreds of Allied ships during World War II, and his lasting legacy came from a health-care plan he set up for his shipyard workers—Kaiser Permanente, the first nonprofit, health maintenance organization, or HMO.

Kaiser's rags-to-riches success began with a love story. The young man taught himself photography and in 1906 owned a small portrait studio in Lake Placid, New York. When Bess Fosburgh came in to get her picture taken, Kaiser was smitten. But when he spoke to her father about proposing, the older man wasn't enthusiastic. He ordered Kaiser to go west and not come back until he had at least $1,000 in the bank and a more "substantial" job than photography. Fosburgh probably thought she'd never see Kaiser again, but a year later, the young man was a top hardware salesman in Washington State, with money in the bank and a ring for Bess.

Kaiser's father in-law must have fired up his ambitions, because the new businessman decided that there was a big future in construction. He started his own road-paving company, which struggled until 1921, when Kaiser took a train to Redding, California. The train didn't actually stop in the town, so Kaiser jumped off while it was still moving. He rolled into a pile of rail-

One in three Californians is Hispanic.

road ties, brushed himself off, and rushed to keep an appointment with Redding city officials. They awarded his company a contract of $527,000 to pave Highway 99—his first big job. Even better, Kaiser liked California so much that he stayed and built the Kaiser Office Building in Oakland, which became the operational center for his many companies.

LABOR LOVER

In 1931, in the midst of the Great Depression, Kaiser and a few other contractors formed a construction firm called Six Companies. Kaiser hoped that by pooling their various strengths and experiences, they could win big federal jobs. As the head of Six Companies, Kaiser went to Washington, D.C., and came back with a prize...a $165 million contract to build the Boulder Dam (now the Hoover Dam).

The Boulder Dam came in ahead of schedule in 1936, but many workers were injured (even killed) in the process because of unsafe conditions. Kaiser learned a lesson during that project, though, because, from then on, he was considered a friend to labor. He brought in his next job, the Grand Coulee Dam, ahead of schedule and with a happy workforce that remained loyal to his company.

CRAZY KAISER

By 1940, Kaiser had a reputation for solving big problems and building things "better, faster, and cheaper." World War II put that reputation to its biggest test. Nazi submarines were destroying British ships three times faster than they could be replaced, and Britain couldn't supply its army. President Franklin D. Roosevelt wanted to help, but the Americans had no shipyards or available builders. So Kaiser bid for the job, even though he had no ship-building experience. He estimated so little time to produce the ships that naval officials thought he was crazy. But they were desperate, so he got the job.

In 1941 Kaiser built a shipyard in Richmond, California, shortly before the Japanese attacked Pearl Harbor. The Americans' need for all kinds of new ships exploded—battleships, aircraft carriers, cargo ships. The navy hoped that "Crazy Kaiser" would be able to deliver and ordered so many ships that Kaiser had to build six more shipyards in the Northwest.

THIS IS WAR!

Kaiser's Richmond yards produced more than 747 ships for the navy, the most produced in World War II. Previously, ships were built individually from the keel up, but Kaiser's were mass-produced using assembly-line techniques. More than 30,000 components per ship were made in factories and shipped to Richmond. Then the parts were fitted together in the yard and moved by cranes to a final assembly point where they were welded together. (Welding was faster than riveting, the way ships were typically made.) To speed things up even more, Kaiser held competitions among his shipyards in California and Oregon. Richmond won by assembling the *Robert E. Perry* in 4 days, 15 hours, and 26 minutes. The average at other companies: 45 days.

Ships couldn't always be put together that quickly, but by 1944, Kaiser's shipyards averaged about one ship every two weeks. Kaiser's ships were also considered to be of better quality than the ones produced in other yards.

NO EXPERIENCE? NO PROBLEM

The ships produced in Kaiser's Richmond yards were originally called Liberty Ships (and later, Victory Ships), merchant marine vessels that carried supplies to the Allies. Their patriotic name was designed to detract from their appearance—the press called them "ugly ducklings." But Kaiser's company was building them so quickly that Germany's submarines couldn't destroy them fast enough to keep supplies from reaching Allied armies.

Liberty and Victory Ships were the workhorses of the war. General Douglas MacArthur relied on them in the Pacific, and said they were his "lifeblood." The public, knowing how important the ships were, began calling Kaiser by the nickname "Hurry-up Henry." Kaiser became a national hero, but he felt that he owed much of his success to the dedicated labor of 100,000 workers, most of whom knew little to nothing about shipbuilding. "If they know one end of a monkey wrench from the other, we'll take them," Kaiser said. "If they don't, we'll label each end." Kaiser's workers had learned on the job to help win the war.

ROSIES AND WENDYS

Kaiser also relied heavily on women in his shipyards. So many men were off fighting during World War II that women became a huge part of the workforce. They were usually known as "Rosies," named after Rosie the Riveter, the national symbol of women who worked in the factories as part of the war effort. But because there weren't actually any riveters at the Kaiser shipyards, the women at the Richmond Shipyards were also nicknamed "Wendy," for Wendy the Welder.

Despite their inexperience, the Wendys knew that lives depended on their ships, and they became well known for careful work. Some of the early Liberty Ships cracked in the cold waters of the Atlantic, and the welders were blamed. But close examination revealed that the welds had actually held; it was the steel that made the ships susceptible to cracking in the cold. Further proof of the Wendys' good work: The SS *Red Oak Victory*, which was built in Richmond in 1944, survived the war, and was docked at the Richmond Shipyards. Sixty-five years later, its welds were still intact.

HENRY AND HEALTH

Along with helping to win World War II and employing women and minorities (despite objections, Kaiser hired African Americans too), the shipyards' biggest legacy was health care. Kaiser started an HMO in Richmond, partly because it helped to attract good workers, but also because of his own life experiences. His mother had died when he was 17, and Kaiser always believed that if the family could have afforded health care, she could have been saved.

In 1942 Kaiser teamed up with Dr. Sidney Garfield, a Los Angeles physician. They'd worked together before at the Grand Coulee Dam to set up a health-care plan for the 15,000 Kaiser construction workers. The cost of that plan: 5 cents a day. During World War II, Garfield opened a hospital in Richmond and formed the Kaiser-Garfield plan for shipyard workers. (It was eventually extended to all shipyards and a Kaiser steel mill in Fontana, California.) Many workers had never seen a doctor, but now they could get unlimited medical care for just $2 a month (about $27 today).

In 1945, after the war ended, Kaiser and Garfield expanded their care of shipyard workers to the general public by founding a general HMO called Kaiser Permanente. It wasn't the first HMO in the United States, but it was revolutionary in several ways: In

There are approximately 8,200 people per square mile in L.A.

those days, most Americans didn't pay for a doctor unless they were sick, few people had any kind of medical insurance, and many couldn't afford medical care at all. The Kaiser plan worked a lot like today's medical insurance: people paid while they were healthy, but by pooling the prepayments together, the company could afford to pay for expensive care if they got sick. Kaiser also brought groups of doctors together under one roof—that meant patients had access to specialists from all areas of medicine as well as to laboratories and hospitals. The most revolutionary idea, though, was probably that Kaiser emphasized preventive care. Doctors didn't make more if people were sick or injured because they were salaried. So it was to everyone's financial advantage if most members stayed healthy.

The new medical plan grew quickly. Between 1945 and 1956, membership rose from 130,500 to more than 300,000 in Northern California alone. By 1990 more than 6 million people were enrolled across the state. Today, Kaiser Permanente is the largest nonprofit HMO in the country. Henry Kaiser probably wouldn't be surprised. He once said, "Of all the things I've done, I expect only to be remembered for…filling the people's greatest need—good health."

* * *

SOLD ON EBAY

ITEM: Lunch with Warren Buffett

STORY: Each year for more than a decade, the nonprofit Glide Foundation in San Francisco has auctioned off a private lunch with legendary investor Warren Buffett, one of the wealthiest people in the world. In 2011 Buffett dined at a steakhouse with the anonymous American who won the auction (and up to seven friends), discussing anything but his current business transactions. The proceeds help the Glide Foundation provide meals, health care, and job training to needy people in the Bay Area. Buffett says he participates because he's impressed by Glide's success in helping people recuperate after they've hit rock bottom.

SELLING PRICE: $2.63 million

HEROISM AFTER THE QUAKE

Disasters often bring out the best in people.

RESCUE ME
At 5:12 a.m. on Wednesday April 18, 1906, an earthquake rocked San Francisco. For the next four days, fires ravaged the city, and city officials, police, firefighters, and even the army all worked together to put them out. But the city might not have survived without the extraordinary efforts of ordinary people who stepped up and helped. Here are some of their stories.

• The **post office** remained standing after the quake but was soon threatened by the growing blaze. Many postal workers risked their lives by using wet mail sacks to beat out the smaller fires. Then, as soon as the danger had passed, they began sorting the thousands of pieces of mail city residents wanted to get out to worried relatives. Survivors scribbled messages on boards, newspapers, even shirts, and as long as it had a legible address, it was delivered—no stamp needed.

• Of the city's five newspapers, only the ***Daily News*** managed to put out an edition the afternoon of the quake. The other four newspapers, long bitter rivals, joined forces with the *Daily News* to put out a combined issue on Thursday. The editors never bothered to ask permission of the owners, knowing it would be denied. The most important task at that moment was to get out the information that citizens needed to find food, shelter, services, and loved ones.

• The **Southern Pacific Railroad Station** depot was saved by brave men with one pump, a single stretch of hose, some wet gunny sacks, and a few buckets. Volunteers carried water from the bay three blocks away. Over the next few days, thousands of tons of food, blankets, clothing, and medical supplies passed through this depot—as well as 300,000 refugees fleeing the city. All traveled free of charge.

Before Clint Eastwood landed the part, Steve McQueen, Paul Newman, and...

- The **San Francisco Mint** was built of steel and concrete, with metal windows. It was fireproof on the outside, but the rampaging flames blew out the windows and set fires inside. Firemen and employees frantically hauled water from a cistern to put out fires in interior woodwork and on the tar-paper roof. Seven hours later, the mint—and all the money inside—was safe.

- The **Hopkins Art Institute** contained thousands of dollars' worth of paintings and statues. All day after the quake, teachers and students removed hundreds of pictures to the lawn, where they were carried in wheelbarrows, wagons, and on shoulders to safe spots around the city. Navy men arrived to help that night, and a young lieutenant used his service pistol to "encourage" other people from the passing crowds to assist.

- Bank owner **Amadeo Giannini** walked 17 miles to inspect the damage at his Bank of Italy. When he arrived, the fire was approaching fast. His clerks swore the fire would never reach that far, but Giannini wasn't so sure. He loaded all the bank's money into two wagons and hauled them to his house, where he hid it underneath his fireplace. When the fires were out, Giannini hauled the money to a new location in the financial district. Giannini's bank later expanded to become one of the largest in the nation—the Bank of America. Another bank president, **William Crocker**, had workers load all of his bank's records into sacks, stack them in a wagon, and take it to the docks. Then he put all the sacks on a boat, which sailed to the middle of San Francisco Bay until all the fires were out. Why was this so important? It meant that he'd be able to identify his customers when survivors came to withdraw much-needed funds.

- **Alice Eastwood** made her way downtown to the California Academy of Sciences. She was the curator of botany and managed to save many treasured plants while her own home and possessions burned. She decided it was easier to buy new furniture than to replace the botanical specimens. All she had left after the fire was the dress she was wearing.

- **The Ultimate Sacrifice:** Police Sergeant Behan saved much of the city's paperwork by wetting it down with beer collected from nearby stores.

STRANGEFEST

Californians have some really bizarre traditions.

FULL MOON

Like many time-honored traditions, the annual Laguna Niguel Amtrak train mooning started in a bar. In 1979 K. T. Smith, a customer at the Mugs Away Saloon in Orange County, offered to buy drinks for anyone who dashed out to the railroad tracks, dropped their pants, and showed their bare behinds to the next train. A handful of people took him up on it. Now held every July, the moon show attracts some 10,000 participants and spectators who bring chairs, coolers, and picnics. They all line up along the fence near the saloon, on the east side of the tracks between the San Juan Capistrano and Irvine stations. Every 20 minutes, a train rolls by—and slows down so passengers can get a good view of the mooners, who range in age from children to seniors. (Some creative participants even decorate their derrieres.) After sunset, pants-droppers bring lanterns to attach to the fence so their rears can be seen clearly. It was all good-natured fun until 2008, when some people flashed *all* their naked parts. Police helicopters and 50 officers came to break up the party, so in the years since, the participants have generally stuck to their buns.

KINETIC SCULPTURE TRIATHLON

The only race in the United States (we think) whose participants are allowed help from interplanetary beings takes place every May in Humboldt County. The Kinetic Grand Championship requires that teams create moving sculptures and pedal them 42 miles from Arcata to Ferndale through water, mud, and sand. The #1 rule: It's mandatory to have great fun. Rule #2: Sculptures must be powered by humans, but "it is legal to get assistance from the natural power of water, wind, sun, gravity, and friendly extraterrestrials (if introduced to the judges)." The contest has been going on since 1969, when sculptors Hobart Brown and Jack Mays raced their creations (one was a five-wheeled cycle) down Main Street in Ferndale. Today, each sculpture has a pilot to steer, a pit crew for maintenance, and "pee-ons" who handle the rest, including any necessary bribing of spectators and judges. Past entries include a giant lobster, a dragon boat, and a Day of the Dead decorated taco truck. This contest doesn't just recognize the team that is the fastest. Sculptures can win for taking the middle spot (the Mediocre Award), for being the first to break down (the Golden Dinosaur), and for not cheating (Ace the Race). However, the organizers make it clear that the race condones cheating only "if it is done with originality and panache."

ODE TO THE ODD

Every spring, as many as 12,000 weirdos gather in San Francisco for the How Weird Street Faire. With annual themes like "the UFO Arrives" or "Bollyweird: the Cosmic Dance," the gathering aims to promote a safe place for eccentric people to gather and be seen. Filling nine city blocks of the SoMa (South of Market) District, the festival features art, a Maypole, a hula-hoop area, and an official flying saucer landing zone (coordinates: 37°47'10.88"N, 122°23'53.50"W). More than 100 bands and deejays play music as diverse as dubstep, world beat, and bhangra, while people dance on elaborate stages. Attendees wear rave gear, disco outfits, stilts, roller skates, colored wigs, bunny ears, or almost nothing at all. Vendors sell unique fairy accessories, bear and cat hoodies, light-up jewelry, and costumes for dogs and kids. Hugs are free!

DON'T HOLD YOUR BREATH

In 1968 Prairie Creek Redwoods State Park in Northern California hosted its first Banana Slug Derby. Banana slugs are one of the largest slug species, growing up to 10 inches long, and they leave a trail of slime as they move—at a speed of six inches per minute. Billed as one of the slowest races on earth, the derby was the idea of bored ranger Paula Pennington. She explains: "We found some banana slugs and raced them. It was so much fun that I talked to my coworkers about having a banana-slug race as a park event to spice up the end of summer." The annual August festival came to include the slug race, a parade, and games, including a slime toss (yeah, we don't know how it works either, but it sounds gross). The main goal is education about banana slugs and their importance to redwood trees—the creatures help fertilize soil and eat other plants that compete with redwoods for nutrients. Rangers are quick to note that the racing slugs are returned to the forest after the derby, and are not harmed in any way. (Just don't tell them about the Slugfest in Monte Rio, where people eat banana slugs in everything from chili and cake to martinis and lime Jell-O.)

DRINKING AND DRIVING...A SHOPPING CART

Usually held in March, the Urban Iditarod began in 1994, the brainchild of the Cacophony Society—a group that unites people "in the pursuit of experiences beyond the pale of mainstream society through subversion, pranks, art, fringe explorations, and meaningless madness." The idea was based on the Iditarod sled dog races across Alaska. But since this race is in San Francisco, the people are the dogs, they wear costumes, and they pull shopping carts full of beer instead of sleds...and most of them are drunk. The four-mile course includes stops at watering holes (bars) where the "dogs" take breaks. Teams consist of one to 100 people, and although most have canine themes—like Underdogs or Dogs Playing Poker—there are teams of Teletubbies, circus freaks, wrestlers, and *Jersey Shore* stars. In 2006 the event drew almost 700 participants. The Urban Iditarod has spawned races in other cities, including Los Angeles, where, unlike the cops in San Francisco, the LAPD doesn't seem to appreciate the spirit of the event and issues tickets for disturbing the peace and possessing stolen carts...but no DUIs so far.

* * *

IT'S A GEEK THING

You've got to appreciate Fry's Electronics. Not necessarily for its bins of obscure electronic bits and bytes, but for the Silicon Valley chain's creativity. Each store has its own theme—most notably King Tut (Campbell), railroads (Roseville), the ruins of Rome (Fountain Valley), Atlantis (San Marcos), *Alice in Wonderland* (Woodland Hills), and the Mayans (San Jose). But the cream of the crop has got to be the Burbank store, with its theme of retro 1950s UFO films. The storefront itself looks like a spectacular disaster scene, complete with a huge flying saucer embedded in it. Just some sort of interplanetary miscalculation, or the result of a defective electronic component? Hope they kept their receipt.

The state reptile, the desert tortoise, can survive for a year without water.

MORE GHOST COAST

California is known for sun, surf, sand...and some of the most haunted real estate in the United States. (Part I appears on page 69.)

WHO: Jonny Johnson
WHERE: Toys 'R Us, Sunnyvale
STORY: Ghosts don't always haunt ancient, gloomy castles. In fact, one of the nation's most famous paranormal photos comes from a warehouse built in 1970. Supposedly, a ghost haunts the Toys 'R Us in Sunnyvale, where toys fly off the shelves and footsteps traipse in empty aisles. Faucets in the women's restroom also turn on by themselves and shoppers claim to feel someone stroke their hair or touch their shoulder when there's no one nearby. The most notorious aisle is 15C, where shoppers have been surprised by the strong fragrance of fresh flowers.

TV psychic Sylvia Browne first visited the store in the 1970s and claimed the ghost was a Scandinavian immigrant named Jonny Johnson. The Toys 'R Us was built on the site of an old ranch, and Johnson was a preacher who worked on the farm. Around 1869, while chopping wood, he accidentally struck his leg with an axe and bled to death. Browne believes Johnson's still around because he's looking for his unrequited love, Beth, the boss's daughter who hardly noticed the immigrant and married an East Coast lawyer.

In 1978 Browne and the TV show *That's Incredible* held a séance in the building. They took high-speed and infrared photos of the event in the unlighted store. One of the infrared photos showed a young man in farmer's clothing standing in an aisle. The séance members said they never saw him. After seeing the photo, Browne returned to the store and encouraged Johnson to find peace by heading toward the light...but lots of people in Sunnyvale say he didn't listen.

WHO: William and Maria Reed; Joseph Peter Lynch and his gang
WHERE: Mission San Miguel, San Miguel
STORY: Spanish priests founded the Mission San Miguel in 1797, but after Mexico won control of California from Spain, it confiscated all the missions from the Catholic Church and decided to

sell them off. In 1846 entrepreneur William Reed bought San Miguel with some surrounding land. Reed turned the building to an inn and, during the gold rush, required that patrons pay for their meals and lodging with gold.

By the end of 1848, Reed had made a fortune and claimed he buried it on his property. He then made the mistake of bragging about his success in front of Joseph Peter Lynch, who was spending the night at the inn with his five companions. Lynch was an army deserter and his pals were outlaws. They left in the morning, but returned the next night and killed 10 people, including Reed, his pregnant wife Maria, their four-year-old son, Maria's brother, and several employees and guests. Then the outlaws got drunk on Reed's liquor and went looking for the gold...but never found it.

A posse caught up with them a few days later, killed two, arrested the rest (including Lynch), and then executed them. The mission was returned to the Catholic Church in the 1850s and, in the 20th century, became a museum too. But the story didn't end there. More than 150 years later, many people who visit Mission San Miguel—even people who don't know the story of the murders—claim to feel an overwhelming sense of melancholy there. Visitors have heard cries and screams and seen strange flashing lights. Many also say they've seen a "Lady in White," thought to be Maria Reed, and a ghost thought to be her husband William (because it wears a pea coat like the one he wore in life). The killers have been spotted, too, supposedly still searching for the buried gold that has never been found.

WHO: Sarah Winchester
WHERE: Winchester House, San Jose
STORY: Sarah Pardee Winchester was incredibly wealthy...and incredibly wacky. In 1862 she married William Winchester, whose family made a fortune manufacturing the Winchester rifle. The couple had a daughter, who lived only a few weeks, and in 1881 William died of tuberculosis. That left Sarah with $20 million and half of the Winchester company, which brought in an income of $1,000 a day (about $22,000 in today's dollars).

Soon after William died, Sarah started visiting psychics, hoping they could help her contact her dead family. Instead, one medium in Boston told her that she was cursed by all the people who had been killed by Winchester weapons. To foil the curse, she had to move west and build a new home...and never stop building on that home—not even for an hour. Sarah listened. She moved to San Jose, hired construction workers and contractors, and built a 160-room Victorian mansion.

The carpenters worked in shifts around the clock. According to legend, Sarah held a séance every night at midnight, in the hopes of contacting the spirits for guidance on how the construction should progress. There were no master plans. Rooms were built around other rooms, and doors opened into walls. There were trapdoors, upside-down stair posts, and chimneys that didn't work. By 1906, the house stood seven stories high. Then on April 18, a strong earthquake struck, and the top three floors collapsed, trapping Sarah in her bedroom. She was eventually freed, but believed that the incident was the spirits' way of telling her they were displeased with the home improvements. So she boarded up 30 rooms in the front of the house and kept going.

Sarah Winchester died on September 5, 1922. When told of her death, the workmen quit what they were doing immediately—some even left half-pounded nails in the walls. But many people say Sarah never left the house. Supposedly, she still plays the piano and walks the many twisting corridors. Visitors have even reported smelling chicken soup cooking in the empty kitchen.

*   *   *

MICKEY NEVER GETS A DAY OFF

As of the end of 2011, Disneyland has had only three unscheduled closings since it opened in 1955:

1. In 1963, after President John F. Kennedy was assassinated.
2. In 1970, when the Youth International Party ("Yippies") mounted an in-park political protest against the Vietnam War.
3. On September 11, 2001, when Disney management worried that the amusement park might become a terrorist target.

Along the same lines, the drawbridge to the Sleeping Beauty Castle has been publicly closed and opened only twice: the day the park opened on July 17, 1955, and when Fantasyland was renovated and rededicated in May 1983.

REAL OR RUMOR?

*Misinformation runs rampant on the Internet. Uncle John considers
it his duty to chase it down and set the record straight.*

RUMOR: The 1976 song "Hotel California" by the Eagles is
about a Christian church that was taken over by a Satanic
group. (And the devil appears on the album cover with his
arms outstretched, beckoning followers.)

TRUE? No

REAL STORY: It's all just a metaphor. According to Eagles
drummer and lead vocalist Don Henley, the song is about corruption and greed—in the music industry and the world at large. In
2007 Henley said, "Some of the wilder interpretations of that song
have been amazing. It was really about the excesses of American
culture and certain girls we knew. But it was also about the uneasy
balance between art and commerce." In another interview, he
explained further: "We were all middle-class kids from the Midwest. 'Hotel California' was our interpretation of the high life in
Los Angeles." (The character with outstretched arms on the cover
was just a model hired for the photo shoot.)

RUMOR: Former U.S. president Ronald Reagan was a tree hater
who said, "If you've seen one redwood, you've seen 'em all."

TRUE? Essentially

REAL STORY: In 1966, as governor of California, Reagan
opposed expanding Redwood National Park, and he was quoted in
the *Sacramento Bee* as saying, "A tree is a tree. How many more do
you have to look at?" Everyone didn't share Reagan's view,
though—Redwood National Park was expanded by 48,000 acres
in 1978.

RUMOR: Thanks to a 2005 law, it's illegal to drive a car in the
state during the day with the windshield wipers on and the headlights off.

TRUE? Sort of

REAL STORY: The law says that drivers have to turn on their headlights during the day if there is 1) "a condition that prevents a driver of a motor vehicle from clearly discerning a person or another motor vehicle on the highway from a distance of 1,000 feet," or 2) "a condition requiring the windshield wipers to be in continuous use due to rain, mist, snow, fog, or other precipitation or atmospheric moisture."

RUMOR: The wildfires that ripped through Southern California in 2003 created a toilet paper shortage in the United States.
TRUE? No
REAL STORY: The origin of this rumor was an e-mail that claimed the Clappington toilet paper factory in Southern California, which made 97.5 percent of all American-used toilet paper, burned down in the fires. But as we at the BRI know, toilet paper manufacturing is not confined to a single factory...in a single area...of a single state. Plus, most of the U.S. papermaking industries are located in the Pacific Northwest (where the trees are), not in the Southern California desert. Plus, there's no evidence that a Clappington factory ever even existed.

RUMOR: The fire chief in Berkeley banned the city's fire trucks from displaying American flags.
TRUE? Well, yes, but...
REAL STORY? He instituted the ban because of safety concerns. After 9/11, the firefighters in Berkeley started flying American flags on their trucks as a show of patriotism. But Assistant Fire Chief David Orth was afraid that antiwar protesters—of whom there are many in Berkeley—scheduled to attend a September 20 rally at UC Berkeley would target the fire trucks, possibly causing injuries. So Orth did order all the flags removed from the trucks for the rally. They went back up the next day.

RUMOR: The U.S. Geological Survey predicted that a massive earthquake would destroy Los Angeles on September 30, 2010.
TRUE? No
REAL STORY: No one can predict earthquakes, and L.A. is still there.

Artist R. Crumb sold his first comics from a baby stroller on SF street corners.

NOVEL CONSEQUENCES

No novel has had more influence on Southern California than Ramona... *though it wasn't the kind of influence that the author had hoped for.*

AMERICA...MEET RAMONA

The first novel ever written about Southern California was a blockbuster called *Ramona*. Penned by Helen Hunt Jackson in 1884, *Ramona* became an immediate best-seller, and it's *still* selling. In the more than 100 years since its publication, the book has been reprinted about 300 times.

For many years, even people who didn't read the book still knew the plot: An orphan and the child of a European father and an Indian mother, Ramona is raised by the wealthy owner of a vast California *rancho* (a sheep and cattle ranch). When she grows up, she falls in love and elopes with Alessandro, a handsome, courageous Native American. But the story turns tragic when Alessandro's family and tribe are thrown off their land, and the novel ends shortly after Ramona sees Alessandro murdered by a white settler who is never brought to justice.

FACT OR FICTION?

Historians debate how much of *Ramona* was made up, but at least two parts were based on real events: The 1875 eviction of the Luiseno tribe from Temecula, California, inspired the story of Alessandro's family being removed from their land, and Alessandro's murder was based on the 1883 shooting of a Cahuilla Indian named Juan Diego, who lived in the San Jacinto Mountains. Diego's wife watched helplessly as a wagon driver named Sam Temple summoned her husband to their cabin door and then shot him several times because he believed Diego had stolen one of his horses. Historians believe the whole thing was a misunderstanding and that Diego accidentally rode off on one of Temple's horses at a common corral instead of his own. But given the racism and anti–Native American feelings of the 19th century, Temple simply claimed self-defense (he said Diego came at him with a knife), and got off without even going to trial. That injustice made author Helen Hunt Jackson incredibly angry.

A CALL TO ACTION

When Jackson checked into New York's Berkeley Hotel to write *Ramona*, the shooting of Juan Diego was very much on her mind. She'd spoken to a court official who explained that no jury in California would ever convict a white man for murdering a Native American if the only witness against him was another Native American. Jackson was outraged and wrote to her editor, "If I could write a story that would do for the Indian a thousandth part that *Uncle Tom's Cabin* [Harriet Beecher Stowe's 1852 antislavery novel] did for the negro, I would be thankful for the rest of my life."

It didn't seem like such a far-fetched hope. Jackson had made a name for herself as a writer of poems and travel pieces, but she gave that up in 1879 after hearing Chief Standing Bear from the Ponca tribe speak about the theft of reservation land in Nebraska. After doing some research, she decided to dedicate her life and her writing to improving the legal standing of Native Americans. In 1881 Jackson wrote *A Century of Dishonor*, a history of federal mistreatment of Native Americans that she sent to every member of the U.S. Congress. Then in 1883 she traveled to California to investigate the living conditions of the Native Americans there. In the report she wrote to Congress, she told stories of rampant theft, brutalization, and even murder. But the representatives didn't seem to care. So Jackson decided to bypass them altogether and make an emotional appeal directly to the American public. In March 1884—while suffering from stomach cancer—she checked into the Berkeley Hotel in New York, determined to write a book that would "move people's hearts."

WELCOME TO RAMONALAND

Four months later, Jackson emerged with a novel that did move people. In fact, the book made such an impression on readers that many of them believed Ramona was a real person. But their call to action wasn't as noble as Jackson had hoped. Readers were so enchanted by the descriptions of life on California's missions and ranchos that they didn't pay much attention to the moral point of the story: the plight of the Native Americans who lived there. Instead, they became enthralled with Southern California.

That misunderstanding wasn't entirely the readers' fault. Although Jackson was tough on the white settlers, she idealized the area, the missionaries, and the Mexican landowners. (By all accounts, she didn't realize that they brutalized the Native Americans, too.) In *Ramona*, wise, kindly padres ran the missions, and the land in California was like paradise. As the book described it: "All was garden, orange grove, and almond orchard; the orange grove always green, never without snowy bloom or golden fruit; the garden never without flowers summer or winter."

"Ramonaland"—as people started to call Southern California—sounded like a lovely place, and East Coasters wanted to see it for themselves. Luckily, in the late 19th century, railroad lines were just opening up the area to the average traveler, and thousands of tourists flocked to the California sites where they thought Ramona grew up, fell in love, and got married. Jackson's novel helped fuel the biggest tourist and real-estate boom in Southern California's history. Between 1880 and 1890, Los Angeles's population grew from 11,000 to 97,000, and San Diego swelled from about 2,600 people to 30,000.

The Americans who already lived and worked in those areas made a lot of money, too. Stores sold Ramona face cream, Ramona perfume, and even Ramona beer. Towns attracted tourists by claiming to be the "real" settings of the book: The city of San Diego called itself "Ramona's marriage place, the most beautiful and romantic spot in California." San Gabriel encouraged tourists to visit and to see "the San Gabriel mission, where Ramona worshipped." A huge postcard industry evolved around the places in the book—one card depicted a photo of "Ramona's garden" in eastern Ventura County. The novel also gave names to Southern California hotels, elementary schools, streets, and towns. Even the San Bernardino and Glendale freeways used to be called the Ramona and Alessandro freeways.

THE GOVERNMENT MAKES THINGS WORSE

None of this was what Jackson had intended, and she died 10 months after *Ramona* was published, thinking that she'd inadvertently inspired a tourist boom instead of activism. One reader did take up her cause, though also in a way Jackson would not have liked. Senator Henry Dawes of Massachusetts sponsored and gave his name to the 1887 Dawes Act, which divided up tribal lands into individual plots and granted them to Native American families. In theory, the goal was to assimilate Native Americans into white society by giving them a piece of what all Americans wanted: land. But in reality, because the land was no longer protected as reservations by the government, whites pushed for their own opportunity to settle it. The government also used the Dawes Act as an excuse to award the Native Americans less land overall and to take more back for railroads and development. Plus, many of the regions where the Indians were living (having been relocated throughout the 19th century) were difficult to survive on and worthless for farming anyway, so Native American families often abandoned their plots. Thanks to the Dawes Act, the amount of land allocated to native tribes decreased from about 140 million acres in the 1880s to just 48 million in the early 1930s.

RAMONA'S IMPACT ON RAMONA

At least one Indian woman was helped by the novel, though. She was Ramona Lubo, the wife of Juan Diego, the man whose murder inspired Jackson to write *Ramona*. Tourists often came to San Jacinto to see her, paying money for a visit and buying the woven baskets she made as souvenirs. Lubo also charged fees to go "on display" at fairs, selling her baskets behind a sign that said, "The Real Ramona." The money kept her going, but she never said much to the tourists about the death of Juan Diego (whom they often mistakenly called Alessandro).

THEY GO WAY BACK

In an interesting bit of literary friendship, it turns out that *Ramona* author Helen Hunt Jackson was close friends with the poet Emily Dickinson. The pair met as children, but lost touch and reconnected in the 1870s. Both women were from Amherst, Massachusetts, and Jackson was one of the people who consistently encouraged Dickinson to publish her poems.

*　　*　　*

"I don't want yes men. When I say no, I want you to say no too!"
—Jack Warner, head of Warner Bros.,
to an underling

PEACE, BROTHER...
AND KEEP OUT!

Marin County's reign as a center of counterculture has ended...
except in the little village of Bolinas, where the kindly
hippie residents ask you to please get lost.

THE GREAT HIPPIE MIGRATION

In 1967 it was the Summer of Love in San Francisco. Young hippies wearing tie-dye and bandannas gathered in the city's Haight-Ashbury neighborhood to celebrate "new values" for their generation. Instead of the pursuit of money and possessions (which they felt had led to the Vietnam War), hippies wanted to live peaceful lives with no restrictions on their love for one another. They'd respect nature and practice self-discovery with the help of religion and psychedelic drugs. By the end of that summer, the movement was supposed to be over. All the indiscriminate sex and drug use caused problems, and critics believed the hippie lifestyle had burned itself out from immorality and irresponsibility.

But hippie culture was far from dead. In the late 1960s and early '70s, lots of hippies took their ideas and simply moved north across the Golden Gate Bridge into Marin County. Marin offered a combination of spectacular natural beauty with wealthy San Francisco suburbs, and those bland 'burbs underwent some changes after the hippies arrived. In 1978 most of America was shocked to see a documentary called *I Want It All Now*, which showed Marin's "swinging lifestyle," complete with hot-tub orgies, peacock feather massages, plenty of marijuana, and that new drug, cocaine.

But that documentary missed the hippie invasion in a much less wealthy area of the county. Although there weren't all the hot tubs or peacock feathers, a definite hippie vibe had taken over the tiny fishing village of Bolinas. Located on the edge of the Point Reyes National Seashore, Bolinas was a hamlet of 19th-century homes, colorful flower gardens, and clean, sandy beaches overlooking the Pacific. But in January 1971, two oil tankers collided near the Golden Gate and drenched the coast in an estimated million gallons of oil. Idealistic hippie volunteers rushed to Boli-

---

The Siskiyou County town of Mugginsville was named for a card game.

nas hoping to save the dying birds and clean up the polluted beaches—and once they saw this lonely little paradise surrounded by water and wilderness, a lot of them stayed.

THE ROAD SIGN WAR

Young hippies and artists flocked to Bolinas for the relatively cheap rent and the tolerance for their lifestyle. Some planted organic gardens, raised chickens and goats, and lived off the land. Hippie celebrities moved in, too: Paul Kantner and Grace Slick of Jefferson Airplane lived in Bolinas, as did San Francisco beat poet Lawrence Ferlinghetti and acclaimed writer Richard Brautigan.

But around the same time, Bolinas also began to be discovered by developers who wanted to build vacation homes, yacht clubs, and tourist attractions in the beautiful spot only an hour from San Francisco. These ideas horrified the counterculture community, who foresaw the end of Bolinas's unspoiled beauty and the permissiveness that allowed them to thrive. And so, determined to keep their neighborhood undeveloped and undiscovered, the Bolinas crowd turned to some unique tactics—like the sign war.

In the 1970s, some of the Bolinas hippies formed the "Border Patrol," a group that went on the offensive against the California Department of Transportation (Caltrans). Every time Caltrans put up a road sign directing drivers to Bolinas from Highway 1, the Border Patrol took it down. (Some residents said the signs made good coffee tables.) Over the next two decades, about 36 signs were stolen, and no sign demarcating Bolinas stayed up for more than 48 hours. Caltrans finally tried to paint "Bolinas" on the asphalt, but the letters were blacked out with tar. The sign war went on for years, but even though Caltrans brought in officers from the California Highway Patrol to help locate perpetrators, no one was ever caught and prosecuted for sign theft.

POWER TO THE PEOPLE

Taking down the Caltrans signs was the most well known tactic Bolinas used against unwanted visitors, but there were others. It was rumored, for instance, that some Bolinians put tire-slashing debris on back roads. In 1973 the community put up its own signs featuring a skull and crossbones. Those signs announced that the beach was polluted and forbade any swimming, clamming, or surfing. (It probably galled Caltrans that those pollution signs also included clear warnings that tampering with them was punishable by law.) Spokespeople for Bolinas also often exaggerated the polluted state of their town, the poor county services, and lack of welcome or activities for outsiders—why, they implied, would anyone want to visit?

The least known and probably most successful tactic at keeping Bolinas from growing, however, had nothing to do with roads or signs. As an unincorporated community, Bolinas was under Marin County's authority. It had no mayor, city council, police department, or city hall, but it did have a water board. So some hippies cleaned themselves up and began to study water politics. Then they got themselves elected to the Bolinas Community Public Utility District.

Not surprisingly, once the hippies dominated that group, the board declared that Bolinas had an emergency water shortage (which actually was true at the time). But rather than figure out a way to get more water, the board issued a moratorium on installing any new water meters. That meant that if anyone built a home or business in Bolinas, they wouldn't be able to hook into the municipal water supply. There would be no water for new homes—let alone for swimming pools at a hotel or country club. And so, by the late 1970s, the little village of Bolinas was happily cut off from tourists and had nixed any development.

HEY! IT'S NOT THE SIXTIES ANYMORE!

Over the decades, in most of Marin County, the influence of the hippie residents faded. More than 40 years have passed since the Summer of Love, and Marin is once again another wealthy suburban community with great scenery. But what about Bolinas?

By 2011 the hippie enclave had also gone through changes. The road sign war wasn't really relevant anymore, since anyone with a GPS could find the town. In fact, the village earned a reputation of getting *more* visitors because it was "known for being unknown." Tourists wanted to see just what the residents were trying so hard to keep secret. Bolinas was also discovered by a new subculture that refused to be intimidated—surfers. Its beaches are now filled with beginning surfers, and Bolinas is considered one of the best places on the coast to learn the sport.

But, according to residents, many things haven't changed. In the 1970s, Bolinas was a small village of about 1,600 people, and that's what the population was in 2011. The no-growth contingent still rules the water board, and the water hookup moratorium continues. Many Bolinians declare they still have the same goals they had back in the '70s: "Limit tourism, slow growth, discourage land speculation, protect wildlife, and 'accept a wide range of lifestyles.'" And the Border Patrol is still patrolling, though it's changed its name to the more politically correct "Bolinas Community." In 2005 England's Prince Charles and his wife Camilla took a trip through Bolinas because Charles wanted to see the famous organic gardens grown there. But in Bolinas, Charles was still a tourist, and the Border Patrol managed to disable the GPS system on the front of his limo.

* * *

UNIDENTIFIED SWIMMING OBJECT

Scotland's Loch Ness has Nessie, and Lake Tahoe has Tessie: a 60-foot serpent. Or maybe it's 80 feet, some say, or only 10 feet. Or maybe it's really a supernaturally huge eel or sturgeon. Or it's something so horribly frightening that oceanographer Jacques Cousteau allegedly confronted it underwater and was quoted by somebody somewhere as saying that "the world's not ready for what's down there." There's not much substantiated fact associated with Tessie, however. Here's what we (think we) know:

• According to legend, her skin is smooth and black...or turquoise or maybe green.

• Two off-duty police officers in a boat in the 1950s claimed she outran them...at speeds of more than 60 mph.

• Supposedly, Tessie is capable of changing her size, shape, and color at will.

So what is she? In 2004 Dr. Charles Goldman of UC Davis offered on explanation. He analyzed all the reported Tessie sightings and found that the witnesses always said they just saw a long dark shape, no specific head or tail. So he took pictures of certain wave patterns on the lake and discovered that they came out looking a lot like the reported descriptions of Tahoe's Tessie.

NASHVILLE OF THE WEST

Bakersfield is probably best known around the world as a birthplace of country music. Yes…really.

THE BAKERSFIELD SOUND

Country music came to the United States with immigrants from Germany, Ireland, Scotland, Wales, England, Italy, and Africa who brought their folk songs and Old World instruments (fiddles, banjos, mandolins, etc.) with them. Originally, it was the music of the poor, mostly people who lived in Appalachia and the South. But by the 1950s and '60s, country had become so popular that it had a capital city (Nashville, Tennessee) and was a multimillion-dollar industry, fronted by artists like Elvis Presley, Marty Robbins, and Dolly Parton.

Some country musicians, though, thought the Nashville sound was too sleek and polished, and strayed too far from country music's outlaw and everyman roots. So they created their own loud, raw, raucous style. Driven by the piano, steel guitar, and the newly invented Fender Telecaster, they stood in direct contrast to the more refined music produced in Tennessee. These men established their capital in the Southern California desert city of Bakersfield, and they became the founding fathers of the "Bakersfield sound."

BUCK OWEN

No one deserves more credit for bringing the Bakersfield sound to mainstream audiences than Alvis Edgar "Buck" Owens. Born in Sherman, Texas, in 1929, he moved to Bakersfield in 1951 after visiting there during a stint as a truck driver and liking the place. With his band the Buckaroos, Owens immediately became a fixture on the local music scene, playing a type of twangy honky-tonk that was full of fiddles, pedal steel guitars, and drumbeats. In 1957 Capitol Records signed him, and Owens went on to score 15 consecutive #1 hits. His spirited, upbeat songs made him one of the greatest stars of his era and led to a job hosting the popular CBS variety show *Hee Haw*, which lasted from 1969 to 1986. A member of the Country Music Hall of Fame, Owens enjoyed one final chart-topping hit in 1988 when he recorded the duet "Streets of Bakersfield" with future Grammy winner Dwight Yoakam. The song's success sent him back to the studio—he recorded three more albums before passing away at his Bakersfield home in 2006.

Cool fact: Owens nicknamed himself "Buck" when he was about four. It was also the name of one of the family's mules.

MERLE HAGGARD

Haggard went by many names—including Hag, Mighty Merle, and the Poet of the Common Man—and he was among the most influential singer-songwriters in country music history. He also personified the life of a rebellious, lawless country music man. Born just outside of Bakersfield on April 6, 1937, to parents who had fled the Oklahoma dust bowl, he spent his teenage years in and out of juvenile institutions and county jails. In 1957 he was arrested for attempting to rob a bar in Bakersfield and served three years in California's San Quentin State Prison. Haggard didn't lose his edge in prison—he brawled with other inmates and ran a gambling ring out of his cell—but he also discovered music. When he got out, Haggard started writing songs and playing around Bakersfield, contributing sincere lyrics and a raw, edgy sound to the city's music scene. Since then, Haggard has recorded more than 600 songs and has had 38 number-one hits. His music has even been played in outer space, thanks to American astronaut Charles Duke, who brought one of Haggard's tapes aboard *Apollo 16* in 1972.

Cool fact: In 1958 country music powerhouse Johnny Cash played his first prison concert...at San Quentin. Inmate Merle Haggard was in the audience and so enjoyed the show that he was inspired to start playing himself.

TOMMY COLLINS

Before there was Buck Owens or Merle Haggard, there was Tommy Collins, known for being one of the earliest musicians to use strong backbeats and electric guitars. Born just outside of Oklahoma City in 1930, he moved to Bakersfield in 1952 and soon began churning out top-10 hits, including "You Better Not Do That," "Whatcha Gonna Do Now," "Untied," and "It Tickles."

San Francisco columnist Herb Caen coined the term "beatnik" in 1958.

Collins's career came to an abrupt halt in 1956 when he experienced a religious epiphany and enrolled in a seminary. He eventually returned to the music business in 1963, but his new songs never found an audience, so he started writing for others. Merle Haggard, in particular, recorded many of Collins's songs, including the hits "Carolyn" and "The Roots of My Raising" in the 1970s. Collins continued to write new compositions throughout the 1990s before passing away in March 2000.

Cool fact: Tommy Collins's real name was Leonard Raymond Sipes. In 1981 Merle Haggard told his life story in a hit song called "Leonard."

THE SECOND STRING

• A native of Denison, Texas, Bill Woods moved to Bakersfield in the 1940s and established himself as the bandleader at the Blackboard Café, a popular nightclub with music seven nights a week. The venue allowed the Texan to rub shoulders with many of the town's most promising young artists, and Woods was responsible for giving both Buck Owens and Merle Haggard some of their earliest paying gigs. Haggard never forgot the generosity and wrote a song about Woods in the early 1970s.

• It was nearly impossible to turn on a television set in the 1950s without seeing Billy Mize. This talented bandleader and steel guitarist found fame in Bakersfield as the host of two local variety radio and TV shows: *The Trading Post Gang* and *Gene Autry's Melody Ranch*. By 1957 Mize appeared regularly on seven different weekly shows in the L.A. area and was later named the Academy of Country Music's "TV Personality of the Year" on three separate occasions. Mize eventually left the airwaves, but he never stopped performing or playing steel and rhythm guitar on many of Merle Haggard's hits throughout the 1970s.

* * *

"I found a sound that people really liked—I found this basic concept, and all I did was change the lyrics and the melody a little bit. My songs, if you listen to them, they're quite a lot like Chuck Berry."

—**Buck Owens**

Country singer Merle Haggard was born in an abandoned refrigerator car in Bakersfield.

SUPERSTAR FOODIES

These four celebrity chefs changed our lives...
well, at least our meals...forever.

JULIA CHILD

Claim to Fame: Bringing French cooking to the American mainstream

California Hometowns: Pasadena and Santa Barbara

Story: Julia McWilliams Child was born in Pasadena, but considered herself a "Southern California butterfly." Of his wife, husband Paul Child wrote in a letter to his brother, "She frankly likes to eat." In 1948 Paul's job took the couple to Paris, and Julia immediately fell in love with classical French cuisine. In 1950 at the age of 38, she enrolled in Paris's famous cooking school, Le Cordon Bleu.

In Paris, Julia Child made two French foodie friends—Simca Beck and Louisette Bertholle—who asked her to collaborate on a French cookbook for Americans. After 10 years of cooking, writing, and rewriting, *Mastering the Art of French Cooking* was published in 1961. It became a best-seller, partly because of an American interest in all things French, but also because, by then, Child had become a TV phenomenon: an appearance on Boston public television to promote her book and demonstrate how to make an omelet led to a huge fan following and her own cooking show, *The French Chef.*

In 1981 Paul and Julia—who missed California—bought a winter home in Santa Barbara. (They spent most of their summers in Massachusetts.) Child became "a landmark in Vons markets," taught cooking in the wine country, and in 1983 launched another TV show. Instead of just cooking on this show, Child also showed her viewers where the food she made actually came from. On an episode where Child served salmon, for example, she was first seen in a yellow rain slicker actually catching the fish from a boat in Seattle's Puget Sound. For other dinners, she picked mushrooms, harvested dates, and went out on a crab boat. Child split her time between California and Massachusetts for the rest of her life; she died at her home in Montecito in 2004.

CECILIA SUN YUN CHIANG

Claim to Fame: Founding the Mandarin Restaurant and bringing authentic Chinese cuisine to California

California Hometown: San Francisco

Story: Born around 1920 in a Beijing palace to a family that had two cooks but never allowed its upper-class children in the kitchen, Chiang went from riches to rags in 1942 when she and her sister fled Japan's World War II occupation of China. They walked nearly 1,000 miles, starving and covered with fleas, to safety in the city of Chungking, where the girls had relatives. By 1960 Chiang was married and living in Tokyo when she visited San Francisco to help her widowed sister. There, she met two old friends who asked her to translate for them; they were starting a restaurant on Polk Street and needed to sign a lease.

Chiang translated the document, cosigned, and also lent the pair the $10,000 that the landlord required up front to rent the business. Ultimately, the friends backed out of the deal, and Chiang was stuck with the lease. She'd already managed a successful restaurant in Tokyo and she knew a lot about cooking, so in 1961 she opened her own restaurant, the Mandarin.

The Mandarin served spicy Mandarin and Sichuan dishes, a contrast to the bland Americanized Chinese food common at the time. Chiang introduced dishes like pot stickers, hot-and-sour soup, sizzling rice soup, and Peking duck. She also tutored cooking stars like Oregon chef and food critic James Beard and Berkeley restaurater Alice Waters. The Mandarin's space was also upscale—instead of dragons or red lanterns, Chiang's restaurant sported Chinese antiques. Until 2006, when the Mandarin closed, it was one of the most famous Chinese restaurants in San Francisco.

ALICE WATERS

Claim to Fame: Inventing California cuisine

California Hometown: Berkeley

Story: In the turbulent 1960s, Alice Waters was a student at UC Berkeley, working toward a degree in French cultural studies, but she also had an interest in cooking. In 1965, she studied abroad in France, where even simple meals included fresh, high-quality ingredients. When Waters returned home and graduated

Early whalers nicknamed the California gray whale the "devil fish" because...

from college, she worked as a Montessori teacher, but at night she cooked for her friends and talked about wishing Americans would desert big agriculture for small-farm, organic ingredients.

In 1971 Waters opened Chez Panisse (named for Honoré Panisse, a character in the French films of Marcel Pagnol) in Berkeley. At a time when most California restaurants had formal dining rooms and standardized fare, Chez Panisse broke the rules. Waters created what's now called "California cuisine"—an intimate, friendly bistro where friends could meet and talk Berkeley politics. The menu changed daily as the restaurant's "forager" (aka, buyer) bought fresh seasonal foods. And to get proper mixed greens for salads, Waters bought the vegetable seeds in France and planted them in Chez Panisse's backyard.

THOMAS KELLER

Claim to Fame: Opening the French Laundry, one of the most celebrated French restaurants on the West Coast

California Hometowns: Oceanside and Yountville

Story: Born in Oceanside, Thomas Keller grew up in Florida, where his single mom Betty managed restaurants. As a teenager, Keller often helped out by peeling potatoes or washing dishes. In 1974, when he was 18, one of Betty's chefs got sick and she handed Thomas an apron, telling him to learn how to cook. He did. Eventually Keller apprenticed with classically trained chefs at renowned restaurants in America and France. By the mid-1980s, he was a partner in an upscale New York City restaurant, and getting a reputation for putting his own spin on classic French food. But then came the 1987 stock market crash. Keller's restaurant partner decided to turn their eatery into an inexpensive bistro because so many of their customers were broke. Dissatisfied, Keller left New York for California.

After spending some time in Los Angeles, Keller landed in the scenic Napa Valley town of Yountville, where he found a rose-covered 19th-century building called the French Laundry—in the 1920s, it had been home to an actual French steam laundry. (It also once housed a saloon and a brothel.) He bought the building and opened an upscale French restaurant there in 1994. With ingredients from his own gardens and small organic farms, Keller calls his food "American with French influences": his mac and cheese, for example, was actually orzo in coral oil with mascarpone topped with lobster and a parmesan chip, and he serves an "ice-cream cone" that's actually savory cornet (a cone-shaped pastry) filled with salmon tartar and red onion crème fraiche.

Keller turned tiny Yountville into a center of world-class dining. The French Laundry is one of only a few restaurants around the globe to win the *Michelin Guide*'s coveted 3-star rating, and in 2003 and 2004 *Restaurant Magazine* honored it as the "Best Restaurant in the World." And then there's Travel Channel chef Anthony Bourdain, who calls it "the best restaurant in the world, period."

* * *

THE U.S. CAMEL CORPS

When the Mexican-American War ended in 1848, the U.S. government realized that it had won a whole lot of desert in Texas, New Mexico, and California, and now had to defend it. Nobody was sure how to do that because there was no grazing land and water for the mules and horses the army used. So the War Department bought some camels.

In 1856, to see how the animals would perform in the American desert, the army asked Edward Beale (who was surveying a trail from New Mexico to California) to use 25 camels on the job. He was aided by handlers who'd come with the camels from the Middle East. During one famous trip, his party was attacked by Mojave Indians. The men all mounted the camels, and camel trainer Hadji Ali (the Americans called him "Hi Jolly") led a camel charge at their attackers, who fled at the sight.

In 1859 the government sent the camels to Fort Tejon, north of L.A., hoping to use them to deliver mail. But that was a failure: The animals weren't fast enough, and their hooves were so ill-suited for the rocky terrain of the Mojave that they sometimes went lame. They were also difficult to work with, often refusing to move when asked or dumping their riders. In 1863 the army sold the camels at an auction, and the state's camel corps experiment was over. Today, however, California has a new camel experiment, the nation's only camel dairy, located in the small mountain town of Ramona, about 30 miles northeast of San Diego.

Real name of the L.A. Angels' "Rally Monkey" mascot: Katie.

HOW TO SPOT
A VALLEY GIRL

Some people believe that the curious California creation—the Valley Girl—went out with the 1980s. Not true. Here's, like, our guide to spotting one.

If you answer yes to at least three of these questions, you have indeed spotted a Valley Girl. Proceed with caution, don't mention that you shop for clothes at Target, and keep quiet about that flip phone in your pocket.

• Does she have blond hair, an even tan, and a fit body? A Valley Girl will never sport a muffin top, and skin cancer is a small price to pay for beauty.

• Is she carrying an iPhone? (Not a Droid, BlackBerry, or other smartphone knockoff.)

• Does she speak seriously about what a genius Paris Hilton is?

• Do a disproportionate number of phrases include "duh," "like, whatever," "as if," "like, oh my god," or "beyotch"?

• Does she begin most stories with the word "so"?

• Is she willing only to be friends with the wealthy and beautiful, all the while constantly mentioning how all her friends are wealthy and beautiful?

• Does she name-drop?

• Is she unwilling to ever leave the house without makeup?

• Do all her sentences end like questions?

• Does she consider *Clueless* and *Wayne's World* to be high cinematic achievements, and *People*, *In Style*, and *Vogue* must-reads?

• Does she own a small, fluffy white dog (or chihuahua) that she carries around in a purse? She may also ask for a high chair for the animal at outdoor cafés and handfeed the dog from the table.

Approximately one in five San Franciscans is a Chinese immigrant.

A TOUGH CLIMB TO THE TOP

What would San Francisco look like without its iconic cable cars? The city almost found out.

A HORSE'S BEST FRIEND

San Francisco is a city of steep hills, and in the 1870s, teams of horses were the primary way that residents and their cargo got up and down those hills. The animals pulled streetcars that rolled on steel rails set in the middle of cobblestone streets. It was a tried-and-true system, but in 1869, when Andrew Smith Hallidie looked at those streets, he saw "the difficulty and pain the horses experienced in hauling the cars." As the horses pulled their streetcars up the steep grades, they struggled with the heavy weight of the cars and passengers. Hallidie also watched drivers whipping and screaming at the animals, and he saw a gruesome accident with horses "falling and being dragged down the hill on their sides, by the car loaded with passengers sliding on its track."

The sight of the exhausted, suffering animals convinced Hallidie that there had to be a better way to get people up and down San Francisco's hills. So he set to work inventing machinery to replace the horses.

INTRODUCING...THE CABLE CAR

Hallidie was a Londoner who had come to California in 1852—another miner hoping to get rich in the gold fields. Unfortunately the amount of gold that he discovered was "just enough to starve on." So Hallidie decided to put his English schooling to work (he'd studied mechanical engineering) and get jobs building suspension bridges. He also designed the Hallidie Ropeway, an aerial tram that used a wire rope, or cable, that he invented. Running on tall towers, the cable ran in a loop that was always moving as it hauled heavy buckets of gold or silver ore over rough terrain—down mountains, over rivers, and above steep ravines. That way, the ore could be moved quickly from the mine to a processing plant.

Q: Which town was home to California's first private school, theater troupe...

As more mines were dug in California, there was an increased demand for the trams and cables. By 1865 Hallidie had settled in San Francisco to devote himself to making and selling the cable. So in 1869, when he wanted to help the horses, he decided to design a cable that was strong enough to haul San Francisco's streetcars up and down its hillsides.

In 1872 Hallidie and three business partners formed the Clay Street Hill Railroad. They planned to send horseless cable cars along a route that began at the intersection of Kearny and Clay Streets and went up the steep grade of Nob Hill to Clay and Leavenworth Streets. The company's contract with the city required that the cars be up and running by August 1, 1873...they were just one day late.

On August 2, at 5:00 a.m., the Clay Railroad began its test run. It was scheduled before dawn so there would be no traffic or bystanders who might be injured if the cable system failed. According to legend, the hired driver—whose job it was to get the cable car from the top of the hill to the bottom and back again—looked down the steep grade, imagined what would happen if things didn't go right...and then he refused to drive the car. What's known for sure is that Hallidie took over and drove the car down the hill and back up again himself. The trial run was a success, and cable cars began welcoming plenty of paying customers on September 1, 1873.

THE INNER WORKINGS

None of Hallidie's cars had an engine. They ran on a loop of cable that was constantly turning (via steam power) under the street. Today the steam engine that turned the cable has been replaced with electric motors, and improvements have been made to make the process easier and safer. But the system basically still works much as it did over a century ago.

• The cars are powered by the moving cable under the street. That cable is made up of six strands of wires wrapped around a core of sisal rope. A system of pulleys keeps the cable in place underground, and at the end of the line, the cable comes into a powerhouse, where huge pulleys driven by electric motors pull it along at a constant speed of 9.5 mph.

• A mechanical device called a grip keeps the cars attached to the

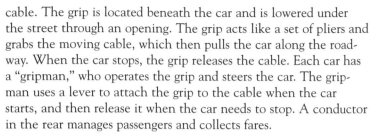
cable. The grip is located beneath the car and is lowered under the street through an opening. The grip acts like a set of pliers and grabs the moving cable, which then pulls the car along the roadway. When the car stops, the grip releases the cable. Each car has a "gripman," who operates the grip and steers the car. The gripman uses a lever to attach the grip to the cable when the car starts, and then release it when the car needs to stop. A conductor in the rear manages passengers and collects fares.

• Cable cars are also equipped with wheel brakes, track brakes, and an emergency brake. The emergency brake, used only as a last resort, jams a steel wedge into the opening between the rails, forcing the car to a jarring stop.

CABLE CAR WARS

Hallidie's Clay Street Railroad was so successful that by the late 1880s cable cars operated on 53 miles of track in nearly every part of San Francisco. Then disaster struck—the 1906 earthquake and its fires destroyed more than 100 cable cars. These were replaced by a new invention: electric streetcars, which were cheaper to run.

As the century progressed, San Francisco's fleet of cable cars kept shrinking, and in January 1947 the city's mayor ,Roger Lapham, decided they were old-fashioned. He announced that diesel buses were cheaper to operate and "the city should get rid of its cable cars as soon as possible."

People were outraged—the cable cars were seen as a part of the city's culture and personality. Friedel Klussmann, a wealthy woman often seen on newspaper society pages, spoke out in defense of the cable cars and formed a committee to save them... while the mayor continued to campaign to get them out of San Francisco. When Lapham gave speeches about the high cost of running the cable cars, Klussmann countered with arguments about cable cars bringing millions to the city as a tourist attraction. The mayor's supporters claimed they could prove the cable cars were dangerous and the city might lose big money paying out potential damages. Cable car supporters had government endorsements of cable car safety and accusations that the mayor's supporters were in the pocket of oil companies who would make millions on the diesel buses. Letters poured into newspaper offices all

At 25,000 square miles, the Mojave Desert is larger than...

around the country, and national magazines even took sides. Celebrities also put in their two cents—actresses Irene Dunne and Katharine Cornell said they'd never return to San Francisco if it abandoned the cable cars.

Klussmann and her supporters managed to get Measure 10 (the cable car bill) on the fall ballot, leaving the decision up to the voters. In November 1947, Measure 10 passed with 170,000 votes for the cable cars and just 50,000 opposed. The cable cars would stay in San Francisco. Today, there are 40 cars and three separate lines. Plus, the city's cable car system is the only transportation system listed on the National Register of Historic Places. More than 9 million people ride them every year.

* * *

DORIS DUKE VS. MIKE LOVE

Doris Duke (1912–93) was once "the richest girl in the world," the sole heir to tobacco and electricity magnate James Duke. Mike Love (1941–) is a distinctive voice on Beach Boys songs. There's no evidence that the two ever met (although there is a Thai restaurant in Hawaii that includes a picture of each on its Celebrity Diners' Wall). Yet they both loved the ocean, and Love's life paralleled Duke's in some unexpected ways:

• Love was born in the Los Angeles area. Duke died there.

• In the 1930s, Doris Duke became the first woman to participate in surfing competitions. In the 1960s, Mike Love became the world's first lyricist and lead singer in a band that played surf music.

• Duke learned to surf from Hawaiian wave champ Duke Kahanamoku and his brothers, leaders of a group of full-time surfers who called themselves the Beach Boys. Love joined with surf music pioneers Brian Wilson and his brothers Carl and Dennis, in a group that also called itself the Beach Boys.

• In 1968 Mike Love went to India with the Beatles and other celebrities to study Transcendental Meditation with Maharishi Mahesh Yogi. The ashram where he studied was built with money donated in 1963 by an earlier celebrity meditator. You guessed it: Doris Duke.

WE ♥ LODI

In 1969, Creedence Clearwater Revival equated getting "stuck in Lodi again" with having life's dreams fall through. Okay, maybe not everybody loves this central California town, but here are some reasons you should at least consider it.

- Some California cities named themselves after angels (Los Angeles), saints (San Francisco, Santa Barbara), philosophers (Berkeley), or European tourist magnets (Venice). But the Central Valley's Lodi modestly got its name from Lodi, Illinois, where some of its early settlers probably came from.

- Lodi is a wine region, and vineyards in the area produce about 40 percent of California's zinfandel grapes.

- Lodi is the birthplace of the first 1980s trendy wine cooler. Michael Crete and Stuart Bewley mixed up the first professional batch of their California Cooler—a sangria-like mix of white wine, carbonated water, fruit juices, sweeteners, flavorings, and citric acid—in 1981. As the big manufacturers got into the business, Crete and Bewley got out, selling the business to a whiskey distiller for about $146 million four years later.

- The Lodi area has been populated for about 4,000 years—the first known settlers in the area were a prehistoric people called the Windmiller culture (sonamed because archaeologists found evidence of them on an area of land that was once home to a family called Windmiller). They were supplanted later by a group of Hokan speakers, who were at some point replaced by the Plains Miwok, who were living in a good-sized village just east of Lodi when the Europeans arrived.

- And what about that "Lodi" song by Creedence Clearwater Revival, about a musician unable to raise bus money to leave a boring town? Over the years, the song's author, John Fogerty, has contradicted himself about its origins: In concerts, he often claims to have been stuck there. But Fogerty also once admitted in an interview that he had never actually been to Lodi before slandering it in song—he just chose it because it had "the coolest sounding name" of two-syllable California farm towns.

California was the 31st state in the union.

GET SPORTY

California has more than 15 professional sports teams. How much do you know about them? (Answers on page 369.)

1. Name the state's five pro baseball teams.
Bonus: Which two teams were the first and most recent to bring the World Series to California?

2. The Lakers are, by far, the most famous basketball team in the state, but L.A. has another NBA franchise…which has had only two winning seasons since moving to the City of Angels in 1984. (Ouch.) Who are they?
Bonus: What former Laker once worked as an assistant coach for the "other L.A. team"?

3. The Bay Area lacked a pro hockey team from 1976, when the Golden Seals left Oakland, until 1991, when this team arrived. Who are they?
Bonus: Name their mascot.

4. What is the only California football team never to have won a Super Bowl?
Bonus: Who is their biggest rival?

5. The Walt Disney Company founded this pro sports team in 1993 and named it after a fictional amateur sports team in one of its movies. What's the pro team's name?
Bonus: What movie were they named for?

6. In 1996, in their first game of their first season, this San Jose soccer team beat D.C. United 1–0. What's the team's name?
Bonus: What was their name for that first season?

7. Oakland has a basketball team…no, really, they do! What's it called?
Bonus: Where do they play?

A cave in L.A.'s Griffith Park served as the Batcave for the 1960s TV series *Batman.*

THIS OLD $HACK, PART II

Our tour of California's most lavish homes continues.
(Part I appears on page 15.)

(Part I appears on page 15.)

THE MANOR
Address: 594 South Mapleton Drive, Los Angeles
Rich residents: Aaron Spelling and family (Candy, Tori, and Randy)
Why it's famous: Better known as the Spelling mansion, this 57,000-square-foot behemoth in L.A.'s wealthy Westwood neighborhood sports 14 bedrooms, 27 bathrooms, parking for 100 cars, and several rooms just for gift-wrapping. Mogul producer Aaron Spelling (of *Charlie's Angels*, *Dynasty*, and *Beverly Hills 90210* fame) ticked off a lot of people in 1988 when he tore down Bing Crosby's old house to build this one. But over the years, the property became a staple on Hollywood's "Homes of the Stars" maps and tours. In 2011 Candy Spelling sold the property to 22-year-old heiress Petra Ecclestone (her father made a fortune in Formula One racing). The selling price: $85 million.
Can I visit? Tourists can drive by (and attempt to peek over the gates from the sidewalk), but the home itself and the grounds are private property.

THE ALBION CASTLE
Address: 881 Innes Avenue, San Francisco
Rich resident: Sculptor Adrien Voisin
Why it's famous: In 1870 an English immigrant named John Hamlyn Burnell built the structure and opened it as the Albion Ale & Porter Brewery. He created the whole thing out of stone and modeled it after old castles in Great Britain. Burnell's business thrived until 1919, when Prohibition effectively killed it; the building sat abandoned for years. In the early 1930s, Adrien Voisin—a sculptor most famous for his busts of Native Americans—bought the decaying property and restored it to use as a home and studio. Today, the castle is a private residence. With just two bathrooms, it may not seem like much of a mansion, but there's more! A hidden spring runs beneath the building through

caves and aquifers built by Burnell himself, all the while gushing 10,000 gallons of fresh water daily.

Can I visit? Tourists can drive or walk by, but the castle and grounds are private property.

THE PLAYBOY MANSION

Address: 10236 Charing Cross Road, Beverly Hills

Rich residents: Hugh Hefner and various *Playboy* Playmates

Why it's famous: This gothic-style mansion was built in 1927, but *Playboy* magazine founder Hugh Hefner put it on the map in the 1970s when he moved in and turned it into the most famous party house in America. The 21,987-square-foot home has seven bedrooms, a wine cellar, a swimming pool grotto (where the Playmates and their male companions swim nude), a secret "Elvis" room, a zoo, and a game room. Over the years, the Playboy Mansion has made the news many times—as the host of a Legionella outbreak, a dead body (found on the grounds), and famous guests such as Pamela Anderson, Tommy Lee, Jenny McCarthy, Shia LaBeouf, and Elvis Presley. Hefner, by the way, also owns the house next door...and the one across the street.

Can I visit? If you can score a ticket to one of the mansion's famous parties, sure. Otherwise, you'll have to gawk from the street; it's private property.

MORE FAMOUS HOLLYWOOD ADDRESSES

• 750 Bel Air Road, Los Angeles, home of *The Beverly Hillbillies*.

• 11222 Dilling Street, North Hollywood, home of *The Brady Bunch*. (Rumor has it, though, that the current residents hate gawkers, so don't dawdle.)

• 1675 East Altadena Drive, Altadena, home of Brandon and Brenda Walsh in *Beverly Hills, 90210*.

• 565 North Cahuenga Boulevard, Los Angeles, home of Richie, Joanie, Marion, and Howard Cunningham (and the Fonz) in *Happy Days*.

• 675 Arden Road, Pasadena, home of Don and Betty Draper (and their kids) pre-divorce in *Mad Men*.

THEY DO IT
WITH MIRRORS

*Thanks to solar power, the Mojave might
soon be the greenest desert in the world.*

THE SHINING

California's Mojave Desert stretches from the Tehachapi, San Gabriel, and San Bernardino mountain ranges past the Nevada border. Temperatures on the desert floor often reach upwards of 120°F, and the area gets less than six inches of rain a year. But the Mojave also gets twice as much sun as most of the United States, which means that solar energy is just there for the taking.

The Mojave Desert has been generating electricity for more than 25 years. In 1985 the first solar power facility was built near Barstow to provide electricity to the Southern California Edison power company. By 1991 eight more were in operation. These power plants form the largest thermal solar-generating facility in the world and provide power for more than 200,000 homes.

HOW DOES IT WORK?

To create electricity from sunlight, most solar power plants use *solar thermal collectors*, long, curved mirrors with computerized controls that rotate the mirrors so they always face the sun. The mirrors concentrate the sunlight (like shining it through a magnifying glass) to create intense heat. That heat is then aimed at pipes filled with oil. When the oil reaches about 735°F, it flows into a boiler that generates steam to drive an electricity-producing turbine. The solar power plants store the electricity and then send it out as needed. They can even deliver the stored power at night or on cloudy days.

In 2011 newly elected governor Jerry Brown signed a law requiring California's utility companies to convert to 33 percent renewable energy by 2020. So as California scrambles to find reliable sources of renewable energy, filling up the sun-baked Mojave with solar farms seems like a perfect solution. By late 2011, the state had already approved plans to build enough solar farms in the Mojave to produce about as much energy as four nuclear power plants. And unlike fossil fuels, solar energy never runs out.

A FEW GOOD MIRRORS

Not everyone sees solar energy as a perfect solution, however. Solar power plants require huge amounts of land, and some environmentalists worry that they will take over federal land originally set aside to protect fragile desert ecosystems, endangered plants, and endangered species like the Mojave tortoise, which is already close to extinction. Other critics argue that solar power is just too expensive, pointing out that new solar plants can cost up to six times as much to build as coal-burning facilities. But the benefits can be tremendous: estimates are that even one large solar power plant can reduce carbon dioxide emissions by nearly 2 million tons per year. That's like removing more than 300,000 cars from the roads.

Solar power from the Mojave has a powerful champion—in 2009 the U.S. Defense Department signed on to build a solar power plant at Fort Irwin in San Bernardino County. Once constructed (hopefully by 2022), the facility will power Fort Irwin and its army training center…and there will still be energy left over for California's civilian power grid. Maybe one day, the state's sun-soaked climate will help to free Americans from using fossil fuels altogether.

* * *

LORD OF THE RINGS

As a gripman, or driver, maneuvers a cable car through San Francisco, he rings a large bell to warn traffic and pedestrians that the vehicle is approaching. He also uses a smaller bell to communicate with the conductor. Here's what those rings mean:

- **One ring:** The cable car needs to stop at the next regular stop.
- **Two rings:** The car is ready to start moving again.
- **Three rings:** The car has to stop immediately.
- **Four rings:** The car is about to back up.

Arcadia city laws give peacocks the right of way.

VIVA LA CAUSA!

"Our goal is a national union of the poor dedicated to world peace and to serving the needs of all men who suffer." —César Chávez

MISSION IMPROBABLE

César Chávez met Dolores Huerta in the 1950s when they were both community organizers bringing services to Mexican American farmworkers. Chávez and Huerta provided help with basics like literacy, citizenship, and voter registration. The families they helped worked long hours in California's agricultural fields, yet made so little money that they often couldn't afford enough food or decent housing. Eventually both Chávez and Huerta decided that the main things farmworker families needed were higher wages and better conditions.

Agricultural laborers have always been California's poorest and least-protected workers. Before Chávez got involved, farmworkers had no access to clean drinking water or bathroom facilities in the field, no work breaks, and no minimum wage. There weren't even laws against child labor. Since the early 1900s, there had been many attempts to unionize farmworkers and improve their situation, but all had stalled. One reason was the power of California agribusiness, a multibillion-dollar industry with plenty of political clout. The growers' influenced politicians to exempt farmworkers from labor protection laws. Also, most unions organized workers who stayed in one factory or manufacturing plant; they had trouble organizing farmworkers who traveled to follow the harvests.

In 1962 Chávez, Huerta, and several colleagues cofounded a labor union called the National Farm Workers Association (NFWA) in the Kern County town of Delano. Chávez was the executive officer and led and shaped the organization's goals. Huerta was his second-in-command; she oversaw practical operations and became the union's chief negotiator. Feeling that they understood the needs of farmworkers, the pair hoped to succeed where so many others had failed.

NOT YOUR BEAST OF BURDEN

Born to a farm family in Arizona, Chávez was the perfect man for

California's first winemakers were Spanish missionaries.

the job. In the 1930s, his father managed to secure 40 acres of land as his own, but a series of swindles by white landlords and lawyers lost the man his property. By 1938, when Chávez was around 11, his family had left Arizona for California, where they worked in the state's agricultural fields.

Chávez experienced plenty of discrimination in his new home. At school, teachers punished him for speaking Spanish, and he saw signs around the Central Valley that read, "No dogs or Mexicans allowed." These experiences cemented his determination as an adult to fight for civil rights and higher wages for farmworkers. Chávez said, "We are not beasts of burden, we are not agricultural implements or rented slaves, we are men." And he wanted them treated as such.

The NFWA motto, "Viva la causa!" ("Long live the cause!"), referred to the group's struggle for civil rights. Its flag was red with a black, square-edged eagle on a white-circled background. It represented hope for many workers that one day the eagle would "fly" above farmworkers who were respected and paid a living wage. Chávez also insisted that the NFWA be a nonviolent movement.

On September 8, 1965, Filipino farmworkers in Delano went on strike against grape growers to demand a livable minimum wage. Eight days later, the NFWA got its first real opportunity to take its message to the people when Chávez's group joined them. Their rallying cry was "Viva la huelga!" ("Long live the strike!"), and unfortunately the strike did live for a very long time—the battle between workers and growers lasted five years. It was one of the largest and longest struggles in U.S. labor history.

WITH A LITTLE HELP FROM OUR FRIENDS

When the strike began, the NFWA had about $87 in its treasury. The union's poverty-stricken members could barely pay dues. By contrast, California's grape growers were among the wealthiest corporations in the state. In one year, the Di Giorgio Corporation, for example, made about $231 million (more than a billion in today's dollars). Corporations like Di Giorgio also had the support of politicians, banks, and local law enforcement, who seemed oblivious when union picketers were beaten or even shot at.

With little money and powerful opposition, the strikers seemed doomed to fail, but Chávez proved to be a powerful morale booster. He pled for justice for all farmworkers and convinced non-union laborers to leave the vineyards and join picket lines. His nonviolent ideals also inspired urban Americans, reminding them of Martin Luther King's struggle for civil rights for African Americans, which was already taking place in the South. NFWA leaders and members endured arrests, jail time, and intimidation. But seeing photos of the peaceful picketers beaten and harassed also brought young people, clergymen, politicians, and large labor union advisors to Delano with offers of help.

Chávez and Huerta needed all the help they could get. In 1966 a group of people who supported the growers sprayed the striking workers with pesticides, which outraged the NFWA. Finally, the union decided to appeal to the general public. The group organized a protest march that wove through the state from Delano to Sacramento and ultimately covered 340 miles. They began with 75 people, but by the time, the march arrived in Sacramento, more than 10,000 Californians had joined in.

EVERY GRAPE YOU BUY KEEPS A CHILD HUNGRY

Even more successful was Chávez's decision to ask his supporters to boycott growers' products. They first put pressure on the Schenley Vineyards Corporation with a boycott of its wines and liquor. That was a huge success, bringing about a 1966 contract—the first union contract for farmworkers in U.S. history. The next fight was harder. The union (which had renamed itself the United Farm Workers, or UFW) struck at the Di Giorgio Fruit Corporation, the largest grape grower in the Central Valley. That strike and the boycotting of Di Giorgio grapes finally forced the company to sign a contract in 1967.

The UFW next went after the Giumarra Corporation, the biggest grape producer in the United States—and the company with the fiercest opposition to the union. Giumarra tried to avoid the boycott by using labels from other companies on its products, so Dolores Huerta came up with a work-around: The UFW would boycott *all* California grapes nationally, regardless of who grew them. Supporters signed on, passing out boycott flyers featuring a photo of a small child in a farmworker's shack. The flyer declared, "Every California Grape You Buy Keeps This Child Hungry."

In 1990 Davis became the first U.S. city to install bicycle-specific traffic signals.

In 1968 Chávez went on a 25-day fast that brought even more attention to the boycott. Eventually, over 14 million Americans, as well as people in Canada and Europe, stopped buying California grapes. The combination of the UFW's ability to keep workers from harvesting grapes and its ability to keep consumers from buying grapes hurt the growers' profits. In 1970 the union won. Giumarra and almost all California grape growers signed three-year contracts with the UFW. The strike ended in victory for La Causa.

THE WORK (AND THE FIGHT) CONTINUES

The contracts gave the workers many of the rights they wanted: representation by a union, health-care benefits, and a raise in pay. Fresh water to drink and proper sanitation were provided in the fields. The victory also led to California's 1975 Agricultural Labor Relations Act, the nation's first bill of rights for farmworkers. Not all the problems were solved, however. Today, many farmworkers and their families still live in poverty—by one estimate, the numbers hover around 30 percent—and child labor is common. But the UFW continues to work to improve working conditions and pay for workers across the country.

Chávez played an active role in the union until his death in 1993. In 1994 President Bill Clinton awarded him a posthumous Medal of Honor. Dolores Huerta, who turned 81 in 2011, is still an activist—that year, she grabbed a picket sign and urged a boycott of the Long Beach Hilton Hotel, standing in solidarity with workers who had been striking since 2009.

*   *   *

CHÁVEZ WORDS OF WISDOM

- "We cannot seek achievement for ourselves and forget about progress and prosperity for our community...Our ambitions must be broad enough to include the aspirations and needs of others, for their sakes and for our own."

- "You are never strong enough that you don't need help."

- "Students must have initiative; they should not be mere imitators. They must learn to think and act for themselves—and be free."

Tallest player ever on the L.A. Lakers: Chuck Nevitt (7'5").

LOONY LAWS

Most of the time, laws are important: They keep us safe and maintain order. But laws like these make us go, "Huh?"

• In the city of Burlingame, it's illegal to spit outside... except on a baseball diamond.

• People in Chico may throw hay into cesspools only if they have the proper permit.

• It used to be illegal to eat ice cream while standing on the sidewalk in Carmel. But in 1986, when Clint Eastwood became the town's mayor, he repealed that law. (Thanks, Clint.)

• Statewide, vehicles without drivers cannot exceed 60 mph.

• Dogs are not allowed to mate within 500 yards of a church. Punishment for breaking this law: $500.

• In San Francisco, you may not use underwear to wash or dry your car.

• The city of Long Beach forbids cursing on a mini golf course. Number of mini golf courses in Long Beach: 0.

• Statewide, it's illegal to keep snapping turtles, skunks, wolf-dog hybrids, and lions as pets. (OK. Maybe that one isn't so loony after all.)

• Downey forbids people from washing their cars on the street.

• In L.A., a man may beat his wife with a strap wider than two inches only if she consents. (Straps less than two inches wide don't require consent.)

• Despite what the Internet tells us, it *is* perfectly legal to set a mousetrap without a hunting license. According to Section 11615 of the California Health and Safety Code, "Any person possessing any place that is infested with rodents, as soon as their presence comes to his or her knowledge, shall at once proceed and continue in good faith to endeavor to exterminate and destroy the rodents by poisoning, trapping, and other appropriate means."

The famous lingerie store Frederick's of Hollywood was established in 1947...

FIRST LADIES

These California women broke stereotypes, smashed through glass ceilings, and invented new rules.

CHARLOTTE CRABTREE (1847–1924)
Hometowns: San Francisco and Grass Valley
Claim to Fame: First American millionaire entertainer
Story: When Charlotte (Lotta) Crabtree was four years old, she and her mother, Mary Ann, left New York and headed for San Francisco to be with Lotta's father, who was mining in the California gold fields. In 1853 the family moved to Grass Valley to a house two doors down from the very scandalous (and wealthy) actress, dancer, and former courtesan Lola Montez, who gave young Lotta singing and dancing lessons.

The little girl was a natural, and at the age of six, encouraged by Montez, she performed songs and Irish jigs for enthusiastic gold miners. By eight, she was touring the gold fields as a dancer, singer, and banjo player. The homesick miners loved the sight of children, who were rare in the gold fields, and they showered the little girl with praise…and gold. Mary Ann swept up all the gold dust and nuggets and put them into a large trunk. As the trunk filled up, Mary Ann used the gold to invest in local real estate so that by the age of 12, Lotta was an incredibly wealthy little girl.

Lotta went on to star on Broadway and tour Europe as a singer, actress, and comedienne. She never married and managed her money and career with only the help of her mother. (Her father had been cast aside after trying to steal her gold-filled trunk.) By the time she retired in 1892, Lotta Crabtree was worth more than $4 million. She shunned the spotlight in her later years and lived quietly, painting, raising horses…and smoking cigars, a habit, legend says, she picked up from Lola Montez.

AGGIE UNDERWOOD (1902–84)
Hometowns: San Francisco and Los Angeles
Claim to Fame: First female city editor of a major newspaper
Story: Born in San Francisco and shuttled among foster homes, Agness "Aggie" Underwood finally settled in Los Angles at 17.

She married the next year and had two children, but the family struggled to make ends meet, so Underwood got a temp job as a switchboard operator for a small newspaper, the *Record*.

Watching the reporters work, Underwood quickly realized that switchboards were not her calling—she wanted to be out in the field chasing stories. So she went after a job as a crime reporter and within a couple of years was among the paper's most celebrated staffers. One reason was that Underwood knew that to hook readers, a story needed a little flair—she once dropped a white carnation on the body of a waitress who had been stabbed to death, just so she could call her story "The White Carnation Murder." She also wrote so well and scooped other newspapers so often that in 1935 media magnate William Randolph Hearst offered her a job at his L.A. paper, the *Herald Express*. After 12 years as the paper's top crime reporter, Underwood became its city editor, the first woman to hold that job at a major American newspaper (and the first female city editor in Hearst's entire media empire).

City newsrooms were famous as being male bastions of cursing and boozing, but Underwood held her own. She had a gun and shot off blanks when her reporters seemed to move too slowly, and she was beloved for treating her staff to cold beers when their office got hot. She was also willing to go to extreme lengths to get a story: Underwood once invited a murderer into her home for an interview while her daughter's Girl Scout troop meeting in the next room.

SALLY RIDE (1951–)

Hometown: Encino

Claim to Fame: First American woman in space

Story: Growing up, Sally Ride loved both sports and science and wanted to be a professional tennis player. But when it came time to choose a career, she settled on science and Stanford, where she earned a PhD in physics. As graduation approached, she was looking for a job when she read that NASA needed astronauts. As a long shot, she applied—along with more than 8,000 others. Only 35 applicants were accepted, and Sally Ride was one of them. In 1979 she joined "TFNG" ("thirty-five new guys"), the nickname for the freshman astronaut class.

For about three years, Ride underwent flight training, weightlessness training, water survival, and parachuting. She also learned to use a 50-foot robotic arm that was attached to the space shuttle and moved things in space. Finally, in 1983, she was chosen for the crew of the *Challenger* space shuttle mission. Despite protests that Ride had been chosen simply because she was a woman, not because she was the best candidate, Shuttle Commander Robert Crippen said, "There is no man I would rather have in her place."

That mission launched on June 18, and the crew spent 147 hours in space. In 1984 Ride went into space again, but her third mission was canceled after the 1986 *Challenger* disaster, which killed all seven crewmembers on board. After helping to determine that the explosion was caused by poorly designed seals in the rocket booster, Ride left NASA to work at Stanford and, later, as a physics professor at UC San Diego. Today, Ride is CEO of Sally Ride Science, a company that provides entertaining programs and publications to get young people, especially girls, involved in science.

*   *   *

DID YOU KNOW?

• A Kern County oil town didn't have a name yet, so its railroad station was labeled "Siding Number 2." Locals asked the Southern Pacific Railroad to change the name to Moro, but a railroad official didn't want it to be confused with Morro Bay to the west. So he added an "n," giving the town the unfortunate name of Moron, California. In the 1920s, after "moron" became a word to describe someone of low intelligence, a fire burned much of the town, including the railway station. After that, the town got a whole new name...Taft, after President William Howard Taft.

• In Carpinteria, in Santa Barbara County, you'll find a popular producer of wax for surfboards and snowboards whose name and logo have been causing confusion, controversy, and laughs since the product was first made in 1972. The brainchild of surfer Frederick Charles Herzog III and chemist Nate Skinner, "Mr. Zog's Sex Wax" was named simply to grab attention and poke some fun at modern advertising's prolific use of sex to sell products.

FAST-FOOD QUIZ

How well do you know the fast-food icons that have graced California's landscape? Put on your thinking cap and pretend you're on a family road trip, looking through the windshield of a 1968 station wagon. (Answers on page 369.)

1. What was the name of the animated chef who winked on McDonald's marquees during the 1940s and '50s?

a. King Burger VI

b. Ronald

c. Winkee

d. Speedee

2. What California chain's logo was modeled after a child who one day walked into its flagship restaurant?

a. Big Boy

b. McDonald's

c. In-n-Out

d. White Castle

3. Thirty 6-foot fiberglass dachshund heads rotating on poles: What San Francisco Bay Area business was being advertised?

a. Big Dog Restaurants

b. Doggie Diners

c. Pink's Hot Dogs

d. Weiner-Doggs

4. A small chef holds a chisel-like wedge above single pea while a beefy chef prepares to split the pea in half with an oversized mallet—it's the Pea Soup Andersens Restaurants. On what two California highways will you find the restaurants?

a. I-5 and Route 101

b. I-5 and I-40

c. Route 66 and the Lincoln Highway

d. I-8 and I-10

Movie director Francis Ford Coppola is an honorary ambassador to Belize.

5. In 1978, what Downey, California chain replaced its ethnic-stereotype logo when PepsiCo bought it out? (The move was not, they explained later, to please the activists who objected, but because they wanted to make their restaurants more attractive to mainstream white Americans.)

a. Sambo's
b. Round Table Pizza
c. Chun King's
d. Taco Bell

6. What restaurant chain, founded in Santa Barbara, tried to salvage its reputation in the 1970s by changing its logo to a light-skinned Indian, and then even changed its name, but still found itself in hot water?

a. Tonto's
b. Sambo's
c. Gunga Din's
d. Mingo's

To read about California's fast-food founders, turn to page 90.

*   *   *

ROUGHING IT

Where did author Robert Louis Stevenson spend his honeymoon? Although the Scottish author pretty much invented pirates as we think of them—peg legs, parrots, even pirate songs and patois ("Arggh, matey!")—he didn't take a ship to some exotic treasure island. Instead, in 1880 he and his bride went to Calistoga, where their honeymoon suite was an abandoned bunkhouse at a derelict mine. Being an author, he wrote a book about the experience, of course. Called *The Silverado Squatters*, it gives a lively look at life in the Napa Valley during the late 19th century, complete with descriptions of eccentric winemakers and Calistoga's Petrified Forest.

There's an underwater canyon in Monterey Bay that's twice the depth of the Grand Canyon.

MOVIES, MOGULS, AND MAYHEM

What do you get when you combine a millionaire media mogul, a rumored affair, a lot of illegal liquor, and wild party aboard a tricked-out yacht? A murder mystery for the ages…of course.

MEET MOGUL #1

Thomas Ince was an innovator and a Hollywood legend. In 1912 he built Inceville, one of the first modern movie studios in Los Angeles, located on what is now Sunset Boulevard at the Pacific Coast Highway. The studio also owned land in the nearby canyons, where Ince built a city of movie sets. He introduced the idea of the movie script, a written record of the plot and action, instead of making up the story as he went along (the way many other early filmmakers did). He also employed writers, directors, cameramen, producers, and others to contribute to the different parts of filmmaking, instead of doing all the work on his own. And he pioneered the Hollywood studio system, shooting multiple films at the same time with a group of creative types who were always at his disposal.

In 1912 alone, Ince directed 29 movies at Inceville; modern directors rarely make more than one. Granted, Ince's movies were much shorter than the ones we're familiar with today, but back then, nothing was digital and everything—from cutting the film to edit scenes to creating the special effects—had to be done by hand. Over his career, Ince made hundreds of movies.

By 1924 Ince had sold that first studio and built (and sold) another one in Culver City. (That second studio ultimately became the home of MGM.) He was the head of his own production company and was on the verge of signing an incredibly lucrative production deal with media mogul William Randolph Hearst. So how is it that a man so prosperous, with a career so promising, ended up dead after attending a party on Hearst's yacht? And why didn't the famed newspaper publisher attend Ince's memorial service…or even bother to send flowers?

MEET MOGUL #2

William Randolph Hearst was the only child of California senator George Hearst, a self-made multimillionaire. In 1887, William took over one of his father's businesses, the struggling *San Francisco Examiner*, and turned it into a success. How? Yellow journalism. Hearst invented the concept, and sensationalist, exaggerated, and sometimes phony reporting became his trademark. (One of his writers described Hearst's publications as "a screaming woman running down the street with her throat cut." And a political cartoonist immortalized him as the "Wizard of Ooze.") Hearst continued to buy newspapers until he owned one in almost every major city, and then he used them to try to gain political power.

After moving to New York in the 1890s, Hearst won election to the U.S. House of Representatives. But he really wanted to be president and used his newspapers to aid his climb to power. First, he published sensationalized stories aimed at stirring up public anger about Spanish colonization in the Caribbean, an area that the United States was also interested in settling. Hearst's papers carried unsubstantiated tales of executed prisoners, starving women and children, and heroic rebels battling the Spanish for freedom. It was the first war covered and driven by the media, and the stories worked. As more people read about Spanish "atrocities" in Hearst's papers, support for American intervention heated up, eventually sending the U.S. military into what became the Spanish-American War. Hearst then used the war to make himself a political hero. He hired reporters and filmmakers to record his every move, and sailed to Cuba, where he made grandstanding efforts to capture Spanish soldiers and win the war. As Hearst reportedly said, "You can crush a man with journalism."

For a while, the sensationalism worked, but Hearst's approach ultimately backfired when his newspapers mercilessly attacked President William McKinley during his 1900 reelection campaign. One editorial in a Hearst paper even went so far as to call for the president's assassination, writing, "If bad institutions and bad men can be got rid of only by killing, then killing must be done." A few months later, McKinley *was* assassinated, and many Americans blamed Hearst for fueling the fire.

Hearst's personal life was equally dramatic. In 1919, without bothering to divorce his wife Millicent (mother of his five sons),

Hearst returned to California to live with a young movie star named Marion Davies. Many saw this as a flagrant disregard of morality and evidence that the newspaper mogul felt he could get away with anything.

THE PLOT THICKENS

During the 1920s, the beautiful Marion Davies was one of the most famous performers in the world, but Hearst met her in 1918, when she was just getting started. The 55-year-old millionaire immediately fell for the 21-year-old Davies, and he developed Hollywood's Cosmopolitan Studios specifically to make her a star. She was cast in most of Hearst's silent films and in his radio productions. And of course, she was favorably reviewed in all the Hearst papers.

In 1919 Hearst began construction on a 56-bedroom, 61-bathroom "castle" on his ranch in San Simeon so that he and Davies could have a place to entertain. He also built her a multimillion dollar mansion in Santa Monica. But he couldn't completely buy the young actress's affections. In the summer of 1924, while Hearst was away working and Davies was making the circus film *Zander the Great*, comic actor Charlie Chaplin began picking her up in his limousine. According to the rumor mill, they were having an affair. Hearst was furious and jealous. He sent angry telegrams to Davies, but she wouldn't admit to any wrongdoing or stop being friends with Chaplin.

AN UNEXPECTED SURPRISE

On Saturday November 15, Hearst boarded his luxurious yacht *Oneida* for a short trip. The boat left Los Angeles for San Diego to pick up Thomas Ince, who had celebrated his 43rd birthday 10 days before and for whom Hearst had arranged an onboard party. The yacht was already filled with various guests, including Hearst's New York movie columnist, Louella Parsons; a group of young actresses; the famous silent leading man Theodore Kosloff; and Marion Davies' supposed lover, Charlie Chaplin. Why Chaplin? Hearst wanted to keep an eye on the pair.

The *Oneida* was as luxurious as Hearst could make it. There was a lounge for watching movies, a dining room that seated 12, and bathrooms with gold-plated faucets. Davies and Hearst also each had separate staterooms belowdecks. (Their rooms were also close to the central stairway and a glass case that held guns. Hearst liked to shoot seagulls.) And even though Prohibition was the law of the land, the yacht's hold was filled with illegal liquor.

Ince's birthday party was in full swing until about midnight, when passengers suddenly heard the producer moaning. They were told he'd suffered a heart attack, and he was rushed by motorboat to San Diego. Daniel Goodman (a licensed but nonpracticing doctor who was also Hearst's studio manager) and Ince boarded a train to L.A., but the producer took a turn for the worse en route so they had to stop briefly at a hotel in Del Mar. The story gets sketchy here: Either they all got back on the train and continued on to Los Angeles, where Ince's wife Nell was waiting for them, or Nell picked them up in Del Mar. Either way, the producer never recovered, and died in L.A. on November 19. The official cause of death: "heart failure caused by indigestion."

People started whispering immediately. The most often repeated rumor was that Ince hadn't died of heart failure at all. Instead, Hearst had shot and killed Ince by mistake after the millionaire caught Chaplin and Davies canoodling. In a jealous rage, Hearst ran to get his gun. Davies's screams brought Ince to the scene, where he got between Chaplin and the bullet. But was it true?

SMELLS LIKE A COVER-UP

There was certainly plenty of circumstantial evidence against Hearst. In the hours after Ince was rushed from the yacht, Hearst's newspapers published blatant lies, saying the producer had fallen ill at the Hearst Castle in San Simeon and was taken to Los Angeles by train. Then the papers admitted that Ince was on a yacht, but never mentioned that the yacht belonged to the boss. About a month later, Hearst created a trust fund for Nell Ince, and gave Louella Parsons (a guest on that fateful voyage) a promotion, making her a syndicated Hollywood gossip columnist instead of a lowly writer for a small New York paper, presumably to keep them both quiet.

The *L.A. Times*, a paper not owned by Hearst, supposedly ran a headline saying Ince had been shot on Hearst's yacht, but then

...but for a lumber mill owner named Abner Weed.

the story mysteriously vanished from its archives. There were also rumors that Chaplin's private secretary said she saw Ince removed from the ship suffering from a bullet wound to the head. But no one could actually pin down anyone who could (or would) officially contradict the story that Ince had suffered a heart attack. So the San Diego District Attorney's office never did an autopsy, and Ince's body was cremated.

Still Hearst seemed worried. His Chicago newspaper was investigating a possible police cover-up in the city following the murder of an assistant district attorney named William McSwiggin. After Ince's death, one Chicago official announced that if Hearst newspapers didn't stop daily headlines like "Who Killed McSwiggin?" he'd be forced to ask "Who Killed Thomas H. Ince?" Suddenly Hearst's papers were silent.

BAD BOOZE, OR MURDER?

Most historians admit they'll probably never know if Hearst shot Ince on the *Oneida*. Many people in Hollywood believe he did, though, and the 2001 movie *The Cat's Meow* shows that version of events. However, if Chaplin was afraid Hearst might kill him, he didn't show it. He continued to visit Hearst and Davies and was filmed at their beach house in 1928.

Several biographers suspect Hearst's illegal liquor might have actually been the cause of Ince's death. The doctors and nurse who attended to Ince before he died said he was drunk and complaining that "bad liquor" had made him sick. During Prohibition, accidentally buying poisonous liquor was always a danger, and Hearst might have feared an investigation because he was also a bootlegger. He had a business in place where he used a motorboat to load up on liquor from British ships in the San Francisco Bay and brought the booze to various California ports. Hearst most certainly wouldn't have wanted that illegal—and very profitable—operation exposed.

However it happened, Hearst was never really able to move beyond the suspicion that he'd killed Thomas Ince, and rumors dogged him until his death in 1951. In fact, Ince's death led to a famous, but unsavory, nickname for the *Oneida*: "William Randolph's hearse."

HARD-TIME HARDBALL

*The crowd cheers and jeers as the pitcher winds up and launches a fastball...
while armed guards keep watch from the towers of San Quentin.*

FIELD OF DREAMS

San Quentin State Prison in Marin County—home to California's death row—seems like an unlikely place for a baseball team. But San Quentin began hosting baseball games in the 1920s, when inmates organized themselves into teams, set up a diamond in the prison yard, and played each other. The fun stopped in the '70s, when a riot caused a lockdown of the yard, but in 1994, prison chaplain Reverend Earl Smith decided to revive the sport. Seven months later, the inmates had created a ball field in the yard at San Quentin. A donation of $10,000 in 2003 from the band Metallica allowed officials to level and smooth the all-dirt surface. During that renovation, engineers unearthed dozens of metal shanks that had been hidden in the yard since the prison opened in 1852.

The San Quentin Giants (named for the San Francisco Giants, who donated their practice uniforms) host about 30 games a year...all home games...and the dirt field is surrounded by concrete buildings and armed guards. But for the inmates who play on that field—called "San Quentin's Field of Dreams"—it's an opportunity and a privilege just to suit up.

PLAY BALL!

The San Quentin squad consists of men, mostly in their 30s and 40s, who are prison veterans like convicted murderer Chris Rich, who killed his wife in 1995. Once a college baseball player, Rich requested a transfer to San Quentin, specifically so he could play baseball. And he stays out of trouble because, he says, "I'm thankful for every game."

Of the more than 5,000 prisoners San Quentin houses, only the 1,800 or so who make up the general population are allowed to play sports—none of the 600 death row inmates are even allowed into the yard. (The rest of the prisoners are transitional,

San Quentin has its own ZIP code: 94974.

waiting to be sent to other facilities.) The team holds tryouts like any other team, and as many as 60 hopefuls show up each year. But only about 20 are able to shed their prison duds in exchange for a baseball uniform.

GROUND RULES

The Giants play other amateur adult teams from the Bay Area. As soon as the visitors arrive at San Quentin, they're told the first rule of prison baseball: Under no circumstances will prison officials negotiate should they be taken hostage. It's a rule the guards apply to all visitors; if prisoners know they won't gain anything by taking hostages, they're less likely to do it.

After that, the game proceeds pretty much like any other. The inmate "fans" who watch the game from behind the chain-link fence have been known to hurl a steady stream of expletives at the visitors, and the home team plays competitively. After the game, the inmates line up to shake hands with the visitors.

Playing baseball at San Quentin has been a transformative experience for many inmates. Away from the baseball diamond, men of different races don't generally interact with each other, and race-based gangs flourish. But once they step on the field, the men have to put aside their racial biases and play together as a team. According to inmate Troy Williams, "Everyone wants to play, but you can't if you're not good. Doesn't matter what color you are. Once you start breaking it down like that, that your race won't hurt you or help you, it starts to change the way you think about it."

AMERICA'S FAVORITE PASTIME

The San Quentin baseball program has a lot of detractors. Many people believe that convicted murderers, rapists, and thieves shouldn't enjoy any of their time behind bars. But others push for recreation programs as a way to help rehabilitate the prisoners. Proponents cite the benefits of social interaction and the team-building skills that can be gained from playing sports. Prison officials claim that sports make the inmates easier to supervise, keep them from getting bored, and motivate them to be on their best behavior—participation is a privilege, not a right. For the inmates, though, the benefits are simpler—baseball offers, says pitcher David Baker, "a way to kind of escape prison."

In 2010, Jim Morrison's original lyric sheet for "L.A. Woman" sold for $20,371.

BRAGGING RIGHTS, PART II

On page 197, we introduced you to two of California's most "famous" landmarks. Here are two more.

CLAIM TO FAME: Toad tunnels and Toad Hollow
WHERE: Davis
STORY: In 1995, the city of Davis built a tunnel under the I-80 freeway. Why? The freeway split the western toad's habitat in half: their breeding pond was on one side, and their living area on the other. Wildlife activists wanted a way for the toads to move between them without getting squished on the highway. Made of metal, the tunnel was 21 inches wide and 18 inches high, a seemingly respectable size for a toad tunnel.

Many Davisites were proud of their tunnel and also wanted to create a safe place for their hopping residents to live, an area they called Toad Hollow. Postmaster Ted Puntillo crafted and donated a selection of miniature buildings for the toad town, which was set up near the tunnel. He also wrote a children's book, *The Toads of Davis*, about the tunnel from the toads' point of view.

But then in 1998, *Daily Show* correspondent Stephen Colbert conducted an "investigation" of the Davis tunnel...and found no toads anywhere near it. Town officials admitted there were problems. The city had put in lights to help lure toads into the tunnels, but they made the tunnels too hot—in fact, on hot days, the metal tunnels were too warm even without the lights. Worse, when some toads did use the tunnels to get to the breeding pond, they were greeted on the other side by predatory birds that had figured out they were coming and swooped in for an easy meal.

However, the Davis toad tunnel did call attention to an American wildlife problem. In 2005, *National Geographic* published an article quoting experts about amphibians such as frogs, toads, and salamanders needing help across roads to survive their breeding season. Biologists said the animals needed...tunnels. But to really help the creatures, the tunnels had to be fitted with iron grates to let in air, light, and moisture. Without tunnels, the scientists said, roadkill will continue to cause the decline of many amphibians.

CLAIM TO FAME: The home of Bigfoot
WHERE: Willow Creek
STORY: The Salish Indians (located mostly in Oregon, Washington, and Canada) told stories of Sasquatch, a large, hairy ape-man (seven to nine feet tall and weighing about 500 pounds) who walked upright. According to legend, this shy creature smelled bad and lived on berries, nuts, fish, and deer. Scientists have yet to give credence to the tale, but since 1884, there have been hundreds of reported Sasquatch sightings in California's northern forests. The most famous have been around the tiny town of Willow Creek, which calls itself "the Gateway to Bigfoot Country" and "the Bigfoot Capital of the World."

In 1958 logger Jerry Crew was working in an area called Bluff Creek when he found a collection of huge footprints. At about 16 inches long and 7 inches wide, these impressions were too large to belong to a human, and their depth indicated a creature that weighed much more than an ordinary man. Crew's discovery made national news and gave the creature the name Bigfoot. Then, in 1967, Roger Patterson and Robert Gimlin, two Bigfoot researchers, shot what they said was a short film of a female Bigfoot walking through the woods in daylight. It was compelling footage—the creature even turns midstride and looks back toward the camera. But was it real? Over the years, several people claimed to have participated in the creation of the film and said that the Bigfoot was actually a person dressed in costume. But others say the "confessions" themselves were hoaxes, given by people seeking fame.

The controversy over Bigfoot doesn't bother Willow Creekers, though, who honor all ape-men, real or mythical. The town boasts a famous "life-size" eight-foot statue of Bigfoot carved from redwood, and the Willow Creek–China Flat museum features Bigfoot exhibits that include plaster casts of the creature's footprints and a rare handprint. And every Labor Day weekend, the town holds Big Foot Days, a festival celebrating the Sasquatch where costumed shaggy ape-men eat local baked goods, visit petting zoos with their kids, and dance to rock bands.

The Richter scale was invented at Caltech in Pasadena.

MEEK WIVES AND CARVING KNIVES

Uncle John wonders if the legends he's heard about the Santa Ana winds are just a lot of hot air.

DEVIL WINDS

Every year from September through March, hot, dry winds called Santa Anas sweep through Southern California. But they've also got plenty of less-than-desirable nicknames: red winds, devil winds, evil winds, and devil's breath. Santa Anas are blamed for everything from sinusitis to mental problems and have even been said to make some people just plain murderous. The movie *White Oleander* opens with the narrator explaining, "The Santa Anas blew in hot from the desert that fall...Maybe the wind was the reason my mother did what she did." (Spoiler alert: Mom poisoned her ex-boyfriend.) In an essay on the Santa Anas, author Joan Didion wrote that the winds makes people act strangely—like her neighbor who suddenly prowled his property with a machete looking for trespassers. But the most famous description of the winds' unsettling power came from Raymond Chandler's *Red Wind*: "It was one of those hot dry Santa Anas that come down through the mountain passes and curl your hair and make your nerves jump and your skin itch. On nights like that, every booze party ends in a fight. Meek little wives feel the edge of the carving knife and study their husbands' necks. Anything can happen."

But what exactly are the facts behind these devil winds? And why do they have everyone so hot and bothered?

BORN IN THE DESERT

A Santa Ana begins in the high-altitude deserts of the Great Basin that sprawls across Utah, Nevada, and California. Santa Anas are often thought to be hot because they come from the desert, but they actually start out cool. From fall to early spring, the Great Basin is cooler than Southern California. As cold, dry air chills the desert, it also builds up high pressure, pushing toward the earth's surface. The weather is warm on the West Coast, though, so the basin's high-pressure mass of heavy, cold air turns into a wind that rushes to fill the vacuum caused by the lighter, warmer low-pressure air. The wind sweeps westward from the high desert through gaps and canyons in the San Bernardino and San Gabriel Mountains and then heads down toward the ocean.

Santa Anas compress as they blow toward the lower altitudes, which makes them lose humidity and gain warmth. For every 1,000 feet, they descend (from a starting point of more than 6,000 feet above sea level), they pick up about 5°F. So by the time the Santa Anas arrive in Los Angeles, Orange, and San Diego Counties, they're hot and dry. They're also fast—moving at anywhere from 30 mph to more than 80 mph.

Santa Anas whip up high waves that are a boon to surfers, and they often blow L.A.'s smog out to sea. But that's about all the good they do. As they rush through Southern California canyons, the winds have been known to topple trees, trucks, trailers, and power poles—and start fires.

Santa Anas dry out vegetation in undeveloped areas. Then if a wildfire starts, the winds fan the flames. They can turn small brush fires into devastating blazes within hours and push them along at tremendous speeds. The destructive Cedar Fire that broke out in San Diego County in 2003 was fanned by Santa Anas. It spread over 30 miles in less than 17 hours and burned more than 270,000 acres.

SICK, GRUMPY, AND JUMPY

Wind damage and lethal fires are more than enough to earn Santa Anas their title of evil winds, but science shows that the winds also have a profound affect on people. For one thing, Santa Anas make many Southern Californians sick. The winds stir up pollens, and for allergy sufferers, that can make it difficult to breathe. They also cause a sudden drop in humidity that swells mucus membranes, causing some people to get headaches and sinus pain. Even worse, Santa Anas carry a dust-borne fungus called *Coccidioides immitis* that causes valley fever, or "California disease." Most sufferers of valley fever just experience flulike symptoms for about a month, but for others, the disease causes pneumonia, meningitis, and even death.

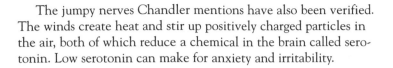

The jumpy nerves Chandler mentions have also been verified. The winds create heat and stir up positively charged particles in the air, both of which reduce a chemical in the brain called serotonin. Low serotonin can make for anxiety and irritability.

THE SANTA ANAS MADE ME DO IT

But can the Santa Anas really create killers? And do they raise the murder rate in Southern California? In an interview with *Blogging Los Angeles*, Craig Harvey, L.A. County's chief coroner, says he hasn't found any connection between the winds and local murder rates. Over the years, the coroner's office has kept records of deaths from homicides, suicides, and accidents and has found spikes in those events during the holiday months of December, January, and July. But Santa Anas also occur in October, November, February, and March, and those months have average rates. So the Santa Anas can legitimately be blamed for a lot of grief, but if you feel like killing someone, you're unlikely to get a judge to believe that the devil winds made you do it.

* * *

HORSE THIEVES!

• California was plagued by horse thieves in the 1800s. Tens of thousands of stolen horses were herded east along the Old Spanish Trail to New Mexico or north via the Siskiyou Trail to Oregon, and then dispersed for sale all over the North America. Various locations still carry names that speak to their thieving pasts...like Horse Thief Canyon in Corona and Horse Thief Camp in Needles.

• In the old days, horse thieves were hanged. The rationale? Stealing a traveler's horse could cause his death. Nowadays, though, stealing a horse is just grand theft, no hanging involved.

• One reformed horse thief was poet and novelist Joaquin Miller, who moved to California in the 1850s hoping to make a fortune in the gold rush. He was also a mining camp cook and, perhaps most damning of all, a lawyer.

WELCOME TO SLAB CITY

Here's a look at one of the most unusual, most unlikely, and, strangely, most beloved campgrounds in the entire United States.

OPEN...AND CLOSED

When the United States entered World War II following the bombing of Pearl Harbor, it was just a matter of time until American soldiers would go into battle against the German and Italian forces occupying North Africa. So in 1942, the Marine Corps opened a base called Camp Dunlap on 630 acres of desert land in Southern California, where it trained troops to fight in conditions similar to those in North Africa.

Camp Dunlap wound down after the war and closed for good in 1956. The military stripped the base of everything of value, and after they cleared out, the citizens of the nearby city of Niland tore down the few remaining buildings and used the lumber to build a church. All that was left were the concrete slabs that had served as the floors for dozens of portable buildings and tents. A few ex-marines decided to stay behind, roughing it on campsites they built on the slabs. "The Slabs," or "Slab City," as it's called, has been occupied ever since.

FOR THE BIRDS

Only the toughest and most determined "slabbers" could stand to live at the site year-round; in summer the temperature can climb past 120°F in the shade, what little there is. But over the years, the site became a popular wintering spot for RV "snowbirds." By the 1980s, more than 3,000 campers, travel trailers, and motor homes were descending on the site each October and staying until April, when they packed up and headed north again before it got too hot. Slab City had a lot to offer its "citizens," most of whom were on limited or fixed incomes: It was warm in winter but not unbearably hot, and because it was owned by the state (and not private property) it was legal to stay there. It didn't cost a penny in rent, and because it was just 50 miles north of the Mexican border, affordable prescription drugs and medical care weren't far away, either.

Most popular tattooed words in the California prison system: "Harley Davidson."

...AND NOW THE FINE PRINT

Before you quit your job and hit the trail for Slab City, there are a few things you need to know. For starters, there's still no water, electricity, or sewage service. There's not much fresh air, either: Slab City is just three miles from the Salton Sea, a dying body of water that's bigger than Lake Tahoe. Fed by salty runoff from the irrigated fields of the Imperial Valley (known as the Valley of the Dead before the irrigation went in), the Salton is already saltier than the Pacific Ocean, and by 2017 it will be so salty that nothing will be able to live in it. The fish die-off is already well under way, and as migratory birds eat the diseased and dying fish, they die, too, and end up in the lake. The overpowering stench has been compared to a combination of cow manure, skunk spray, rotten eggs, urine-soaked hallways, and vomit.

And while Camp Dunlap has been closed for more than 60 years, the adjacent Chocolate Mountain Gunnery Range is still open for business. It's attacked day and night by bombers and fighter planes using real ordnance. As if the loud noises and trembling ground weren't enough, some Slab City denizens make extra money sneaking onto the range at night to collect shrapnel that they sell for scrap metal. The military sends out patrols to stop them, but the county sheriff has caught more than one "scrapper" red-handed trying to bring unexploded cluster bombs, antitank rockets, and even Sidewinder missiles back to Slab City. A few of the scrappers have been blown to bits by the bombs.

DIFFERENT STROKES FOR DIFFERENT FOLKS

So is Slab City the last bastion of true freedom and independence in America, or is it a stinking, sunbaked, postapocalyptic ticking-time-bomb vision of hell on earth? It depends on who you ask. It's certainly not for everyone: A 1989 survey of visitors to the Salton Sea area found that not only did most of them say they'd never want to return, more than half said they were *afraid* to return.

And yet in spite of it all, people keep coming back. They've created quite a thriving community in Slab City, complete with swap meets, a library, a singles club, a Christian center, a church, a pet cemetery, and an outdoor stage where people gather to listen to live music every night. Nearly everyone has a CB, and they're usually tuned to channel 23, the unofficial Slab City channel, especially for the 6:00 p.m. nightly news bulletins and announcements. Many residents are better known by their CB handles (Stargazer, Brain Dead, Cardboard Johnny) than they are by their real names.

When groups of snowbirds start arriving in October, they tend to cluster their rigs in groups for security. But the various factions at Slab City—snowbirds, year-round slabbers, migrant laborers, the Apple Dumpling Gang (dune buggy enthusiasts), and even the local sheriff's deputies, who patrol the area regularly—manage to interact on a daily basis without much fuss. Many slabbers have built small businesses that provide services to other residents. Does your rig need a new fan belt? Do you need water hauled in, or your garbage hauled out? Is your TV on the fritz? Do you want to replace your electric generator with solar panels? Someone in Slab City can take care of it for you. They even have an Avon Lady.

STAY TUNED

Imperial County isn't crazy about Slab City, and neither is the State of California, which owns the land. But nobody wants the responsibility—or the expense—of closing it down and cleaning it up. Forty years' worth of abandoned cars, burned-out trailers, and other junk would have to be hauled away, and the hundreds of "gopher holes" (makeshift septic tanks) scattered around the site would have to be dealt with. And who knows how many unexploded bombs are still lying around?

On more than one occasion the state has tried to sell Slab City, perhaps to someone who would clean it up, put in utilities, and turn it into a commercial campground. But who would *pay* to camp between the stinky Salton Sea and a live bombing range? And as much as the county must hate to admit it, when all those RVs roll into town each October, they pump a fortune into the economies of Niland and other small towns in the area. Even if the county could get rid of Slab City, would it really want to?

Every year the conversation in Slab City fills with speculation and worry that this season might be the last, and every year the old-timers laugh it off. "Somebody's always got a plan to clean up the Slabs," one resident said in 1994. "I'm 87 now, and if I live to be 100, I'll still be coming here."

The Hollywood sign read "Hollywoodland" until 1941.

FIELD OF DREAMBOATS

During Hollywood's golden age, the city's stars weren't only in the movies. They showed up on the baseball field, too.

STAR POWER

The Pacific Coast League (PCL) is a minor league baseball organization founded in 1903. Because its teams play Triple-A baseball (just one level down from the majors), the PCL has produced some of the most talented players in history, including Joe DiMaggio and Ted Williams. The league is still going strong today, but the first half of the 20th century was its heyday and that's when it produced its most glamorous team—the Hollywood Stars.

The first incarnation of the Hollywood Stars lasted from 1926 to 1935, but it wasn't until the team was bought by Robert H. Cobb in 1939 that it truly began to capture the country's imagination. Cobb, the owner of L.A.'s famous Brown Derby restaurant (and the man after whom the Cobb salad is named), gave the Stars a touch of glamour by selling stock in the team to celebrities like Gary Cooper, Bing Crosby, Gene Autry, Barbara Stanwyck, Robert Taylor, George Burns, Gracie Allen, Harry Warner, and Cecil B. DeMille. Their involvement brought in loads of free publicity and attracted other Tinseltown glitterati to the Stars' home games. On any given day, you were apt to see celebs like Gregory Peck, Natalie Wood, Spencer Tracy, Milton Berle, Rosemary Clooney, Danny Kaye, Jack Benny, Clark Gable, and Elizabeth Taylor cheering on the home team from the grandstands.

The Stars played in Hollywood until 1957, when they were pushed out by the arrival of the Los Angeles Dodgers. Despite its fans and prestige, the club couldn't compete with a big-budget major league franchise and were sold to a group based in Salt Lake City for $175,000. But during their time in Hollywood, the Stars racked up some pretty cool achievements. Here are a few.

THEIR BEST PITCHER WAS A CHEATER

Playing for the Stars was nothing to spit at, especially for pitchers like Frank Shellenback, who needed every bit of saliva he could muster to become the finest hurler in the PCL. This talented right-hander played two seasons with the Chicago White Sox (1918–19) before the major leagues banned the spitball and deprived him of his most effective pitch. Fortunately, the pitch was still legal in the PCL, so Shellenback packed his bags and headed for the West Coast, where he won 205 game for the Stars between 1926 and 1935. Shellenback was later elected into the league's hall of fame and, with 295 career victories, remains the winningest pitcher in PCL history.

THE HOME-FIELD ADVANTAGE

Part of the appeal of seeing the Stars play was soaking up the atmosphere at Gilmore Field, a 12,500-seat stadium that had a reputation for being one of the most intimate parks in the PCL. Opened on May 2, 1939, at 7700 Beverly Boulevard in Los Angeles, the cozy park practically put the fans into the action with seats that were just 24 feet from first and third base, and 34 feet from home plate. (The distance between home plate and the backstop at most contemporary major league ballparks is 52 feet.) The close proximity at Gilmore Field encouraged a high level of interaction between the fans and players, and it wasn't unusual for the two groups to carry on conversations throughout the game. Gilmore Field was torn down in 1958 and today is home to a CBS studio.

FIRST IN FLIGHT

In 1928 the Stars became the first professional baseball team to travel by airplane. They didn't do it regularly, however, and continued to travel mainly by train over the next two decades. Other baseball teams finally started flying on a regular basis in 1946 when the New York Yankees began shuttling their players in a United Airlines plane nicknamed the "Yankee Mainliner."

MADE FOR TV

In 1939 the Stars were the first professional baseball team to appear on television for an interview with a local station. They became the first club to regularly televise home games in the late 1940s.

California's state seal includes a miner, a grizzly bear, and...

INNOVATION WAS THE NAME OF THEIR GAME

• The Hollywood Stars tried to get a leg up on the competition in 1950 when they became the first professional baseball team to replace their standard trousers with shorts. The "shorties," as they became known, were supposed to allow players more speed and mobility, but the uniforms proved unpopular with the public and were phased out after the 1953 season.

• The Stars were one of the first professional baseball teams to regularly use batting helmets and to employ cheerleaders.

• The team also came up with a brilliant way of improving their concession sales in the early 1950s when they became the first professional baseball team to drag the infield after the fifth inning of each game. The activity, which involved moistening and raking the infield dirt, typically took 10 minutes and prompted many fans to grab a beer or hot dog while they waited for the game to resume. The ensuing spike in revenue was so significant that dragging the infield became a staple at all levels of professional baseball.

A SUPERSTAR MASCOT

The Stars were a Hollywood team, so it's not surprising that they raised eyebrows throughout the league in 1955 when they held a Miss Hollywood Stars pageant to select their first mascot. The winner: a blonde bombshell named Jayne Mansfield.

* * *

CALIFORNIA Q & A

Q. Who was the last California governor to live in the governor's mansion?

A. Ronald Reagan in 1967. When Jerry Brown succeeded Reagan as governor, he decided that he didn't want to live in a swanky home, and instead took a small apartment with a mattress on the floor to show his frugality. The governor's mansion became a museum and state park after Reagan moved out, and all the governors since have been responsible for making their own living arrangements while in office.

NOVEL CALIFORNIA

The Golden State has inspired some great writers.

"The Mojave is a big desert and a frightening one. It's as though nature tested a man for endurance and constancy to prove whether he was good enough to get to California."
—**John Steinbeck,**
***Travels with Charley: In Search of America* (1962)**

"Come down to Big Sur and let your soul have some room to get outside its marrow."
—**Richard Brautigan,**
***A Confederate General from Big Sur* (1964)**

"This is the Pacific that Balboa looked at from the Peak of Darien, this is the face of the Earth as the creator intended it to look."
—**Henry Miller,**
***Big Sur and the Oranges of Hieronymus Bosch* (1957)**

"After school I played in orange groves and in Little League and in the band and down at the beach and every day was an adventure. I grew up in utopia."
—**Kim Stanley Robinson,**
***Pacific Edge* (1990)**

"San Francisco has as pleasant a climate as could be contrived, take it all around, and is doubtless the most unvarying in the whole world."
—**Mark Twain,**
***Roughing It* (1880)**

"A grapy dusk, a purple dusk over tangerine groves and long melon fields; the sun the color of pressed grapes, slashed with burgundy red, the fields the color of love and Spanish mysteries."
—**Jack Kerouac,**
***On the Road* (1951)**

"And this hill, looming up above the southern corner of the city, rising like a pregnant belly above the green patchwork of houses and gardens and paths and the blue waters of San Francisco Bay."
—**Starhawk, *The Fifth Sacred Thing* (1993)**

"There are no real Californians. Only people who live there and people who don't."
—**Laura Kalpakian,**
***Steps and Exes: A Novel of Family* (1999)**

Q. Who was president when California became a state? A. Millard Fillmore.

JOHN MUIR'S YOSEMITE, PART III

Naturalist John Muir first visited Yosemite in 1868, and he wrote all about it in the 1912 book The Yosemite. *Here are some excerpts from that book. (Parts I and II appear on pages 85 and 176.)*

THE REDWOODS

T"Between the heavy pine and silver fir zones towers the Big Tree (*Sequoia gigantea*), the king of all the conifers in the world, 'the noblest of the noble race.' The groves nearest Yosemite Valley are about twenty miles to the westward and southward and are called the Tuolumne, Merced and Mariposa groves."

BIG AND OLD

"The height of 275 feet or thereabouts and a diameter of about twenty feet, four feet from the ground is, perhaps, about the average size of what may be called full-grown trees, where they are favorably located. The specimens twenty-five feet in diameter are not very rare and a few are nearly three hundred feet high. In the Calaveras grove there are four trees over 300 feet in height, the tallest of which as measured by the Geological Survey is 325 feet.

The very largest that I have yet met in the course of my explorations is a majestic old fire-scarred monument in the Kings River forest. It is thirty-five feet and eight inches in diameter inside the bark, four feet above the ground. It is burned half through, and I spent a day in clearing away the charred surface with a sharp ax and counting the annual wood-rings with the aid of a pocket lens. I succeeded in laying bare a section all the way from the outside to the heart and counted a little over four thousand rings, showing that this tree was in its prime about twenty-seven feet in diameter at the beginning of the Christian era. No other tree in the world, as far as I know, has looked down on so many centuries as the sequoia or opens so many impressive and suggestive views into history. Under the most favorable conditions these giants probably live 5,000 years or more though few of even the larger trees are half as old...So harmonious and finely balanced are even the mightiest of these monarchs in all their proportions that there is never anything overgrown or monstrous about them."

YOSEMITE'S FLOWERS

"Yosemite was all one glorious flower garden before plows and scythes and trampling, biting horses came to make its wide open spaces look like farmers' pasture fields. Nevertheless, countless flowers still bloom every year in glorious profusion on the grand talus slopes, wall benches, and tablets, and in all the fine, cool side-cañons [canyons] up to the rim of the Valley, and beyond, higher and higher, to the summits of the peaks. Even on the open floor and in easily reached side-nooks many common flowering plants have survived and still make a brave show in the spring and early summer. Among these we may mention tall œnotheras, Pentstemon lutea, and P. Douglasii with fine blue and red flowers; Spraguea, scarlet zauschneria, with its curious radiant rosettes characteristic of the sandy flats; mimulus, eunanus, blue and white violets, geranium, columbine, erythraea, larkspur, collomia, draperia, gilias, heleniums, bahia, goldenrods, daisies, honeysuckle; heuchera, bolandra, saxifrages, gentians; in cool cañon nooks and on Clouds' Rest and the base of Starr King Dome you may find Primula suffrutescens, the only wild primrose discovered in California, and the only known shrubby species in the genus. And there are several fine orchids, habenaria, and cypripedium, the latter very rare, once common in the Valley near the foot of Glacier Point, and in a bog on the rim of the Valley near a place called Gentry's Station, now abandoned. It is a very beautiful species, the large oval lip white, delicately veined with purple; the other petals and the sepals purple, strap-shaped, and elegantly curled and twisted."

*   *   *

OUT OF REBOUNDS

In the 1967 Crosby Golf Tournament at Pebble Beach, Arnold Palmer hit two balls off the same tree at the 14th hole, landing both balls out of bounds and ruining his chances for a win against Jack Nicklaus. Maybe to make it up to him, a storm that night uprooted "Palmer's tree" and blew it to the ground.

Dried grapes (raisins) hold 25% of their original weight.

ALL HAIL THE EMPEROR OF SAN FRANCISCO

San Francisco is known for being accepting of nonconformists, but few people better exemplify the city's love of eccentricity than Joshua Abraham Norton, the self-proclaimed "Emperor of these United States."

HOW RICE MADE ROYALTY

Few monarchs have ruled as kindly or been as revered by their subjects as Joshua Abraham Norton—aka his Imperial Majesty Norton I. Calling himself the "Emperor of these United States" (he later added "Protector of Mexico"), Norton "ruled" from 1859 to 1880 from his home in San Francisco. True, Norton was out of his mind at the time, and by "ruled," we mean "made a lot of laws that no one ever followed." But in San Francisco he was so popular that he's still celebrated to this day.

Norton was born around 1819 to a Jewish family in London, England, and grew up in South Africa, where he served in the military and worked in his father's retail business. After his parents died, he moved to San Francisco in 1849 with an inheritance of $40,000. But instead of hunting for gold like most 49ers, he opened an office to seek his fortune in commodities and real estate. Norton soon became well known and successful around the city. By 1852 he'd managed to acquire a fortune of more than $200,000 (about $5 million today). But then came the bad investment.

In the 1850s, there was a famine in China, and the country banned any of its farmers from exporting rice. China, though, was America's main rice supplier, and in San Francisco, Chinese immigrants considered the grain a staple. Seeing what he thought was a great opportunity, Norton put a down payment on an incoming shipment of rice from Peru. He planned to buy it cheap and sell it high. But the Peruvian rice turned out to be of poor quality, and other cargo ships brought more and better rice to San Francisco within weeks. Suddenly, there was a glut of rice in the city, and prices tanked—Norton's purchase was worthless. He felt misled and went to court arguing that he shouldn't have to pay for a shipment whose quality had been misrepresented. But after a long and costly legal battle, the California Supreme Court decided against him. He had to sell his real estate at a loss to pay creditors, and by 1856, he was broke. Destitute and depressed, Norton left town.

BUILDING AN EMPIRE

By 1859, though, Norton had returned to San Francisco a new man...literally. Instead of a poverty-stricken former investor, he declared himself to be an emperor. No one knows exactly what prompted Norton's change of status, but his "official" reign began when the *San Francisco Bulletin* published (as a humorous story) a "proclamation" he wrote for them. It began, "I Joshua Norton... declare and proclaim myself the Emperor of these United States." He went on to call for American leaders to meet in San Francisco and said his goal was to make laws that would "ameliorate the evils under which the country is laboring." Norton dressed the part, too. He wore old uniforms with gold epaulets on the shoulders—usually given to him by soldiers at the Presidio. He also carried a cavalry sword and a walking stick and, on special occasions, donned a beaver hat with an ostrich plume.

Norton behaved like a true king. He announced his new laws regularly in the local newspapers. These included dissolving the U.S. Congress, the California Supreme Court (which had decided against him in his rice catastrophe), and the Republican and Democratic parties. To keep religious peace, Norton attended synagogue on Saturday and went to a different Christian church every Sunday—so that all the country's religions felt equally honored. He also patrolled San Francisco's streets to make sure things were in order—sidewalks were clear of obstructions, police were on patrol, and city ordinances were enforced.

THE EMPEROR'S LOYAL SUBJECTS

There's no question that Norton was a bit crazy, but many San Franciscans humored and honored him anyway. They often even bowed when he passed by. He got free meals at restaurants. He rode on public transit for free and got complimentary front-row seats to lectures, plays, and concerts. He even paid bills with currency he invented. His friends, supporters, and locals also paid "taxes" to the poverty-stricken Norton...to help him pay his rent.

One reason for Emperor Norton's popularity was the fact that San Francisco had several competitive newspapers that always needed a good story. Emperor Norton—with his uniform, city inspections, and creation of new laws—made great copy and sold papers. The newspapers turned Norton into a local celebrity.

But San Franciscans also genuinely respected and cared for Norton, whom they considered to be kind and harmless. According to one newspaper, "The Emperor Norton has never shed blood. He has robbed no one, and despoiled no country. And that, gentlemen, is a hell of a lot more than can be said for anyone else in the king line." Many San Franciscans also believed that Norton had better ideas, more compassion, and much more common sense than their elected officials.

A BENEVOLENT MONARCH

Norton's "laws" (proclaimed in letters that he sent to local papers) were often ahead of their time. Even before the Civil War was declared, he'd wanted to dissolve Congress so it couldn't bring the country to "ruin" over the question of slavery. Other Norton ideas included the development of a flying machine and calling for a League of Nations to solve disputes instead of going to war. (When President Woodrow Wilson finally did establish a League of Nations in 1919, a precursor to the United Nations, he won a Nobel Prize.)

In 1872 Norton decreed that a suspension bridge be built between Oakland and San Francisco and that a tunnel be constructed through the bay. Those wishes were finally fulfilled with the Oakland Bay Bridge in 1936 and the Bay Area Rapid Transit (BART) Transbay Tube railway service in 1972.

THE KING IS DEAD

In 1880 Norton collapsed and died while walking to Nob Hill. The city raised money to bury him, and newspapers reported that the line of people in his funeral parade was two miles long. Even after his death, Norton wasn't forgotten: In 1934, his remains were moved from San Francisco to Woodlawn Cemetery in Colma. Thousands attended this second burial too, which featured full military honors. His tombstone is engraved with his title of "Norton I, Emperor of the United States, Protector of Mexico."

WHAT'S BREWING?

Wine shmine. California has some great beers.

THE STEAMIEST. Gold Rush "steam beers" were so named because brewers used primitive equipment and had no ice. San Francisco's Anchor Steam was the only one of these breweries to survive Prohibition, but the beer had a poor reputation, nearly causing the company to fold in 1965. Then came Fritz Maytag (from the appliance company). He took over and refined the brewing process, not only giving Anchor Steam new life but helping to start the microbrew craze of the 1980s.

THE MEANEST. The Stone Brewing Company in Escondido was created in 1996 by beer lovers Steve Wagner and Greg Koch. Their most infamous brew is Arrogant Bastard Ale. From the description: "It is quite doubtful that you have the taste or sophistication to appreciate an ale of this quality and depth." Despite this warning, the beer (7.2% alcohol) has won many awards.

THE WEEDIEST. Weed's Mt. Shasta Brewing Company prints "Try Legal Wee" on its bottle caps. In 2008 the Alcohol and Tobacco Tax and Trade Bureau ordered brewer Vaune V. Dillmann to remove the slogan because it "advocates the use of illegal drugs." Dillmann (a former Oakland cop who's never smoked weed) refused. It's his First Amendment right, he claimed, plus he received permission to use the name from the descendants of town founder Abner Weed. After threats from the ACLU, the bureau backed down.

THE GREENEST. What ingredient would you expect to find in a beer from Humboldt County? Hemp, of course. The seeds give Hemp Ale a nutty taste. Due to legal restrictions, this beer is only available in California. (And no, it doesn't get you high.)

THE OLDEST: In 2006 the brewers of Fossil Fuels Beer, including Cal Poly scientist Paul Cano, isolated a yeast strain that had been preserved in real amber for 45 million years. The ancient yeast gives Fossil Fuels Beer a "smooth and spicy taste," and reportedly goes well with chicken strips.

Largest park in the continental U.S.: Death Valley National Park (3.3 million acres).

WE ♥ SOLVANG

*If you've ever blundered into Solvang after taking a wrong turn from Santa
Barbara, you'll be excused for thinking you somehow wandered into
The Twilight Zone as visualized by Hans Christian Andersen.*

• **Couldn't cope with Copenhagen.** Solvang was founded and settled by a group of Danes in 1911. Like most good Scandinavian
immigrants, they first headed to the Midwest. But after a few years
of braving bitter winters, they decided to move west to a warmer,
milder climate. Those first settlers included a small contingent of
educators, farmers, and (luckily) a carpenter who headed to California to locate a good spot for and then set up a town for new
Dainish arrivals. They bought about 9,000 acres outside Santa
Barbara, settled in, and named their town Solvang (Danish for
"sunny field").

• **The media changes everything.** In the first half of the 20th
century, Solvang didn't look like it does now (with all the windmills and old-style architecture). It looked like a regular farming
town—the only difference was that the people spoke Dutch and
held the occasional Danish festival. Then the media discovered
Solvang. In 1947 the *Saturday Evening Post* ran a photo feature
about the town. The article was called "Little Denmark," and it
referred to Solvang as a "spotless Danish village that blooms like a
rose in California's charming Santa Ynez Valley." This sparked the
curiosity of day-trippers from Los Angeles, just two hours away.
But when they arrived in Solvang, they often looked a little lost
because there really wasn't that much to see.

But the ever-resourceful Danish residents saw an opportunity
and rushed to promote their annual Danish Days festival. The
town also began spiffying up its storefronts and public buildings,
retrofitting them to look like early 1900s Denmark. Hotels and
windmills were built, restaurants opened, horse-drawn carriages
took to the streets, and tourist shops opened their doors. Outside
town, an upscale dude ranch named the Alisal attracted city slick-
ers and Hollywood celebrities. Soon tourism became the town's
biggest industry.

The Beatles gave their final concert in 1966 at San Francisco's Candlestick Park.

- **Hans tributes.** Few Danish authors are more beloved than Hans Christian Andersen, and Solvang is proud of its homeland's most famous son. In town, there's a statue of the fairy-tale character the Little Mermaid (a copy of the famous one that stands in Copenhagen), a park, a museum, and a square all dedicated to the writer's memory.

- **On-screen antics.** Solvang has appeared on-screen too many times to mention, but a couple of recent notables include the movie *Sideways*, filmed at and around several local wineries, and an episode of *The Simpsons*, in which Milhouse's Solvang-dwelling uncle arrives in an airplane.

- **By the numbers.** The ratio of Solvang residents to tourists who arrive each year is about 5,000 to 2 million...in other words, 400 tourists for every townsfolk.

- **Solvang cyclists.** Not everything about Solvang has to do with Dutch kitsch. The town is also well known among cycling enthusiasts as a great place to train (even Lance Armstrong has trained there), and it's appeared many times as a stop on the annual Tour of California cycling race.

* * *

THE FIRST ARTICHOKE QUEEN

In 1948 a then-unknown Marilyn Monroe arrived in Salinas to help promote a diamond sale at Carlyle's Jewelers. (The company had hired another starlet who canceled at the last minute, so Monroe stepped in as a replacement.) She drew such large crowds that extra police officers had to be called in to keep order. While in the area, Monroe also agreed to lend her magic to nearby Castroville, the self-proclaimed "Artichoke Capital of the World." She visited the town's artichoke fields, posed with the vegetables, and wowed growers, who crowned her their Artichoke Queen. She brought in so much good press that after Monroe became famous in the 1950s, Castroville decided to make the tradition an annual event; it's been held every year since 1959.

Master of ceremonies for the 1960 Winter Olympics in Squaw Valley: Walt Disney.

MINE, ALL MINE

They brought California great big riches...and great big problems.
Here are three of the most profitable mines in the state's history.

T HE NEW ALMADEN MINES
Where: Santa Clara Valley
Story: California's first and most profitable mine wasn't a
gold mine. New Almaden opened two years before gold was even
discovered, and by the time it closed in 1976, it had generated
more than $70 million. Its haul? Quicksilver (aka, mercury).

In 1845 a group of Ohlone Indians led Mexican captain
Andrés Castillero to their source of cinnabar, the rock that contains mercury. The Ohlone had long used cinnabar to make body
paint, but Castillero knew that the mercury was where the money
was. He dug several mines in the area and sold them to a company
that named them after some famous mercury mines in Almaden,
Spain, which had been operating since Roman times.

For centuries, mercury has been used in medicines, cosmetics,
thermometers, and scientific tools, and in 19th-century California, it was also used in gold mining. Mercury attracted gold like a
magnet, and prospectors used it to extract gold from gravel or
crushed rock. By 1865 the busy New Almaden Mines supported
an entire community with doctors, churches, schools, and a population of 1,800.

But there was a problem: Mercury is incredibly toxic, and
can poison people who touch it or inhale its dust. As that danger
was discovered in the mid-1900s, mercury mining declined. Then,
finally, in 1976, the County of Santa Clara bought and closed the
mines, creating the Almaden Quicksilver County Park in their
place.

Cool Fact: The ancient Chinese believed mercury was a miracle
medicine that could heal broken bones and promote a long life.
Every day, Emperor Qin Shihuangdi, who ruled China during the
third century BC, ingested a mixture of mercury and jade (probably in pill form) that he believed would make him immortal. It
didn't. He died of mercury poisoning in 210 BC.

First private American citizen to own a Humvee: Arnold Schwarzenegger.

THE EMPIRE MINE

Where: Grass Valley

Story: When California's gold was first discovered in the 1840s, miners were panning for it in streams. But as those "easy pickings" disappeared, gold seekers turned to hard-rock mining—digging out ore that contained veins of gold. The oldest, largest, and richest hard-rock gold mine in California was the Empire Mine, which produced more than 5.6 million ounces of gold, estimated at well over a $100 million.

In 1850 logger George Roberts noticed flecks of gold on his boots. It came from gold lodged in quartz rock, but Roberts lacked the money and technology to remove the gold from the quartz. He also had no idea that he'd found such a huge, rich vein of gold, so in 1851 he sold his claim for $350 to a group of investors. They started the Empire Mine. By the time San Francisco businessman William Bourn and his son took it over in 1869, Empire had produced well over a million dollars' worth of gold.

Some of Empire's mining methods were unique: Its tunnels sank about a mile underground, and steam pumps were used to keep those passages from filling up with water. The mine also tried to be modern and constantly improved its technology and safety methods. In World War II, President Franklin D. Roosevelt ordered all gold mines closed because he wanted their manpower to go to the war effort. The Empire reopened briefly after the war, but by 1956 operating costs were just too expensive...even though only 20 percent of the mine's gold had been removed. So the Empire was shut down, and today it's a state park. Now, visitors can see the mine and dream about all the gold that's still in there.

Cool Fact: For many years, the Empire Mine ran almost entirely on mule power. The animals were lowered into the ground at the age of one and spent their entire lives down there, pulling carts of ore. Although they lived in almost complete darkness, the mine always claimed they were well cared for and enjoyed special treats from the miners—oats, whiskey, and...snuff.

THE HIMALAYA MINE

Where: Santa Ysabel

Story: With all the attention paid to the gold rush in Northern

California, it's easy to miss the fact that Southern California was also world-famous for its mines filled with semiprecious jewels like garnet, topaz, and especially tourmaline. Tourmaline is a gem that comes in a range of colors, and San Diego County mines produced a pink tourmaline that became very popular thanks to one very powerful woman. Tzu Hsi (Cixi), the dowager empress and ruler of China in the early 1900s, adored tourmaline. She made it so popular that the Chinese used it for jewelry, for the buttons and toggles of their clothing, and in carved figurines for their homes.

One of the richest tourmaline mines in North America was discovered by an unusual pair of New Yorkers: German gemologist Lippman Tannenbaum and his African American foster son, J. Goodman Bray, who had studied geology at Cornell University. Bray led the pair's search for a rich source of tourmaline. They found it in Mesa Grande, an area northeast of San Diego that was well known as a source of colored crystals. The New Yorkers bought a ranch and set up the Himalaya Mine, at one time the largest producer of tourmaline in the world.

For about 12 years, the Himalaya was at the heart of a Southern California gemstone mining boom, and Bray was nicknamed the "Tourmaline King of California." In 1904, the Himalayan mine produced 5.5 tons of tourmaline—a record that's never been broken. But the empress died in 1908, and soon after, the tourmaline boom died with her.

Gem mining in Southern California was nearly forgotten until 1957, when the Himalaya's new owner hit a valuable strike and led to a gradual rebirth of gem mining in the region. Today, for the (some say) exorbitant price of $75, tourists can sift through ore from the Himalaya in a hunt for their own crystalline treasures.

Cool Fact: The world's rarest tourmaline is called *paraiba*. Mined in Brazil, it's a brilliant, shimmering blue, the result of excess copper in the ore. Today, Paraiba tourmaline sells for tens of thousands of dollars...per carat.

ANIMAL TALES

*The skinny on some of California's most
beloved feathered and finned residents.*

FISH THAT FLY

Every summer since the late 1890s, Catalina Island skippers have been taking passengers out on night cruises to see the *Cheilopogon pinnatibarbatus californicus*, better known as the California flying fish. The fish, which arrive off the Catalina coast in late May and usually stay through September, are the largest species of flying fish in the world—18 inches long and weighing up to two pounds. They can jump 30 feet out of the water and glide for up to a quarter mile before dropping back into the water. The secrets of their aerodynamic ability are their large pectoral and posterior fins, which spread out like wings from their torpedo-shaped bodies.

The fish spend their days in the ocean but approach shorelines at night to feed on plankton and small fish. In turn, schools of larger fish such as tuna go after them. Their spectacular jumps are attempts to flee the predators. Fishermen use lights to lure flying fish into their boats at night, and Catalina skippers use flying fish to lure customers to their boats. Sometimes the fish even jump into the boats.

BIRDS FAMOUS FOR THEIR RETURN VISITS

In 1812 the church at the mission in San Juan Capistrano was nearly destroyed by an earthquake—today its stone ruins remain one of California's most impressive architectural sites. But the ruins are actually more famous for the birds' nests hanging from their eaves, nests belonging to the mission's cliff swallows.

Every spring, the swallows fly 6,000 miles from Argentina, to winter and find shelter in the ruins. (Argentina is in the Southern Hemisphere, so the swallows' winter is in the North American summer.) In 1910 Father John O'Sullivan came to the mission and spent years observing the swallows' migration. He noticed that first a few "scout swallows" appeared and then the large flocks followed, nearly always arriving on March 19, St. Joseph's Day. They stayed through the summer and usually left on October 23.

California's coastline is more than 1,264 miles long.

O'Sullivan considered the swallows' annual return to be miraculous, and he wanted to share it with others (he also hoped publicity would bring badly needed money to repair the mission). So in the 1930s, he asked a radio show to visit the mission and do a broadcast about the swallows' return. To the amazement of radio listeners, the swarms of swallows arrived punctually. Word spread and the mission got the fame (and much-needed funding) it needed. In the years since, thousands of visitors have descended on San Juan Capistrano every March 19 to watch the swallows return, and the city honors the day with an annual festival.

Unfortunately, in recent years, visitors have had a hard time actually seeing the swallows because many of the birds have headed for the hills—Chino Hills, that is. In 2010 the birds made nests in the eaves of buildings at Chino Hills' ritzy Vellano Country Club. According to mission officials, urbanization has destroyed the swallows' original feeding grounds in San Juan Capistrano, so they're working with an ornthinologist to set up conditions that will encourage the birds to return and thrive there again.

WAS THAT A PARROT?

From San Diego to San Francisco, flocks of wild parrots fly the urban skies—an estimated 7,000 parrots of at least 10 different species. There are many stories to explain how the tropical birds got here: Two common legends are that they were released from pet stores during fires or escaped from storm-damaged aviaries. But all we know for sure is that the flocks began with wild parrots brought in to California to be sold as pets before a 1992 ban outlawed the practice. With plenty of tropical plants growing on California properties, the parrots thrived. One of the largest flocks inhabits the area around Pasadena, and at least five types of parrots have interbred to make the flock a uniquely California breed.

Not everybody likes the parrots, however. The birds tend to screech to communicate...and often begin at dawn. Other members of the state's anti-parrot contingent worry the birds will endanger the survival of native fowl (experts haven't yet found that to be the case). But most cities enjoy their parrot flocks—especially in San Francisco, where the wild birds were the subject of a popular documentary, *The Wild Parrots of Telegraph Hill*, which followed a San Franciscan who befriended the birds.

Charles Lindbergh's *Spirit of St. Louis* was built in San Diego.

WATERWORLD

Located at the very tippy-top western corner of the state, the tiny seaside town of Crescent City is a wild place…geologically speaking, anyway.

• **Crescent City has been hit by a record 31 tsunamis** since the town started keeping records in 1933. The worst came on Good Friday 1964, after an earthquake registering 9.2 on the Richter scale hit Anchorage, Alaska. It was the largest earthquake ever recorded in North America, and it sent a tsunami rushing down the West Coast and all the way out to Hawaii. Washington and Oregon sustained some damage, but Crescent City (pop. 3,000) bore the brunt of the waves, which began to come ashore just after midnight on March 28. Peggy Coons, one of the keepers at the town's Battery Point Lighthouse, described the tsunami this way: "The basin was sucked dry. At [the dock], the large lumber barge was sucked down to the ocean bottom. In the distance, a black wall of water was rapidly building up, evidenced by a flash of white as the edge of the boiling and seething seawater reflected the moonlight." In all, the tsunami killed 11 people in Crescent City and caused about $15 million in damage, making it the deadliest and most destructive tsunami ever to hit the continental United States.

• **California has about 840 miles of coastline,** so why do tsunamis gravitate toward Crescent City? According to scientists, it has to do with a geological formation called the Mendocino Fracture Zone. Basically, a fracture zone is an underwater landmass that extends into the ocean from the coastline and marks the spot where two tectonic plates meet—in this case, the Gorda Plate and the Pacific Plate. The landmass is elevated from the ocean floor, like a mountain, and it creates something like a basin in the ocean off the shore of Crescent City. When a tsunami moves south from Alaska, it is stopped by the fracture zone and redirected toward the shore. Add to that the fact that Crescent City's natural harbor is shaped like a crescent (hence the town's name). Once a mass of water enters the harbor, it gets caught in the crescent and has nowhere to go but onto the shore.

THE ALMOND COOKIE REVOLUTION

When it comes to cleaning up the planet, California is usually on the front lines, but sometimes, even this state needs to be reminded to think twice about environmentalism. Here's the story of how three genteel housewives used tea parties and cookies to save San Francisco Bay.

THE HOUSEWIFE BRIGADE

THE HOUSEWIFE BRIGADE San Francisco Bay is an estuary where large amounts of freshwater from rivers empty into the Pacific and mix with saltwater. As the largest estuary on the Pacific Coast, the bay supports more than 750 species of fish and wildlife. Today, Californians know that the health of the bay affects the region's climate, agriculture, fishing, and the quality of life for the millions who live nearby. But that wasn't the case in 1960, when two Berkeley housewives met for tea.

Esther Gulick was well known in her neighborhood for her almond cookies, and just before Christmas, she took a batch to her friend Catherine "Kay" Kerr. Over tea and cookies, the two women discussed a map they'd seen in the *Oakland Tribune*. Drawn by the Army Corps of Engineers, it showed plans for the bay that would eventually make it a riverlike shipping corridor completely surrounded by landfill. In Berkeley, there were plans to fill more than 2,000 acres of wetlands so the town could double in size and have its own airport.

Kerr told Gulick that she and another friend, Sylvia McLaughlin, planned to take action to protect the bay, and Gulick quickly said she'd help. That agreement launched one of the nation's most powerful environmental movements. In the coming years, the three women would be called all kinds of names: "enemies of progress," "posy pickers," "eco-freaks," "enviromaniacs," and even "almond cookie revolutionaries." But their grateful supporters just gave them the nickname "the ladies."

FROM GOLD TO GARBAGE

San Francisco Bay's environmental problems had been growing for more than 100 years. Before the mid-19th century, the bay covered about 680 square miles and was filled with fish and wildlife. Its shores were lined with freshwater marshes, saltwater marshes, and mudflats. But in 1850, runoff from hydraulic mines began to fill the Bay with gravel and sand. Then the U.S. government passed the Swamp Land Act, authorizing the sale of tidelands for $1 an acre. More than 2 million acres of tidelands all over the country were sold and "reclaimed" for agricultural and real-estate purposes and to create ponds to produce salt. And as California's population exploded, the bay itself was seen as having great real-estate potential.

By 1960, 90 percent of the tidelands in San Francisco Bay were gone, and so much landfill had been dumped into its waters that the bay had shrunk by a third. The estuary carried untreated sewage, and there were at least 40 garbage dumps along its shoreline. In Berkeley the waters gave off a smell politely called the "East Bay stink." Politicians tired of dealing with the environmental problem and big businesses that stood to make fortunes from construction supported fill plans for shopping malls and subdivisions. Any objections were silenced in the name of progress.

HOLDING THE BAG

Any objections, that is, except the ones from the ladies. Kerr, Gulick, and McLaughlin thought a conservation organization might be willing to demand a halt to filling the bay. They had a few contacts because the University of California often did conservation research and their husbands were employed by the state's universities—Kay Kerr's husband Clark was president of the entire UC system.

In January 1961, the women held a historic meeting of conservation leaders at Esther Gulick's home. Representatives from the Sierra Club, the Save the Redwoods League, Audubon, and the Nature Conservancy were all there, and journalist Hal Gilliam, who had written a best-seller about San Francisco Bay, also attended. The meeting didn't go as the women had hoped, though. Everyone agreed that the estuary should be saved, but none of the groups had the resources to take on a new project. According to Gilliam, "Kerr, McLaughlin, and Gulick, to their surprise and dismay, were left holding the bag."

Beverly Hillbillies star Buddy Epson was originally cast as the Tin Man in...

So in 1961—at time when women were discouraged from working outside the home, participating in politics, or running important organizations—the three friends founded the Save San Francisco Bay Association, later known as Save the Bay. And they pooled their talents to do it: Kerr wrote the pamphlets and flyers and made use of her social clout. Gulick did the books, the paperwork, and made her almond cookies for meetings. McLaughlin was a dynamic public speaker who lectured to civic groups and performed community outreach. The three agreed to learn all they could about the bay from anyone—biologists, engineers, city planners—who could educate them about the needs of the estuary.

HATS, GLOVES, AND RADICAL CHANGE

The three women strategized that their first job would be to stop the Berkeley fill project, but to do that, they would need more than three members. So they went on a recruiting campaign, reprinting the Army Corps map with the added caption "Bay or River?" and sending it off with 1,000 letters asking $1 for membership. They soon had more than 900 new members (and dollars). The women thought they'd just been "lucky" to get such a successful response, but other fund-raising groups maintain that the strategy was actually brilliant. The map was a shocking wake-up call to all who loved San Francisco Bay, and the $1 membership fee encouraged participation even among people who had little money to give. It turned out that the three women were excellent grass-roots organizers.

They also had a unique style: Kerr, Gulick, and McLaughlin invited members to their homes and made protest plans over tea, coffee, and cookies. They dressed well—for one visit to the California state legislature, McLaughlin recalled wearing a blue linen suit, a red straw hat with flowers, red shoes, "and probably gloves too." They had impeccable manners and avoided confrontation. But the forces that wanted to develop San Francisco Bay soon discovered that the women were also tough and tenacious.

FIGHTING FOR THE BAY

In 1962 Save the Bay lost its first battle when the Berkeley City Council passed an amendment that allowed companies to fill the bay for commercial purposes. But instead of giving up, Kerr,

---

...The Wizard of Oz, but he had to quit after having an allergic reaction to the silver makeup.

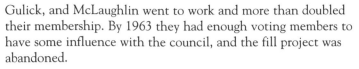

Gulick, and McLaughlin went to work and more than doubled their membership. By 1963 they had enough voting members to have some influence with the council, and the fill project was abandoned.

But what they really wanted was for elected officials in Sacramento to protect the entire bay from being filled. In 1964 Kerr called on State Senator J. Eugene McAteer and asked for his support. By then, Save the Bay membership included thousands of active voters. To please those voters, McAteer agreed to help. He sponsored a law that would protect the entire estuary and appoint an oversight commission to do it. Save the Bay members did their part by traveling to Sacramento in buses, filling legislature halls, and lobbying for the law.

The next year, the law passed and the Bay Conservation and Development Commission (BCDC) was established. Today, the BCDC oversees the preservation of the bay; there can be no filling, building, or dumping without its permission. BCDC was the first coastal protection agency in the United States. And thanks to its efforts and to those of Save the Bay, the estuary is now 40,000 acres *larger* than it was in 1960.

A TURNING TIDE

Although their most famous accomplishment was stopping the filling of the bay, Kerr, Gulick, and McLaughlin did much more. In 1960 there were only four miles of access to the hundreds of miles of shoreline in the Bay Area. The women worked to create shoreline parks and more than 500 miles of trails.

But perhaps their greatest legacy is that the city that once wanted to pave San Francisco Bay is now trying to restore it. On April 16, 2011, during an Earth Day celebration, Sylvia McLaughlin (the only surviving member of the original founders) was honored at the dedication of the Berkeley Meadow. The 72-acre green space is a former Berkeley landfill that's been turned back into wetlands. It's now a thriving habitat for native plants and animals, and offers walking paths for the public.

The state grass of California: purple needlegrass.

UP THE DOWN RAILROAD

Got a minute? In L.A., you can use it for a trip back in time.

A HEAVENLY RIDE

On the morning of December 31, 1901, a new train opened for business in downtown Los Angeles. There were crowds and many speeches about progress, and Mayor Meredith Snyder took one of the first rides. Wealthy women who lived in the Victorian mansions atop Bunker Hill served free punch to the passengers. The new railroad's official name was the Los Angeles Incline Railway, but a nearby metal archway already contained the words, "Angels Flight," so that's what everyone called it. Passengers paid a penny for a one-way ride that lasted just 50 seconds. Advertised as "The Shortest Railway in the World," Angels Flight's track was only 315 feet long. It wasn't a typical train, either, and didn't have an engine car, boxcars, or a caboose—there were only two small, 32-passenger trams.

The cars were named Olivet and Sinai (for two mountains in the Bible). They traveled on an incline between Hill and Olive Streets that was so steep their floors and seats had to be built on different levels like stairs, to keep people from sliding off their benches. Painted white with black trim, Olivet and Sinai worked in tandem: one car carried passengers up from the corner of Third and Hill to Olive, while the other car was heading down. Some people complained that the ceremonies in 1901 made too much fuss over a train that just traveled a couple of blocks. But Angels Flight went on to carry more passengers per mile than any other railway in the world. More than 100 million people traveled on its tracks in the first 50 years.

THAT MAN WITH A PLAN

The man who brought Angels Flight to L.A. was Colonel James Ward Eddy, a Civil War hero and a friend of President Abraham Lincoln. Eddy lived in the downtown area with his teenage grandson—a kid who often complained it would be a lot easier to climb

---

California produces 99.5% of all dates grown in the U.S.

Bunker Hill if the city would put in a cable car.

The colonel was an entrepreneur, always looking for a new business. He knew that the wealthy families who lived in the expensive Bunker Hill neighborhood would be willing to pay to not to have to climb the dirt road between Hill and Olive. Eddy had practiced many professions, including railroad construction and engineering. He knew that a cable car would be impractical on the short, steep slope to Bunker Hill, but certain types of railways might work very well.

In May 1901, the city gave Eddy permission to build the railway if he also included steps for pedestrians. By the end of the year, Bunker Hill residents returning from downtown shopping sprees could either haul their packages up 123 concrete steps or zip up the hill on Olivet or Sinai. Needless to say, Angels Flight was a success.

To entice tourists up to Bunker Hill, Eddy also built a 100-foot tower behind the Olive Street railway terminal. He called it Angels Rest and advertised its viewing platform as "grand beyond compare overlooking city, sea, and mountains." Eddy also put a camera obscura in the tower. This dark room worked like the inside of a camera, using a pinhole light to project the view of the street outside onto the room's walls.

FUN WITH FUNICULARS

Part of the charm of Angels Flight was that it was a funicular railway. *Funicular* is Latin for "cord" or "cable," and the Angels Flight cars traveled up to Bunker Hill on heavy steel cable, with Sinai attached to one end and Olivet to the other. An electric power motor turned the cable and hoisted one car up the hill, while gravity pulled the other car down. The two cars counterbalanced each other, so that when Olivet went down the hill, Sinai's weight prevented gravity from sending Olivet down too quickly, and vice versa.

The cars were guided along by their railway tracks. They had no brakes, but each had an extra safety cable in case the main cable broke. There was one derailing in 1913 when a winch axle snapped, but all passengers except one were unhurt...and that woman broke her collar bone only because she jumped off the train. Otherwise, the funicular system worked safely as Olivet and Sinai each made 400 trips a day, seven days a week.

The head on the Oakland Raiders' logo is a rendering of actor Randolph Scott.

CLIPPED WINGS

By 1969 Angels Flight had operated continuously for 68 years. During that time, the railway saw only a few changes: There were new owners, the fare went up to a nickel, the cars' colors were now orange with black trim, and the observation tower had been torn down in 1938. (It was too rickety.)

What changed most was Bunker Hill. The wealthy residents moved to the suburbs, and the fancy Victorians became multiunit rooming houses that didn't age well. After World War II, the City of Los Angeles considered Bunker Hill to be a crime-ridden slum. In the late 1950s, L.A.'s Community Redevelopment Agency (CRA) knocked down the old Victorians to make way for high-rises and skyscrapers.

As Bunker Hill was demolished, preservationists fought to keep Angels Flight going. They lost in 1969, when CRA dismantled the railway and put Olivet and Sinai in storage, though the agency promised that they'd be back on their tracks "in a couple of years."

TRAGEDY STRIKES

Twenty-seven years later—in 1996 and after lots of public pressure—CRA finally reinstalled Angels Flight...but it moved the station to the corner of Fourth and Hill, about half a block from the original site. The new track was 298 feet long, but the steep grade was the same. So were Olivet and Sinai, which had been cleaned and restored. What CRA contractors changed, though, was the funicular hauling system. They hired Lift Engineering to "improve" the railway with a drive system that used separate gears, cables, and brakes for each car.

Then, in 2001, Sinai derailed. Its cable broke, its brakes failed, and it plummeted backward down the hill, crashing into Olivet. An 83-year-old tourist and Holocaust survivor named Leon Praport was killed. His wife and seven other passengers were injured. The National Transportation Safety Board blamed the accident on Lift's faulty design and construction, and an investigation revealed that Lift's owner, Yanek Kunczynski, had already been sued twice because two ski lifts he'd built had failed and caused passenger deaths. After the accident, Kunczynski fled the country, the City of Los Angeles paid a million dollars in damages to the Praport family, and Olivet and Sinai were grounded again.

Largest Cambodian population outside of Cambodia: Long Beach.

THIRD TIME'S THE CHARM

It took nine years, but a nonprofit foundation, which now owns Angels Flight, raised enough money to restore it. They kept the original funicular system and added safety features, including rail brakes.

On March 2010, Olivet and Sinai began their ups and downs once again. After a little more than a month, they'd carried nearly 60,000 riders. Today, passengers can still experience a ride on the "world's shortest railway" (though technically, it's now the second-shortest: at 298 feet long, the Fourth Street Elevator in Dubuque, Iowa, just edges out Angels Flight). And it's all much the same as it was a century ago...except (thanks to inflation) a one-way ride now costs a quarter.

FAMOUS FLIGHTS

Angels Flight has made its mark in movies and novels—usually showing the nonglamorous side of L.A. The railway has been featured in many crime films, including *Hollow Triumph* (1948), where a murderer is on the run; *Criss Cross* (1949), about an armored car robbery; *Cry of the Hunted* (1953), about an escaped prisoner; and *Kiss Me Deadly* (1955), a murder mystery. It even had a place in Hollywood's first monster horror musical: *The Incredibly Strange Creatures Who Stopped Living and Became Mixed Up Zombies* (1964).

Mystery writers also liked Angels Flight. Raymond Chandler put it in two of his books—*The King in Yellow* (1938) and *The High Window* (1942)—and so did Michael Connelly, in his popular police novel *Angels Flight* (1999).

*　　*　　*

SUCH A LOVELY PLACE (SUCH A LOVELY PLACE)

Camarillo State Hospital, a mental institution from 1936 to 1997, was long rumored to be the inspiration for the Eagles' song "Hotel California" (the place that "you can never leave"), but that's been debunked by the song's author. It was, however, the inspiration for troubled jazzman Charlie Parker's "Relaxin' at Camarillo," written there while Parker was detoxing from a heroin addiction.

Francis Ford Coppola wrote large portions of *The Godfather*...

THE ORIGINAL TREE HUGGER

In the 1850s, a miner and mountain man named Galen Clark set up a homestead in the Yosemite Valley and began a life as one of the area's most ardent advocates. Here's a classic first published in Uncle John's Bathroom Reader Plunges into National Parks.

GO FOR THE GOLD

Galen Clark journeyed to California's Mariposa County in 1853 after hearing stories of miners who found gold in the state's northern hills. But like so many before and after him, prospecting for gold never panned out, so he supplemented his meager income by surveying government land on the west side of the San Joaquin Valley.

Mining wasn't only a bust when it came to riches; the cold, dusty, damp conditions of the underground caverns also made Clark sick. In 1855, doctors diagnosed him with tuberculosis and gave him only six months to live. Hoping to heal his lungs (or at least live out his days in what he believed was America's most beautiful valley), Clark headed for Yosemite.

In 1857, he settled along the Merced River and built a modest cabin. Away from the mines and surrounded by fresh air, Clark's health improved dramatically and his tuberculosis went into remission.

THE BIG DEAL ABOUT BIG TREES

Clark explored the area around his homestead and soon stumbled on the Mariposa Grove. Then, as now, this grove near Yosemite's south entrance was home to more than 500 giant sequoia trees, the second-oldest trees on earth—some are more than 2,000 years old. (Bristle-cone pines are the oldest.) Although Clark certainly wasn't the first person to see the giant sequoias, he was the first to explore the grove extensively. He counted the trees and measured each one, and he was the one who called it "Mariposa," after the county where the trees are located (and where he lived).

The big trees soon became Clark's passion. He'd always been an avid outdoorsman; Sierra Club founder and Yosemite champion John Muir called him "the best mountaineer I'd ever met." But Clark's dedication to the grove was unwavering. He began offering up his homestead to travelers who wanted to see the trees. For a small fee, nature enthusiasts could sleep in his log cabin (which was called "Clark's Station" and later became the site of the Wawona Hotel) and follow his horse trail to the grove.

Clark also lobbied the federal government on behalf of the Mariposa Grove and Yosemite Valley. In the 1850s, Yosemite hadn't yet been set aside as a national park. So Clark, Muir, and others who wanted to preserve the valley wrote to Congress asking that the area be protected from commercial interests. Their efforts were successful. Congress created—and President Lincoln approved—the Yosemite Grant in June 1864. Although the grant didn't technically make Yosemite a national park (in 1872, Yellowstone was the first area to be called a "national park"), it did protect the Yosemite Valley and the Mariposa Grove for "public use, resort, and recreation . . . to be left inalienable for all time." And it laid the foundation for the National Park System.

THE GUARDIAN GETS TO WORK

With Yosemite and the Mariposa Grove protected by the government, the new preserve needed an overseer, someone who knew the valley well and felt passionate about its well-being. President Lincoln chose Clark. He became the "Guardian of the Valley," a job that required him to keep roads, trails, and bridges in good repair and to relocate homesteaders who encroached on the area. Clark served in this position for 24 years, and under his watchful eye, bridges were built, roads were constructed, and trails were connected to local points of interest, improvements that made Yosemite and the Mariposa Grove accessible to visitors from all over the world.

Clark also wrote three books about his beloved trees and their valley home: *Indians of the Yosemite Valley and Vicinity* (1904), *The Big Trees of California* (1907), and *The Yosemite Valley* (1910). Although each volume is small, they all helped to promote the beauty and history of the area and encouraged tourism, which helped pay for upkeep.

AT HOME IN THE BIG WOODS

Galen Clark died on March 24, 1910, after battling a severe cold. He was just four days shy of his 96th birthday and had recently been crowned "Mariposa County's Oldest Citizen," an impressive feat for a man doctors had written off 50 years before.

Clark had also spent the previous 24 years planning his own grave site. He planted and nurtured at least four sequoia seedlings in the Yosemite Valley Cemetery and is buried there beneath a simple headstone. He's also memorialized by the Mariposa Grove's Galen Clark Tree, one of the grove's largest trees and, some think, the first sequoia Clark saw when he arrived there in the mid-19th century.

* * *

THE NO-SAILING SOLUTION

Located in the Imperial Valley, the Salton Sea is California's largest body of water, almost 400 square miles, but this is no refreshing spot. It's saltier than the ocean and lies 228 feet below sea level atop the San Andreas fault. The Salton wasn't always a sea. It used to be an enormous sinkhole that, through the 19th century, was a major source of salt.

That changed in 1904 when the Colorado River flooded, knocking down the earthen dams of the Alamo Canal, which had been built to release a measured amount of water to irrigate nearby farmland. Suddenly, instead of a controlled stream of water, the entire river began draining into the Salton Sea, destroying towns, erasing a railroad line, and inundating residences and salt mines.

It took two years to stop the flow, but by then, the water had created a huge, shallow freshwater lake. For a few decades, the new lakefront thrived as hotels and yacht clubs popped up on its shores and tourists flocked to fish in its waters. But the lake had no drainage to the ocean, so salt levels just increased from the deposits under it. Even worse, the water turned brown and dangerous from a toxic mix of industrial waste, fertilizers, and pesticides from irrigation ditches that drained into it. The ever-increasing salt and pollution killed millions of fish and birds, stinking up the beaches with their carcasses, and the hotels and marinas of the "Riviera of California" quickly went belly up, too.

The oldest L.A. suburb: the Palms, incorporated in 1886.

THE PHYSICS OF SURFING

On page 155, we told you about the history of surfing. Here's how they do it.

CATCH A WAVE

When a surfer rides a wave toward shore, it may look as though the board and rider are being propelled by the rushing water. But they're not. In fact, the act of surfing is more like riding a skateboard down a hill. The difference is that a surfer is sliding down the face of a hill made of water.

An ocean wave moves through water that stays relatively still. Think of a gull floating in the ocean. When a wave comes along, the gull floats up to the top and then back down without being carried along with it. Waves don't carry water—or anything else—with them until they break on the beach.

When a wave breaks, it's because it has run into land. Half of a wave is above the water's surface and the other half is below. As the wave approaches the beach, it moves into shallower water. The bottom of the wave slows down when it begins to run into the ocean floor, but the top keeps going just as fast. As the top of the wave outpaces the bottom, the moving hill of water gets steeper until it breaks into white water and falls in front of itself with incredible weight and force. It's as the wave stands up and gets ready to break that a surfer wants to begin sliding down its face.

GET ON BOARD

• Surfboards come in all shapes and sizes, but are divided into two broad categories: long boards and short boards.

• Long boards generally range from 9 to 12 feet long. Because of their greater size and mass, they offer more stability but are not as maneuverable as short boards. Beginning surfers usually start with long boards and move up to smaller boards as their skills improve.

• Why is there a fin on the bottom of a surfboard? It provides stability and prevents the board from sliding sideways.

Koko, a gorilla in the San Francisco Zoo, has a sign-language vocabulary of 1,000 words.

WHO'S THAT BAND?

More stories behind some of California's most-beloved musical groups.

NO DOUBT. At the age of 11, Gwen Stefani recorded the first song her brother Eric ever wrote: "Stick It in the Hole." (It was about a pencil sharpener.) Six years later, in 1986, Eric and his friend John Spence formed a band they named No Doubt (after their favorite phrase) and asked—Gwen says "forced"—her to join as a background vocalist. Over the next eight years, the group gained members (bassist Tony Kanal, guitarist Tom Dumont, and drummer Adrian Young), lost members (Spence to a tragic suicide and Eric Stefani, who got a job as an animator for *The Simpsons*), and then hit it big in 1995 with the album *Tragic Kingdom*. (The title is a play on Disneyland's nickname "the Magic Kingdom," which was just a few miles away from the Stefani family home in Anaheim.) That record sold more than 20 million copies, and *Rolling Stone* called it one of the greatest albums of all time.

MÖTLEY CRÜE. Heavy metal muscians Nikki Six, Tommy Lee, Vince Neil, and Mick Mars were indeed a motley crew, playing around Los Angeles in the early 1980s. When Mars mentioned that someone had once actually referred to his previous band that way, the guys thought it would make a good name for their group. Even better: Add umlauts in honor of the German beer they were drinking when the conversation began.

CREEDENCE CLEARWATER REVIVAL. Although he grew up outside of San Francisco, John Fogerty loved Southern blues and listed to a lot of Elvis Presley, Muddy Waters, and Hank Williams. So when he formed a band with his brother Tom in the late 1950s, it made sense that the music they played also sounded a lot like Southern rock. The group went through some names that sounded Southern, too: First they were called Tommy Fogerty and the Blue Velvets, and then the Golliwogs. But their third name came from three separate places: Creedence was the first name of someone Tom Fogerty knew, Clearwater came from a beer ad, and Revival paid homage to the fact that the band was finally coming into its own. (Also, it sounded cool.)

THE BLACK DAHLIA

A young woman is murdered, her body mutilated and dumped next to an L.A. sidewalk. Sensationalized newspaper reports call her everything from a manipulative tease to a naive young girl. But who was she, and who killed her? Here's a murder mystery, L.A.'s most notorious cold case, ripped from the headlines...of 1947.

GRISLY FIND

A On the chilly, foggy morning of January 15, 1947, an L.A. housewife out for a walk with her young daughter stumbled upon a gruesome crime scene. Amid the weeds and grass of a vacant lot, a few feet from the sidewalk, lay the body of a woman. To add to the horror, the body had been cut in two at the midsection, the intestines removed and stuffed underneath the bottom half. The woman's face had also been disfigured, her mouth cut into a wide, Joker-like grin.

The shocked housewife grabbed her daughter and ran to a neighbor's house to call the police. By the time investigators arrived, however, reporters and curious residents were already there...and had trampled all over the scene, destroying a lot of evidence. Still, the LAPD made some interesting discoveries:

• The woman was about 5'6" tall, had black hair and green eyes, but no identification.

• There wasn't any blood at the scene—not in, on, or around the body. In fact, the medical examiner would later say that the body appeared to have been drained of blood and scrubbed clean. So the police knew the woman had been killed elsewhere.

• Besides the cuts to the woman's face, she had rope burns on her wrists and ankles, indicating that she'd been restrained.

• There was dew under the body, meaning she had to have been placed there after 2:00 a.m., when the temperature in the area dropped below 38°F, the dew point (temperature at which dew forms) that day.

• The body had been cut cleanly in half, leading police to believe the murderer was someone skilled at dissection...like a surgeon, medical student, or butcher.

Hollywood child star Shirley Temple became U.S. ambassador to Ghana and Czechoslovakia.

But as interested as the investigators were in what had happened to the young woman, initially they had a more pressing question: Who was she?

BIRTH OF THE BLACK DAHLIA

The officers took the woman's fingerprints and sent them off to the FBI lab in Washington, D.C. Pretty soon, they had an answer: Elizabeth Short, age 22. She'd been fingerprinted a few years before for a job at Vandenberg Air Force Base (then called Camp Cooke) and again for an arrest for underage drinking.

To the police, Short was a crime victim, plain and simple. But to the reporters sniffing around the case, she became a media star. The details of Short's brief life were mysterious—she had no real friends and seemed to prefer the company of strangers. As details of her personality emerged, reporters began to sensationalize the case: She hadn't just been murdered, she was slaughtered! She hadn't just been pretty, she was a hauntingly beautiful, aspiring starlet! Newspapers implied (or even outright said) that Short's good looks and lifestyle had led to her murder. Pretty quickly, they nicknamed her the "Black Dahlia," for her dark hair and a movie, *The Blue Dahlia*, that was popular at the time.

A SHORT STORY

Short first came to the state in 1943–44, and lived in Vallejo and Lompoc with her father and various roommates. After being arrested for underage drinking, she was sent home to her mother in Massachusetts and spent some time traveling the East Coast. She'd been engaged to an airman who was killed in World War II, and in mid-1946 followed another boyfriend back to California.

The descriptions Short's former roommates gave to police became fodder for the press. According to one, she had "a different boyfriend every night." Another said she liked to "prowl" Hollywood Boulevard looking for men. She also had no job and had been staying with new friends in San Diego until just before she was murdered.

It was in San Diego that she met Robert "Red" Manley, the last person police could find who had spent any real time with Short while she was alive. His story went like this: On the evening of January 8, Manley saw Short on a street corner. He'd never seen

---

California had four different state capitals between 1850 and 1854.

her before, but was worried about her well-being. (A woman out at night alone in 1947 was, for many, cause for immediate concern.) He pulled over and asked if she needed a ride. At first, he said, Short ignored him. Eventually, she relented and got into his car. They spent a platonic night together at a San Diego hotel, and he dropped her off at the Biltmore in downtown L.A. the next day. According to Manley, Short said she was heading up to Berkeley. That, he always maintained, was the last he ever saw of her.

But there was a big problem. Short was murdered on the night of January 14 or the early morning of the 15th. If Manley had last seen her on the 9th, where had she been for the five or six days in between? Nobody knew...or would admit to it.

ODD DEADENDS
Meanwhile, the police continued investigating, knocking on doors and interviewing residents in the neighborhood where the body was found. Had anyone seen or heard anything suspicious? Did anyone know Elizabeth Short? Most answers were no, but they did find out that Short's father lived within a couple of miles of where her body had been discovered. At first, that seemed like a fantastic lead, but Cleo Short said he hadn't seen his daughter in three years, ever since they'd had a falling-out over housework and the fact that she preferred to spend her time partying in Hollywood instead of finding a nice husband and settling down. Police had no reason not to believe him.

There were a few other leads, too. Police found Short's purse and shoes in a trash can a few miles from the crime scene. They also eventually received 10 letters from someone claiming to be the killer. (Over the course of the investigation, police got hundreds of letters, but these 10 seemed legitimate.) And an anonymous package had been mailed to an L.A. newspaper several days after news of Short's death broke. The package smelled like it had been doused in gasoline, a technique criminals sometimes used to obscure their fingerprints on paper. It included pictures of Short, her birth certificate, her social security card, an obituary, and an address book containing the names of 75 different men. As the press went wild with that salacious detail, the police questioned all the men. Their stories were a lot like Manley's: They'd met Short briefly (often on the street at night) and had a few drinks with

Calipatria is the lowest town in the U.S. (184 feet below sea level).

her. But after figuring out that she wasn't interested in a relationship, they never saw her again.

ANYONE'S GUESS

To this day, more than 60 years after the crime, the LAPD and FBI have no official suspects in the murder of Elizabeth Short, and the case has never been solved. It has remained a media sensation, though. Over the years, dozens of books have been written about the case, and two movies have been made, the most recent in 2006. The list of unofficial suspects remains long and, in some cases, ridiculous—one woman even went so far as to accuse actor/director Orson Welles because he'd once performed a magic act in which he sawed a woman in half. But here are three suspects on the "real possibility" list:

• **Robert Manley.** Because he was the last person to see Short alive, Manley has always topped the various suspect lists. But he had an alibi for the night of the murder and passed a polygraph test shortly afterward.

• **Walter Bayley.** In the late 1990s, LAPD detectives got a new piece of evidence: In 1947, Walter Bayley, a surgeon, had lived just one block away from the crime scene. His daughter was friends with Elizabeth Short's sister, clearly connecting him to the victim. But Bayley had no history of violence, and no other evidence linking him to the crime has ever turned up.

• **George Hodel.** Retired LAPD detective Steve Hodel claimed in a 2003 book that his father George, a brilliant surgeon, killed Elizabeth Short. According to Steve, his father was a sadistic man who had molested his own 14-year-old daughter (a crime for which George was tried and acquitted in 1949). Both Steve and his sister claim their father held wild parties at his Hollywood mansion in the 1940s and that there was even a secret room inside the house that was off-limits to the kids. Steve also offered as evidence a family photo album, which he said included a blurry picture of a woman who resembled Short. (No one has been able to tell for sure.) And one long-ago witness reported seeing a black sedan in the neighborhood near the abandoned lot shortly before the body was found. In 1947 George Hodel drove a black Packard.

REAL CALIFORNIA CUISINE

Sure, Californians love fresh local ingredients, fusion cuisine, and a striking presentation on the plate. But that's not all the state is known for. Here are some...er...lower-brow foods that originated here.

RICE-A-RONI

Today, Rice-A-Roni is owned by Quaker Oats, a subsidiary of PepsiCo, and is made across the San Francisco Bay in San Leandro, but there really was a time when it was (as advertised) "the San Francisco treat." From 1958 to 1986, the rice and pasta meals were put together in a small family factory in the city's Mission District. The DeDominico family (father Charlie, mother Maria, and sons Tom, Vince, Anthony, and Paskey) based the dish on a recipe for Armenian pilaf that Tom's wife learned from her landlord. Since the main ingredients were rice and little rice-size pieces of macaroni, Rice-A-Roni seemed like the perfect name.

JELLY BELLIES

Jelly Bellies were a collaboration between Northern and Southern California: conceived in Los Angeles and born in Oakland. In 1976, 29-year-old David Klein, a candy distributor in Los Angeles, had a revelation one night while watching *Happy Days*: jelly beans could be more than just cheaply made chunks of overly sweetened pectin covered with an artificially flavored shell. He dreamed of naturally flavored jelly beans with half the sugar of the originals and that tasted like actual food: cherry, grape, lemon, and so on. He contacted Herman Goelitz, who owned a candy manufacturing company in Oakland, and handed over the specs. Goelitz's company used fruit juices to flavor the new jelly beans, and the pair came up with a catchy name: Jelly Bellies.

But the candy didn't take off right away. For years, Klein promoted the gourmet jelly beans all over the country. But the beans were a tough sell—at $2 a pound ($7.66 in today's money), they cost a lot more than generic jelly beans. The tide finally turned in 1980 when Ronald Reagan, a big fan of Jelly Bellies, was elected

---

Mendocino was the first county in the U.S. to ban genetically modified crops (2004).

president. He outfitted his office, meeting rooms, and *Air Force One* with jars of them. (He'd turned to the candy to quit smoking.) Sales took off, but by then, Klein had sold his trademark to Goelitz. In 2010 his company (now called the Jelly Belly Candy Company) made an estimated $193 million in profits.

WHITE ZINFANDEL

California is known for producing good wines, but the only type actually invented in the state is White Zinfandel...and that was by mistake. Zinfandel grapes are deep purple and normally make a hearty red wine, so it takes a lot of processing to turn them into the sweet pink concoction we know it as today. From the end of Prohibition through the 1960s, wine in America was cheap and of poor quality (*more about that on page 53*). Sophisticated Americans typically stuck to beer or cocktails. But in the late 1960s, small family wineries began appearing in Napa Valley. One of them was the Sutter Home Winery, which specialized in Zinfandels. Part of the process of making a Zinfandel is bleeding off some of the grape juice and leaving the grape skins soaking in what's left. Sutter Home didn't want that light-colored juice to go to waste, so in 1972, winemaker Bob Trinchero set it aside and fermented it too, making a dry white wine...even though its color was pink. He called it "White Zinfandel."

HAWAIIAN PUNCH

Hawaiian Punch first appeared in Fullerton in 1934, the brainchild of three guys trying to come up with a sweet, fruity ice cream topping. Soon they discovered that, diluted with water, the syrup made a better drink than a topping. But if the beverage was California-born, why did the guys call it "Hawaiian" Punch? When they named the drink, Hawaii was a remote place that was exotic for most Americans. Plus, the syrup used the juices of several fruits found on the islands: guava, orange, papaya, passion fruit, and pineapple. (It also included apple and apricot juice.)

FORTUNE COOKIES

Despite their ubiquity at Chinese restaurants, fortune cookies are an American invention, and the man who first sold them in the United States was Japanese. Makoto Hagiwara of the Japanese Tea

Wineries are the second most popular tourist destination in California. (Disneyland is first.)

Garden in Golden Gate Park started offering fortune cookies in the early 1900s, and by 1915, they were massively popular in San Francisco. Hagiwara's cookies included little "thank-you" notes instead of wise sayings. The cookies moved south around 1918, when Chinese baker George Jung, who later owned the Hong Kong Noodle Company, began serving them at his L.A. restaurant.

But who came up with the idea of putting the notes inside? No one's sure, but according to legend, in the 13th century, the Chinese began to hide notes inside small pastries called mooncakes. They were fighting the Mongolians at the time, and most Mongolians didn't like the taste of the mooncakes and so would ignore the treats...making them a perfect way to pass secret messages.

THE EGG McMUFFIN

It makes sense that a McDonald's product would start in California—after all, McDonald's itself technically started in Southern California (before the McDonald's of San Bernardino sold their business to Ray Kroc of Illinois). But it's not that simple. A goal of the McDonald's organization has always been to make every restaurant identical so that consumers know exactly what to expect when they drive up to the take-out window or walk in the door. As a result, it is absolutely forbidden for a franchise owner to try a new product without the blessing of the headquarters. So in 1972, when Herb Peterson, who later ran six franchises in Santa Barbara, broached the subject of expanding the restaurants' hours to include breakfast (and to sell a new egg sandwich he'd come up with), he should have run into trouble. But fortunately for Peterson—and Egg McMuffin lovers everywhere—he had a few things going for him: He was well-known at headquarters and was respected as someone who knew McDonald's culture and rules. He had been a vice president at D'Arcy Advertising in Chicago, which worked closely with McDonald's. Peterson himself wrote one of the chain's advertising slogans: "Where Quality Starts Fresh Every Day."

Peterson got the go-ahead to try out the new sandwich in one of his restaurants. He chose the one in Goleta, and the new egg sandwich—and breakfast in general—was a hit. It was Ray Kroc and a friend who actually named the Egg McMuffin, but the sandwich introduced a huge new revenue stream: breakfast items are now responsible for up to 30 percent of each restaurant's business.

TAKE ME TO YOUR LEADER

The rest of the country likes to say California is populated by fruits and nuts.
Little do they know that it's actually the lizard people and flying
ancient Egyptians who are really strange.

STRANGE POPULATION: The Lizard People
WHERE: Below Los Angeles
STORY: The Hopi Indians tell the following legend:
About 5,000 years ago, a huge meteor shower rained down on the
Southwest, frying anything in its path and terrifying the Hopis'
ancestors, known as the "Lizard People." But the Lizards were an
intellectually advanced species, and they were determined never
to be caught off guard that way again. So they started digging tunnels, eventually carving out 13 underground cities on the West
Coast that would act as shelters in future disasters and would also
hold all of the Lizards' academic and archaeological artifacts. One
of the cities was below present-day Los Angeles.

Fast-forward to 1933, when a mining engineer named G. Warren Shufelt, who had heard the Lizard People legend, went looking for the city under L.A. On January 29, 1934, the *Los Angeles
Times* declared that he'd found it, using a special radio frequency
device…thing. Supposedly Shufelt mapped the maze, which
showed a network of tunnels that stretched 20 miles below Santa
Monica Bay to Pasadena and beyond. He said the city was in the
shape of a lizard, the Hopi symbol of long life. Shufelt even
brought in Hopi chief Little Green Leaf to inspect the tunnels.
The chief said that 1,000 Lizard families lived in them and stored
life-sustaining herbs, plus piles of gold and tablets with the history
of the world etched upon them. (Note: No one else ever actually
saw the tunnels.)

The L.A. City Council required that any riches found on city
land (or beneath it) had to be shared by the city and the finder, so
(likely hoping for a big haul) the council gave Shufelt and Chief
Green Leaf permission to sink several shafts to try to bring up the
Lizards' spoils. One shaft was at 518 Hill Street, about two miles

from present-day Dodger Stadium. By lowering his radio X-ray attached to a pendulum, Shufelt hoped to take pictures of the tunnels. But alas, the Lizards' city was too deep, and the men had to give up when they hit water and their holes flooded. The shafts were filled in and abandoned, and no treasure was ever recovered. **WHAT HAPPENED TO THEM:** Shufelt and Chief Green Leaf simply disappeared. No one seems to know where they ended up. The Lizard People's fate is equally mysterious. One account says they all died after a natural gas leak below the city. Other reports claim they moved to other Lizard cities...including one beneath Vandenberg Air Force Base in Santa Barbara County, where they supposedly help the military.

STRANGE POPULATION: The Hav-Musuvs, or Suvians
WHERE: Beneath the Panamint Mountains, Death Valley
STORY: The Hav-Musuvs come from the Mojave's Paiute Indians, who have a legend that a race of Egyptian-like people colonized massive caverns in the Panamint Mountains 3,000 to 5,000 years ago. At the time, Death Valley was part of an inland sea connected to the Pacific (that part's true, but it was more like two to eleven *million* years ago). When the sea dried up, the intellectually gifted, seafaring Hav-Musuvs arrived. They're described as humans with bronze skin who wore flowing robes and headbands that pulled back their dark hair. Over time, they even developed winged "silvery flying canoes" and branched out deeper into the caves.
WHAT HAPPENED TO THEM: Supposedly the Hav-Musuvs are still around—they come and go via interplanetary space travel.

For the story of the Lemurians who live inside Mount Shasta, turn to page 38.

*   *   *

ALTARED STATES

Considered by many to be the crown jewel of California's missions, the Carmel mission has walls that taper inward, forming an arch, rather than the usual flat ceiling. California mission founder Junipero Serra called Carmel his favorite mission, and fittingly, he's buried under its altar.

The original idea for San Diego's SeaWorld was that it would be an underwater restaurant.

THE BEST-LAID SPANS

Miles from the closest road, California's Bridge to
Nowhere sits abandoned, used only by wildlife,
hikers, and the occasional bungee jumper.

INTO THE WILD

As California grew, it often became too big for its bridges. Most were torn down or replaced, but the state also has dozens of bridges that have been long abandoned but are still standing: railroad bridges, highway bridges, city street bridges, horse path bridges, even half a dozen rickety wooden covered bridges. But the most intriguing abandoned bridge is the Bridge to Nowhere, located 17 miles north of Ontario. It's been there since 1936, spanning the San Gabriel River's East Fork in what's now the Sheep Mountain Wilderness.

The bridge is a great example of what architects call an "open-spandrel arch," a series of connected concrete arches with a roadway on top. There's only one thing missing from that roadway—traffic—and two things missing from either end of the bridge—a road. In fact, the Bridge to Nowhere is located five miles from the nearest road in a popular hiking area, about 4.5 miles in from a trailhead.

OVER-ARCHING PLANS

The bridge wasn't supposed to be a wilderness site, though. In the 1920s, L.A. County officials dreamed of a direct highway from the San Gabriel Valley to the mountain town of Wrightwood. The existing route was circuitous, but the most direct route went through rugged mountain terrain and had to cross an especially big hurdle: a 2,800-foot-deep gorge called the Narrows.

Still the officials pressed on. They hired an architect who came up with a design that mixed old and modern technology—an arch bridge modeled after the stone bridges of ancient Rome and Greece, but made from concrete molded around a core of thin steel rods. For a bridge being built in the middle of nowhere, the choice was ideal because it used a lot less material than a *closed spandrel arch* made of solid concrete or stone. The contractor needed to bring in only a few truckloads of reinforcing rods, lumber, and cement. The rods would be assembled and welded together on the spot, with the lumber built around them to serve as molds. Best of all, the concrete could be created in the mountains using mostly materials found at a riverbank—one barrel of powdered dry cement became six barrels of concrete by mixing in two barrels of sand, three barrels of gravel, and a half barrel of water. The process was labor-intensive, but providing local jobs during the middle of the Great Depression was considered a good thing.

CAPTIVATING WORK

County prisoners made up a good portion of the work crew too, and they began building a road toward the bridge in 1929. By the mid-1930s, they'd reached the Narrows, and the bridge building began. The project finished a year later, and then the workers began the next big part of the job: blasting a tunnel through the solid rock on the far end of the bridge.

That should have been the beginning of a magnificent bridge, but there was one thing wrong with the road leading up to it—the plans didn't anticipate a massive rainstorm like the one that hit in March 1938. The bridge survived, but the road didn't. When the San Gabriel River rose 20 feet into a fast-moving torrent, it pulled much of the road off the canyon walls. With the roadway lost and too expensive to replace, the project was abandoned.

"TRY AGAIN?" ARE YOU INSANE?

Two decades later, in 1954, not wanting to waste a perfectly good bridge, CalTrans tried one more time to build a highway along the route, but the effort was abandoned after just a few miles—the area was too remote and the project too expensive to complete. Some of its pavement still exists, though, blocked by gates on both ends that are easily circumvented by hikers. Bungee jumpers also usually appear on weekends since the Bridge to Nowhere is the only bridge in California that's officially "licensed for jumping."

*   *   *

The L.A. Dodgers have had 16 Rookie of the Year winners—more than any other major league team.

The California grizzly bear (*Ursus californicus*) was designated the state animal...

THE LITTLE GANGSTER KING

Mickey Cohen was one of L.A.'s most notorious gangsters, and sometimes he seemed to get more pleasure from taking shots at law enforcement than from his actual dirty deeds.

A BAD BEGINNING

The first time mobster Mickey Cohen committed a crime in Los Angeles, he was nine years old. Meyer "Mickey" Cohen had moved with his mother and siblings to East L.A. in 1920. Prohibition was in full swing, and two of Mickey's older brothers ran a black-market gin mill behind the family's drugstore. Mickey delivered the illegal booze, and on one outing, he was caught and arrested. (While the cops were bringing him in, he threw punches, his first attempts to evade the police.) A family friend with connections convinced the city to drop those charges, but Mickey continued to get into trouble.

His hot temper got him tossed out of Hebrew school, and he ditched public school so often that he never really learned much math or how to read. Mickey decided his talents were in his fists. In 1929, at the age of 16, he ran off to the Midwest and New York to compete as a boxer. He amassed a respectable 76 wins and 29 losses, but his career essentially ended two years later when world featherweight champion Tommy Paul knocked him out in the first round. Mickey decided then that boxing wasn't the career for him after all, but he'd met a few mobsters who hung out at the boxing events and liked their flashy clothes, cars, and girlfriends. So he decided to take up a life of crime.

THE ERA OF MICKEY AND BUGS

Cohen first moved to Cleveland, Ohio, where he hooked up with mob boss Lou Rothkopf and started robbing illegal casinos that hadn't paid Rothkopf to protect them from other criminals. Next, he headed to Chicago, got a job protecting a mob-owned casino... and killed two men who threatened the place. The corrupt police in Chicago released him with no charges, and Cohen continued

...in 1953, more than 30 years after the species went extinct.

his fighting mobster ways—until he bloodied up a member of a rival gang and was arrested for attempted murder. Cohen never went to trial but decided to leave town. He headed west to Los Angeles to work for Benjamin "Bugsy" Siegel, who was involved with the city's illegal gambling, drugs, and prostitution rackets. In 1937 Cohen got a job as Siegel's main enforcer.

Tall, handsome, and charming, Siegel liked to hobnob with movie stars and other Hollywood glitterati. He kept his Mafia work quiet, posed as a legitimate businessman, and left the shooting, bone breaking, and drug dealing to the short (5'5"), pudgy Cohen. It was Cohen who brought in heroin from Mexico to sell on L.A. streets and Cohen who attacked gambling rings, killing any leaders who didn't pay Siegel protection money.

Siegel made big money on these L.A. rackets, and he grew fond of his attack dog. He launched Cohen on a self-improvement course so the little gangster would fit in better with Hollywood society. As Cohen put it, "He tried to evolve me." But while Cohen bought better clothes and improved his diction, Siegel ran into problems with other gangsters. In particular, some were angry that he'd lost their money in his mismanagement of the Las Vegas Flamingo Hotel—there was suspicion that he was also skimming off profits. In 1947 he was shot dead.

CATCH HIM IF YOU CAN

Cohen had mixed feelings about Siegel's death: "Naturally, I missed Benny, but to be honest with you, his getting knocked off was not a bad break for me. Pretty soon, I was running everything." *Life* magazine called Cohen "the Gangster King of Los Angeles." Meanwhile, rival L.A. mobster Jack Dragna decided that with Siegel gone, it was time to kill Cohen and take over everything himself.

At the time, Cohen owned a men's clothing store that included a basement office for his illegal businesses. In 1948 a Dragna gunman sneaked into Cohen's office and shot two of his associates. Cohen wasn't injured, though—he was compulsive about germs and had been in the bathroom washing his hands. So Dragna's hit men tried again: Another day, a sniper tried to shoot Cohen on the street, but just as the man fired, Cohen knelt to examine a scratch on the bumper of his Cadillac and the bullet

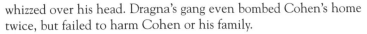

whizzed over his head. Dragna's gang even bombed Cohen's home twice, but failed to harm Cohen or his family.

The mobster had less luck with the U.S. Senate Committee investigating organized crime. In 1951 evidence uncovered by the Senate put Cohen in prison for income-tax evasion.

NOT READY FOR PRIME TIME

Four years later, Cohen emerged from prison claiming he was a changed man. He became good friends with Reverend Billy Graham and professed interest in becoming a Christian. He even opened businesses like flower shops and ice cream parlors. But it soon became clear that his conversion was in name only.

During a television interview, Cohen said, "I have killed no man in the first place that didn't deserve killing. In all of these here killings, there was no alternative." He also ranted against L.A. police chief William Parker, calling him a "sadistic degenerate of the worst type." Most importantly, though, the mobster never gave up his illegal activities or his violent ways. In 1958 he was arrested for punching a waiter. In 1959 he killed rival gangster Jack Whalen. Only bungled witness testimony and perjury from one of his henchmen kept Cohen from being tried for the murder.

In 1961 Cohen was again convicted of tax evasion and sent to Alcatraz. After the prison closed down in 1963, he was transferred to various U.S. prisons until his release in 1972. Cohen died of stomach cancer in 1976, but he hadn't changed much since he got out of jail and, in 1974, managed to take one last famous swipe at the law: That year, Patricia Hearst, heiress to the Hearst newspaper fortune, was kidnapped by the Symbionese Liberation Army (SLA), a group of radicals bent on overthrowing the U.S. government. Cohen claimed that the Hearst family wanted him to find her (they denied asking, but thanked him for his help). He also insisted that he did find her, but chose not to bring her home. Why? While Hearst was an SLA prisoner, she participated in a bank robbery. Some people believed she'd been brainwashed by the SLA into doing it, but the police thought she was acting freely and Cohen said he refused to do anything that would help the cops send her to prison.

WE ♥ SUMMERLAND

Driving along the coast just south of Santa Barbara, you might notice some small houses jammed together on the hillside. That's Summerland, a small community with a lot of spirit...or, if you believe its founder, a lot of spirits.

• **Surreal estate.** Summerland was the brainchild of H. L. Williams, a real-estate speculator and spiritualist who bought the small parcel of hilly land in 1883, divided it into tiny lots measuring just 25' by 60', gave it an idyllic name, and invited his fellow spiritualists to buy in. They did.

• **Stairways to heaven?** It seems that Summerland's architects may have studied the Winchester Mystery House, located 300 miles up the coast in San Jose and designed on the fly by Sarah Winchester. Why? Well, like the Winchester house, many of Summerland's tiny homes include some strange features...like stairways leading to nowhere and doors that open to reveal walls.

• **The ghost of oils past.** In the 1800s, it wasn't hard to believe that Summerland was blessed. After all, tar seeping up from the ground had long been used by nearby Native Americans to waterproof boats, and locals quickly discovered that they could produce excellent firepits simply by poking a pipe into the ground and lighting the escaping gases.

In the 1880s, an oil company discovered why—there was a vast oil and gas field under the town and nearby beach. In 1896 the town built the world's offshore oil well, and in 1957, the Standard Oil Company founded the Summerland Off-Shore Oil Field, which gave the town the dubious distinction of being the world's first place to have its views ruined by offshore oil rigs. Oil production lasted for about a century, until public outrage led to the wells' closure in the 1990s.

• **Central coast superstar.** Despite being a small community of only about 1,500 people, Summerland was memorialized in a 1995 Everclear song titled "Summerland," and in a short-lived WB Network television show, also titled *Summerland*.

Santa Monica collects about $5 million annually in parking fees.

CALI-FOLKS, PART II

On page 5, we introduced some of the key personalities who shaped California culture. Here are a few more.

ROBERT MONDAVI
Who's that? Mondavi's family owned the Charles Krug Winery, where Robert worked as a wine marketer. He and his brother Peter disagreed over how to run the winery, and in 1965, things got so bad they had a fistfight. When the family sided against him, Robert left Krug and started his own winery.

Mondavi was the first major winery in Napa since Prohibition, and its owner spared no expense making it famous for world-class wines. Mondavi became the most famous winery in Napa, inspiring a partnership with renowned French winemaker Baron Rothschild. In 2004 Mondavi sold for over $1 billion.

California legacy: Mondavi trained some of the region's best winemakers and almost single-handedly turned Napa away from producing cheap jug wines. Instead, he encouraged Napa to show off its wines and invite in tourists. He marketed California's wine country as a center for gracious living where visitors would find luxurious accommodations, beautiful scenery, and gourmet food as well as fine wine. Mondavi's influence was instrumental in creating today's $20 billion California wine industry.

JOHN MUIR

Who's that? Muir was a prize-winning inventor who gave up on his own inventions in the 1860s to become a naturalist and "study the inventions of God." He was one of the first naturalists to understand how mountains were formed and was a philosopher who wrote numerous books about the wonders of the natural world. Muir was also one of America's first conservationists, fighting to preserve the country's wilderness.

Shaping California: Muir arrived in Yosemite in 1868 and was so "overwhelmed by the landscape" that he lived there for six years, studying the Yosemite Valley and the surrounding Sierra Nevada mountains. At a time when many Americans considered the

wilderness important only as a resource for gold, lumber, farming, hunting, or pastureland, Muir's poetic descriptions helped the public understand nature's positive effect on the human spirit.

Muir wanted beautiful wilderness sites kept free from development, and in 1890 his efforts led to the establishment of Yosemite National Park. In 1892 Muir founded the Sierra Club, which continued his work to protect the California wilderness. (*For more about Muir's descriptions of Yosemite, turn to pages 85, 176, and 273.*)

KATHY KOHNER ZUCKERMAN

Who's that? Fifteen-year-old Kathy Kohner was drawn to surfing as a way to conquer her feelings of not fitting in. But in the 1950s, only guys surfed, and few people practiced the sport in California at all. Still, Kohner bought a board and bribed some dedicated Malibu surfers with peanut-butter-and-radish sandwiches until they taught her to ride the waves. Nicknamed "Gidget" (meaning a girl-midget, because she was so short), Kohner loved the sport, and her father, screenwriter Fredrick Kohner, used her adventures as the basis for his 1957 novel *Gidget*.

California legacy: During its first year of publication, *Gidget* was #7 on the best-seller list. In 1959 it became a movie starring Sandra Dee. That hit spawned two more movies and a television series. Suddenly, wannabe surfers crowded Southern California beaches. Into the 1960s, the fad only intensified: The girls wore bikinis, the guys drove woodies, and everyone began using surf slang. Beach songs, movies, and parties became the norm, and today California is known for its surf culture. Hang loose, Gidget!

ANDRE "DR. DRE" YOUNG

Who's that? Andre Romelle Young is a pioneer of West Coast gangsta rap (rapping about street life and violence from the point of view of gang members). He grew up in the South Central L.A. neighborhood of Compton surrounded by gangs—though he managed to avoid them. Instead, he focused on music. Adopting the moniker "Dr. Dre" ("Dr." for the basketball player Julius "Dr. J" Erving, and "Dre" for Andre), Young became famous as part of N.W.A., the first top-selling West Coast gangsta rap group. He then became famous as a solo artist at Death Row Records, where he also produced other hip-hop artists.

California's state fossil: the saber-tooth cat.

California legacy: N.W.A.'s 1988 album *Straight Outta Compton* was extremely controversial because it included a lot of profanity and many descriptions of street violence. But the album was such a big seller that record companies started searching L.A.'s inner cities for more rap stars. Often, those new stars put out albums produced by Young. The track "Let It Ride," from Young's own album *The Chronic* (slang for potent marijuana), won a Grammy in 1993 and helped bring gangsta rap into the mainstream. The controversies remained, though: Some people said gangsta rap glorified violence; others, that it shone a spotlight on L.A.'s troubled inner cities. Either way, Young helped make the music—and South Central L.A.—the center of a huge cultural phenomenon.

HARVEY MILK

Who's that? In 1977 Milk won a seat on the San Francisco Board of Supervisors, the first openly gay man to be elected to an important political position. His first order of business was to initiate two pieces of legislation: one guaranteed homosexuals equal rights as citizens, and the other was a popular pooper-scooper law that his constituents badly wanted. But before he could do more, Milk was murdered (along with the city's mayor, George Moscone). Their killer was Dan White, a former supervisor who quit his job and then blamed Milk and the mayor when he couldn't get reappointed. In 2009 Milk was posthumously awarded the Presidential Medal of Freedom, the first openly gay civil rights leader to receive the award.

California legacy: When Milk ran for office, gays in the United States often lost their jobs or went to jail because of their sexual preference. Psychiatric studies labeled homosexuality a mental disorder. Not surprisingly, many San Francisco gays felt a need to "stay in the closet" by hiding their sexual identity.

Milk believed gays wouldn't get equal rights until they came out, organized, and worked for political clout. Elation over Milk's election and his ability to get an equal-rights law passed—as well as the pain and anger over his murder—influenced the gay community in San Francisco to unite and become a powerful political force for equal rights.

In "Surfin' USA," the Beach Boys mention 14 California surfing locations by name.

KEYS TO A BYGONE ERA

If you're going to make it in the desert, you need to be smart, resourceful, and creative. Like this guy.

HOME ON THE RANGE

Few people would willingly live in the Mojave Desert— fewer still before the advent of air-conditioning. But one person who loved the desert and managed to turn it into a comfortable home was Bill Keys, whose family became an icon of the rugged Southwest. Today, the Keys Ranch is part of Joshua Tree National Park, but in the early 1900s, there was nothing there except the Desert Queen Mine.

Bill Keys (a former Rough Rider and Arizona sheriff's deputy) arrived in Joshua Tree in 1910 at the age of 30, reporting for duty as the superintendent of the Desert Queen. His boss was Jim McHaney, a onetime cattle rustler who had sent a band of thugs to "convince" the mine's previous owner to turn the place over. When the owner refused, one of the thugs shot him. Crying self-defense, the thug got off, and McHaney (and his brother) got the mine. But by 1917, the Desert Queen was deteriorating and McHaney was deeply in debt. He hadn't been able to pay superintendent Bill Keys for several years and finally turned over the deed to the mine—and its five acres—instead.

Keys built a small wooden cabin and moved in. The next year, he married Frances May Lawton, a young sales clerk from Los Angeles, and she moved in too. And then, for the next 50 years, the couple expanded their ranch and mine to 160 acres. Along with their four children, they called that isolated, sweltering, rocky patch of land their home.

THE FATHER OF INVENTION

The Keys ranch had no modern plumbing or electricity, and Twentynine Palms, the nearest town, was a two-day wagon ride away. The family did some trading with merchants to get supplies they couldn't make themselves—sugar, coffee, things like that—but most of what they had, Keys made himself. And some of it was genius:

It took four years and $35 million (more than $525 million today)...

- A five-stamp mill that processed gold more quickly and efficiently than other mills of the time. That meant that Keys not only owned the ranch where the gold was mined, but he also owned the only way to extract the gold from the rock for miles.
- The Keysmobile, a modified iron-wheeled truck that was able to travel over the desert terrain and rarely broke down.
- The very first elementary school in Joshua Tree. In 1933 Keys hired a teacher and brought her to the ranch, giving her a small cabin to live in. He built the one-room schoolhouse himself.
- A stone dam behind the house collected water in a manmade reservoir. The stones were all cut and fitted by hand; Keys made his own stonecutting tools. The Keys children even ice-skated on the pond in the winter.
- A scrapyard filled with whatever Keys scavenged from old mines or the homesteads that less-hardy settlers left behind when they fled the Mojave. Tools, old car parts, bolts, screws, metal canisters, and much more was laid out on the Keys ranch. The family used what they needed, and sold or bartered the rest to other miners and pioneers passing through.
- A piping system that brought water from the well into the house.
- A mailbox on the road to Twentynine Palms...a half-day's horse ride from the Keys ranch. According to Bill's son Willis, in 1935 that mailbox was the only man-made structure for miles around.
- A bunkhouse and restaurant. In the 1920s and '30s, tourists started flocking west to see California for themselves, and one of the spots they visited was the Mojave Desert. Keys built several small cabins for visitors, and his wife cooked them meals.
- A traction machine to realign his back. In his 60s, Keys sustained a back injury on the ranch and needed to keep working. He lay on the wooden contraption while his wife cranked a wheel that pulled his spine back into place.

A SHOT ACROSS THE BOW

Bill Keys found his share of trouble in the desert, too. Around 1943 he got into a turf war with a neighbor named Worth Bagley, a former L.A. deputy sheriff who retired to the desert. The biggest point of contention: a road that passed through Bagley's property.

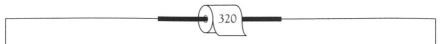

Keys had been using it for years and didn't stop. That irritated Bagley, who started covering the road with broken glass and felled trees. On May 11, 1943, as Keys once again ignored the warnings, Bagley came after him with a gun. The former lawman fired and missed—Keys shot back and didn't.

Keys immediately reported the killing to the police. He stood trial and was convicted of manslaughter. At 64 years old, he was sentenced to 10 years in San Quentin, and his wife went to work seeking a pardon. She wrote many letters—one to an old friend, lawyer Erle Stanley Gardner, who had met Keys years before while camping in the desert. Since then, he had become famous for creating the character Perry Mason. He also wrote a magazine column called "The Court of Last Resort," which featured stories of men who may have been wrongfully convicted. Gardner ran a column on Keys, and the response got the case reopened. After five years in prison, Keys was released and eventually pardoned. He later recalled his time in prison as his "education," since he spent it reading and teaching himself to play guitar. As soon as he got home to Joshua Tree, he set up a marker at the site of the Bagley shooting and carved the inscription himself. It read, "Here's where Worth Bagley bit the dust at the hand of W. F. Keys." The marker is still there.

Keys became a local celebrity after that. Walt Disney Studios even cast him as an old prospector in the 1960 film *The Wild Burro of the West*, which was filmed in Joshua Tree. Frances Keys died in 1963, and Bill six years later. They are buried next to each other on the Desert Queen Ranch.

*   *   *

TAKE THIS KLAN AND SHOVE IT

Anaheim suffered a serious political problem in the 1920s, when four Ku Klux Klan members were elected to the city's five-member board of trustees. Once the men's Klan connections were exposed, however, a whopping 95 percent of the city's population showed up for a recall election in which they were soundly defeated. Ten Anaheim police officers were also fired when they turned out to be Klan members. They hadn't been hard to identify, though—at the urging of the new board members, they'd begun wearing their KKK uniforms while on duty.

Every year, smog costs California $71 billion in health-care expenses.

KEEPING SECRETS UNDER WRAPS

Ancient occult societies, alchemy, and magical chanting—how much do you really know about your nice neighbors in San Jose?

MUMMY DEAREST

Tucked away in an area of San Jose best known for its green lawns and high-end homes are ancient mummies of everything from cats to catfish, including a few mummified people. These mummies rest in San Jose's Rosicrucian Egyptian Museum with more than 4,000 other artifacts (originals and replicas), the largest collection of Egyptian artifacts on exhibit in the western United States.

The museum building, designed to resemble the ancient Amon temple that once stood in Karnak, Egypt, is part of a beautiful, but somewhat baffling, complex built by the Ancient Mystical Order Rosae Crucis (AMORC). The what? They're a group devoted to self-improvement and the study of mysticism. Rosicrucian Park takes up an entire city block in San Jose and features a planetarium, a research library, a temple, a shrine, and a peace garden replete with Egyptian plants, a pond, and fountains. All the buildings—except the Moorish-style planetarium—have exteriors inspired by Egyptian structures.

How this blend of ancient Egypt and New Age mysticism came to be located in a San Jose suburb is a strange story. For some, it begins in 1915 when Harvey Spencer Lewis, a former advertising illustrator from New Jersey, founded the AMORC to "study the elusive mysteries of life and the universe." For others, though, the story really begins in 1500 BC, when some of those mummies in the museum were still alive.

EGYPT, BY WAY OF GERMANY?

The AMORC is an offshoot of the Rosicrucian Society, which has puzzled, intrigued, and sometimes angered people for years. Like the Freemasons and the Knights Templar, the Rosicrucian Society has been linked to secret symbols, famous people, and conspiracy theories. The first Rosicrucians appeared in 16th-century Germany, supposedly founded by Christian Rosenkreutz. According to legend, he was both an enlightened mystic and a successful alchemist (he could turn lead into gold, though we have no idea *how*), so he had a lot of clout in the worlds of religion and mysticism.

But many historians now believe that Rosencreuz was a mythical figure, rather than a real person. Three pamphlets appeared in the 17th century—one about Rosencreuz, a second about his secret society, and a third about alchemy and spiritual enlightenment. No one knows exactly who wrote the pamphlets, but the authors may have been German Protestants who started the society themselves. Regardless, those pamphlets spawned elaborate legends about the Rosicrucians, elite Christian mystics who clandestinely practiced magic and alchemy while trying to bring about spiritual enlightenment. Meanwhile, conspiracy theorists accused the Rosicrucians of trying to dominate the world.

By the 20th century, new groups had formed whose beliefs strayed from those of the original Rosicrucians. As leader of the AMORC, Lewis taught that Rosicrucian knowledge actually originated much, much earlier...in ancient Egypt, around 1500 BC. He was fascinated by that culture and believed he'd been an ancient Egyptian in a past life. Lewis claimed that pharaohs like Thutmose III and Akhenaten were the first masters of the secret mysteries that became the Rosicrucian doctrine.

DOES HE KNOW THE WAY TO SAN JOSE?

Lewis decided to make the Rosicrucians' secrets available to regular people, so in 1915 in New York City, he founded the AMORC as an educational and philosophical organization. It was New Age before "New Age" was even a term, teaching everything from out-of-body travel to meditation. All members had to do was pay a monthly fee, and they'd get their lessons through the mail.

Lewis's intentions have been criticized over the years. Some considered him to be an important mystical teacher, but others just called him a marketing genius. Either way, Lewis headed a growing organization that became the most popular Rosicrucian sect in the United States and attracted prestigious members— Walt Disney and *Star Trek* creator Gene Roddenberry both belonged for a time. As the AMORC grew, Lewis had to decide

---

where to establish the group's home. Buried "treasure" led him to consider California.

According to the AMORC, the first Rosicrucians to come to America arrived in Carmel, California, in 1602 on the ships of the Spanish explorer, Sebastian Vizcaíno. They then carefully buried sacred texts in the area for a future Rosicrucian master to find so that he could spread their knowledge. Lewis claimed to be the master who found the texts. He decided to base the AMORC in nearby San Jose, which was more accessible than Carmel, but not too far away from the special site.

MUMMIES THE WORD

Lewis brought his belief in ancient Egypt's effect on the Rosicrucians with him to San Jose. He built Rosicrucian Park in the ancient Egyptian style, and also began an Egyptian artifact collection. His first piece: a small Sekhmet (lion goddess) statue. Eventually, the collection grew large enough to warrant a museum.

In 1971 the museum acquired a sarcophagus listed in a Neiman-Marcus Christmas catalog as a gift for "people who have everything." The museum bought the supposedly empty coffin, but when a Neiman-Marcus worker was preparing it for shipment, he found that it contained a male mummy. He shipped it anyway, and the museum had its first famous piece…made even more famous after specialists found an iron pin in the mummy's knee that had been inserted surgically nearly 2,600 years earlier.

The other mummy that made a name for the museum was only a child when she died. Using CT scans, researchers were able to figure out that she died whens she was four years old and was born about 2,000 years ago. She didn't suffer from chronic illnesses, but died suddenly, probably from an infection like dysentery. Her gold leaf mask indicated that she'd been born to a wealthy family.

Today, those mummies and the other Egyptian exhibits bring many visitors to Rosicrucian Park, though the AMORC also still holds meetings and meditations there. Tourists might be interested to know that there are more remains at the park than just the ones wrapped up in linens in the museum. At the park's Akhenaten Shrine are the ashes of Harvey Spencer Lewis himself, who—despite all his respect for ancient Egypt's mysteries—opted out of being mummified.

THE PREPOSTEROUS PLATE OF BRASS

A Berkeley professor gets punked—1930s-style.

DRAKE WAS HERE?
In 1936 a pheasant hunter discovered a metal plate near San Quentin State Prison, which overlooks San Francisco Bay. When he cleaned it up a bit, he noticed some writing on it that looked like the plate had been left there in 1579 by Sir Francis Drake, a sea captain and privateer in Elizabethan England. Engraved on it was the explorer's claim of having found the land he called Nova Albion for "Herr Majesty Queen Elizabeth." Finally, here was the proof that some historians had been waiting for. That Drake explored the western coast of North America is well known, but exactly how far north he went is unclear and had long been debated among historians. The plate seemed to prove that he'd at least gone as far as San Francisco.

The marker was called Drake's Plate and was quickly accepted as a part of American history. It was exhibited at the 1939–40 Golden Gate International Exposition, and photographs of it showed up in books and magazines.

Some scientists were suspicious. The plate appeared to have been hammered, carved with a chisel, and heated over a wood fire to create a dark patina that made it look old. But most people thought it was the real thing.

BERKELEY GOES BERSERKELEY

One of the believers was a Berkeley history professor named Herbert E. Bolton. Fascinated by a legend about Drake creating a brass plate marking his entry into California, Bolton used to tell his students to be on the lookout for it when they were in Marin County (home of San Quentin). The discovery of the plate was a dream come true for Bolton, and before anyone had a chance to tip him off about the possible hoax theory, he announced the discovery to the world and stored the plate safely in the school's Bancroft Library.

California's deepest recorded ground snow cover: 451 inches in Tamarack (1911).

Besides being a history buff and member of the California Historical Society, Bolton was a Clamper...a member of E Clampus Vitus, a playful fraternity of Western history lovers that was originally founded to poke fun at stuffy secret societies like the Freemasons. The Clampers were well known for spoofing each other, especially on historical matters, and Professor Bolton's preoccupation with Drake's landing made him a tempting target. But when it got out that the plate might be a phony, the Clampers emphatically denied having anything to do with Drake's "plate of brasse."

ANALYZE THIS

In 1977 the plate was finally proven to be a hoax. Two Berkeley scientists, hired to analyze it in honor of the quadricentennial of Drake's landing, immediately saw things that made them suspicious. The plate's thickness was too consistent for something that had been hammered out. Drilling into the plate turned up no corroded metal, and a high level of zinc (which had not even been identified in the 16th century) suggested that the brass was a mixture of high-purity copper and zinc, which would not have been available at the time. The scientists concluded that the plate had probably been manufactured between the last half of the 19th century and the early part of the 20th.

THE PLOTTERS

But who had done it? Researchers now point the finger at a band of respectable gentlemen of the day—only one of whom was known to have been a Clamper.

• G. Ezra Dane, a Clamper and member of the California Historical Society.

• George Haviland Barron, curator of California history at San Francisco's De Young Museum until 1933, was a prominent member of the California Historical Society. He lifted most of the text on the plate from *The World Encompassed by Sir Francis Drake*, a book about Drake's voyage that was first published in 1628.

• Art critic, appraiser, inventor, and friend of Barron's, George C. Clark designed the plate's layout and chiseled the lettering.

• Lorenz Noll, an art dealer and restorer, and Albert Dressler, a dealer in Western artifacts, were also accused.

The state's first cathedral: Old St. Mary's Church, San Francisco (est. 1854).

They didn't just fool Bolton. The California Historical Society's directors authorized publications about the plate, and the group's president donated $3,500 so that UC Berkeley could buy the plate for its library.

FESSING UP

Because everyone belonged to the same small world of California history buffs, a public confession after the fact was tricky. The perpetrators of the hoax did try to warn Bolton indirectly, but he was so excited about the discovery that he either didn't notice or chose to ignore the warnings.

Three of the tricksters—Dane, Barron, and Clark—died in the early 1940s, freeing up Lorenz Noll to confess the real story to the Clampers and at least one well-respected honcho at the California Historical Society. After Bolton died in 1953, Noll started telling the truth to a wider circle. But the facts didn't reach the right ears until that 1977 study.

Finally, the connection was made; attention was turned back to Lorenz Noll's story. An article on this final chapter of the hoax was published in February 2003.

THE MAN LEFT HIS MARK, IF NOT HIS PLATE

Some modern historians think the hoax had a positive impact—they point out the increased public awareness of California's explorer-era history and a wide range of related historical research. The fake plate is still on display at the Bancroft Library, and no one's quite given up hope that the real thing is still out there... maybe lying deep beneath the water, rocks, and sand of Drake's Bay near Point Reyes...and will be discovered someday.

Even if it isn't, Sir Francis Drake still left his mark on Marin County: Drake's Bay; the Drake's Landing Office Park; Sir Francis Drake Boulevard, which runs from the neighborhood around San Quentin all the way to the Pacific Ocean; and Sir Francis Drake High School (Go, Pirates!) were all named for him.

* * *

The only performer to have five stars on the Hollywood Walk of Fame is Gene Autry.

World's largest unsupported wooden structures: two hangars in Tustin...

STICKING AROUND

How much do you know about the Angelenos of the
Pleistocene? Yeah, us either. Read on.

FANCY TAR?

Hancock Park, an affluent area of Los Angeles, is well known for its celebrity sightings, million-dollar homes, and the famous Hollywood sign in the distance. But some of the neighborhood's "residents" are even cooler. World-famous fossils—like the extinct dire wolf, saber-toothed tiger, and Columbia mammoth—are among the millions of specimens that have been excavated from the La Brea tar pits.

Located on Wilshire Boulevard in the Miracle Mile, the tar pits contain one of the richest deposits of late Pleistocene era (the last ice age) fossils in North America. The fossils date from 10,000 to 40,000 years ago, and more than three million of them—including plants, mammals, birds, lizards, and insects—have been excavated since paleontologists first began digging there in the early 1900s.

The tar pits on display today were once excavation sites where workers dug for asphalt or scientists dug for fossils. Over the years, humans dug more than 100 pits throughout Hancock Park, but most of them have been refilled with dirt, debris, asphalt, and water. About 13 tar pits remain—the largest, called the Lake Pit, measures 28 square feet and is approximately 14 feet deep.

STICKY, GOOEY DEATH TRAPS

The La Brea tar pits formed thousands of years ago, when gas and oil beneath the ground came under pressure. The molten mixture pushed up through vents in the earth's crust. Once it reached the surface, the oil pooled in natural depressions aboveground. The lighter part of the pooling oil evaporated—left behind was a heavy, sticky oil. Then rain and underground springs added water, forming ponds and lakes on top of the oil and creating what we now call the tar pits.

The water on the tar pits' surface was especially attractive to thirsty animals, and during the warm spring and summer, the thick oil underneath was especially sticky. Animals that ventured into to the pits couldn't escape. Often predators chased their prey into the pits and got stuck too. Paleontologists once found a large bison fossil surrounded by a pack of fossilized wolves. The dead animals eventually sank completely, and their bones and teeth turned brown from the oil. But otherwise, they were almost perfectly preserved for more than 30,000 years.

THOSE STRANGE CATTLE BONES

Hundreds of years ago, local Native Americans used the thick oil at the tar pits as waterproof caulking for their baskets and canoes. When the Spanish arrived in the 18th century, they used it to waterproof their houses. In 1828 the tar pits were part of a Mexican land grant called Rancho de la Brea (*brea* means "tar" in Spanish). When the United States took over California in 1848, the area was part of the deal, and ultimately, it came into the possession of lawyer and surveyor Henry Hancock and his family. The Hancocks sold the oil from the tar pits, and their workmen often found fossils, which they assumed to be the bones of unlucky cattle. It wasn't until 1875 that a geologist identified a collection of bones as belonging to a saber-tooth tiger that had been extinct for 10,000 years.

By 1906 a paleontologist from UC Berkeley named John C. Merriam was busily excavating fossils from Rancho de la Brea. He published a paper on his findings and listed so many different types of prehistoric animals that the tar pits became a focus of study for paleontologists around the world. In 1913 fossils from the La Brea pools went on display at the newly opened Los Angeles County Museum of History, Science, and Art, and three years later, the Hancock family donated the tar pits to Los Angeles County. Scientists have been studying them ever since.

PALEONTOLOGY IS THE PITS

So many fossils have been discovered at the La Brea tar pits that scientists call the last 300,000 years of the Pleistocene era the "Rancholabrean land mammal age." Thanks to the sticky pits, we now know that, during the ice age, creatures like saber-tooth cats, mammoths, long-horned bison, horses, bears, wolves…even camels and lions once prowled what is now Wilshire Boulevard. In 2006 workers were digging up ground along Wilshire Boulevard to enlarge a parking lot when they found Zed, a Columbian mammoth skeleton that was 80 percent complete, resting in what used to be a riverbed. Work on the parking lot was halted to allow the creature (and his 10-foot tusks) to be excavated.

But it's not just the exotic animal fossils that excite scientists. Tiny bugs, with their wings still attached, have been preserved in the oil. And the partial skeleton of an 18-to 25-year-old woman shows that humans were living in L.A. more than 9,000 years ago. The skeleton from the tar pits is known as "La Brea Woman," and she's earned the distinction of being "the oldest Californian."

Plant fossils are also important. The oldest La Brea fossil is a piece of wood that dates back 40,000 years. By examining the plant material (even pollen has been preserved in the oil), scientists are able to tell that, during the last ice age, Los Angeles was cooler and moister than it is now. Redwoods that prefer the foggy climate of the Northern California coast once thrived in Hancock Park.

IT'S ALIIIIVE!

Of course, what all these great discoveries of La Brea have in common is that they're dead. Very few things actually live in the tar pits—there is an insect called the oil fly that lays its larvae there. But in 2007, environmental scientists at UC Riverside found another living creature where it wasn't expected.

The researchers were studying the large bubbles of methane that appear on the tar pits' surface. They took samples of oil from the pools and looked to see if they could find any bacteria that might be creating the methane. To their surprise, they found more than 200 types of as-yet-undiscovered bacteria living in the oil. These bacteria were eating the oil and excreting methane gas that bubbled up to the pits' surface. One of the bacteria is related to a type that survives 50 miles above the surface of the earth, where ultraviolet rays sterilize almost everything else. Another resembles bacteria that can withstand high levels of radiation. Scientists hope these bacteria will help them understand how life can exist in extreme environments, including those on other planets. Researchers also hope that studying the oil-munching bacteria may lead to their use in cleaning up oil spills. And so it seems that even after decades of excavation at the tar pits, scientists still never know what they'll dig up next.

A California doctor holds the world record for eating 17 bananas in two minutes.

THE GREAT AMERICAN DREAM HOUSE

It wasn't everybody's idea of home sweet home, but it was the right house at the right time for thousands of West Coast families after World War II.

MASTER BUILDER IN THE MAKING

All Joe Eichler wanted to do was build some low-cost housing for World War II veterans and their families: small, ranch-style homes with basic amenities. What he ended up with were stylish, iconic homes that are still in demand today. The reason? Eichler, though he didn't know it at first, was a modern man in every way. For one thing, he was an equal-opportunity builder who opened the doors of his houses to people of all races and colors, a pretty daring prospect in the pre–civil rights era. If someone wanted to buy one of his houses, all they had to do was come up with the down payment (anywhere from $500 to $2,650) and qualify for a mortgage.

In fact, the only colors Eichler cared about were the colors of his houses. His son Ned tells the story of how his father, while cruising through one of his developments, called a halt to a house-painting job because the color the owners had chosen didn't look right with the colors of the houses on either side of it. The house-painter told Eichler that the owners really wanted that particular color and added, "After all, it's their house." Eichler said, "Like hell it is. It's my house. Change the g**damn color."

THE HOUSES THAT JOE BUILT

Eichler started his business—Eichler Homes—in 1947. He bought some land in Northern California and built his first subdivision: a planned community of conventional-looking little boxes with cramped rooms, wood floors, Sheetrock walls, and forced-air heat. When an outspoken architect from San Francisco told Eichler the houses were "crap," the builder reluctantly agreed. So he challenged his architect, Robert Anshen, to design a stylish house that would appeal to young families and would still be affordable.

Anshen came up with the first in a series of open, airy contemporary houses that Eichler eventually became famous for: a house that was perfectly suited to the California climate and lifestyle.

Those first homes were built in 1949 in Sunnyvale, 40 miles south of San Francisco. Anshen's plan called for the siding to be upgraded to redwood, but the exteriors of the 50 ranch-style houses were otherwise unremarkable—they looked square and utilitarian. The interiors were another story. Inspired by homes Frank Lloyd Wright had designed in the Bay Area in the 1930s, the interiors were exceptionally modern for suburban houses of their time. Gone were the chopped-up floor plans and teensy rooms. In their place was a redwood-paneled living area with an open floor plan that made the houses seem much bigger than the 1,044 to 1,230 square feet they actually were. The floor-to-ceiling glass walls on the rear facade made the homes feel even larger and seemed to bring the outdoors in. The house was set on radiant-heated concrete floors, and all of it could be yours (or your grandparents') for just $9,500 (about $90,000 today).

Eichler's houses evolved over the next eight years: By 1957 most of them had four bedrooms, two baths, and a family room and, depending on the model, sold for $18,000 to $25,000 ($144,000 to $200,000 today). But the exteriors changed only slightly: taking advantage of the relatively warm, snowless winters, the roof stayed either flat or low-pitched, and the floor-to-ceiling glass at the back of the house remained standard so that homeowners could take in the view, even if it was only of a fenced-in suburban patio and garden.

THE BALL IS IN YOUR COURTYARD

The recession of 1957–58 hit most businesses hard, and home sales were no exception. Joe and Ned Eichler met with their architects for weeks, trying to figure out how to attract more customers and save their languishing business. As one of their many meetings was about to close, Anshen once again saved the day. He showed Eichler a scribbled floor plan of a house built around a small courtyard. When Eichler asked, "What...is that thing in the middle?" Anshen said, "An atrium. The Romans used to use them."

Adding an atrium made no sense to Eichler; in fact, it seemed

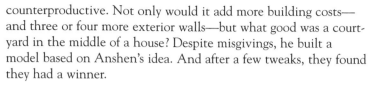

counterproductive. Not only would it add more building costs—and three or four more exterior walls—but what good was a court-yard in the middle of a house? Despite misgivings, he built a model based on Anshen's idea. And after a few tweaks, they found they had a winner.

From the street, an Eichler with an atrium looked the same as the previous models: angular and nondescript. But now, when prospective buyers opened the front door, they were greeted by an open-to-the-sky atrium; glass doors on the other three walls looked into the kitchen, living room, or bedroom wing. The houses were a huge success. Nearly every Eichler from then on was built around an open-air courtyard. The company went public in 1959 and continued to earn steady profits, building about 700 houses a year, and expanding into Southern California. But change was on the way, and it didn't bode well for Eichler Homes.

WHAT KILLED THE EICHLER?

A variety of factors contributed to the bankruptcy of Eichler Homes in 1967: the growing expense of glass and redwood, competition in the marketplace, and the high cost of air-conditioning a house with an open floor plan and huge walls of glass. Also, some young couples who'd bought Eichlers as starter homes had more money by the '60s and no longer wanted tract housing; they were looking for something more unique. But perhaps the most important factor was simply that the classic Eichler home had gone out of style.

After the bankruptcy, Joe Eichler built a few more custom and tract homes, but another recession in 1973 did him in. He died in 1974.

Decades later, however, the houses that Eichler built are more popular than ever. Even in the depressed real estate market of the late 2000s, Eichler homes were selling for $600,000 and up—and often for more than their asking price.

*   *   *

At 147 feet, Disneyland's Matterhorn Mountain is exactly 1/100th the height of the real Matterhorn in the Alps.

REAL OR RUMOR: THE HOTEL DEL CORONADO

Built in 1888, the Hotel del Coronado (or Hotel Del) near San Diego has been the site of ghost hauntings, movie filmings, celebrity getaways, and all kinds of other legendary stuff. Let's separate the facts from the fiction.

RUMOR: In December 1904, the Hotel del Coronado lit the first electric outdoor Christmas tree in the United States.

TRUTH: The hotel itself makes this claim, but it's unlikely. Electric lights on trees probably came sometime in the late 1800s. However, in 1904 the hotel did wire 250 lights to its 50-foot tree. It may have been the first in Southern California and was certainly done at a time when few people lit outdoor trees at all and indoor ones were still fire hazards with candles. The tree remained on display for a three hours each night from Christmas Eve through New Year's.

RUMOR: Every U.S. president since Lyndon B. Johnson has stayed at the Hotel Del.

TRUTH: This is true. The hotel has been the temporary home to 15 presidents, including the eight since Johnson. Seven presidents before Johnson also stayed at the Hotel Del: Benjamin Harrison, William McKinley, William Taft, Woodrow Wilson, Franklin D. Roosevelt, Dwight Eisenhower, and John F. Kennedy.

RUMOR: At a 1920 Hotel Del banquet in his honor, the 26-year-old Prince Edward of Wales met 24-year-old Wallis Spencer, a U.S. Navy captain's wife who was destined to (scandalously!) become Edward's Duchess of Windsor.

TRUTH: Years later, the couple did have an unsanctioned relationship (he had a thing for married women, and she was about to be twice-divorced). He briefly became King Edward VIII, but abdicated his throne to marry her, and they lived in exile as the

---

The California condor has a wingspan of 10 feet.

Duke and Duchess of Windsor. Wallis Simpson did live in San Diego in 1920 while her first husband was stationed on Coronado. But aside from a brief meeting at a party's receiving line, historians find no proof that Edward and Wallis ever spent time together at the Hotel Del.

RUMOR: Each winter, the hotel's staff leaves a Christmas party invitation for the Hotel Del's resident ghost, Kate Morgan.

TRUTH: Back in 1892, a beautiful young woman (whose real name, many believe, was Kate Morgan) checked into room 302. After trying (and failing) to repair her marriage, she fatally shot herself on the hotel's beach. For more than a century since, visitors claim to have seen her ghost and other strange happenings. But there's no truth to the holiday party invites, according to the hotel.

RUMOR: The Hotel Del inspired writer L. Frank Baum's fictional Emerald City of Oz, and Baum himself designed part of the hotel.

TRUTH: Baum first visited San Diego in 1904 and stayed at the Hotel Del several times, writing *Dorothy and the Wizard of Oz*, *The Road to Oz*, and *The Emerald City*. But the Emerald City first showed up in the series' original book, *The Wonderful Wizard of Oz*, which was published in 1900...four years before Baum came to Coronado.

However, it is true that Baum designed part of the hotel's interior. The author was a fixture at the hotel in the early 1900s, reading to children and writing from a rattan rocking chair outside the formal Crown Dining Room. The room was grand—with a sugar pinewood ceiling built using pegs and notches, no nails—but Baum thought it needed a more regal, luxurious feel to live up to its name. So he created the room's elaborate chandeliers, which he shaped like the crown worn by the lion in the Oz books. They're still hanging in the dining room today.

RUMOR: Marilyn Monroe had a thing for the hotel's pudding.

TRUTH: This is also true. A former chef at the hotel dished that Marilyn Monroe requested the same treat every day while she filmed 1959's *Some Like It Hot* on the property—the vanilla soufflé pudding decorated with an egg white.

WELCOME, SPACE BROTHERS! PART II

On page 133, we introduced you to two of California's famous space cults. Here are three more.

WHAT: The Ground Crew
WHERE: Walnut Creek
WHAT THEY'RE ABOUT: The Ground Crew believes its purpose is to wait for spacecraft to arrive and then assist them in their landing. Their leaders also channel messages from outer space. For example, Mira from the Pleiadian High Council got in touch on September 14, 2011, through the group's founder, Valerie Donner, to reassure the Ground Crew that the Pleidians were still planning to come...someday. According to Donner, the message went like this: "We ask you to be patient as we make way to brighten your skies...The Earth is the most diverse planet. This makes the ascension process complex...Your space family admires and adores the Earth."

Donner began the group in 1996 and shares about two messages a month, channeled mostly from Mira. But occasionally there are others: Mary (mother of Jesus), Kuthumi (an enlightened being who is the master of animals, Earth, nature spirits, and fairies), and Hilarion (another enlightened master of teachers, missionaries, doctors, scientists, engineers, musicians, and those who work with computers or space travel).

Until the spaceships come, members of the Ground Crew work as "light workers," serving humanity, raising its consciousness, and protecting the world. Some Crewmembers also believe they were sent from outer space as "star seeds" to help backward Earthlings ascend to higher spiritual levels.

WHAT: Universal Industrial Church of the New World Comforter
WHERE: Stockton
WHAT THEY'RE ABOUT: In 1954 church founder Allen

The oddly shaped trees in San Diego's Scripps Park inspired many plants in Dr. Suess's books.

Michael Noonan saw an alien in the Mojave Desert. He claimed, though, that he'd been speaking telepathically with space creatures since 1947, when he was enveloped in a purple-and-gold light and transported to a mother ship where a voice told him of his new mission as messenger and world comforter. Despite this dramatic wake-up call, Noonan didn't rush out and immediately start a church. He continued his job painting signs in Long Beach until the late 1960s, when he got word that there was a groovy scene happening up in San Francisco and headed north.

Noonan—now calling himself Allen Michael—decided to stay in the Bay Area, opening a vegan restaurant and commune in San Francisco before moving them both to Berkeley. In 1973 he wrote a book about various space people who spoke to him psychically, and then founded the Industrial Church. Two years later, he moved the commune, restaurant, and church inland to Stockton, where they remain today. Noonan ran for president (of the United States) in 1980 and '84 on the Utopian Synthesis Party ticket, but didn't win. He likewise lost his attempt to become California's governor in 1982.

WHAT: Heaven's Gate

WHERE: San Diego

WHAT THEY'RE ABOUT: Most of California's space cults are harmless in their eccentricities, but Heaven's Gate was an exception. After recovering from a heart attack in the early 1970s, cofounder Marshall Applewhite believed he had survived a near-death experience, and he somehow convinced his nurse, Bonnie Nettles, that the two of them should start a new religion. Their ideology combined Biblical apocalyptic prophecy, space aliens, and alternative dimensions. Traveling around the country to drum up recruits, they fine-tuned their group's theology and settled on a name: Heaven's Gate (which was also, coincidentally, the title of a famously bad 1980 movie about life in the Old West).

Nettles died of cancer in 1985, and Applewhite took over the group. He believed that Earth was imminently due to be wiped clean of all life in order for God to start over. The only hope was to get off of Earth by way of the approaching Hale-Bopp comet, due to pass Earth in the spring of 1997. The comet, he said, was

The Richard Nixon Library in Yorba Linda can be reserved for private weddings.

just a cover for a vehicle that had been sent by his extraterrestrial patrons to get the most worthy humans—i.e., members of his group—off the planet before it was destroyed. To prove their worthiness and advanced spirituality, Heaven's Gate members gave away all of their things, cut off relationships with family and friends, and ended sexual activity of all kinds, going so far as a trip to Mexico during which Applewhite and five other male members were castrated. Then the group rented a luxury home in the affluent San Diego suburb of Rancho Santa Fe, dressed in identical athletic outfits, and killed themselves in three groups over three days. Their poison of choice? Arsenic and cyanide mixed into applesauce, and washed down with phenobarbital and vodka. Before the poison took hold, they placed plastic bags over their heads. By the time the police arrived on March 26, 1997, 39 people, including Applewhite, were dead.

IRONIC? One of the dead Heaven's Gate members was Thomas Nichols, whose sister Nichelle Nichols played Lieutenant Uhura in the original *Star Trek* TV series.

* * *

A CALIFORNIA TREASURE

Where? The Spyglass Hill Golf Course, Pebble Beach

Claim to Fame: The Pebble Beach Company, which owns several golf courses around town, was founded in 1919 by Samuel Finley Brown Morse, a distant cousin of Massachusetts-born telegraph inventor Samuel Finley Breese Morse. The California Morse was a friend of author Robert Louis Stevenson, and legend has it that one day the writer went on a brainstorming stroll around Monterey Peninsula and came up with the idea for the book *Treasure Island*. Half a century later, when it came time to build the Spyglass Hill Golf Course in 1966, the designer named each hole after something from the pirate fantasy. Golfers start on "Treasure Island" before "Billy Bones" brings them to the ocean. Then it's on to "The Black Spot," the third hole, where instead of a fairway, there is only a vast 100-yard wasteland of shrubs and sand.

World's largest blooming plant: Sierra Madre's lavender lady, a wisteria with 500-foot branches.

THE GOLDEN STATE'S FIRST MILLIONAIRE

Want to know how to make money in California?
Don't dig for gold. Sell the shovels.

T"HAT DAMNED AMERICAN FLAG!"
Samuel Brannan earned his fortune in the California gold
rush without ever setting foot in a mine. In fact, he hadn't
come to California in search of wealth at all. Brannan moved to
San Francisco to serve his religion—only to renounce his faith
later when it interfered with his becoming the richest man in
California.

Brannan was a teenager in the 1830s when he met Mormon
missionaries from the Church of Jesus Christ of the Latter Day
Saints (LDS). At 23, he converted to the faith, joined the LDS
community, and eventually moved to New York to put out a Mormon newspaper called *The Prophet.*

During the mid-19th century, the LDS faced violent opposition in America, and in 1844 an angry mob murdered the group's
founder, Joseph Smith. A close associate of Smith's, Brigham
Young, became the new LDS leader, and to protect his followers,
he wanted to get out of the United States altogether. So Young
began encouraging groups of Mormons to emigrate west to Utah,
California, Nevada, and other territories owned by Mexico at the
time. In 1845 Sam Brannan and his wife Anne Eliza agreed to
lead a group of more than 200 Mormons to California. They set
sail from New York on a ship called the *Brooklyn,* traveled around
Cape Horn, and on July 25, 1846, docked at a tiny pueblo called
Yerba Buena (now San Francisco).

But when they arrived, Brannan and the others got a surprise.
During the nearly six months the *Brooklyn* was at sea, Mexico
and the United States had gone to war. Mexico lost, and American soldiers had just taken control of San Francisco Bay. Bitterly
disappointed that they were under U.S. rule once again, Brannan
supposedly shouted, "By God, there is that damned American
flag!"

LIFE'S BETTER IN CALIFORNIA

Still, Brannan believed he'd found a happy home for the LDS. Yerba Buena's population was so small that the newly arrived Mormons more than doubled it. They were the majority in a region filled with redwoods for lumber, fertile land for agriculture, and a port that could make a good commercial shipping center. Brannan couldn't wait to tell Brigham Young, who was leading 15,000 Mormons west on foot, that he'd found their perfect home.

As the head of the LDS in California, Brannan got busy. He bought land, built flour mills, and established a community called "Mormon Island" near modern-day Folsom. Brannan also ran San Francisco's first newspaper, the *California Star*, and started the area's first school. Then, in 1847, he rode off to find Young and tell him about his new settlement on the coast.

In July Brannan met up with Young's group and accompanied them to the Great Salt Lake in what's now Utah. Appalled at the harsh climate and barren soil there, Brannan tried to persuade Young that they'd all be better off in California. But Young brushed Brannan off. He argued that the land might be unyielding in Utah, but there would also be fewer settlers there, making it a place that the church could grow in peace. Brannan returned to California, angry with his leader and determined to change his mind.

THERE'S GOLD IN THAT THAR RIVER!

Brannan immediately got back to business, opening a general store outside Coloma, near a small settlement called Sutter's Mill. In 1848, when some customers started paying for their goods in gold dust, Brannan went looking for the source and found a group of men happily mining nuggets along the American River.

The fact that gold had been discovered in California was kept quiet at first. John Sutter, the mill's owner, didn't want anyone to know about it because he feared a mass influx of prospective miners...who would ruin his plans to create a vast, profitable farming community in the area. But Brannan jumped on the opportunity immediately. He bought up all the mining equipment he could find, put some gold into a quinine bottle, and returned to San Francisco. There, he ran through the streets with the flask of

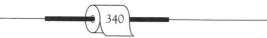

gold above his head, yelling, "Gold! There's gold on the American River!" Within days, the city was nearly deserted as every able-bodied man left for the gold fields.

Everyone except Brannan, that is. Instead of digging for gold, Brannan ordered more shovels and opened more stores. By 1849 his store at Sutter's Mill sold about $150,000 in goods per month (about $4 million today). He made even more by charging exorbitant interest on loans when miners needed cash. He even charged them 10 percent on their earnings so he had a claim to the land they were mining.

BREAKING FAITH

Brannan was also getting fed up with the Mormon church. Busy settling Utah, Brigham Young hadn't showed much interest in the California settlement. An offended Brannan decided that Young sent him to California "to get me out of the way, supposing, it being a Spanish country, that I would be killed."

When Young finally did send a message to Brannan, it was to ask the new millionaire for donations to the "Lord's Treasury." Brannan's legendary reply to the messenger was, "You go back and tell Brigham Young that I'll give up the Lord's money when he sends me a receipt signed by the Lord, and no sooner." The store-keeper would later become known for generous contributions to many kinds of charities—except the ones that involved the Latter Day Saints.

NEW MONEY, NEW DREAMS

By the 1850s, Brannan was the richest man in California. He went into real estate development and owned about 20 percent each of San Francisco and Sacramento. He also owned land in Hawaii and ran all kinds of businesses—everything from railroads and distilleries to a large tea plantation.

When Brannan discovered Napa's hot springs in 1859, he bought about 2,000 acres around them to build a resort like the one he'd seen in Saratoga, New York. As legend has it, at his resort's opening in 1862, Brannan got so drunk that, instead of declaring the place "the Saratoga of California," he called it "the Calistoga of Sarafornia"—giving the town of Calistoga its name.

Brannan became a powerful man in California, both for good and for bad. He developed the cities of San Francisco and Sacramento and was elected to the state senate in 1853. But he also formed "the Committee of Vigilance," a vigilante group that drove undesirables out of San Francisco—and held several hangings without fair trials.

BAD LUCK FROM SAINT POLYGAMY

Brannan also had a drinking problem that got him into trouble. He had a reputation for being a brawler and was shot several times. One wound forced him to walk with a cane for the rest of his life. He was also such a womanizer that many miners claimed Brannan's new religion was "praying to Saint Polygamy."

In the end, all that drinking and womanizing cost Brannan his fortune. In 1872, when Anne Eliza got tired of her husband's many mistresses, she divorced him, and he had to pay her half of his wealth in cash. But since most of his money was tied up in real estate, Brannan had to liquidate in a terrible market. His fortune took a hit, and it gradually disappeared into investments that did not pan out. By 1887 Brannan was selling pencils door-to-door. Two years later, he died broke just north of San Diego. But his mark on California remained: Many places around the state are named for him, including San Francisco's Brannan Street and Brannan Island in Sacramento County.

* * *

HERE SHE COMES, MISS CELANEOUS

Debbie Reynolds was the perky *Singin' in the Rain* movie star who inspired millions of parents in the early 1950s to name their daughters "Debbie." But in 1948, she had been lured to sign up for the Miss Burbank pageant by the promise of a free silk blouse and green scarf. Before the big day, Reynolds changed her mind, but her father insisted that she keep her word about participating. So the 16-year-old Debbie Reynolds showed up for the contest and found that the crowd went wild when she sang and imitated *Annie Get Your Gun* star Betty Hutton. Reynolds's performance not only won her the Miss Burbank title, but also earned her a seven-year contract from Warner Bros.

DIM STARS

California is full of celebrities…just not necessarily the smart ones.

"Smoking kills. If you're killed, you've lost a very important part of yourself."
—**Brooke Shields**

"It's really hard to maintain a one-on-one relationship if the other person is not going to allow me to be with other people."
—**Axl Rose**

"Fiction writing is great. You can make up almost anything."
—**Ivana Trump**

"Whenever I watch TV and see those poor kids starving all over the world, I can't help but cry. I mean, I'd love to be skinny like that but not with all those flies and death and stuff."
—**Mariah Carey**

"If I go down, I'm going down standing up."
—**Chuck Person, L.A. Lakers assistant coach**

"I don't diet. I just don't eat as much as I'd like to."
—**Linda Evangelista**

"I am for the death penalty. Who commits terrible acts must get a fitting punishment. That way he learns the lesson for the next time."
—**Britney Spears**

"Nobody deserves to be treated like a princess 100 percent of the time…not even me."
—**Jessica Simpson**

"I've got taste. It's inbred in me."
—**David Hasselhoff**

"So, where's the Cannes Film Festival being held this year?"
—**Christina Aguilera**

"I think that gay marriage is something that should be between a man and a woman."
—**Arnold Schwarzenegger**

"[Kabbalah] helps you confront your fears. Like if a girl borrowed my clothes and never gave them back, and I saw her wearing them months later, I would confront her."
—**Paris Hilton**

THE TOWN OF MISFIT WRITERS

Glen Ellen is a charming little town that straddles the Sonoma Highway. Its population is only about 800 people, but the town has served as home to three of the 20th century's most famous writers: Jack London, M. F. K Fisher, and Hunter S. Thompson.

M. F. K. FISHER

Background: Mary Frances Kennedy was a Californian for most of her life, moving to Southern California with her family in 1911 when she was three. She grew up working at her father's newspaper and then dubbed herself M. F. K. Fisher in 1929 after marrying her college sweetheart, Alfred "Al" Fisher. While Al attended school in Dijon, France, Fisher studied art and gourmet cooking. Returning to California during the Great Depression, she got a job at a card shop and began writing short pieces about travel and food. The couple eventually divorced, but Fisher's career path was set. Ultimately, she published 16 books before moving to Glen Ellen.

Glen Ellen goings on: When Fisher moved to Glen Ellen in 1971, she was 63 years old and wasn't sure she had anything more to write. A friend named David Bouverie offered to build Fisher a house on his Glen Ellen property. She designed the home herself and—fitting her sense of finality and impending mortality—called it Last House.

Epilogue: Fisher apparently found new energy in the Sonoma County town. She used it as a springboard for frequent trips to France, and as a place to come back and write about her travels. (She also protected herself from unwanted visitors with a sign that read "Trespassers will be violated.") Despite suffering from Parkinson's disease and arthritis, she wrote another 10 books in the 21 years she lived in Last House. The property still stands at 13935 Sonoma Highway. Another seven books were published posthumously from her letters and journals.

Largest county in the continental U.S.: San Bernardino (13 million acres).

HUNTER S. THOMPSON

Background: American journalist and author Hunter S. Thompson wrote books like *Fear and Loathing in Las Vegas* and *The Rum Diary*, and invented gonzo journalism, a genre in which journalists let go of all objectivity, involve themselves in the action they're investigating, and actually become a part of their stories.

Glen Ellen goings on: In February 1964, Thompson arrived in Glen Ellen with his eight-month-pregnant wife, Sandy. They had driven 1,200 miles from Colorado and ended up at 9400 Bennett Valley Road, in what he called the Owl House. He wrote that it was "a sort of Okie shack" where he spent "most of my day in a deep ugly funk, plotting vengeance." By early April, he was suffering from a bad case of writer's block, not selling any freelance articles, and telling friends that he was considering a job as a laborer to get "out of debt and desperation." He wrote that his move to Glen Ellen was a "disaster" and vowed to leave as soon as possible. In the end, though, he stayed for eight months before moving to an apartment in San Francisco.

Epilogue: Thompson's time in Glen Ellen happened just before his career took off. In San Francisco, he began covering the nascent countercultures of the Beat and hippies. He rode with the Hell's Angels and wrote about it for *The Nation* and later in his first published book. He also pulled a notorious stunt while living in Glen Ellen: Sent by the *National Observer* to Ernest Hemingway's home in Ketchum, Idaho, to look for any new answers as to why Hemingway committed suicide, Thompson stole a pair of elk antlers that hung above the cabin's door. (His wife planned to return them...eventually.)

JACK LONDON

Background: Glen Ellen's biggest kahuna, though, was definitely Jack London, author of classics like *Call of the Wild* and *White Fang*. When London breezed into Glen Ellen with his wife Charmian in 1905, he was flying high in life, the best paid and most famous writer of his time, though not necessarily the richest—the couple seemed to blow through his money as fast as he earned it.

Glen Ellen goings on: One of their biggest expenditures was

More sourdough bread is produced in Oakland than any other city in the world.

$7,000 (roughly $179,000 today) for 129 acres of land on the outskirts of Glen Ellen, next to what was then called the California Home for the Care and Training of Feeble Minded Children (today, it's the Sonoma Developmental Center). London promptly dubbed the land the Beauty Ranch. They moved into a small cottage on the property, and Jack immediately began planning what he called the Wolf House, a multistory home big enough to hold large gatherings and allow guests to stay overnight. He wrote to a friend, "It's not a mansion, but a big cabin, a lofty lodge, a hospitable teepee"—built from redwood and volcanic rock, and including a large reflecting pool in the middle of its courtyard.

London also hoped to turn the property into a model of modern farming. He built California's first-ever silos made from concrete. He built the state's first humane pig farm—the Pig Palace, which featured clean floors and sanitary drainage. London also experimented with terraced farming and green mulches.

That's not to say all his ranching ideas worked well. Around 1903, he befriended horticultural genius Luther Burbank, who lived in nearby Santa Rosa. Burbank had bred some prickly pears that weren't prickly; instead of having barbs, the cactus's skin was smooth. London thought the plant would make a great cattle food, so he bought them all. Only one problem: The cactus actually did have barbs; they grew under the skin. Several of his cattle died as a result of eating them.

Epilogue: London died of kidney failure in 1916 at age 40. Charmian lived until age 83 in 1955. Both were cremated, and their ashes are buried under a mossy rock at the former Beauty Ranch.

* * *

WELCOME TO GLEN ELLEN

The town that became Glen Ellen began in 1846 as a eight-square-mile gift (or payment) by Spanish landowner General Mariano Vallejo to his children's piano teacher. Later, pioneer and politician Charles V. Stuart bought the land and named it after his wife Ellen. The vineyards and wineries appeared soon after, and many of the residents are direct descendants, just a few generations removed, of the original Sonoma Valley wine families of 150 years ago.

In the 1950s, Bob Hope served as honorary mayor of Palm Springs.

BEWARE FALSE COLONELS BEARING GIFTS

Los Angeles has had its share of shocking celebrity criminals—O. J. Simpson, Robert Blake, Christian Brando, Phil Spector. But one of the earliest, and most influential, may have been businessman Griffith Jenkins Griffith, the father of Griffith Park.

EVERYBODY KNOWS HIS NAME
Griffith Jenkins Griffith was one of L.A.'s wealthiest men—he often strolled the city carrying a gold-headed cane—and he was also one of the most generous, donating the land and money for Griffith Park, the Griffith Park Observatory, and the Greek Theatre. But Griffith also had a dark side, which was exposed in 1903 when he nearly murdered his wife.

Griffith was born in the United Kingdom on January 4, 1850. He arrived in New York 16 years later, alone and broke, but with plenty of ambition. He managed to get some schooling before moving to San Francisco in 1873, where he taught himself about mineralogy and mining.

In 1878 Griffith got a job at San Francisco's *Alta California* newspaper, reporting on mines in California, Nevada, Oregon, and Washington. But he didn't really want to be a reporter—he wanted to be rich. So he used the information he learned from his job at the paper to launch a new career instead.

Mining was big business in California in the late 19th century, and mining syndicates (partnerships that ordinary people could buy into) were making huge fortunes. There were also no laws against insider trading at the time. So Griffith used his inside knowledge of the mining industry to make investments in companies that he knew were going to soar in value. By 1882 the formerly penniless immigrant was a millionaire, and he took up residence in Los Angeles.

The state's first newspaper: *The Californian* (Monterey), launched in 1846.

A GIFT FOR THE "PLAIN PEOPLE"

Once established in L.A., Griffith made even more money investing in real estate. Pretty soon, he was so wealthy that instead of just buying a mansion, he bought part of Rancho de los Feliz, more than 4,000 acres of what is now the neighborhood of Los Feliz. In 1887 Griffith came into even more money when he married socialite Mary Agnes Christina "Tina" Mesmer, a descendant of one of the earliest (and richest) Spanish land barons in California.

Griffith and his wife were well known around Los Angeles, and they became local celebrities in 1896 when they gave residents a unique Christmas gift. The couple donated 3,015 acres of Rancho de los Feliz to the city. Griffith insisted on only one condition: The land had to be made into a public park, "a place of recreation and rest for the masses, a resort for the rank and file, for the plain people." Griffith had seen great urban parks in Europe and New York, and he wanted Los Angeles to have one too.

LIAR, LIAR, PANTS ON FIRE

Newspapers praised Griffith's "princely gift," but those who knew him had other things to say. Several former acquaintances and associates called him "pompous" or "a midget egomaniac" (because he was short). They also said he was a liar. For one thing, even though he called himself a colonel, Griffith had only served in the reserves, not the active military. And the closest he ever came to an official title was "Major of Riflery Practice," an honor bestowed on him by some of his friends in the California National Guard. The phony colonel made boring speeches at his exclusive men's club...but the club couldn't throw him out because he gave so much money. Griffith also complained about being so admired that people wanted him to be president of the United States—a job he insisted he really didn't want.

In 1903 while vacationing in Santa Monica with Tina, Griffith's reputation went from bad to dangerous. He tended to lose his temper and was prone to delusions—in this case, Griffith believed his Catholic wife and the pope wanted to poison him so they could steal his money for the church. In a hotel suite, he confronted his wife with a loaded gun. Despite her protests, he demanded that she get down on her knees, and then he put the revolver to her head.

First wild-card team to win the Super Bowl: the Oakland Raiders (1980).

THE BOOZE DID IT

Tina Griffith jerked her head away just before her husband fired, but she was still shot through the left eye. To escape him, she threw herself out the hotel window and landed on an awning two stories below. She broke her arm in the fall, but somehow managed to crawl through a window to get help. She survived, and her husband was arrested.

Griffith went on trial for attempted murder in 1904, and the proceeding quickly turned into a spectacle—reporters crowded the courthouse, and hundreds of gawkers were turned away daily. The prosecutor was district attorney John D. Fredericks, aided by former California governor Henry Gage. But for the defense, it was Earl Rogers—the inspiration for the title character in the *Perry Mason* book series—who took the reins. Rogers defended 77 murder cases during his career...he lost only three.

Rogers's defense for Griffith? Alcoholism. The tactic was untried, but Rogers argued that even though Griffith was a self-professed teetotaler who gave money to support Prohibition, he was actually a closet alcoholic (he was) who secretly drank "two quarts of whiskey a day" (that might have been an embellishment). Rogers then called witnesses who testified to Griffith's "insane" behavior. One witness told a story about the paranoid colonel complaining that someone had poisoned his wine. (No one actually had.)

To hide her disfigured face, Tina Griffith wore a veil throughout the trial. She lifted it only once to show her scars to the jury. Her husband responded by laughing, which outraged the public. Los Angeles wanted him to pay for what he'd done. But in the end, Griffith was acquitted of attempted murder and convicted only of a misdemeanor—assault with a deadly weapon. He served two years in San Quentin.

SOBER BUT UNLOVED

As soon as the trial ended, Tina Griffith sued for divorce. A sympathetic judge granted her request in just under five minutes...the fastest divorce proceeding in L.A.'s history. In prison, Griffith sobered up and seemed humbled. He turned down an easy job in San Quentin's library to do menial work instead, and he served his full prison term without applying for parole. In 1906 he returned

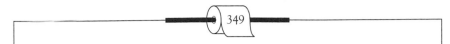

to L.A.—now sober, still rich, and fully determined to improve his image with the "plain people" who enjoyed Griffith Park. Unfortunately, the plain people despised him.

Before his arrest, Griffith had planned to build a 2,000-foot railway tram up Mount Griffith, the peak where the Hollywood sign is. But after the trial, the peak was renamed Mount Hollywood and the tram was never built. Then, in 1912, Griffith tried to give the city $100,000 to build an observatory in the park. The public protested taking money from a villain and convinced officials to turn Griffith down. The next year, he offered the city $50,000 to build the Greek Theatre, but city officials put him off, delaying the vote to reject or accept the money. Griffith finally thwarted the public and got his way when he died in 1919: In his will, he left a trust fund for both the theater (built in 1929) and the observatory (built in 1935).

*   *   *

RO-DE-OH...OR RO-DAY-OH?

The pronunciation of Beverly Hills' fancy Rodeo Drive has been confusing tourists for years. In a country that mostly says "RO-de-oh," it's a surprise to discover that this rodeo is actually pronounced "ro-DAY-oh." Many people also wonder where exactly the rodeos were on what's now one of the most famous shopping streets in America. But there were never any rodeos here. A local merchant was once quoted as telling tourists that the name comes from the time when there was a horse path down the center divide instead of palm trees, but that's not true either.

So how did the oddly pronounced street get its name? It helps to know that it's actually a Spanish/Native American translation hybrid. In Spanish, the word *rodeo* (pronounced "ro-day-oh") has nothing to do with ropin' and ridin'. It means "rounding up, gathering, detouring around, surrounding, or enclosing." The original Tongva Indian name of the area, which was once covered in swamps, was translated into Spanish as *El Rodeo de las Aguas* ("The Gathering of the Waters."). We suppose that name is still fitting—although the waters are no longer around, the gathering continues today...of shoppers penned in by the expensive stores that make up the street's famous three blocks of retail indulgence.

JOHNNY ORANGESEED

When people told Charles Chapman that he was mixing apples and oranges, he took it as a sign that he was headed in the right direction.

ORANGES DON'T FALL FAR FROM THE TREE
California's Charles Chapman was a descendant of John Chapman, better known as Johnny Appleseed. Johnny traveled the Midwest in the 1700s and 1800s, sowing apple seeds, creating local nurseries, and introducing the apple tree into Indiana, Ohio, and Illinois. He dressed simply, walked long distances in raggedly clothes and bare feet, and didn't make much money. He was also a vegetarian and very religious, following the teachings of Swedish Christian mystic Emanuel Swedenborg.

Charles Chapman was deeply religious, too, but he didn't want to live simply—Charles wanted to make a lot of money. His product of choice? Valencia oranges. Just like Johnny Appleseed didn't plant the original apple seeds he distributed, Charles Chapman stumbled upon a small Valencia orange grove in Fullerton around 1900 and turned the fruit into a national staple.

JUICY

Oranges thrived in Southern California's mild climate, and Chapman recognized that the sweet fruit had great selling potential. So he expanded his grove and marketed "Chapman's Old Mission Brand" oranges all over the United States. By the 1920s, oranges had replaced walnuts as Fullerton's primary crop, and Chapman was known as the "Father of the Valencia Orange Industry." (He also became Fullerton's mayor.) Today, oranges aren't grown much in Fullerton—development gobbled up all the groves. But Chapman is still an important part of Orange County's landscape: Chapman University in Orange and Chapman Avenue in Fullerton both bear his name.

FUN FACT: Before Chapman marketed Valencia oranges to a mass audience, a cowboy and agricultural scientist named William Wolfskill was the first to cultivate them in Southern California. Named after the city in Spain, Valencias were so common in the area that they gave Orange County its name.

THE DUST BOWL REVOLUTION

Imagine what life would be like if you and your entire family lost everything and were forced to move across the country to an unfamiliar new place. Would you survive and even thrive? If you lived during the Great Depression and moved to California, the surprising answer is...probably yes.

PARDON OUR DUST

One of the most enduring images of 1930s America is of the migrant farm family—their old car stuffed with possessions, hungry children with dusty bare feet, mothers trying desperately to put together a meal, fathers with signs begging for work. Between 1930 and 1940, more than 2 million people left the American interior, and about 25 percent of them headed to California alone. They were lured by rumors of plentiful jobs, great weather, and fertile fields. What they discovered when they arrived, however, wasn't exactly the paradise they'd hoped for.

The crisis began with good intentions and bad weather. As immigrants poured into the United States in the late 19th and early 20th centuries, many of them settled in the middle of the country and started farming. Southern plains states like Oklahoma and Texas had seen several decades of plentiful rain—something the newcomers figured was normal—so the new arrivals planted fields of wheat and other crops to feed their new countrymen and to contribute to America's effort in World War I. When farmers from other parts of the United States heard about the agriculture boom in the Great Plains, many of them packed their families into wagons and cars and headed for the plains, prepared to borrow some money, stake a claim, and make a fortune.

But the wet weather was an anomaly. In fact, the Great Plains were notoriously dry, and beginning in 1930—and lasting for about 10 years—the area plunged into a terrible drought. The lack of rain combined with years of overplanting, no crop rotation, deep plowing, high temperatures, and no real effort at conservation meant that the soil lacked nutrients and simply baked. In Texas, Oklahoma, Arkansas, Kansas, Colorado, and Missouri, the topsoil turned to dust. When the wind kicked up, and with no natural grasses to keep the soil where it belonged—because the grass had been removed to create farmland—the dust blew everywhere.

"Black blizzards," swirling dust storms with clouds more than a mile high, became the norm. Dust whistled through crevasses and windowsills into homes, causing blackouts, asthma, dust pneumonia, bloody noses, and a mess that could never be cleaned up. Even meals were covered with dust. Residents put wet towels around door frames to try to stem the flow, but the dust could not be stopped. In 1934 some of it even blew all the way to New York City, where it fell like snow. A hundred million acres of Great Plains farmland had turned into powder.

WHEN YOU GOTTA GO, YOU GOTTA GO

Their farms destroyed, deeply in debt, and facing an economic catastrophe made worse by the Great Depression, thousands of farm families packed what little they had left and headed out. Many of them had one destination in mind: California. Flyers advertising jobs for migrant workers called it the "Land of Sunshine and Opportunity." Although the migrants came from several states and different cultures (surprisingly, a third of them were white-collar workers), the media lumped them together. California's newest residents were mostly known—with a great deal of derision—as "Okies."

California's need for workers wasn't a ruse. The state's enormous farms produced many fruits, vegetables, and other crops and used a lot of migrant labor to do it. Typically, growers relied on homeless men and Filipino and Mexican immigrants who, for decades, had traveled from farm to farm picking up jobs as needed. But the flood of dirt-poor, newly homeless families in the 1930s created a labor glut, and jobs quickly became scarce. The state was so overwhelmed with migrant workers that, for several months in 1936, state police patrolled California's borders, turning destitute migrants away.

THAT'S LIFE, HERE IN DITCH CITY

Those who actually made it past the borders initially found that life in California offered little improvement. The overabundance of cheap labor meant that wages had dropped (in some places, by 60 percent) and with them went the standard of living. In the midst of the Great Depression, the state wasn't prepared for all those new people—20 percent of L.A. County was so poor it was on government assistance. So camps were hastily set up, and Okie families moved into tent cities, ditch camps (in ditches along the sides of roads), or cardboard houses. Many slept in their cars.

Discrimination was also a problem. California growers were accustomed to using mostly immigrants as field laborers. One prejudice of the time was that Mexican and Asian workers were better suited for "stoop labor" (working in fields) than white workers were. Many growers refused to hire Okies in the fields, preferring to bring them on only for "ladder jobs" (like apple picking), further reducing the job opportunities.

Local Californians also often resented the new arrivals, who used up resources, contributed little, and were considered a drain on already low supplies of taxpayer money. Some hospitals refused to treat Okies, and one town's mayor even spread the fear that the migrants were Communist spies. He said, "The whole proposition is Communist through and through. It stinks of Russia…The Reds are burrowing from within."

PROUD TO BE AN OKIE

And yet the Okies stayed. Certainly, they were poor and had few resources, so moving would have been difficult. But they had left their homes on the Great Plains with just as little. The fact was that many of them liked California. The weather was nice, and by the late 1930s, the U.S. government had started building official relief camps that included simple houses with indoor plumbing (something that was often lacking on the plains). But more importantly, the Okies could see opportunity in their new home. The Depression would end eventually, they reasoned, and then things would pick up. They were right. Life began to change dramatically as the country got involved with World War II.

The Okies left a huge cultural imprint on the state. For the most part, the migrants were hardworking but progressive, tending to support the rights of laborers and unions, which became hot political issues in California during the latter 20th century. During World War II, they contributed greatly to the state's economy as a rise in government defense contracts pulled workers off the farms and into factories, where the pay was much better. And Okie artists like

James Dean, Jim Morrison, and Kareem Abdul-Jabbar all attended UCLA.

Woody Guthrie brought Dust Bowl blues and folk music to the mainstream. Today, despite the fact that many of their ancestors once hid their heritage in order to fit in, some grandchildren of the Dust Bowl have embraced the term "Okie" with pride and are even making a reverse migration back to their roots on the plains.

*　　*　　*

WHO WAS CARL SR.?

In 1941 Carl Karcher opened several food stands in Los Angeles and Anaheim; four years later, when the stands got too small, he opened a full restaurant and called it Carl's Drive-In Barbecue. That place was too big, though, and too expensive to maintain, so he closed up shop and decided to open some new restaurants around L.A. He scaled them down to "just the right size" and, because they were the second generation, called them Carl's Jr.

Karcher's restaurants did very well in the post–World War II boom years, expanding throughout California. By 1981 he passed the 300-restaurant mark and started selling stock to investors. That's when the trouble began. In 1984 the Karcher family sold off large quantities of stock right before announcing that the company was having financial trouble and the value of its stock was about to be cut in half. That looked suspicious to the Securities and Exchange Commission, which accused the Karchers of insider trading. In 1988 Karcher ended up paying more than $500,000 in fines.

Then in the 1990s, Karcher and his board of directors got into a dispute about marketing, strategy, and business practices, leading to Karcher's sudden involuntary "retirement." The founder, a conservative man, was left to watch from the sidelines as the company began relying on racy ads to go after a new customer base of young men. First, basketball bad boy Dennis Rodman made a commercial in which an animated version of one of his tattoos ate a tattoo hamburger. In 2005 came the notorious commercial in which Paris Hilton ate a hamburger while crawling and writhing atop a Bentley in a wet swimsuit. And finally, in a 2007 commercial, two rappers compared the delights of their teacher's and the sandwich's "flat buns." Carl Karcher never regained control of his namesake restaurants. He died in 2008 after years of fuming about the marketing of Carl's Jr.

California is home to more native species of conifer trees than any other state.

L.A. CONFIDENTIAL

Before there was Gawker, TMZ, or the National Enquirer, there was Confidential magazine.

TELLING "FACTS" AND NAMING NAMES

Founded in 1952, *Confidential* was the first tabloid gossip magazine to focus on Hollywood's bad behavior. In the prim and proper 1950s—when Hollywood still portrayed married people as sleeping in separate beds and tried to emphasize family values in the private lives of its stars—other magazines published only stories approved by the movie studios. But *Confidential* published any scandal it could find, and the staff paid special attention to the private lives of Hollywood's most glamorous celebrities.

Confidential's founder was New York writer and magazine publisher Robert Harrison. In 1950, while watching U.S. Senate hearings on organized crime on television, Harrison was struck with an idea: Americans were glued to their TV sets as the senators grilled gangsters about their bad behavior and illegal operations. There was clearly a market for crime and scandal in the United States, thought Harrison. So he put together a new magazine (printed on cheap paper), filled it with unflattering celebrity photos, and gave it the subtitle: "Tells the facts and names the names."

THE MONEY'S IN THE SNOOPING

At first, Harrison did plenty of stories on corrupt politicians and suspected communists in government, but he quickly learned that what really sold magazines were juicy facts about a misbehaving Hollywood celebrities. So he created Hollywood Research Inc., a Los Angeles–based company that snooped-out scandals. Hollywood Research hired detectives to wiretap stars and take photos of them with zoom lenses. They also had a network of paid informants: private detectives, starlets, wannabe stars, cabdrivers, waiters, and call girls.

Confidential paid for information on stories like "My Night with Elvis Presley," "Bob Hope and That Naughty Blonde," and "Here's Why Sinatra Is the Tarzan of the Boudoir" (a woman who spent the night with Sinatra said that he noshed on Wheaties to keep up

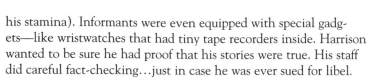

his stamina). Informants were even equipped with special gadgets—like wristwatches that had tiny tape recorders inside. Harrison wanted to be sure he had proof that his stories were true. His staff did careful fact-checking...just in case he was ever sued for libel.

Since Harrison was a New Yorker who had no desire to live near Hollywood, he hired his niece Marjorie Meade and her husband Fred to run Hollywood Research. Soon anyone who had something sleazy to say—and sell—came to the Meades.

THE KING OF LEER

Harrison's instincts paid off: The American public was captivated by the tales of movie star misdeeds, and *Confidential* became the best-selling magazine in the country. Humphrey Bogart once said of the rag, "Everyone reads it, but they say that the cook brought it into the house." Bogart also nicknamed Harrison "the King of Leer."

The studios hated Harrison. Until he came along, they'd been able to use their money and clout to keep the newspapers and magazines from spilling any secrets, and bribes to police and politicians buried stories that reflected badly on glamorous stars. But Harrison didn't need the studios' money. He made about half a million dollars on each issue of his magazine.

Confidential wielded a lot of power in Hollywood. The magazine didn't really care about exposing wrongdoing—it just wanted a salacious story and often preyed on the public prejudices of the day. One of its mainstays was "exposing" interracial relationships. But that approach affected the studios' bottom line and the stars' reputations. After *Confidential* wrote that (Caucasian) Ava Gardner was romancing (African American) Sammy Davis Jr., for example, some movie theaters refused to show Gardner's films. The magazine also often threatened to out homosexual male stars—Tab Hunter and Rock Hudson both had run-ins with *Confidential*. And that ran the risk of costing them their fan bases of young women.

Pretty quickly, the studio moguls became fed up with losing money, and rumors flew that they sent gangsters to Harrison's office to scare him. More rumors said that the gangsters hung Harrison by his heels out of a high-rise window. (But no one ever proved that.)

FIGHTING BACK

Some Hollywood stars lived in fear of Harrison, but not all of them did. When *Confidential* accused Groucho Marx's quiz show *You Bet Your Life* of being rigged, Marx wrote the following letter: "Gentlemen: If you continue to publish slanderous pieces about me, I shall be forced to cancel my subscription."

Actor Robert Mitchum didn't have Groucho's sense of humor. In 1955, he filed a million-dollar libel suit against *Confidential* after the magazine published a story claiming the inebriated star had removed his clothes at a party, poured ketchup on himself, and announced that "this was a costume party and [he] was a hamburger." Mitchum lost the libel case on a technicality, though: Harrison and the magazine's publishing company were based in New York State, not California, and therefore couldn't be held responsible there.

But the attempt inspired other celebrities to sue—actresses Maureen O'Hara and Dorothy Dandridge both filed libel suits against the magazine. Hollywood executives turned to the courts, too. They asked California's attorney general, Edmund Pat Brown, to investigate Harrison. Brown's office did and found at least two stories the state considered to be "obscene" and in violation of California's business code. In May 1957, a grand jury indicted *Confidential* and Hollywood Research for conspiracy to publish criminal libel and obscene material. New York still wouldn't extradite Harrison for the trial, but California prosecutors proceeded against Hollywood Research anyway.

The prosecutor threatened to demand jail time, but defense attorney Arthur Crowley hit back, sending out subpoenas to more than 100 Hollywood stars. Crowley intended to question the stars about whether the scandals published about them in *Confidential* were true. That way, Hollywood would be forced to admit that the magazine was accurate, not libelous. But so many celebrities fled California to avoid being served with subpoenas that Crowley compared it to the Bible's story of the Israelites' exodus from Egypt.

SCANDAL ON TRIAL

The trial began in August 1957. Prosecutor Clarence Linn accused *Confidential* of libel in six stories: the Robert Mitchum hamburger story and articles that detailed the love affairs of Maureen O'Hara,

Dorothy Dandridge, Gary Cooper, Mae West, and June Allyson. The prosecution's star witness was Howard Rushmore, a fervent anticommunist who'd written and edited for *Confidential* and then quit the magazine. Rushmore had wanted to include more right-wing politics and less celebrity trashing, but Harrison refused and the two had a falling-out. Rushmore got back at his old boss by testifying that Harrison entrapped stars with his network of spies. Rushmore was so angry and bitter, though, that he seemed to turn jurors off.

The prosecution witness who packed the most punch was probably Maureen O'Hara, famous for starring in films like *How Green Was My Valley* and *Miracle on 34th Street*. According to a *Confidential* article, O'Hara and her "south-of-the-border sweetie" were all over each other ("practically having sex," said the magazine) in the balcony of Grauman's Chinese Theatre. O'Hara admitted that she did have a boyfriend who had been born in Mexico, and theater employees testified that they saw the couple behaving shockingly in row 35. But O'Hara produced a passport that showed she was in Spain on the day the magazine said it had caught her in the act. For once, Harrison's fact-checkers had slipped—either O'Hara was never there or (more likely) the magazine got the date wrong. Either way, the damage was done.

The defense took another blow when the judge forbade Crowley from calling all those movie stars he'd subpoenaed. The judge insisted that Crowley limit himself to defending the six stories introduced by the prosecution. After that, many relieved stars, including Frank Sinatra, finally came home.

NO JUDGMENT AT THE MAYFLOWER

The trial of Hollywood Research lasted six weeks, and the only other major celebrity to testify was Dorothy Dandridge. The article about her claimed that she'd "frolicked in the woods" of Lake Tahoe with white bandleader Hal Terry. According to Dandridge, Tahoe was so prejudiced against African Americans that she barely left her room when she performed there, so "frolicking" with Terry would have been impossibly dangerous and out of the question.

The trial finally ended, but after 15 days of deliberations, the jury remained deadlocked. The judge declared a mistrial. Both the prosecution and defense declared victory, but neither side really wanted to fund a retrial...so they made a deal instead.

CONFIDENTIAL TO THE END

No one admitted any wrongdoing, but Harrison agreed to stop writing about Hollywood, paid a small fine, and the State of California dropped the charges. As soon as Harrison announced that his magazine would focus on politics, circulation plummeted and he sold Confidential in 1958. Maureen O'Hara and Dorothy Dandridge both won private lawsuits against the magazine, but Harrison managed to settle those and others for relatively small amounts. The prosecution's star witness didn't fare as well: Drinking heavily, Rushmore shot and killed his wife and himself in a New York taxi in 1958.

Despite the end of Confidential, Harrison predicted that Hollywood would never again be able to control the gossip industry because the public would always want to know what lurked behind Hollywood's facade. He declared that scandal publications would soon return, and with today's celebrities openly stalked by paparazzi and scandalous headlines dominating the tabloids, Harrison has certainly been proven right.

ONE OF THE BIGGEST SCOOPS

In the magazine's heyday, no one was exempt from Confidential's spies...not even baseball hero Joe DiMaggio. One night in 1955, a terrified Florence Kotz Ross screamed as the door to her Los Angeles home was broken down with an ax. A drunken DiMaggio, two private detectives he'd hired, and a couple of pals—including Frank Sinatra—came rushing in.

They were looking for DiMaggio's ex-wife Marilyn Monroe, whose car was parked across the street. It had been only nine days since DiMaggio and Monroe's divorce, and since he thought she'd left him for another man, he was still jealous and looking to catch the guy. But DiMaggio broke down the wrong door. Ross called the police, reporting the break-in as a burglary, but the cops had no lead—the apartment was dark and Ross didn't actually see who broke in. It all would have ended there, but one of the private detectives who had been with DiMaggio needed money and sold the story to *Confidential*. When the article came out in September 1955, DiMaggio, who was usually considered a hero and a stand-up guy, seemed like a boozy, jealous bumbler. When Ross found out who'd broken down her door, she sued DiMaggio, Sinatra, and the others. She won $7,500 (more than $50,000 today). The kicker: Marilyn Monroe *had* actually been in the building, in another apartment at the home of an actress friend…who, some biographers claim, was helping to conceal the blonde bombshell's affair with her handsome voice coach.

*   *   *

DINOSAUR WRECKS

Once upon a time—like the mid-20th century—dinosaurs could be found throughout California. Artists and others hoping to create something big and lasting settled on dinosaur structures that became roadside attractions. Here are some of the biggest, baddest, and best:

• About 20 miles southeast of Arroyo Grande, along winding, dead-end Huasna Road, a pair of rusty iron dinosaurs—a "Brontosaurus" (which has since lost its dinosaur status) and a Tyrannosaurus rex—stand alone in a rural valley. Where they came from is a mystery, though. Not even the locals know who built the creatures.

• Even though these dinosaurs are smaller than life-size, we still like them…and since they're on a miniature golf course, it makes sense. Built in 1948, the Guerneville Pee Wee golf course was the first goofy-sculpture miniature golf course ever created, designed, and put together by Lee Koplin, a welder who went on to create novelty golf courses all over the country. Besides the dinosaurs, this one features weird stuff like cannibals and a sun god.

• Then there was the headless dinosaur in Dinosaur Caves Park in Pismo Beach. Now a city park, the spot was originally an attempt to create a tourist attraction. But the sea caves that were part of the attraction collapsed in the 1970s, and the concrete dinosaur remained headless for many years after the owner was told to stop work because nearby residents complained. Sadly, the headless dinosaur has since been torn down.

Four most common non-English languages in CA: Spanish, Chinese, Tagalog, Vietnamese.

VASQUEZ ROCKS!

About 25 million years ago, a violent earthquake in northern L.A. County uplifted sandstone at a 45-degree angle. Today that area is known as Vasquez Rocks County Park in Agua Dulce, and it's been featured in thousands of TV shows, movies, commercials, and music videos.

• One of the first movies filmed there: 1931's *Dracula*. In *Werewolf of London* ('35), the Rocks double as Tibet. Classic Westerns include John Wayne's *Dakota* ('45), and Burt Lancaster's *Apache* ('54).

• Many people call the area "Kirk's Rock." Why? Because it's the location of the cheesy *Star Trek* scene where Captain Kirk fights the lizardlike Gorn. Vasquez doubled for several planets in the *Trek* shows and films: It was Vulcan in *Star Trek IV* ('86) and the 2009 reboot *Star Trek*. Kirk's fight scene was also re-enacted at the Rocks in the sci-fi spoofs *Bill and Ted's Bogus Journey* ('91) and *Paul* (2011).

• Classic Western TV shows shot at the Rocks: *The Lone Ranger*, *The Gene Autry Show*, *Cheyenne*, *Gunsmoke*, *Broken Arrow*, *Bonanza*, *The Wild Wild West*, and *Hondo*.

• In 1994's *Flintstones* movie, the park was transformed into the town of Bedrock.

• Other classic TV shows to use the location: *The Six Million Dollar Man*, *Battlestar Galactica*, *Buck Rogers in the 25th Century*, and *MacGyver*.

• Recent shows to film scenes there: *Numb3rs*, *CSI*, *Monk*, *Buffy the Vampire Slayer*, *24*, *The X-Files*, and *Friends* ("The One with Joey's Big Break").

• More films: *Blazing Saddles* ('74), *Army of Darkness* ('92), *Austin Powers: International Man of Mystery* ('97), *Jay and Silent Bob Strike Back* (2001), *Bubble Boy* ('01), *Holes* ('03), and *Little Miss Sunshine* ('06).

• Vasquez makes an animated cameo in Pixar's *Cars* ('06). The familiar triangular rocks also show up in the *Shrek* movies and on *Futurama*.

• In the 1991 *Black or White* music video, Michael Jackson dances with Native Americans at the Rocks. In the 2008 *Rehab* music video, Rihanna and Justin Timberlake look really, really hot there.

The California Academy of Tauromaquia in San Diego teaches courses in bullfighting.

THE THINGS
MONEY CAN'T BUY

*A man, a museum, and a whole lot of stolen art—welcome
to the wild world of the J. Paul Getty Museum.*

THE SKINFLINT FOUNDS A MUSEUM

The J. Paul Getty Museum consists of two locations—the
Getty Center in Los Angeles and the Getty Villa in Pacific
Palisades. Together, they house some of the most important pieces
of art from around the world. Both were the brainchild of Jean
Paul Getty, an American industrialist who made billions of dollars
in oil. In 1957 *Fortune* magazine named him the "richest living
American," yet Getty was known as much for being an incredible
tightwad and miser as he was for his money. In his palatial London
mansion, he installed a pay phone so that no one could run up his
phone bill. He also made international headlines in 1973 when he
refused to pay a ransom for his teenage grandson, who had been
kidnapped in Italy. Only after one of the boy's ears was sent to the
media did Getty agree to pay $2.2 million (the amount that would
be tax-deductible) of the $2.8 million ransom. The rest he loaned
to his son—the boy's father—at 4 percent interest.

But there was something Getty didn't seem to mind spending
money on: art...especially if he could get a good deal. (Getty even
went so far as to buy artworks from frantic Jewish families desperate to escape the Nazis during World War II.) Getty called his collecting an addiction, and bought so much art that a financial
consultant finally advised him that he could get some big tax
breaks if he founded a nonprofit museum to house all the art and
then allowed the public to view the collection. So in 1954 Getty
opened his museum to the public in a special wing of his home in
Pacific Palisades. When his collection outgrew that museum,
Getty built another, larger one on his estate, and some of his most
prized possessions were antiquities (art from ancient civilizations).

MONEY, MONEY, MONEY

In 1976, just two years after building the Getty Villa, Jean Paul

Getty died, but he bequeathed $700 million worth of oil stocks to the museum, asking only that it be spent on "the diffusion of artistic and general knowledge." That money made the small Pacific Palisades museum the wealthiest art institution in the world. Plus, the oil stocks kept going up in value. By the time Getty's estate was finally settled in 1982, the museum's stock was worth $1.2 billion. In 1997—even after spending a billion dollars to build the Getty Center in West L.A.—the museum's funds had grown to $4.5 billion. With all that money available, the museum set out to buy a world-class collection, and that's when the trouble began.

The Getty focused on its antiquities department, where the first chief curator, Jiri Frel, developed contacts with some questionable international art dealers who sold "hot" antiquities—artworks that had been illegally excavated and smuggled out of their native countries. In 1985 Frel urged the museum to spend $10 million on a group of antiquities that included a five-foot-tall marble statue of Apollo and a painted marble statue of a pair of mythical, winged griffins devouring a deer. At the time, both Frel and the Getty's directors suspected the pieces had probably been stolen, but they were so rare (and would bring so much traffic and prestige to the museum) that they took a chance and bought them anyway.

LOVELY LOOT FOR SALE

Frel wasn't the only curator buying questionable antiquities. Nearly all the top museums had them on display because no one ever asked many questions about the history of the works they bought. Sometimes the stolen artifacts were found by ordinary citizens who, instead of notifying local authorities, took them to a smuggler for quick cash. But many of the works came from criminals who looted ancient tombs and ruins, stole the art, and then smuggled it out of the country—usually into Switzerland. There, a piece passed into the hands of an unscrupulous art dealer who forged a document called a provenance that gave the piece a respectable history and made it look as if the art had been in someone's collection for years. When antiquities came from Italy, for example, a phony provenance usually showed that the art had been in a collection before 1939...because 1939 was the year Italy passed a law making it illegal to take antiquities from out of the country without government permission.

Only California-born president: Richard Nixon.

For decades, U.S. museums had been buying antiquities this way. They justified it by saying they performed a public service by displaying the ancient treasures and guaranteed that the works were carefully preserved. But countries such as Egypt, Turkey, Greece, and Italy, where most of the looted pieces came from, found it nearly impossible to prove that an object had been taken illegally.

VIVA LA ITALIA!

That changed for Italy in 1995, when Italian investigators tracked a gang of tomb raiders to a Swiss art dealer's warehouse. Inside, they found incriminating photos of many looted antiquities that had been moved out of Italy. The Getty had bought most of them.

Included in the incriminating photos were snapshots of the Getty's prized statues: the Apollo and the griffins. (Those rare griffins had been photographed while stuffed in the trunk of an old car and partially wrapped in Italian newspapers.) The Italian government pressured the Getty to return the stolen pieces. When the museum resisted, the Italians began investigating its buying practices. Their focus: a woman named Marion True.

TRUE'S TRIALS

In 1986 Dr. Marion True took Frel's place as chief antiquities curator at the Getty. She launched a $275 million renovation of the museum and was asked to spend millions to fill the Villa with a magnificent collection of ancient Greek, Roman, and Etruscan art. In 1988, for the price of $18 million, True made one of her most famous purchases: a 2,400-year-old, 7.5-foot-tall marble-and-limestone statue believed to be of the goddess Aphrodite. In 1993 True had the Getty pay $1.1 million for another treasure, a funerary wreath dating back to Alexander the Great that included solid gold leaves and molded glass flowers. With purchases like the golden wreath and the marble goddess, True was creating a great antiquities museum. But she was also unknowingly ending her career. True and her bosses at the Getty either didn't know—or just ignored—the likelihood that their celebrated treasures were stolen.

In 2005 the Italian government indicted True for participating in a criminal conspiracy to buy stolen art. Among the charges was her purchase of the Aphrodite. Italian prosecutors could prove

---

Creedence Clearwater Revival began as the Blue Velvets, a high-school band in El Cerrito.

that the statue had been stolen in Sicily in the late 1970s...and smuggled to Switzerland in a truck filled with carrots. Next, Greece indicted True for buying the golden wreath, which had been illegally excavated by a farmer in northern Greece and then smuggled into Germany.

True resigned from the Getty, but she still faced up to 10 years in prison for essentially doing the same job that other curators did. Suddenly, U.S. museums—including the New York Metropolitan Museum and the Boston Museum of Fine Arts—began worrying that their curators could be put on trial for buying antiquities. So they made agreements to return stolen antiquities to Italy. In 2007 the Getty got on board, returning the gold wreath to Greece and 40 works (including Aphrodite) to Italy. Greece dropped the charges against True, and the Italians allowed the process to move so slowly that the statute of limitations ran out in 2010.

NOT FOR SALE

Among the objects that the Getty returned to Italy were some of its most celebrated treasures, including the Apollo statue and those marble griffins. The museum also lost the millions it had spent to buy them. Today, Getty officials say that the scandal changed the way they acquire antiquities. They now rely more on donations from long-held private collections and arrange loans with other museums. In a market full of illegal antiquities, museums can no longer just write big checks and ship ancient art home for display without being extremely careful about the object's origins...especially since the source countries have made it clear that they will go to great lengths to get their stolen masterpieces back.

THE FIGHT GOES ON

But not everything is so cut and dried. In 1964 Italians fishing in the Adriatic Sea off the coast of Yugoslavia pulled up a life-size bronze statue of a Greek athlete, called the *Statue of Victorious Youth*. To keep the barnacle-covered statue away from the government, the men buried it in an Italian cabbage field and later sold it to a middleman, who hid it in a priest's bathtub and eventually smuggled it out of the country. Then the statue was cleaned up and put on the art market.

Victorious Youth is believed to have been created between 100 and 300 BC. It's one of the few life-size ancient Greek bronze statues left in the world because so many were melted down over the centuries to make tools or weapons. The Getty bought *Victorious Youth* for $3.95 million in 1977, and although Italy has asked for its return, the statue remains on American soil for now. Technically, it was found in international waters, so the Getty is waging a legal battle to keep the statue.

*   *   *

WHEN'S MUMMY COMING HOME?

Elmer McCurdy was a pretty lousy train robber. Fresh out of the army in 1911, he held up a passenger train in Oklahoma that he thought was carrying a safe filled with money. It was actually carrying just $46 and a few bottles of liquor. The police caught up with him nearby, put a bullet in his chest, and dropped him off at a local funeral home. The mortician waited, but nobody claimed the body, so after curious townspeople began dropping by to see McCurdy's corpse, the mortician decided to make some money from it. He embalmed McCurdy and put him on display, telling visitors to put a nickel in the corpse's mouth to cover the cost of admission.

After five years of this, a man arrived, expressing outrage that his long-lost brother was being displayed like this. He took possession of the body, saying he planned to hold a decent family burial. It never happened. The "brother" was a fake who worked for a carnival that quickly put the body on display.

What does all this have to do with California? Fast-forward to 1976, when a camera crew for the TV show *The Six Million Dollar Man* was setting up at a haunted house in Long Beach. An assistant moved what he thought was a mannequin...but its arm broke off, revealing human muscle and bones. It was McCurdy. How he got to Long Beach remains a mystery, but the coroner later found a penny and a ticket for an L.A. crime museum in his mouth. It seems McCurdy had been exhibited at carnivals, museums, and haunted houses for more than 60 years. Finally, he was sent back to Oklahoma and buried in Guthrie...under three cubic yards of concrete to make sure no one could get at him again.

There are 43 hills in the city of San Francisco.

THE LAST LIST

All good things must come to an end, just like this
book…and just like these things in California.

L AST TIME THE BEATLES PERFORMED
TOGETHER IN CONCERT: August 29, 1966, at the
Cow Palace in San Francisco.

**LAST TIME YOU COULD SWIM AT THE SUTRO
BATHS:** Technically speaking, June 26, 1966. That was when the
baths—which once covered three acres of San Francisco shore and
included seven swimming pools—burned to the ground. Today, you
can still swim in the ruins, but we don't advise that…people have
been known to be swept away by strong currents.

**LAST TIME ELVIS WAS "ALL SHOOK UP" OVER
PRISCILLA PRESLEY:** October 8, 1973. They divorced the
next day in Santa Monica Superior Court.

**LAST TIME YOU COULD LIVE IN THE STATE OF
JEFFERSON:** 1941…kind of. That was the year that Port Orford,
Oregon, mayor Gilbert Gable decided that, by taking a northern
portion of California and a southern portion of Oregon, he could
make a new state that he called Jefferson. Amazingly, some border
counties supported this notion and the idea took hold. On
December 4, 1941, to great fanfare, Jefferson inaugurated its first
governor. Alas, Pearl Harbor was bombed just days later, and the
idea died.

**LAST TIME TO WATCH THE L.A. RAMS PLAY
FOOTBALL:** Christmas Eve, 1994. After that, they relocated to
St. Louis.

**LAST TIME YOU COULD GET A LETTER BY PONY
EXPRESS:** Officially, October 24, 1861. That was the day
the Overland Telegraph Company and the Pacific Telegraph
Company completed their coast-to-coast telegraph line, and the
day the Pony Express was supposed to end. Because of a little
lagtime, though, some mail trickled in through November.

Orange County's Tiger Woods was named *Sports Illustrated*'s "Sportsman of the Year" twice.

ANSWERS

SINGIN' CALIFORNIA QUIZ, PAGE 36

1. "Oh My Darling Clementine" Extra credit: She hit her foot against a splinter.

2. Folsom Prison, Johnny Cash. Extra credit: *Inside the Walls of Folsom Prison.*

3. "The Little Old Lady from Pasadena". Extra credit: A red Super Stock Dodge (aka, a Dodge Polara or Dodge 330).

4. Santa Monica Boulevard. Extra credit: He peels off the labels.

5. L.A., Watts, and Compton. Extra credit: Chris Tucker.

6. "Save Me San Francisco." Extra credit: Marin.

7. "California, Here I Come." Extra credit: Al Jolson.

8. "I Love You California." Extra credit Sunsets are purple.

9. "I Left My Heart In San Francisco." Extra credit: Dianne Feinstein.

10. In L.A.'s Hollywood hills. Extra credit: Derek Taylor, a journalist who worked for the Beatles.

11. Lodi. Extra credit: Fogerty had never been to Lodi; he just thought it had a cool name.

12. "California Gurls." Extra credit: Katy Perry.

13. Woody Guthrie. Extra credit: Woody's daughter, Nora Guthrie.

SOCAL SANTA ANA-GRAMS, PAGE 97

Los Angeles County: 1. Redondo Beach, 2. Santa Monica, 3. Pasadena, 4. Inglewood, 5. Thousand Oaks

Inland Empire: 1. Riverside, 2. San Bernardino, 3. Palm Desert, 4. Fontana, 5. Temecula

San Diego County: 1. San Diego, 2. Chula Vista, 3. Escondido, 4. Oceanside, 5. La Mesa

Central Coast: 1. Solvang, 2. San Luis Obispo, 3. Simi Valley, 4. Paso Robles, 5. Santa Barbara

From 1907 to 1963, there was a bounty on mountain lions in California.

NORCAL SANTA ANA-GRAMS, PAGE 179

The Bay Area: 1. San Rafael, 2. San Jose, 3. Oakland, 4. Palo Alto, 5. San Francisco

The Central Valley: 1. Bakersfield, 2. Fresno, 3. Stockton, 4. Modesto, 5. Visalia

Gold Country: 1. Sacramento, 2. Yuba City, 3. Truckee, 4. Grass Valley, 5. Elk Grove

Way Up North: 1. Redding, 2. Red Bluff, 3. Crescent City, 4. Susanville, 5. Fort Bragg

GET SPORTY, PAGE 239

1. San Diego Padres, Los Angeles Angels of Anaheim, Los Angeles Dodgers, Oakland A's, and San Francisco Giants. Bonus: The first were the L.A. Dodgers (1959), and most recent were the San Francisco Giants (2010).

2. L.A. Clippers; Bonus: Kareem Abdul-Jabbar

3. San Jose Sharks; Bonus: Sharkie

4. San Diego Chargers; Bonus: Oakland (formerly L.A.) Raiders

5. Anaheim Ducks; Bonus: Mighty Ducks

6. San Jose Earthquakes; Bonus: San Jose Clash

7. Golden State Warriors; Bonus: Oracle Arena

FAST FOOD QUIZ, PAGE 252

1. d. Back in its early days, McDonald's emphasized that its food was fast and cheap. That's why a constantly moving chef (wearing a white hat and apron) and the price of a hamburger (originally 15¢) on its sign made sense at a time when you'd expect to spend twice that much at a comparable hamburger stand. Other prices on the menu: shakes 20¢, fries 10¢, soft drinks or coffee 10¢, and cheese on your burger 4¢.

2. a. Founder Bob Wian remembered the little boy, saying, "He was about six, and rolls of fat protruded where his shirt and pants were designed to meet. I was so amused by the youngster—jolly, healthy looking, and obviously a lover of good things to eat—that I called him big boy."

The world's tallest ponderosa pine stands in **Plumas National Forest** (227 feet tall).

3. b. Doggie Diners was the first fast-food chain to appear in the San Francisco area after World War II, and it lasted until 1986. Nowadays, only 12 of the iconic dogs are known to exist, including one that's on display near the San Francisco Zoo.

4. a. For a short period, there were actually four Pea Soup Andersens' in California, but over the years, two closed down. The two that still survive are located on the major north-south highways between San Francisco and Los Angeles, I-5 and U.S. 101. The strange construction of the restaurant's name, by the way, only makes sense if you know that founder Robert Andersen's nickname was "Pea Soup."

5. d. PepsiCo's research led the company to believe that middle-class Americans thought Mexican restaurants would be dirty and the food too spicy, so it toned down Taco Bell's salsa, emphasized that the ingredients were not "un-American-tasting" (and were pretty much the same as a hamburger "seasoned to American taste"), and got rid of the big sign of a Mexican man taking a siesta in a big sombrero.

6. b. In a real case of "what were they thinking?" the founders insisted that back in 1957, the name Sambo began innocently— they had merely combined their names, SAM Battistone Sr. and F. Newell BOhnett. However, as many pointed out, they could've just as easily come up with Newstone's or Batnet's, instead of the title character of an increasingly controversial children's book titled *Little Black Sambo*, about a resourceful dark-skinned boy from India. As controversy and boycotts hit the chain, the company responded by having its murals repainted with a lighter-skinned Sambo. When that didn't appease the public, they tried changing restaurant's name to No Place Like Sam's, The Jolly Tiger, or Season's Friendly Eating. No one was fooled, and by 1982, only one Sambo's remained: the original one in Santa Barbara. It's still there, at 216 West Cabrillo Boulevard.

The first Super Bowl (Green Bay beat Kansas City) was played in L.A. in 1967.